Readi

Through a
Darwinian Lens

# Reading Edith Wharton Through a Darwinian Lens

## Evolutionary Biological Issues in Her Fiction

JUDITH P. SAUNDERS

McFarland & Company, Inc., Publishers
*Jefferson, North Carolina, and London*

LIBRARY OF CONGRESS CATALOGUING-IN-PUBLICATION DATA

Saunders, Judith P.
  Reading Edith Wharton through a Darwinian lens : evolutionary
biological issues in her fiction / Judith P. Saunders.
      p.      cm.
  Includes bibliographical references and index.

  ISBN 978-0-7864-4002-3
  softcover : 50# alkaline paper ∞

  1. Wharton, Edith, 1862-1937 — Criticism and interpretation.
2. Evolution (Biology) in literature.   3. Darwin, Charles,
1809–1882 — Influence.    I. Title.
PS3545.H16Z876    2009
813'.52 — dc22                                          2009006123

British Library cataloguing data are available

Cover image: (inset) detail of Edith Wharton portrait (Library of
Congress); background ©2009 Shutterstock

Manufactured in the United States of America

*McFarland & Company, Inc., Publishers*
  *Box 611, Jefferson, North Carolina 28640*
    *www.mcfarlandpub.com*

For Nancy Keeler McCormick

# *Acknowledgments*

I am indebted to Joseph Carroll, of the University of Missouri–St. Louis, for his counsel at several stages of this project, in particular for his comments on an early draft of Chapter 1. Elsa Nettels, of the College of William and Mary, has been a source of encouragement from the vantage point of Wharton studies. Special thanks are due to my colleague Victoria Ingalls, of the Marist College science faculty: our ventures in collaborative, interdisciplinary teaching deepened my knowledge of evolutionary biology and confirmed my interest in Darwinian literary criticism. I am grateful to officers and personnel at Marist College who for many years provided an administrative framework for these interdisciplinary collaborative teaching endeavors. Two professional organizations, the Human Behavior and Evolution Society and the Edith Wharton Society, have been valuable sources of intellectual stimulation. Conferences sponsored by these organizations in recent years provided forums in which I was able to test my ideas at different stages of their formulation.

Chapter 6 on *The Children* appeared in a slightly different version in *College Literature 32.2 (2005)* under the title "Evolutionary Biological Issues in Wharton's *The Children*," and is reprinted here with permission of the editors.

# Table of Contents

# List of Abbreviations

BG     *A Backward Glance*. New York: D. Appleton-Century, 1934.

AI     *The Age of Innocence: Complete Text with Introduction, Historical Contexts, Critical Essays*. Ed. Carol J. Singley. Boston and New York: Houghton Mifflin, 2000.

C     *The Children*. New York: D. Appleton, 1928.

GM     *The Glimpses of the Moon*. New York: D. Appleton, 1922.

HM     *The House of Mirth*. New York: Charles Scribner's Sons, 1905.

OM     *The Old Maid (The 'fifties). Old New York*. New York: Appleton, 1924.

R     *The Reef*. New York: Charles Scribner's Sons, 1914.

RF     "Roman Fever." In *The World Over*. New York: D. Appleton-Century, 1936. 215–239.

# Introduction

The goal of this study is to identify evolutionary biological issues central to Edith Wharton's fiction, demonstrating their significance in terms of character, setting, plot, and theme. Although evolutionary thinking has influenced a wide range of fields in recent decades, from medicine to anthropology, infiltrating the popular press and public awareness with considerable thoroughness, its potential to illumine the workings of imaginative literature has only begun to be tapped. Literary texts invite Darwinian scrutiny because they provide a special record of human experience, centering typically on endeavors with undoubted implications for fitness: courtship customs, for example, marital strife, parenting behavior, sibling rivalry, or status-seeking. Like all manifestations of art, literature serves as a forum in which humans employ their complex mental structures to voice awareness and interpretation of their condition. At times, moreover, they utilize that forum to articulate eloquent protests against the biological and psychological constraints of human existence. This project tests the potential of the new but growing field of biopoetics by undertaking an extended examination of evolutionary biological concerns in the work of a single author.

Edith Wharton may seem at first glance to be an unlikely object of attention for Darwinian literary analysis, since the genteel social environments she most often delineates are apparently far removed from stereotypical struggles for survival. Beneath the polished surface of her fictional worlds, however, readers can observe her characters competing fiercely for desirable partners, questing aggressively for status and resources, and plotting ruthlessly to advance their relatives' fortunes in life. Wharton herself highlights her interest in "the nether side of the smooth social surface: actions assiduously concealed or misrepresented, emotions persistently unacknowledged or denied" (*OM* 34).[1] Her narratives are rife with deception and self-deception, with conflicts and competitions no less brutal because they are bloodless. Invariably she provides sufficient information for readers to gauge the success, as measured by fitness, of her characters' actions. She offers evidence, too, that some individuals perceive and resent the biologically-based behavioral tendencies that frustrate their conscious designs. Asking whether and how her characters' behavior is *adaptive*, that is, whether it promotes the passing on of genes, opens the way to richer comprehension of Wharton's view of human nature and human society. Furthermore, she provides richly detailed information about the social environments in which her characters struggle, including particulars of domestic arrangements, kinship networks, leisure activities, and community customs. Creating a convincingly complete social universe, she paves the way for Darwinian analysis of the social animals whose habitat she so thoroughly documents. It is intriguing and instructive to see adaptive mechanisms at work in environments so radically different from that in which humans evolved. For Wharton herself the disjunction is a source, by turns, of ironic amusement, satiric judgment, and resigned acceptance.

The methodology utilized in this study of Wharton's work relies on theory and research now current in the field of evolutionary biology rather than on Wharton's own reading and interpretation of Charles Darwin's ideas. She was familiar with the Darwinian theory of her day, certainly, and acquainted with Darwin's writings first-hand. Indeed, she acknowledges him as "one of the formative influences" in her intellectual development.[2] Her fiction contains direct and indirect references to evolution and related topics, such as inherited traits and differential survival. No doubt her knowledge on such points contributed to her tendency to consider the human condition from a biosocial point of view. A number of her biographers and critics have discussed the history of her engagement with Darwinian thought, tracing her reading in the field, including works by authors such as T. H. Huxley and Herbert Spencer.[3] Readers interested in Wharton's understanding and interpretation of evolutionary theory, as it was framed in the late nineteenth and early twentieth centuries, thus will find considerable material on this topic. That said, it must be emphasized that Darwinian literary analysis is neither dependent upon an author's knowledge of evolutionary biology nor undermined by any misunderstandings of it an author may have harbored.[4] If there is indeed a "universal human nature," as research in evolutionary psychology strongly indicates — that is, if "our thoughts, feelings, and behavior are the product of psychological adaptations" that have evolved over a period of millions of years — then that human nature will prove susceptible to examination in literary representations with or without an author's conscious design.[5] As Joseph Carroll explains, literature "reflects the structure and character of the adapted mind": this is the "central principle" guiding evolutionarily-based literary study.[6] What was known about the operation of evolution via natural selection during Wharton's lifetime has been augmented and modified since then, needless to say, most obviously by research in genetics and cognition, to name two of the areas in which important strides have been made.[7]

Since Wharton's recurrent interests as a novelist and story-writer are so clearly focused on fitness-related behavior, evolutionary biological theory can be applied to her work without strain: the shaping force of reproductive logic is nearly always central to plot and theme in her fiction. As a result, biopoetic analysis of her fiction is inextricably linked to examination of literary elements such as point of view, figurative language, characterization, allusion, and tone. Connections will be drawn throughout to existing Wharton criticism, so that readers can see how biosocial interpretation extends, refutes, enriches, or reconfigures insights derived from other literary critical perspectives. Articles and book-length studies of Wharton's work have appeared steadily over the past thirty years, as she has come to occupy an increasingly important place in American literature. Some of these critical works incorporate Wharton's familiarity with evolutionary ideas into their commentary, often focusing on the application of Darwinism to social theory: see, for instance, studies by Donald Pizer, Claire Preston, and Alan Price, among others.[8] Recently a few scholars have pioneered investigations of Wharton's work that draw on specific features of current research and theory in evolutionary biology, most notably Bert Bender, Richard A. Kaye, and Paul J. Ohler.[9]

The theoretical framework, as well as the intellectual rationale, for undertaking biopoetic investigation of literary texts has been ably laid out by aestheticians and critics such as Ellen Dissanayake, Edward O. Wilson, Joseph Carroll, Robert Storey, Jonathan Gottschall, David Sloan Wilson, Brett Cooke, Frederick Turner, Nancy Easterlin, and Brian Boyd, to name some of the most prominent thinkers in a growing field.[10] Readers unfamiliar with the historical and theoretical foundations of Darwinian literary criticism will find useful commentary in works by these writers (see the notes and the bibliography). Carroll's *Evolution and Literary Theory* (1995), in particular, is a seminal work to which all thinkers and practitioners in the field are indebted. Explaining "the relevance of biology to literary theory," Carroll presents in detail the underlying assumptions of the Darwinian, or Adaptationist, paradigm.[11] At the same time he makes the case for its value in contrast to prevailing poststructuralist schools of literary criticism. Literary works "reflect and articulate the vital motives and interests of human beings as living organisms," he argues, and such an understanding of literature "conflicts fundamentally with the currently pervasive disposition to regard all motives and interests as merely self-reflexive linguistic or cultural functions."[12]

The reluctance of literary scholars to utilize insights deriving from evolutionary biology as a tool of critical understanding reflects more than a bias in favor of poststructuralist theoretical assumptions. There is pervasive anxiety (and not only among humanists) that the Darwinian paradigm presupposes genetic determinism. Such anxiety is based upon fundamental misconceptions, however, as numerous researchers have explained. The complex workings of human adaptations are not the result of any one-to-one correspondence between genes and behavior, nor does the existence of a universal human nature translate into robotically uniform feelings and actions. As John Tooby and Leda Cosmides put it, "the idea that the evolutionary causation of behavior would lead to rigid, inflexible behavior is the opposite of the truth. Evolved neural architectures are specifications of richly contingent systems for generating responses to informational inputs."[13] The human brain is "packed with programs that cause intricate relationships between information and behavior," including "default preferences that are adjusted by experience" and "complex decision rules." In short, the result of the interaction between evolved adaptive "programs" and particular environmental stimuli is "a dazzling variety of behavioral responses."[14]

In addition to general apprehensions about possibly deterministic implications of evolutionary biology, there is specific anxiety that its findings may prove antagonistic to the goals of feminism. If it is proved and acknowledged that there are evolved differences between male and female members of the human species, feminists anticipate that such differences might be used to perpetuate legal, economic, and social inequality. A number of evolutionary biologists have addressed this issue in detail, attempting to allay fears. Anne Campbell's book-length study on the topic includes a point-by-point comparative analysis of feminist and evolutionary theories.[15] She offers careful refutation of the most commonly articulated feminist objections to Darwinism, noting that the existence of gender differences does not, in itself, constitute logical or ethical grounds for social injustice:

> When we can open up new opportunities for expression, enjoyment, and achievement for women, we should do it because it is morally right. But that is very different from saying that gender has no biological basis and that the nature of men and women is wholly constructed by society. The problem with such a position is that it fails to address the issue of why sex differences take the particular form that they do. If gender differences are arbitrary, it is a curious coincidence that they follow such a similar pattern around the world.[16]

If the economically and politically pernicious effects of evolved sexual strategies are to be effectively countered in a contemporary, post-industrial environment, they must be recognized and acknowledged. Armed with evidence from Darwinian studies, women may be in a better position to argue for social change. Notable efforts to integrate Darwinian and feminist perspectives have been made by Griet Vandermassen, Sarah Blaffer Hrdy, Barbara Smuts, and others.[17] Wharton's fiction frequently depicts conflict between the sexes, suggesting that it is deeply rooted in gender differences. Even as she identifies male-female antagonism as the cause of personal miseries and societal problems, however, she targets same-sex competition as an equally significant locus of human unhappiness and strife. Overall, her portraits of conflicts between and within the sexes tend to support David M. Buss's observation that "men cannot be united with all other men as a group for the fundamental reason that men are in competition primarily with members of their own sex. The same is true for women." Conflict between the sexes arises most often simply as "an undesirable by-product of the fact that the sexual strategies of men and women differ in profound ways."[18]

No specialized knowledge of evolutionary biology is needed to follow the lines of discussion in this study. Concepts and terms necessary for preservation of scientific accuracy are explained in context, and a glossary is provided. Information in the notes directs readers to foundational scientific sources: given an audience consisting chiefly of literary scholars and other humanists, documentation aims at efficiency rather than exhaustiveness. The sources named offer detailed bibliographies that will assist interested readers to delve more deeply into primary research on specific topics. Chapters are organized around individual works of fiction and are followed by a conclusion that summarizes the evolutionary biological issues persistently engaging Wharton's attention. Works selected for comment were chosen with two principles in mind. First, they represent a mixture of well known and less familiar works by Wharton: *The House of Mirth*, *The Age of Innocence*, *The Old Maid*, and "Roman Fever," on the one hand, and *The Reef*, *The Glimpses of the Moon*, and *The Children*, on the other. Second, the chosen texts illustrate a wide range of biosocial concerns. As a group, they underline the depth and extent of Wharton's evolutionary psychological acuity as she depicts inherited mechanisms at work in distinctly modern environments.

# 1

# The House of Mirth

## *An Unsuccessful Mate Search*

The story of a frustrated mate search, *The House of Mirth* (1905) addresses issues obviously rooted in human biology and reproduction. Edith Wharton is especially concerned with the inescapable influence of social environment — community and family — upon individual personality and behavior. Her condemnation of the "flatness and futility" of the society she has chosen to portray culminates in her recognition that its pursuit of material luxury has reached a fitness-threatening level (*BG* 207). In the upper-class world inhabited by her characters, the accumulation of resources has been divorced to a considerable extent from the biosocial function it ordinarily serves, namely, the rearing of healthy, viable offspring. The failure of Lily Bart's matrimonial designs points directly to factors in her wealthy, turn-of-the-century American environment that contribute to personal discontent and reduced fitness by promoting maladaptive goals and strategies. It is no accident that much of the sympathy Wharton generates for her protagonist stems from Lily's lingering impulse to resist the "debasing ... ideals" surrounding her and yield instead to "the blind motions of her mating-instinct" (*BG* 207, *HM* 516). The "streak of sylvan freedom in her nature" offers a glimpse of the person she might have become in a different social universe (*HM* 19). The brief moments in which ordinary adaptive mechanisms appear to influence Lily's emotions or actions are also the moments in which she becomes most fully human and most likeable. Examining *The House of Mirth* from an evolutionary perspective can help readers to sort through the frustratingly ambivalent responses its central character provokes.

The opening pages of Book I make clear that matrimony is Lily's goal.

From the clothing she wears, to the parties she attends, to the conversational topics she cultivates, her activities are designed to maximize opportunities to meet and attract eligible men. Her quest for a husband creates suspense in the novel and drives its plot. Inevitably, her failure to achieve her objective raises questions in readers' minds, questions about her ambitions *per se* and about the means she employs to fulfill them. More than anything else, the novel comprises an investigation of Lily's mistakes. Why can't this unusually attractive woman find a husband? Why does her socioeconomic standing sink so precipitously in the space of two short years? Enjoying opportunities that by any ordinary standards seem privileged, why does she end up dead (however accidentally) by her own hand? Enormous narrative energy and space are devoted to analysis of Lily's motives (professed and actual), her anguished ruminations, her frequent second thoughts, her ruefully belated recognitions. An omniscient narrator provides insight into her mental and emotional state, utilizing interior monologue generously.[1] The detailed depiction of Lily's psyche enables readers to identify a pernicious constellation of reasons for the tragic outcome of her efforts.

Lily's mistakes begin with the criteria she invokes in her selection of a long-term mate. Sizing up potential husbands, she places overwhelming importance on material resources, eliminating all but the richest men from serious consideration. Up to a point, her focus on a man's ability to provide for her and any future children is not only adaptive but entirely predictable. As Buss notes, "the evolution of the female preference for males who offer resources may be the most ancient and pervasive bias for female choice in the animal kingdom."[2] At the same time, as Buss's research demonstrates, economic capacity alone is insufficient to render a man worth choosing. Women place importance on additional issues of character and circumstance, such as status, health, intelligence, ambition, stability, commitment, and compatibility.[3] They seek an appropriate combination of such qualities (appropriate, that is, in terms of their own individual traits and situations) for excellent reasons. A prosperous man who lacks health, for instance, may die young or may prove infertile. A wealthy suitor who is deficient in intellectual ability or in emotional stability may lose resources already in hand and prove unable to acquire more. Thus Lily Bart's much discussed ambivalence toward the men she identifies as potential husbands stems in large measure from her disregard, on a conscious level, of selection criteria human females have evolved to consider significant. Lily tells herself, and others, that material prosperity constitutes an all-sufficient criterion, but her behavior suggests that she is in fact unable to conquer her own unacknowledged drive to find a mate who possesses additional biosocially important attributes.

Percy Gryce is the potential husband whose qualities readers are able to assess in most detail, and his "limitations," to use Lily's term, are blatantly conspicuous (*HM* 30). Shy and socially constrained, he lacks intellectual drive, imaginative playfulness, and even physical vigor. He is constitutionally "reluctant and cautious," the kind of young man who is unwilling "to hazard himself abroad in the rain" (*HM* 34). A "vacant passivity," or "dulness," is his habitual state (*HM* 140, 30). Even his strongest enthusiasm, the collecting of Americana, is secondhand, inherited along with the rest of his property. He quite evidently lacks the force of character, as well as the energy and purpose, to acquire resources on his own. He is no dominant male, but merely the passive beneficiary of a more active ancestor's successes. Tellingly, Gryce is held in low personal regard by peers, who frequently refer to him with ridicule or even contempt. His status level is technically acceptable to Lily, since he belongs to the circle in which she seeks a husband, but his personal deficiencies have led to reduced standing within that group. Gus Trenor calls him a "portentous little ass"; Lily compares him at one point to a "baffled beetle"; even the omniscient narrator likens him to "the lower organisms" (*HM* 133, 106, 31). Women typically avoid potential partners "who are easily dominated by other men or who fail to command the respect of the group."[4]

In terms of social gifts, as well as intelligence, vigor, and ambition, Gryce has little to offer Lily Bart. In habits, values, and personalities, moreover, the two are strikingly divergent. Gryce is an arch-conservative. Timid, prudent, and humorless, he attends church with scrupulous regularity, for example, and he abhors the idea of playing cards for money. Lily, in contrast, is something of a rebel and an iconoclast: her perception of the social scene she inhabits tends to be ironic, and she frequently engages in high-risk flouting of conventions. A Darwinian observer would predict that a mating between two such different individuals would lead to personal unhappiness on both sides and hence to marital instability. Even Judy Trenor commiserates with Lily on the prospect of the alliance ("'Oh, Lily, what an awful life you'll lead!'"), and the narrator ensures through repeated negative descriptions that readers will not be rooting for the protagonist to resolve her difficulties by marrying Percy Gryce (*HM* 72). In order to attract Gryce's interest, significantly, Lily must engage in deceptive maneuvers: she pretends to enjoy his company; she feigns interest in his collection of Americana; she claims to be a regular church-goer; she conceals her habits of smoking cigarettes and betting at the bridge table. In order to stimulate his interest in her as a long-term partner, in short, she presents herself as a person dramatically unlike her real self. Most courtships are characterized by some deceptiveness in self-presentation on the part of both partners, for obvious reasons, but the manifold duplicity required of Lily to win serious attention from Gryce signals extreme dissimilarity between the two.

The rich men Lily has targeted for her attentions in the past do not appear to have offered her much better hopes for a successful union. In the opening pages of Book I, for instance, Seldon refers to the most recent candidate dismissively: "'you can do better than Dillworth'" (*HM* 14). When Lily occasionally reviews her history of husband-hunting, she gives no evidence of having formed emotional attachments to any of the men she had hoped to marry. Her regrets are based on financial considerations, "'good chances'" she has bungled, rather than on heartbreak (*HM* 14). The prospective mates she identifies fail to engage her feelings precisely because she is attempting to ignore a whole range of important criteria in the selection of a long-term partner — attempting, in effect, to suppress powerful psychological mechanisms. She has very consciously decided to give nearly absolute priority to the criterion of wealth, with some secondary attention to the closely related issue of social status. But her lack of emotional responsiveness to the candidates she has ostensibly chosen betrays the partialness of her commitment to those choices. Emotions serve, as Robert Wright succinctly observes, as "evolution's executioners," that is, they are the mechanisms through which evolved adaptations express themselves.[5] An individual feels drawn to one potential partner, or repelled by another, as a result of cost-benefit calculations that are largely unconscious. With the notable exception of Lawrence Seldon, Lily's suitors fail to stimulate her ardor, a clear sign that her unconscious assessment of them as mates is negative. Although some critics have tried to argue that Lily herself sizes up the institution of marriage in sociopolitical or in ethical terms, evidence for this is meager.[6] It is, rather, her creator who places marriage under the lens of critical scrutiny, commenting acerbically on evolved behavioral tendencies (here, the impulse to seek a long-term mate) as well as on the social institutions that shape their expression in a given milieu.

Riches notwithstanding, the potential drawbacks of marriage to a Dillworth or a Gryce are greater than the potential advantages. Thus Lily's reiterated failure to secure the wealthy men she works to attract is attributable to inner conflicts she barely acknowledges and is only hazily able to define. She accuses herself of "unsteadiness of purpose" (*HM* 408). As she persistently undermines her own matrimonial schemes, her vacillation attracts comment from those around her. Gerty Farish concludes that Lily has "shrunk" from the kind of marriage she ostensibly seeks, accurately identifying the locus of Lily's ambivalence as sub-rational (*HM* 251); inner forces work to betray her conscious designs. While Lily deliberately seeks a husband who can offer her "a great deal of money" and never ceases to think of material resources as crucial to her future happiness (*HM* 14), she is not nearly so willing as she imagines she is to sacrifice all other considerations to that of wealth. Her on-again-off-again pattern of courtship, like her inability to conquer her inclination for the relatively impecunious Seldon, reflects her struggle to repress emotional responses that have evolved for the precise purpose of guiding choices like those she is in process of making.

The overvaluing of material resources that renders Lily's assessment of potential husbands so lopsided does not take place in a vacuum; it is encouraged and ratified by her environment. Her social circle is dedicated to extravagant consumption. The ability to lavish resources on fashion and entertainment — dinners, cruises, theatricals, clothing, jewels — is of paramount importance; hence the ability to attract a mate with unusually abundant resources is regarded as unquestionably desirable. Despite the manifest personal deficiencies of Percy Gryce, his arrival on the scene "fluttered the maternal breasts of New York," and Lily's pursuit of him earns support and "consideration" from her women friends (*HM* 33, 73). Her cousin Jack Stepney courts and marries one of the plain, dull Miss Van Osburghs for reasons that are chiefly economic. Lily knows Jack feels little personal attraction to the girl, whom he compares to "roast mutton," but she is rich and he is not: "hunger makes any fare palatable" (*HM* 75). Bertha Dorset regularly engages in love affairs with men she prefers to her wealthy husband, but she is careful to conceal her affairs from him and never considers leaving him, "'on account of the money'" (*HM* 70).

Resources are closely allied to status in this environment, as is the case in most human communities.[7] The novel documents a subtly nuanced socioeconomic hierarchy in which loss of resources tends to be accompanied by loss of prestige, while acquisition of new resources leads to increased respect. After his advantageous marriage to a Van Osburgh, Jack Stepney assumes a position of greater prominence in his family and "in his new character as the richest nephew ... tacitly took the lead" (*HM* 355). Being disinherited by her aunt damages Lily socially as well as financially; even those who disapprove of her involvement in the Dorset scandal "wouldn't quite have dared to ignore" or snub her if she had come into a handsome legacy (*HM* 362, 363). The wealthy Bertha Dorset's false accusations prevail over Lily's innocence in part because an "impregnable bank-account" is the basis of "social credit" (*HM* 421). Those with sufficient money also may aspire to ascend the social ladder; wealth is a necessary if not all-sufficient prerequisite for status-climbing. "'Everybody with money can get into society,'" or "'*nearly* everybody'" (*HM* 301). With proper guidance, as Carry Fisher demonstrates, even the Welly Brys may achieve acceptance into a social group not eager to welcome them. By providing elaborately expensive entertainment like the *tableaux vivants*, they lure high-status individuals into socializing with them: "society ... succumbed to the temptation of Mrs. Bry's hospitality" (*HM* 211). Simon Rosedale similarly buys his way into a circle quite determined to exclude him, using busi-

ness "tips" as bait to promote his acquaintance with men like Gus Trenor and
Jack Stepney (*HM* 130). Wishing to profit financially from a connection with
Rosedale, such men influence their wives to offer coveted social invitations.
At every step of her career, in short, Lily is compelled to acknowledge money
as a powerful social force.

The earliest and most intimate environmental influences on Lily Bart are
provided by the parents who reared her, and her upbringing has reinforced
the primacy of wealth with unusual intensity. It is her mother who trained
Lily in profligate habits and expectations, who developed her "taste for splen-
dor" (*HM* 47); indeed, Mrs. Bart considers her own efforts to live beyond her
means "heroic" (*HM* 46). She encourages Lily to "plead" with her father for
special extravagances, to view resources available to her as almost infinitely
renewable (*HM* 49). Husbands are "always to blame" for any financial
insufficiencies (*HM* 46); in his wife's eyes Mr. Bart becomes "extinct" when
he ceases to fulfill his designated purpose as bountiful provider (*HM* 51).
Faced with financial reverses, Lily's mother fails to rally with any kind of
energy to meet the future. She can summon neither courage nor stoicism,
instead offering her daughter a model of "furious apathy" and thwarted entitlement (*HM* 52). She rails "acrimoniously against love-matches," relentlessly
instilling the idea that the only mate worth having is one who can provide a
luxurious lifestyle (*HM* 53). Thus the exaggerated importance Lily places on
resources in a prospective mate is fostered not only by prevailing social norms,
but nurtured with especial keenness by those closest to her during her formative years.

Indictment of Lily Bart's social environment clearly is one of Wharton's
major purposes in writing *The House of Mirth*. Lily herself at one point attributes her flawed values and actions to environmental causes: "'I am bad,'" she
tells Gerty Farish; "'all my thoughts are bad — I have always had bad people
about me'" (*HM* 266). Like most of her peers, she has chosen a life of what
Seldon dubs "stupid costliness" and "showy dulness" (*HM* 347). As the omniscient narrator caustically observes, Lily associates with "a class of old New
Yorkers who have always lived well, dressed expensively, and done little else"
(*HM* 58). They have created a "selfish world of pleasure" in which they discover nothing more than "an infinity of ways of being idle" (*HM* 78, 300).
Throughout the novel, religious metaphor is wielded ironically to criticize
the overvaluing of wealth, as when Percy Gryce is said to have been "initiated with becoming reverence into the art of accumulation" (*HM* 35). The
quest for rich mates similarly is denounced with the narrator's scathing observation that divorce will be countenanced if the parties show "signs of peni-
tence by being re-married to the very wealthy" (*HM* 91). The barrage of scorn
leveled against material excess highlights Wharton's dismayed recognition of

the power of social climate to corrupt potentially fine human material. In *A Backward Glance* she famously explains that "a frivolous society can acquire dramatic significance only through what its frivolity destroys" (*BG* 207).

A critically important element in Wharton's social criticism, moreover, is the dissociation of economic exertions from biological imperatives. Behavior has been reduced to a "show ... staged regardless of expense" (*HM* 295). When exorbitant display becomes an all-sufficient goal, Seldon comments, "it distorts all the relations of life" (*HM* 112). Recurring theatre imagery suggests the essential unreality of social "performance" in this "pallid" world (*HM* 294, 442). Lily notes the absence of "human activities" in Mrs. Hatch's circle, the lack of any "wholesome roughness of life" (*HM* 442). Reviewing her own past on her final evening on earth, Lily recognizes that she has never experienced any "real relation to life" (*HM* 516). The pursuit and display of wealth have been elevated in her community to ends in themselves and all but severed from their adaptive functions — namely, survival and reproduction. Why, after all, do females seek out mates with resources? This preference has evolved because access to resources directly benefits offspring.[8] Social display typically is utilized to signal possession of abundant resources; the adaptive purpose of such display is to acquire a mate and offspring in whom those resources may be invested. Yet children, along with hopes and plans for offspring, are scarcely mentioned in *The House of Mirth*.[9] The small space they occupy in the narrative reflects the smallness of their importance in the lives of the principal characters. When "show" of wealth becomes an end in itself, as in Lily's old New York, we observe cultural norms influencing the expression of evolved behavioral tendencies with no adaptive gain.

Lily recognizes in her final hours that important aspects of her nature ("the blind motives of her mating-instinct") have been prevented by environmental forces from functioning normally ("checked by the disintegrating influences ... about her") (*HM* 516). Her encounter with Nettie Struther triggers this recognition, just as holding Nettie's baby awakens "life-hunger" in her (*HM* 518). Subsisting "on the grim edge of poverty," but glorying in her loyal husband and her healthy baby, Nettie is participating in "the continuity of life" (*HM* 517, 516). She has discovered "the central truth of experience" that has eluded Lily (*HM* 517). Contrasting Nettie's life history with her own, Lily begins to think about the ultimate ends from which her proximal behavior has been so distanced, consciously acknowledging the reality of genetic continuity and the "links of kinship" it generates: "a slowly accumulated past lives in the blood" (*HM* 516). As she slips into a chloral-induced coma, she enjoys a final hallucination of herself cradling Nettie's child. She derives "a thrill of warmth and pleasure" from this sensation of maternity, immediately associating the baby with "something she must tell Seldon ... that should make life clear between them" (*HM* 522). Vaguely imagining the joint reproductive effort she and Seldon might make together, she moves finally toward acknowledgement of the biological consequences of mate choice. With the potent image of the baby, Wharton introduces the strongest possible contrast to Lily's financially driven marital ambitions.

A number of Wharton's readers have interpreted the hallucinated baby as a metaphoric representation of Lily herself, signifying either unfulfilled regressive needs or an emerging new self.[10] Such readings become most plausible when the deathbed hallucination is examined in conjunction with other scenes: the evening visit in Nettie Struther's kitchen, when Lily holds Nettie's daughter and feels "as though the child entered into her and became part of herself," and the night at Gertie Farish's apartment, when Gertie cradles her distraught friend "as a mother makes a nest for a tossing child" (*HM* 510, 270). Considerations of possible metaphoric implications of the baby image offer insight into the gamut of reader reactions to Lily's character, particularly with reference to the question of whether or not she develops, or changes, over time. It is important, nonetheless, to remain alert to the more obvious significance of the fantasized infant as the surfacing of a reproductive impulse, especially given Lily's pondering of her own "mating-instinct" and concomitant realization, just prior to taking the chloral, that Nettie Struther's life is replete with precisely those things her own conspicuously lacks (*HM* 516). Richard A. Kaye accurately observes "that Lily is barren when she dies, that her last thought is of Nettie Struther's child," and "these details enforce a sense of Lily as a female who has forsaken her proper role in a Darwinian procedure ... the principal purpose of which is, of course, procreation."[11]

The exaggerated weight she places on economic resources is not the only mistake Lily makes in her search for a mate. Like any individual embarked on such a search, she considers what she wants in light of what she herself has to offer. Lily's great "asset," to use her mother's term, is her personal beauty (*HM* 53). She is physically attractive to an unusual degree, a fact repeatedly emphasized in the text. Indeed, her appearance elicits a stream of tribute from those around her. She has ample reason to conclude that her looks are sufficiently striking to set her apart from rivals in the competition for mates. As research has demonstrated, physical appearance is as important a selection criterion for males as economic capability is for females. Youth, health, and vigor are critical qualities men seek when assessing a woman's reproductive capacity.[12] Lily's feigned headache, for instance, worries Gryce: "he wondered ... if she was delicate, having far-reaching fears about the future of his progeny" (*HM* 106). Visible indicators of probable fertility include such attributes as "full lips, clear skin, smooth skin, clear eyes, lustrous hair."[13] Descriptions of Lily Bart emphasize precisely these features of her appearance, with emphasis on the "freshness," or youthfulness, of the impression she makes (*HM* 128). Her "radiant" complexion makes other girls appear "sallow-faced" by comparison (*HM* 4, 6); her skin has a "girlish smoothness" (*HM* 6). Her hair is "vivid" in color, with a "crisp upward wave" (6). Her eyes are "charming," "lovely" (*HM* 11, 8); her lashes are "thick" (*HM* 6). "Everything about her" signals vitality: she is "at once vigorous and exquisite" (*HM* 7). She possesses in addition an excellent figure; male characters comment frequently on the unusual shapeliness of her "outline" (*HM* 223). Evidently her waist-to-hip ratio is close to ideal, the universally preferred 0.70. This is yet another important predictor of reproductive capability and therefore functions as "a powerful cue to women's attractiveness."[14] The distinctly plain Gerty Farish recognizes Lily's "loveliness" as "a natural force" that is bound to prevail in intrasexual contests: "love and power belong to such as Lily" (*HM* 268).

Lily is well aware of the advantages she enjoys: "Ah, it was good to be young, to be radiant, to glow with the sense of slenderness, strength and elasticity, of well-poised lines and happy tints" (*HM* 187). She realizes, furthermore, that "beauty is only the raw material of conquest," that "to convert it into success other arts are required" (*HM* 54). She regards herself as highly adept at those "arts," priding herself upon "her skill in enhancing" her beauty, "the care she took of it," and "the use she made of it" (*HM* 178). Employing tact and diplomacy to maximize the "opportunities" her physical attractiveness opens to her, she employs a strategy of calculated "compliances and adaptabilities" (*HM* 54, 39). Throughout her career, she consciously supplements the inborn advantage of beauty with social intelligence and well developed interpersonal skills. When she imagines the possibility of "recapturing" Percy Gryce from a rival, for example, she focuses on the other girl's lack of social intelligence as much as on her homeliness: "What chance could such a simpleton have against her if she chose to exert herself?" (*HM* 148).

Beautiful as she is, Lily nonetheless tends to overestimate, and thus to mismanage, the value of her physical attractions in the exchange of benefits mate selection entails. Her early home environment has taught her to imagine that her extraordinary looks invest her with enormous power, even including the ability to regain the family's lost fortune. "'You'll get it all back, with your face,'" her mother repeatedly tells the growing girl (*HM* 44). Mrs. Bart has "studied" her daughter's developing beauty obsessively, regarding it as a "weapon" to be wielded in the only struggle that matters to her, namely, the struggle to achieve the highest possible economic status (*HM* 53). She successfully impresses upon Lily "the magnitude of her opportunities," encouraging fantasies of future luxury (*HM* 54).[15] As a result of maternal influence, Lily not only aspires to a magnificent lifestyle but assumes it is hers by right; it is "the existence to which she felt herself entitled" (*HM* 40). She is persuaded that "her own jewel-like rareness" deserves an appropriately out-standing "setting," one in which "every tint and line should combine to enhance her beauty" (*HM* 144, 176–77): hence her eagerness to "do over" drawing-rooms, her delight in costuming for the *tableaux vivants*, her enjoy-ment of the stylish "enhancements of dress" financed by Gus Trenor's money (*HM* 14, 187).

Lily has been reared to harness her taste in service to her beauty, to view her own exquisitely developed discernment of nuances and outward impres-sions as a virtue. She considers herself better than those who live by other lights: "Lily imbibed the idea that if people lived like pigs it was from choice, and through the lack of any standard of conduct. This gave her a sense of reflected superiority" (*HM* 47). She never shakes off this early teaching, retain-ing the notion that her standards of style somehow elevate her above her other people; she rejoices in "that artistic sensibility which made her feel herself their superior" (*HM* 176). The incident with the flowers, when young Lily's "sense of fitness" is offended by a fading floral centerpiece, illustrates the pride she takes in her finely tuned sensibilities, the overweening complacency which her mother has nurtured (*HM* 48). To exercise "refinement and good taste" on the scale Mrs. Bart has set requires enormous wealth, obviously, and at the same time appears to justify the ambition to acquire it (*HM* 54): Lily "could not help thinking that possession of such tastes ennobled her desire for worldly advantages" (*HM* 54–55). She deems herself worthy of the life "she long[s] to lead," one of "fastidious aloofness and refinement in which every detail should have the finish of a jewel" (*HM* 133). Thus she is not embarrassed to admit to Selden that she is "very expensive" (*HM* 14). In sum, Lily's early environment has inculcated in her a double sense of entitlement. Because she possesses both natural beauty and exquisite taste, she imagines that she deserves unusually abundant resources to showcase them.

In consequence of this carefully cultivated belief in "her own exception-alness," Lily exaggerates her own value to a prospective husband (*HM* 143). Despite some variation in individual situation and inclination, there are cross-culturally identifiable patterns of preference in human mate selection.[16] Since two well established elements in this pattern include strong male preference for physical beauty, and strong female preference for economic viability, Lily is not wrong to think that her exceptional looks may attract a man with excep-tional wealth. She is mistaken only in setting her goals uncompromisingly high. She restricts her search for a husband to a tiny pool of extremely wealthy men, only to discover, as observed earlier, that men in this pool may not pos-sess other traits important in a long-term partner — such as intellectual capac-ity, emotional stability, or social grace, for example. At the same time, this limited group of men is the focus of intense female competition. "Desirable partners are always outnumbered by those who desire them," Buss points out.[17] Each time Lily hesitates in a nascent courtship with a rich but otherwise less than ideal potential husband, she opens the door to rivals eager to obtain a wealthy mate, rivals who may prove less reluctant than she to overlook a few imperfections. Physically less attractive rivals furthermore may offer some desirable attributes in greater measure than Lily — wealth, for example, or a pliable disposition. Lily's conviction that her beauty empowers her to "attract a brilliant destiny" renders her overly particular, both in defining a pool of eligible men and in assessing individual candidates (*HM* 140). She is "unwise ... in estimating her worth," as Maureen Howard states, with the result that "younger and plainer girls had been married off by dozens" while she has spent more than eleven years in fastidious vacillation (*HM* 60).[18]

In sum, two environmentally fostered psychological tendencies — her overemphasis of a prospective husband's wealth and her exaggerated conviction of unique personal worth — combine to render Lily an absolutist in pursuing her goals, unyielding in a human situation that inevitably requires compromise. Buss observes that "the combined qualities of kindness, intelligence, dependability, athleticism, looks, and economic prospects occur in the same person only rarely and most of us have to settle for someone who has less than the full complement of desirable characteristics."[19] Due to her belief in her own specialness, however, Lily refuses over and over to accept the necessity of compromise. She employs an all-or-nothing strategy, gambling that she will locate and successfully attract an ideal mate before her youth and fertility wane. Since women, unlike men, are confronted with an obviously circumscribed period of fertility, typically they respond to temporal cues by modifying their criteria and strategies for mate selection over time. It may make sense for a girl of nineteen to hold out for better prospects rather than to accept a mediocre suitor, but she is apt to relax her standards if enough time passes, rather than to wait indefinitely for a more desirable man to appear. Not only is her opportunity to pass on her genes slipping away year by year, her reproductive value to potential partners is at the same time declining. Lily demonstrates unconscious awareness of these facts with her anxiety about emerging "lines in her face" and other signs of fading youth (*HM* 43). Although she does not make overt mention of her decreasing reproductive capacity, she realizes that mounting age threatens her beauty and thus imperils her ability to attract men.[20]

When the novel begins, she has already squandered eleven of the approximately twenty-five years of fertility a woman can anticipate. Her response to her growing awareness of temporal constraints on her mate search, however, proves neither typical nor adaptive. "If a woman's excessive self-estimate persist[s] too long," Buss warns, "her actual mating value [will] decline as she age[s]."[21] At age twenty-nine, Lily should be prepared to modify her selection criteria, to accept a husband somewhat less ideal than one her nineteen-year-old self would have contemplated. Yet her pursuit of Percy Gryce, with which the novel opens, does not indicate any inclination on her part to rethink her goals; her ambitions remain focused on a small pool of very rich men. At the same time, her poor follow-through (as when she spends a day with Seldon instead of paying attention to Gryce) demonstrates that she still is reluctant to accept even a rich man if he fails to please her in other arenas of life. Had her mother not instilled in her an abnormally high sense of self-worth, Lily might now exercise the flexibility in strategy necessary for optimal mate choice. Two options for compromise immediately suggest themselves. She can either maintain her standards for economic resources in a husband and accept a man whose personal traits do not altogether please her, or she can reduce her demand for wealth and seek a mate in a larger economic pool, choosing a less wealthy man with more desirable personal qualities. Opportunities for both kinds of compromise are close at hand: she can marry Percy Gryce or Simon Rosedale, opting for wealth, or she can marry Lawrence Seldon, opting for a pleasing constellation of personal traits. Resisting both options, however, she agonizes and procrastinates endlessly, frittering away two more years of fertility.

Lily's behavior constitutes a decision to risk the possibility of obtaining no mate at all rather than to settle for one who is less than ideal. While such a decision might be considered admirable in some lights, it serves neither her immediate survival needs nor her genetic self-interest. More important, she is clearly unwilling to abide by the consequences of her refusal to reframe her goals. As Wolff indicates, she manifests "no capacity to make choices, draw difficult distinctions, or bear hardship."[22] Unwilling to lead the life of a spinster on a modest income, she refuses to consider retreating from the social scene she has identified as her proper sphere of action. She is consistently unwilling to live within her income, and she rejects the prospect of combining resources and setting up household with another single woman. For Lily, there is no Plan B; her ideas about her future all are predicated upon successful achievement of the "brilliant destiny" she has so long anticipated (*HM* 140). In her failure to formulate alternative objectives, we see traces again of Lily's early family environment. Her mother's example has taught her nothing about planning ahead or anticipating setbacks: Mrs. Bart spends extravagantly even when a "thunder-cloud" of financial troubles obviously threatens (*HM* 47). Once her husband is "ruined," Mrs. Bart cannot bear to continue her life in New York on the "little money left," even though doing so probably would be in her debutante daughter's best interest (*HM* 52). To live modestly instead of grandly, and to be observed doing so, would mean settling for "the mere mockery of what she was entitled to" (*HM* 52). Because she can no longer lead a sumptuous lifestyle, she ceases to "manage" at all: "the effort was no longer worth making" (*HM* 52). Reared by a mother for whom there is no middle ground, Lily, too, rejects the idea of second choices and back-up plans. Her inclination to play cards for high stakes is only one expression of the gambler's mentality and penchant for high-risk behavior instilled in her at an early age.

Other individuals in her social circle provide examples of compromise that contrast sharply with Lily's inflexibility. Both Judy Trenor and Bertha Dorset, for instance, appear to have given heavy weight to economic factors in choosing their husbands. Spending relatively little time with their husbands and often speaking deprecatingly of them to others, they give little indication that they value their chosen mates' personal attributes. Judy Trenor immerses herself in her role as societal leader and hostess; lavish entertainment becomes an all-engrossing hobby for her. Bertha Dorset finds solace in extramarital affairs. These women seem quite consciously aware that the bargains they have struck are not perfect. From the matter-of-fact way in which they speak of their mates and carry on their lives, bystanders can infer that they are neither surprised nor disappointed by their marriages. They obtained more or less what they expected when they selected their partners; they were prepared to make do.

The marriage of Lily's cousin Jack Stepney to Gwen Van Osburgh represents an instance of compromise tellingly close at hand. Attractive and vivacious, but lacking riches, Jack appears in many respects to be a male version of Lily Bart; like her, he wants to marry into money. His courtship of Gwen, in progress at Bellomont, represents "the same kind of romance" Lily is conducting with Percy Gryce. Lily regards it, indeed, as "a caricature of her own situation" (*HM* 75). "A large girl with flat surfaces and no high lights," Gwen is as deficient in personal magnetism and social graces as Percy (*HM* 75). She lacks many attributes, both physical and social, that Jack would choose if "his own taste" rather than money were of paramount importance to him (*HM* 75). Lily watches Gwen's face turn to Jack's "like an empty plate held up to be filled," while he gives indications of "encroaching boredom" in her presence (*HM* 75). Unlike Lily, Jack perseveres in his courtship, fully aware that he is forfeiting certain attributes in a future mate in order to secure others.

Although Lily complains that it is easier for Jack, as a man, to achieve marriage to a rich partner than for her, as a woman, to do the same, there is not much evidence to support her complaint. It seems probable that she could have brought her courtship with Gryce to a successful conclusion if she had remained committed to attracting him. Wharton does not present this as a desirable outcome, obviously: readers do not admire, and are not intended to admire, the calculated trade-off a marriage like Jack Stepney's seems (at least through Lily's eyes) to represent. Given his ambition for financial security, however, there is discernible adaptive logic in his choice of a wife, particularly in comparison with Lily's stalled mate search. He has made a decision based on a cost-benefit analysis in the context of an environment that values material resources highly. He reaps economic and social advantages from his marriage, and he demonstrates ongoing commitment to his choice: when Jack appears in Monte Carlo, Seldon notices that he has "thickened" and "grown prudish, as Van Osburgh husbands were apt to do" (*HM* 297). Insofar as the dreary personal characteristics of Gwen Van Osburgh and Percy Gryce may point to poor genetic quality, readers may sympathize with Lily's reluctance to compromise in her choice of long-term mate. The problem, of course, is that she does not choose any mate at all. To procreate with Gryce clearly would benefit Lily's fitness more than procreating with no one.

When she compares Jack's courtship with her own, at Bellomont, Lily is struck by how much the two objects of their attention appear to have in common. Sharing "the same prejudices and ideals," Gwen and Percy are, "in short, made for each other, by every law of moral and physical correspondence" (*HM* 76). Yet these two young people, both in search of mates, "'wouldn't look at each other,'" Lily declares (*HM* 76). She imagines that each yearns for an exotically different partner, "'a creature of a different race, Jack's and mine, with all sorts of intuitions, sensations, and perceptions that they don't even guess the existence of'" (*HM* 76). Events prove Lily's hypothesis wrong, however. Percy Gryce does not marry Gwen Van Osburgh, to be sure, but he does marry her sister Evie, "the youngest, dumpiest, dullest" of the sisters (*HM* 146). Gertie Farish bubbles over with enthusiasm for this union between two people so "'exactly suited to each other'": "'she's such a quiet stay-at-home kind of girl, and it seems he has just the same tastes'" (*HM* 145). Lily, in contrast, is dumbfounded by the match; she cannot conceive how an individual deficient in wit, poise, and *savoir faire* could prefer a counterpart equally deficient in these traits. Her assumption that she must inevitably attract Gryce more than Evie Van Osburgh ever can hope to do is based upon her overestimate of her own value, which causes her to dismiss the importance of compatibility as a criterion in mate selection.

As Buss's research has established, a "sustained cooperative alliance" such as marriage is more likely to succeed between two individuals possessing similar personal characteristics. Thus, "worldwide," men and women tend to select mates holding "similar social and political values" and resembling themselves "in race, ethnicity, and religion," as well as in a host of personal traits (e.g., introversion, extroversion, boldness, energy), "especially intelligence, perceptiveness, and creativity."[23] The fact that Lily and Jack might seem like "creatures of a different race" to Gwen and Percy is likely to lessen their appeal as potential mates in this situation, rather than to increase it. Lily fails to realize that dissimilarity based on her ostensible superiority to the man she hopes to attract (as well as to rivals for his attention) functions as a disadvantage. For all her physical plainness and blunted perceptions, Evie Van Osburgh ultimately proves more attractive to Gryce than Lily because, based on important biosocial factors, Evie is, in fact, a better mate choice for him. Her very inferiority to Lily gives Evie the advantage: the traits Lily derogates constitute important points of compatibility between Evie and her future husband. Here and elsewhere, Lily's exaggerated sense of self-worth prevents her from recognizing that the qualities she has to offer a potential husband do not possess absolute value: such value is situation-dependent and therefore fluctuating.

Wharton's characters make choices indicating that compatibility typically weighs heavily as a factor in mate choice, even against beauty, taste, and brilliance. Similarity in values, interests, and attributes "leads to coordination of efforts, reduces conflict within the couple, avoids the costs of mutually incompatible goals, maximizes the likelihood of achieving success, and reduces the risk of later abandonment or dissolution of the relationship."[24] Even Jack Stepney and Gwen Van Osburgh may be less incompatible than first appears; despite indications of incipient "boredom" in Gwen's presence, Jack later seems contented with the lifestyle the two forge together, "trailing breathlessly in her wake" from one expensive entertainment to the next (*HM* 75, 297). His ability to metamorphose into the typical "Van Osburgh husband" suggests some degree of essential affinity with Gwen, as does a comparable shift in her attitudes and pursuits: "marriage ... emancipated her" from her family's staid tastes (*HM* 475). From a Darwinian perspective, necessarily, the most important measure of "success" in any marriage is its fertility. And Wharton makes a point of establishing the reproductive outcome of the union between the "'exactly suited'" Percy Gryce and Evie Van Osburgh (*HM* 145). In April of the year following the marriage, Lily sees "the new heir to the Gryce millions enthroned ... on his nurse's knee" in a carriage on Fifth Avenue (*HM* 479–80). This detail in the narrative, which is in no way important to development of plot or character, demonstrates the incompleteness of Lily's ideas about mate selection, highlighting a significant fallacy in her theory of her own superiority.

Despite her overtly stated goals, Lily's vacillating behavior suggests that she is, in fact, sensitive to the importance of compatibility in a future mate. The absence of ardency in her response to any of the men she deliberately selects as potential husbands is, as noted earlier, a clear sign that on an unconscious level she finds them poor candidates: certainly Gryce fails the test of compatibility, as does the most aggressive contender for her hand, Simon Rosedale. Rosedale, whose background, education, and ethnicity differ distinctly from Lily's, proposes a marriage frankly conceived as a union of opposites: his pursuit of her is an example of mate selection based upon complementarity.[25] Rosedale argues that his material resources will provide a magnificent backdrop for Lily's beauty, along with opportunity to exercise her extravagant taste. Her existing alliances, by friendship and birth, in the group he aspires to join, in turn will serve his social ambitions, as will her artistically engineered self-display and highly developed interpersonal skills. Although Lily recognizes how the partnership Rosedale offers might prove mutually beneficial, its potential advantages are insufficient to overcome her aversion to the marriage. Her repugnance may be understood as the result of her unconscious assessment of the obvious dissimilarities between them. Thus Lily behaves predictably when approached by a suitor her emotions inform her is incompatible, even though the benefits he offers include those she most desires, at least theoretically, in a mate — enormous wealth, with *carte blanche* to spend money in the most lavish of styles. As she gets better acquainted with Rosedale, interestingly, Lily's appreciation of him grows. Her increased liking and respect are based upon the realization that he and she are not as widely divergent in personal styles and values as she previously had thought. The more she is able to see him as similar to herself, the closer Lily comes to deeming him a possibly acceptable husband.

Unwilling, despite her conscious intentions, to marry a rich man with whom she is in many ways incompatible, such as Gryce or Rosedale, Lily confronts and rejects a radically different kind of compromise in refusing Lawrence Seldon. He proposes to Lily twice in the course of the novel's action, and on the first occasion she comes close to accepting him (for the space of a few seconds, at least), making the well remembered declaration that she will "'look hideous in dowdy clothes'" but can "'trim her own hats'" (*HM* 117). The remark is significant because it addresses issues of primary concern to Lily, in particular her belief that her beauty deserves and requires expensive adornment. The level of material comfort Seldon can offer her is not by any ordinary standards unacceptable, but the emphasis she places on wealth has caused her to omit him from her pool of potential mates, even though she finds him "more agreeable than most men" (*HM* 86). In the opening scene of the book, she comments that she can behave naturally in his company precisely because he is not, in her judgment, eligible: "'you can't possibly think I want to marry you'" (*HM* 11). If she accepted his proposal, she would lead a life necessitating some frugality, forfeiting large houses and elaborate entertainment, expensive restaurants and tours, rich jewels and top-of-the-line clothing. As Marilyn Lyde observes, however, it is clear that such a marriage would not force her into a life of true poverty, comparable to that, say, with which Nettie Struther and her working-class husband must contend.[26] Lily and Seldon would remain members of a narrow community of upper-class New Yorkers, losing neither social ties nor status. As a result of her inflated conception of her own marriage prospects, however, Lily is unable to view marriage to Seldon as anything except a diminution of her expectations.

If her conscious decision to eliminate Seldon from consideration proved sufficient to banish him from Lily's thoughts, the on-again-off-again courtship between them could not become, as it does, the central drama in Wharton's narrative. Lily is drawn to him ("throbbing inwardly") against her own determinations, responding positively to elements in his physical and psychological make-up (*HM* 102). With "a height which lifted his head above the crowd," he is tall — a trait that women typically find desirable (*HM* 104).[27] In addition, his "keenly-modeled dark features" (*HM* 104) give evidence of the symmetry that is a significant part of a man's appeal.[28] These glimpses of Seldon's physical attributes through Lily's eyes suggest that, facially and physiologically, he meets cross-cultural standards for masculine attractiveness. His qualities of character, together with his personal habits and values, furthermore exercise strong appeal for her. His status in his group is distinct but refined ("his popularity was of the quiet kind"), and his "reputed cultivation" pleases her more than more boisterous or shallow predilections might (*HM* 103). His intellectual interests, like his wit and discernment, gratify her: "everything about him accorded with the fastidious element in her taste" (*HM* 104). Lily is particularly impressed by the mental and emotional distance he preserves from his social environment; he shares with her the habit of passing ironic judgment upon members of their community. His "social detachment" enables him to maintain an "air of friendly aloofness," to enjoy membership in a group yet to some degree remain apart from it (*HM* 86, 104). "Most of all, perhaps," Lily admires Seldon "for being able to convey as distinct a sense of superiority as the richest man she had ever met" (*HM* 104). In him she sees a fitting counterpart to her own special value, a man with whom she might forge the exceptional future of her fantasies.

Lily can admire superiority like Seldon's, which is based on something other than money, but she is nonetheless unwilling to make the radical shift in mating goals that would enable her to take him seriously as a potential husband. Her unswerving commitment to a luxurious lifestyle, as contrasted with his easy acceptance of circumscribed means, constitutes the point of greatest incompatibility between them. In his own reflections, and sometimes to her face, Seldon upbraids Lily for embracing mindless extravagance, priding himself on his own devotion to activities and pleasures far less banal than the "showy dulness" she prefers (*HM* 347). When she asks if he doesn't wish he could afford to buy more first editions or to take more exotic vacations, he responds that he can crave such things occasionally without experiencing bitterness or being tempted ("'God forbid!'") to marry for money (*HM* 17). The profound difference in their ideas about financial well-being, which inevitably affect many details of daily life, might well prove to be a source of significant conflict between them if they were to marry, threatening the long-term stability of the union.

Just how insurmountable their dissimilarities may be is a question that assumes increasing importance as the novel progresses. A closer examination of Seldon's attitude toward material resources suggests, for instance, that he is less immune to the charms of easy living than he likes to admit. Early on, Lily implies that his criticisms are tainted by hypocrisy: "you spend a good deal of your time in the element you disapprove of'" (*HM* 111). He may regret Lily's addiction to costly self-display, but his interest is excited nonetheless by the "wonderful spectacle" she creates (*HM* 105). "The Lily unadorned would fail to sustain his interest," Wolff wryly observes.[29] And his evident decision to remain single might be interpreted, at least in part, as a reluctance to dilute his own disposable income by undertaking the support of a family. (Even in identifying a candidate for a short-term liaison he avoids any drain on his income; he chooses Bertha Dorset, whose ample resources ensure that she will not require the monetary inducements short-term partners often demand.) In fact, Seldon's response to wealth is not quite so diametrically opposed to Lily's as sometimes appears to be the case. And Lily, for her part, sometimes does demonstrate sensitivity to non-material values. Under Seldon's influence, she evinces a dawning inclination to appreciate intangibles such as "freedom" (i.e., "from all ... material accidents") and she feels a sporadic wish to join his "republic of the spirit" (*HM* 108). Almost despite herself, she respects Seldon's ethical principles, acknowledging on several occasions that his counsels are morally and pragmatically sound (e.g., his advice to leave the Dorset yacht or to distance herself from Mrs. Hatch's schemes). On the final afternoon of her life, Lily seeks him out to tell him that his moral vision has "'helped'" her and "'kept [her] from mistakes'" (*HM* 496). Despite the harsh judgments he passes on her shallowness, Seldon himself continues to believe that Lily is "better" than her avowed aspirations (*HM* 497). There is room to conjecture, therefore, that the two might, if they made the attempt, overcome the dissimilarity in values that threatens the success of a union between them. For all the questions that readers have raised about Seldon's quality as a potential husband — and there are many — he is clearly the most suitable of the three candidates available to Lily.[30]

Even more important, Lily's positive response to him goes much deeper than rational appraisal, including a "blind groping of the blood" very different from anything Gryce or Rosedale is able to awaken in her (*HM* 103). One measure of her involuntary attraction is the effort she makes to disengage Seldon from Bertha Dorset on Sunday morning at Bellomont. Lily already has decided to devote the day to her prospering relationship with Percy Gryce; she has nothing to gain from breaking her date with him to spend time with a man she has no intention of marrying. Yet she experiences a "keen shock of disappointment" to find Seldon *tête-à-tête* with Bertha, and she can't resist testing his interest in her by attempting to defeat this on-the-spot rival (*HM* 96). "Competition puts her on her mettle," the narrator informs us (*HM* 96). Lily reacts assertively to Bertha's "air of proprietorship" toward Seldon, employing a series of dissimulations and maneuvers nicely calculated to reassure her, as they do, that his "'only engagement at Bellomont'" is with Lily herself (*HM* 95, 104).

Her victory in this intrasexual competition is a pyrrhic one, since she rebuffs the proposal which her signaling of apparently serious interest elicits from Seldon. At the same time she pays the cost of incurring the wrath of her defeated rival. Because Bertha is much richer and socially more powerful than Lily, the negative consequences of Lily's one-upmanship are far-reaching, as Judy Trenor foresees: "'you dragged him away from her. After that she had a right to retaliate — why did you interfere with her?'" (*HM* 119). Bertha avenges herself by spoiling Lily's chances to marry Gryce, first by passing on damaging information about Lily, then by promoting a romance between Gryce and Evie Van Osburgh. Nor is Bertha's enmity fully assuaged by these successful machinations, as her future attacks on Lily's reputation demonstrate. Bertha's efforts to fan Seldon's flagging affections and to vanquish an emerging rival (like her predatory seduction of young Ned Silverton and successful exploitation of Lily as scapegoat later on) are stunningly determined. In creating the character of Bertha Dorset, Wharton illustrates the human female's capacity for sexual and social aggressiveness.

Lily's unwilling preference for Seldon has spurred her to actions that serve only to defeat her consciously defined purposes. Her regard for Seldon manifests itself even more powerfully in her refusal to use Bertha Dorset's letters as a lever to regain her social position and to marry Rosedale. She is leery of incurring the social stigma associated with blackmail, it is true, and she remains reluctant, despite her increased appreciation for him, to marry Rosedale on any terms. Above all else, however, she finds herself unwilling to involve Seldon in a degrading transaction: "to attain her end, she must trade on his name, and profit by a secret of his past" (*HM* 491). It's "'because the letters are to *him*,'" as Rosedale guesses, that she balks at using them against an enemy whose ruthlessness has earned her no consideration (*HM* 419). In destroying the letters, Lily acts protectively on Seldon's behalf; thus her action may be interpreted as an indirect expression of love.[31] Here, too, as in her victory over Bertha at Bellomont, an ardency she attempts to repress continues to prevent her from attaining what she thinks she wants.

In her final hours, she identifies the "sensations" Seldon has evoked in her as "the throbbing brood of the only spring her heart had ever known" (*HM* 491). This metaphor of procreation equates her emotions with offspring, the "brood" of children she and Seldon might have conceived together. Like the baby she is soon to hallucinate, this image reveals Lily's unconscious tendency to associate Seldon with reproductive success and enhanced fitness, strengthening readers' impression that he is, on some primal level, her real choice. Her refusal to act on her feelings for him stems from her unwillingness to sacrifice wealth for compatibility and high genetic quality — just as her hesitation to accept Gryce or Rosedale demonstrates her unwillingness to make the opposite kind of compromise in her selection of a husband.[32] Wharton's final pages, steeped in emotion and certainly open to charges of sentimentality, encourage readers to view the failed romance between Lily and Seldon as the principal example of tragic waste in the sterile environment of the novel.[33]

Lily's mate search effectively is brought to a standstill by counter-biological selection standards, reinforced by narcissistic exaggeration of her own value to prospective suitors. Wharton's novel draws attention to the perhaps unpalatable but nonetheless pragmatic reality that marriage is an exchange of current and projected benefits.[34] As Buss bluntly puts it, "people with higher desirability ... can attract a mate with a higher value. Those with a low value must settle for less."[35] When contemplating marriage, two would-be partners assess their relative worth to each other, each measuring personal assets and liabilities against those of the proposed long-term mate. A union occurs only when each calculates the future benefits of a marriage between them as likely to outweigh the costs. In *The House of Mirth*, as Linda Wagner-Martin emphasizes, "people marry to improve their social or financial position"; hence "beautiful men and women who have no fortunes marry into money in exchange for their own beauty."[36] Gwen Van Osburgh decides, for example, that the possible costs of marrying the impecunious Jack Stepney are outweighed by the benefits of his physical attractiveness, vivacious personality, and social skills. Jack, in his turn, decides that the benefit of Gwen's wealth outweighs the costs of her homely looks and dull personality. Simon Rosedale addresses the transactional nature of marriage straightforwardly when he explains to Lily that her worth has declined due to her loss in status. "'Last year,'" he tells her, "'you wouldn't look at me: this year — well, you appear to be willing. Now, what has changed in the interval? Your situation, that's all. Then you thought you could do better; now —'" "'You think you can?' broke from her ironically" (*HM* 412). As these examples show, it is not women alone who are forced to put a price on themselves.[37] Both partners in the exchange are attempting to get as much value as possible (in terms of such things as fertility, status, resources, fidelity, kindness, intelligence, and parental commitment) given the advantages and disadvantages of their own circumstances. Those who fail to assess the qualities of potential mates with discernment or who miscalculate their own worth are likely to mate unhappily or, like Lily, not at all.[38]

The negative effects of Lily's unrealistic selection criteria are magnified, furthermore, by her poor treatment of kin. Following her mother's example, Lily often ignores or offends the relatives whose support otherwise might benefit her. Indeed, the people whom Mrs. Bart scorns on account of their unrefined tastes are "mostly cousins" (*HM* 47). Foolishly she encourages Lily to develop a "sense of ... superiority" at the expense of individuals whose genetic interest is closely related to her own, individuals with whom she typically would bond for the sake of mutual assistance (*HM* 47). Following Mr. Bart's death, Lily's mother seeks help from kin but at the same time continues behavior calculated to insult them, "paying long visits to relatives whose house-keeping [she] criticized" (*HM* 52). The consequences of her actions are unfortunate: after Mrs. Bart's death "the family council composed of the wealthy relatives whom she had been taught to despise" is not eager to help provide for the nineteen-year-old orphaned Lily (*HM* 56). Mrs. Peniston is the only relative with sufficient nepotistic impulse to offer her protection. Although she is "grateful for the refuge," Lily's thankfulness does not prevent her from disdaining her aunt's taste in household furnishings, her lethargic social habits, and her conservative moral views (*HM* 57). She does nothing to insult her aunt directly, but she risks disapproval by offending Mrs. Peniston's sense of propriety, ignoring her advice, and violating her ethical principles (e.g., gambling, incurring debt, joining the Dorsets' Mediterranean cruise). It is easy for Grace Stepney to arouse Mrs. Peniston's ire against her niece because Lily has taken little trouble to win her aunt's regard or to submit to her expectations. Lily likewise takes no trouble with Grace herself, wounding her cousin's feelings by causing her to be excluded from one of Mrs. Peniston's dinner-parties. The omniscient narrator comments regretfully on Lily's failure to show even "scant civilities" to her drab cousin (*HM* 197). Feeling superior in every way to this "freckled" and "insignificant" being who "sincerely admire[s]" Mrs. Peniston's hopelessly old-fashioned drawing-room decor, Lily carelessly makes an enemy of her (*HM* 196, 197, 161). It would take so little effort, the narrator laments, for Lily to have made a "friend for life" of her cousin, but her self-absorption prevents her from exercising the consideration a kinswoman has a right to expect from her (*HM* 197). As a result, Lily loses her anticipated inheritance, at the same time earning the collective disapprobation of family and the larger community.

Lily's failure to cultivate the good will of her relations is especially self-destructive given her situation: she has no immediate family members to support her in her search for a mate. Like Thackeray's Becky Sharp, she tells herself that she is handicapped in having no mother "to contrive opportunities" for her, a mother whose "unerring vigilance and foresight" would help to "land her ... safely in the arms of wealth and suitability" (*HM* 146). In these circumstances Lily should do all she can to preserve the affection of her remaining kinfolk, but her early training exercises a perversely maladaptive effect upon her behavior. Many small incidents in the novel illustrate the strength and general pervasiveness of nepotistic feeling in the larger community: Seldon, for instance, has "always been kind" to his cousin Gerty, and the middle-aged Silverton sisters pathetically seek employment to "pay Ned's [their nephew's] debts" (*HM* 143, 126). Even Lily's relatives stand by her to some extent — in part, no doubt, to protect themselves from any stigma that might result from her misfortunes. A Van Alstyne cousin enjoins Seldon's silence when the two of them glimpse Lily emerging alone at night from Gus Trenor's house; Jack Stepney reluctantly provides overnight shelter to Lily when Bertha Dorset sends her away without notice. By the time Lily has been disinherited by Mrs. Peniston, however, she has lost all capacity to inspire altruistic response from her relatives: "'my whole family have unanimously washed their hands of me'" (*HM* 380). The adaptive mechanisms inspired by kin selection typically prove resilient, yet Lily has managed to blunt her relations' sense of obligation to her, in large part because she herself was reared to ignore the claims of kin on her generosity and forbearance.

Another significant contributing factor in Lily's failed mate search and precipitous decline in status is her violation of behavioral norms for marriageable girls. She makes a major error at the outset of the novel's action by seeking financial assistance from Gus Trenor. In accepting money from him, she gives the impression that he must have received sexual favors from her in return. Those aware of the one-way flow of resources from Gus to Lily can conceive of no reason for him to spend large sums of money on an attractive young girl, unrelated to him by blood or by marriage, except as inducement or payment for extramarital intimacies. "Immediate extraction of resources is," as Buss's research demonstrates, "a key adaptive benefit that women secure" from short-term affairs."[39] Whether true or not, gossip of Lily's supposed involvement with Gus drastically reduces her desirability as a long-term mate. Men who hear this gossip will be uncertain about her future sexual fidelity which, "despite cultural variations ... tops the list of men's long-term mate preferences."[40] Human males value premarital chastity and post-marital sexual loyalty because these behavioral traits offer assurance that the children a woman bears will be her husband's. All men seek to avoid providing resources and care for children resulting from a wife's extramarital affairs, since to do so would tend to reduce their own fitness. The fear of being duped into mistaken paternal investment is longstanding and potent; in consequence, human males exercise a strong evolved preference for "qualities in a potential mate that might increase the odds of securing their paternity." Premarital chastity has proven to be one of the most reliable indicators of future sexual loyalty, so that "women damage their social reputations as a result of sexual indiscretions," particularly in the eyes of high-status men who can afford to be the most discriminating in their choice of wives.[41]

Lily's social community is extremely sensitive to any hint of failure in female sexual reserve, reinforcing with cultural strictures this adaptive male preference. The behavior of marriageable girls is subject to special standards and scrutiny, as becomes evident in the novel's opening pages. Lily cannot make an unchaperoned visit to the home of a single man without violating etiquette. "'I'll take the risk,'" she decides, in response to Seldon's invitation to tea, and when Simon Rosedale observes her departure from his flat she realizes that her impulsive decision is "going to cost her rather more than she could afford" (*HM* 8, 23). Here, as elsewhere, readers observe that Lily's impetuous, often rebellious, personality makes her impatient with conventions that limit her freedom of action. She lives, as Maureen Howard puts it, "at the edge of permissible behavior."[42] Lily herself fears that this aspect of her character may reduce her chances to attract suitors. She is perceived, she realizes, as sometimes "too eager" in her interactions with potential husbands, and women friends warn her to "go slowly" (*HM* 105). The more unyielding she succeeds in appearing, the more desirable she becomes to men. Rosedale, for example, responds with heightened interest to Lily's "manner of holding herself aloof," "her exquisite inaccessibleness, the sense of distance she could convey" (*HM* 182–83, 410). Displaying the degree of reserve necessary to signal chastity becomes harder, however, as she ages; at twenty-nine she is, in fact, no longer an inexperienced girl. The longer she remains unmarried, the more social poise she acquires and the more personal history she inevitably accumulates. She learns, to her sorrow, that old stories may be interpreted to her disadvantage. Bertha discredits Lily in Gryce's eyes simply by "'rak[ing] up'" tales of her supposed prior involvements ("'she brought up Prince Varigliano — and Lord Hubert'") and by intimating that Lily once "borrowed money" from a man (*HM* 121). Even with this warning fresh before her of the dangers inherent in the mere appearance of indiscretion, Lily proceeds to solicit financial assistance from Gus Trenor.

The penalty she pays for this imprudence is enormous. Like a row of

falling dominoes, the negative consequences pile up. She becomes the subject of unpleasant gossip; she loses Judy Trenor's friendship; her social reputation suffers; she is discredited in her aunt's eyes; she forfeits her inheritance;
Rosedale withdraws his marriage proposal. Her value as a long-term mate
drops irrevocably. It is Rosedale who points out to Lily that "'if there hadn't
been — well — questions asked before'" concerning her dealings with Trenor,
Bertha Dorset's later accusations "'couldn't have touched'" her (*HM* 418). No
one would have believed Lily Bart guilty of improper behavior with George
Dorset if her name had not already been linked ambiguously with Gus
Trenor's. Thus Lily's final social disgrace and exile never could have occurred,
despite Bertha's vengeful scheming, if she herself had not opened the door to
charges of impropriety through her dealings with Gus. This aspect of Lily
Bart's history illustrates the force of evolved preferences in human mate selection: men avoid the potentially costly mistake of choosing any woman, no
matter how desirable she otherwise may be, whose behavior raises questions
about her future sexual loyalty.

Lily is well aware of the "tiresome distinction" prevailing in her community "between what a married woman might, and a girl might not, do" (*HM*
27). She is not ignorant of the conventions: what, then, is she thinking when
she employs "the appeal of her exquisite nearness" to coax Gus Trenor into
offering her monetary aid? (*HM* 35). She knows that it is not "the fraternal
instinct" in Trenor to which she is appealing, and she tacitly concedes that
his promise of material aid gives him the right to "lean a little nearer and rest
his hand reassuringly on hers" (*HM* 36). She seems to assume that because
she plans to cheat him, that is, to take his money without giving him much
in return, her chastity will remain uncompromised. Her intentions are duplicitous: she implies by her subtle seductiveness that she will exchange intimacy
for cash, but she is resolved to offer nothing except sympathetic attention and
a few socially acceptable caresses. The high value she places upon her own
exceptional qualities enables her to imagine that the privilege of helping her
will be sufficient reward for this "coarse dull man," this "mere supernumer-
ary": "it would be easy to hold him by his vanity and so keep the obligation
on his side" (*HM* 137).

As Trenor delivers more and more money, the unevenness of the exchange
Lily has engineered grows ever more pronounced. He becomes irritably impatient for a return on his investment, while she becomes increasingly frightened by the growing vehemence with which he asserts his claim. Few actual
transfers of money are depicted; instead readers are confronted with Lily's
belated "discovery that she had, in all, received nine thousand dollars" (*HM*
273). It is perhaps difficult to believe that any man would give such a large
sum of money, over time, to a woman who does no more than "listen to his

stories ... receive his confidences and laugh at his jokes" (*HM* 137). Wharton evades this difficulty by omitting some scenes in which Trenor might be expected to insist on a show of gratitude. Lily has preserved her chastity, but with the result that Trenor feels ever more ill-used. This is perhaps one reason why he talks about her to Rosedale and others, sparking gossip that quickly damages her reputation. She is naïve, of course, in expecting him to remain silent about the new relationship in which he stands to her, but if she had been less deceptive in their reciprocal exchange he might have demonstrated more gallantry. She is equally naïve in thinking Trenor's wife will remain unaware that resources are being diverted toward Lily. Judy's retaliative behavior towards Lily is entirely predictable, since female jealousy is especially sensitive to possible loss of a husband's long-term investment.[43] Indeed, Judy has already indicated her resentment of such loss in her complaints to Lily about Carry Fisher; she shows no particular concern about her husband's probable sexual involvement with Carry, focusing instead on the money with which Gus has provided her (*HM* 126).

As talk of Lily's dealings with Trenor spreads, she feels she is being treated unfairly, that she is condemned for acts she has not committed. The narrator dryly comments that Lily has been "treading a devious way" (*HM* 205): she enters into an agreement that has every appearance of impropriety but hopes to maintain her reputation because she fails to honor her end of the bargain. It is important to recognize that Lily deceives herself as well as Trenor; indeed, seeks to deceive herself, so as to avoid confronting unpleasant facts about her own motives and conduct. When we "wish to deny something, usually negative ... or 'incriminating' personal facts," Robert Trivers explains, the psychological process of self-deception begins to operate. "Denial will easily engender denial of denial, the deeper to bury the falsehood. Denial may plausibly require a heightened level of arousal, the better to attend quickly to the facts needing denial and shunt them from consciousness."[44] In an effort to interpret her actions as favorably as possible, Lily tries hard to convince herself that her involvement with Gus Trenor is nothing more than a business arrangement: he has offered as a friend to speculate with her capital, she tells herself, and each new gift of money is merely "another dividend" from investments he has made on her behalf (*HM* 147). She is half-aware, in some moments, that this description of their arrangement is a face-saving fiction: "this way of explaining the situation helped to drape its crudity, and she was always scrupulous about keeping up appearances to herself" (*HM* 131). If Lily considered the help she accepts from Trenor perfectly above-board, after all, she would not conceal it, as she does, from his wife; Judy presumably would not object to any reasonable favors her husband might choose to grant her friend. As more money changes hands, and Trenor's efforts to collect what is owed him become more strenuous, Lily's "habits of moral evasion fail her."[45] She seesaws between outraged denial and forthright admission of unpalatable facts.

She paints her behavior in the best possible light when putting her case to Rosedale, yielding to a "passionate desire that some one should know the truth about this transaction" (*HM* 472). The "truth" she is so eager to impart to him emphasizes her own naïveté ("'I knew nothing of business'") and irreproachable intentions: "'it was not the sort of obligation one could remain under'" (*HM* 472). In the privacy of her own thoughts she is less able to sustain such a high degree of self-deception. To herself, she articulates her responsibility much more fully, and "the flimsy pretext" on which she has accepted Trenor's money "shriveled up in the blaze of her shame" (*HM* 273). To Gerty Farish she even acknowledges the element of fraud in her treatment of Trenor, admitting "'I've sunk lower than the lowest, for I've taken what they take, and not paid as they pay'" (*HM* 268–69). Aghast to realize that she is no longer regarded as a respectable and marriageable girl, she describes the "'hideous change'" in her reputation as "'a disfigurement'" (*HM* 265). Since she treasures her beauty as the principal source of her value, she can describe the social damage she has sustained in no more poignant way than to compare it to a loss of physical attractiveness.

Lily's decision to repay Trenor's money represents a desperate effort to "restore her self-respect," as well as to launch social rehabilitation (*HM* 273). She hopes, for instance, that "the rumour of her intention to repay the money should reach Judy Trenor's ears" when she confides that intent to Rosedale (*HM* 472). After Lily's death, the mute evidence of her checkbook does indeed reinstate her in Seldon's good opinion: "It was true, then, that she had taken money from Trenor; but true, also ... that the obligation had been intolerable to her, and that at the first opportunity she had freed herself from it" (*HM* 531–32). Here the laws of reciprocal exchange guide Seldon's analysis: if Lily had already granted sexual intimacies to Trenor in return for his monetary gifts, the account between them would be balanced. Symmetry of exchange would prevail, and therefore she would not treat his nine thousand dollars as a debt to be repaid. Her check to Trenor serves the purpose of exonerating Lily, in Seldon's mind, at least, from charges of having sold her favors. How effective the repayment would have been in restoring her public reputation, if she had lived, is more questionable.

Given its powerfully negative effects on her community status and marriage opportunities, Lily's decision to approach Gus Trenor for assistance is the single most self-destructive act of her career. Readers understand, too, that this particular violation of social convention is not the result of fleeting impulse or genuine naïveté on Lily's part. It is the consequence, rather, of behavioral tendencies encouraged by early influences on her development — in the narrator's phrasing, "inherited tendencies ... combined with early training" (*HM* 146).[46] The larger community has fostered Lily's commitment to luxury; familial "training" has reinforced that commitment while at the same time nurturing a sense of special entitlement and a predilection for high-risk strategies. A young woman more modest in her spending habits, more humble in her self-appraisal, and more prudent in assessing risk would not have entered into dubious financial transactions with a married man. A woman with close relatives on hand to guide and supervise her (that is, one who had not alienated her kin) likewise would have avoided such a socially costly mistake.

At every step of the way in Lily's downward-spiraling career, in fact, Wharton's narrative highlights the powerful effect of early environmental influences upon the developing individual.[47] Genetic differences (those "inherited tendencies" Wharton's narrator identifies) interact with cultural pressures (such as parental training and community values) to shape the degree of ambition, vulnerability, assertiveness, or industry, for instance, that any individual will manifest. The social group to which Lily Bart belongs is responsible for creating personalities driven by cupidity and acquisitiveness. In this social context, Lily has been further influenced by family to place inordinate value on herself, to the point where her self-estimation exceeds her actual worth as a potential wife. The effects of this combination of untrammeled acquisitiveness and immoderate self-regard are indisputably negative. In important respects, Lily's is a cautionary tale, demonstrating what happens to people who think too well of themselves and who demand too much.[48]

The vision of life Wharton expresses in *The House of Mirth* is remarkably consistent with Adaptationist principles. "Conflict, competition, and manipulation ... pervade human mating," Buss has observed, and Wharton's novel illustrates this harsh reality in compelling detail.[49] Readers observe the ferocity and cunning with which individuals struggle to get and keep desirable partners. Wharton's women play an active role in mate choice, moreover, and they wield undeniable social power. They do their share of pursuing, plotting, scheming, and lying to entice partners, gain resources, defend status, and protect investments.[50] Indeed, the assertiveness women exercise in the courtship process is emphasized sarcastically throughout by metaphors drawn from hunting and fishing, e.g., studying prey, effecting capture, landing a prospect, wasting powder on small game (*HM* 26, 38, 44, 12). Even as it depicts relentless competition among individuals, moreover, the narrative points to equally intense struggles between individual and community. With its vivid portraits of gossip and slander, alliance and betrayal, social pressures and penalties, the novel painstakingly documents the plight of a social animal. Since there is no human culture in which the group does not wield power over its members by shaping values, enforcing standards, regulating behavior, and allocating status, Wharton's chilling insight "transcends the limited social environment with which [*The House of Mirth*] is immediately concerned."[51] Lily's fate shows that "ostracism from the class of one's birth is the equivalent of a death sentence,"[52] just as surely as solitary expulsion into the jungle or desert would prove to be for the member of a pre-industrial tribe of hunter-gatherers.

Wharton uses her protagonist's stifled humanity and mishandled matrimonial quest to expose the pernicious effects of cultural "training" in the milieu she has targeted for criticism. Lily Bart is Exhibit A in the gallery of "wasted human possibilities" her creator is concerned to document.[53] Lily attempts to squelch a host of important adaptive criteria in her search for a husband[54]: she fails to exploit her greatest asset — her unusual beauty — to good purpose because she exaggerates its worth; she behaves dismissively to kin and thus forfeits important social and material support; she believes she can flout community mores with impunity and therefore recklessly endangers her reputation. More modest material goals, coupled with humbler self-assessment, would have helped her to identify a larger pool of potential husbands, pursue her matrimonial goals more flexibly, assess suitors more appropriately, and avoid costly, high-risk strategies. Instead she ends up dead at age thirty-one, having achieved a direct fitness of exactly zero. Thus the outcome of her striving is as catastrophic from the perspective of evolutionary biology as it is disastrous in terms of emotional satisfaction. In this novel, maladaptive behavior promoted by environmental forces leads simultaneously to personal misery and to reproductive failure.

# 2

# The Reef

*The Costs of Conflict Between the Sexes*

In *The Reef* (1912), Edith Wharton explores biologically-based differences between male and female reproductive strategies. She builds her plot around courtship, shedding light on the different, sometimes conflicting, objectives that motivate members of each sex and shape their behavior. Interactions among the four principal characters highlight the dynamics of pursuit and evasion, fidelity and infidelity, jealousy and trust. The characters' experiences not only confirm the existence of divergent, gender-specific mating goals and styles, but illumine the suffering these differences can cause in individuals of both sexes. In fact, the novel directs attention more to the psychology of human behavior than to the behavior itself. The bulk of the narrative is devoted to the mental processes of the central couple, portraying individual yearnings, doubts, regrets, remorse, bewilderment, and anguish. Equally ample space is given to dialogue, long conversations in which two or more characters attempt to probe each other's motives, account for their own actions, and promote or uncover deceptions.[1] "What is central ... in this novel," as Cynthia Griffin Wolff was one of the first to point out, is "the immensely convoluted, many-sided problem of sexuality."[2]

The narrative structure gives equal weight, or, at any rate, equal time, to the predicament of each gender. Point of view in the novel is third-person limited and alternates between George Darrow and Anna Leath, the couple whose courtship stands in the foreground of the action. Access to thoughts and feelings of the younger couple, Owen Leath and Sophy Viner, is indirect, although plentiful dialogue compensates to some extent for the absence of interior disclosure.[3] The novel begins from Darrow's point of view, sustaining this perspective for seventy-seven pages. Point of view then alternates between Darrow and Anna, in sections ranging from twenty to fifty pages, until the conclusion: the last ninety pages are narrated from Anna's perspective. The narration achieves nearly perfect equilibrium, in terms of page count, between these two centers of consciousness, the long opening emphasis on Darrow's mental processes counterbalanced by the concluding emphasis on Anna's.[4] Wharton's chosen structure nevertheless appears to imply more sympathy with Anna's plight (and hence with female psychology in general), not only because the concluding section devoted to her point of view is slightly longer than the opening section devoted to Darrow's, but because it does come last. Readers leave with Anna's inner turmoil and intimate concerns firmly impressed in their memories.

The differences between Darrow and Anna can be expressed aptly in Darwinian terms: the two characters serve as prototypes of the ardent male and the choosy female. As Bateman's Principle indicates, evolution by natural selection has promoted "an undiscriminating eagerness in the males and a discriminating passivity in the females."[5] Anna Leath embodies feminine "discriminating passivity" perfectly. She is "kind" and encouraging to Darrow, but at the same time she manages to retard the pace of their courtship: she "contrive[s] to make him understand that what was so inevitably coming was not to come too soon" (R 5–6). Because the initial romance between them (which took place fourteen years before the beginning of the novel's action) failed to reach a happy culmination, Darrow compares their newly growing intimacy with their earlier history as a young courting couple. He has retained a powerful visual memory of Anna walking toward him down a garden path: "she had smiled and signed to him to wait," so that he stood still, admiring her, allowing her to move toward him at her chosen pace (R 6). Her smile encourages him, while the gradualness of her approach inspires the delights of anticipation. Recollecting that moment now, so many years later, he feels Anna again enjoining his patience, this time more metaphorically. "He knew she would come straight to where he stood, but something in her eyes said 'Wait'" (R 6). Now, as before, she exercises a braking influence upon the progress of their intimacy.

Darrow's own inclinations, archetypically masculine, run counter to Anna's. He is eager to press his wooing forward at a more rapid pace than she finds comfortable, and he urges physical intimacies before she is quite ready. As she recalls, "he wanted to kiss her, and she wanted to talk to him about books and pictures, have him insinuate the eternal theme of their love into every subject they discussed" (R 87). This contrast between male and female courtship styles demonstrates how her long-range concern with issues of compatibility and devotion flies in the face of his desire for immediate gratification of his ardor. Later, at Givré, Anna is "not eager to define" their future together, whereas Darrow is filled with "impatience to see their plans take shape" (*R* 116). Anna's "reluctances," "reticences," and "hesitations" serve to postpone the moment when she will commit herself fully to Darrow and accept the risk of a joint reproductive enterprise with him (*R* 25, 28). Her behavior accords with Darwinian predictions that women will be slow to commit and highly selective in assessing prospective mates. Their initial parental investment is much greater than that of men, and the costs to them of a mating mistake are potentially enormous.[6] Thus they have evolved to exercise wariness in screening suitors. By forcing Darrow to proceed more slowly than he would like (with conversations about pictures and books, for example), Anna wins more time to evaluate his qualities as a long-term mate — his ambition and persistence, for example, or his temperament and companionability. Even more important, her delaying tactics enable her to test her suitor's probable future loyalty, to herself and to potential offspring.

Darrow fails this test twice. His original pursuit of Anna ends when his impatience with her continuing inaccessibility causes him to detour into a quick "adventure," a "rapid passage" with the more "irrepressible" Kitty Mayne (*R* 91). Disappointed with his inconstancy, Anna concludes that her positive image of him has been based on "illusions" (*R* 89). Fourteen years later Darrow derails their renewed romance by dallying for a week in Paris with Sophy Viner, an escapade triggered when Anna angers him by postponing his planned visit to her. On both occasions Darrow fails to "wait" faithfully as long as Anna requires; instead he consoles and distracts himself with opportunistic sexual encounters. Her reticence serves one of its most important evolutionary functions by exposing a flaw in her suitor's capacity for sustained loyalty, a flaw that no doubt would have remained hidden if she had acceded to his desire for speedier consummation. Discovery of this weakness in an otherwise desirable suitor makes Anna unhappy, of course, and in the end it may not prevent her from choosing him as a husband, but her decision will be based upon a range of evidence which a hastier courtship could not have provided.

Sexual cautiousness is a strategy that provides women with more than one kind of benefit. In addition to functioning as a screening device, it actually enhances a woman's desirability in the eyes of male suitors. Men value sexual reserve in a long-term mate because it offers assurance of a woman's likely future fidelity. Since cuckoldry presents such a clear-cut threat to male fitness, men look for qualities in a spouse that promise to minimize this danger. To protect themselves from making unwitting investment in another man's offspring, they review a woman's past sexual history, if possible, and also observe her current conduct. A woman known to have indulged in frequent amorous encounters quickly may be rejected as recipient of a man's long-term investment, as may a woman who yields easily to a current suitor's advances.[7] Owen Leath's behavior provides an excellent example of the proprietary concern men typically display toward their long-term mates, actual or potential. He surreptitiously monitors his fiancée's private meetings with another man, watching for signs of possible defection. His mate-guarding behavior grows more assiduous as he observes Sophy and Darrow repeatedly "'shut up together alone'" (R 245). When he detects a lack of reserve in Sophy's behavior toward Darrow, a familiarity suggestive of intimacy, his jealousy becomes acute and he bursts forth with angry accusations. In general, as Buss's research shows, a man in quest of a long-term partner is favorably impressed by manifestations of sexual reluctance (toward himself and toward others) in the woman he woos. The woman herself has much to gain, in any case, by taking time to evaluate a future mate's health, status, prospects, kin, and commitment. Thus she is well served on all fronts by responding with reticence to male ardor. "By withholding sex, women increase its value," Buss points out; hence female reserve exerts a positive effect upon "a man's perception of a woman's value as a mate."[8]

Anna Leath's behavior, which illustrates a high degree of sexual inhibition, predictably elicits a positive response from George Darrow. She is "secluded and different," desirable precisely because she appears more unobtainable than other women (R 2). Even after their youthful courtship is disrupted, she remains for him "the image" of something "sacred" (R 26). Later he marvels at "the strength of the spell she cast" (R 220). He is especially attracted by the impression she conveys that he alone can break through the barrier of her reserve: "she, who was always so elusive and inaccessible, had grown suddenly communicative and kind"; she has "opened the doors" (R 5). He revels in "the sense that he was a being singled out and privileged" (R 5). In her, Darrow imagines he has found the incarnation of every man's ideal long-term mate, a woman who will prove receptive to him alone, remaining unavailable ("reserved," "shy," "cold") to all others (R 129). At one point he compares Anna to "a picture so hung that it can be seen only at a certain angle; an angle known to no one but its possessor. The thought flattered his sense of possessorship ..." (R 129). This metaphor suggests that Anna's reticent behavior serves the same function as does a veil, or claustration, ensuring that she will be fully enjoyed solely by her mate. She appears willing, in other words, "to channel all of her reproductive value exclusively" to her husband.[9] Anna's ability to communicate such selective receptivity clearly increases her desirability to her suitor. He luxuriates in "the high privilege of possessing her" (R 128). Not only is she "the kind of woman with whom one would like to be seen in public," "it would be distinctly agreeable," Darrow thinks, "to say 'my wife' of her to all sorts of people" (R 130).

Conflict arises because Darrow grows impatient with Anna's hesitancy. Her elusiveness frustrates him even as it entices him — and predictably so. Her continued inaccessibility thwarts his ardency. His frustration constitutes a perfect example of strategic interference, which occurs when the sexual strategies employed by members of one sex hinder those employed by members of the other.[10] As an investing male who seeks the kind of partner who will assure him maximal paternal certainty, he is deeply attracted to Anna's reserve. As an amorous male who desires to proliferate his genes as quickly and widely as possible, however, he finds himself balked in his reproductive quest by her insistence on a protracted courtship. The conflict he experiences is not solely intersexual, between himself and Anna (or between male and female reproductive strategies), but also internal, between different evolved tendencies within himself. His impulse to revere Anna's chaste choosiness wars with his irritation at her continued unyieldingness. In depicting Darrow's contradictory feelings, Wharton identifies a major source of human unhappiness: adaptive mechanisms do not always mesh smoothly with one another. If a man wants to marry a sexually reticent woman, obviously it makes no sense for him to rebuke her lack of eagerness. As a result of natural selection working on the complexities of human intelligence, however, individuals frequently harbor incompatible desires.

Darrow's impatience with Anna's reserve peaks in the moment when he receives a telegram postponing his visit to Givré. The novel opens with the text of her message: "'Unexpected obstacle. Please don't come till thirtieth. Anna'" (*R* 1). His disappointment is understandable, particularly since he had intended to use the occasion to propose marriage and formulate definite plans for their joint future. However inconvenient and inconsiderate her request for delay (and it *is* inconvenient, as he has arranged special leave from his work to accept her invitation), Darrow's powerfully negative response nonetheless seems incommensurate to the occasion. He finds the words of the telegram "rattling" in his mind like bullets, or like dice tossed by "the gods of malice" and inspired by a "fury of derision" (*R* 1). These metaphors, which rise unbidden in his consciousness, show Darrow ascribing mockery, hostility, and even violence to Anna. She is deriding and refusing his hopeful love; he experiences this apparent rejection as both insult and assault. Mistrustful of her motives and focused on his own "wounded vanity," he articulates no concern for the problem she may be facing — illness or injury, for all he knows, or fire or flood (*R* 46). He considers the situation solely from his own point of view, as it affects his emotions, hopes, and plans. For him, the delay she now enjoins is the proverbial last straw; it is a test of patience he can not or will not meet. He interprets her telegram as part of a long-range strategy to make him "wait," a tactical move directed toward himself.

By refusing to consider the possibility that the "obstacle" Anna cites may be valid (and may, indeed, concern something unrelated to their courtship), Darrow creates justification in his own mind for his anger and subsequent infidelity. He exaggerates the negative implications of her words in order to relieve himself from self-reproach in future.[11] Readers observe Darrow constructing a self-defense in advance for the casual affair he is about to initiate with Sophy Viner by insisting to himself that Anna's telegraphed message is a final rebuff: "she didn't want him" (*R* 8). If her "'reason'" for putting him off is "nothing but a pretext," after all, his fling with another woman will constitute no breach of faith (*R* 8). He concentrates on his "grievance against her," and in consequence his thoughts are increasingly dominated by critical judgments of Anna (*R* 9): she submits too "tamely" to the needs of others, for example; she is "too readily resigned" to "family duties"; she is "afraid of life" (*R* 7, 8, 28). Picturing the two of them as "the ghostly lovers of the Grecian Urn, forever pursuing without ever clasping each other," Darrow finds a perfect image for the frustration of endlessly deferred consummation (*R* 28). He identifies with the ardent lover in Keats's poem, doomed "never" to "kiss" his beloved no matter now "near the goal" he comes, but he takes Keats's lines in a new direction by blaming his partner for his stymied passion.[12] He is convinced at this point that Anna intends to hold herself eternally out of his reach, maddening him with anticipation of a togetherness that is never to be realized.

Gradually emerging facts demonstrate that Darrow has not gauged Anna's intentions accurately: she does not wish to break off with him or to discourage his courtship; she offers reasons she considers fully adequate for deferring his visit; she explains those reasons in a long letter that reaches him approximately a week after her telegram. When he fails to answer her letter, she overcomes her own reserve sufficiently to write him again, taking the initiative to re-establish their romantic relations. Although her decision to postpone Darrow's visit is entirely defensible from Anna's point of view, and by no means calculated or manipulative, Darrow nevertheless interprets her action as intolerably withholding. In the stand-off between his pursuit and her resistance, the balance shifts decisively at this moment: the price of Anna's sexual reserve now seems higher to Darrow than he is willing to pay. He has lost the impression she earlier conveyed to him that he has been "singled out" for her love (i.e., that she has chosen to make herself "selectively accessible" to him), along with his belief that she views their union as "inevitable" (*R* 5, 6).[13] In this instance of intersexual competition, each party is motivated by gender-related concerns, and each feels confident of having behaved justifiably. The woman feels serenely certain that her suitor should trust in her love and be patient; the man fumes that if she really cared for him she would let nothing disrupt their growing intimacy. Thus the interval between Anna's abrupt telegram and her follow-up letter (somewhere between a week and ten days) seems reasonable to her but interminable to Darrow. His urgency conflicts with her circumspection, and each feels small understanding, let alone empathy, for the impulses driving the other's responses.

Darrow's prototypical ardency, plainly evident in his intolerance for the delays Anna imposes upon their courtship, manifests itself with special clarity in his pursuit of short-term mating opportunities. Twice in his acquaintance with Anna Leath he responds to her reticence by initiating affairs with more easily obtainable partners. His meeting with Sophy Viner coincides with his anger at Anna's apparently rejecting telegram, and he is attracted immediately to the girl's physical appearance. He notices her youth and "favourable" looks, zeroing in on two of the qualities men most desire in a mate ($R$ 14).[14] At the theatre he exults in the admiration her appearance elicits from other men, illustrating Buss's finding that "men seek attractive women as mates not simply for their reproductive value but also as signals of status to same-sex competitors" ($R$ 59)[15]: he "knew the primitive complacency of the man at whose companion other men stare" ($R$ 48). From the beginning he thinks of Sophy in explicitly amorous terms. On the second night they spend in adjoining rooms at a Paris hotel, for instance, he fantasizes her undressing just a few yards away from him: "his imagination followed her ... traced the curve of her slim young arms ... pictured the sliding down of her dress to the waist and then to the knees" ($R$ 56).

As he lures her into ever greater intimacy, Darrow experiences "the excitement of pursuit" ($R$ 70). Evidently he is stimulated as much by the chase itself, and the renewed proof it offers of his masculinity, as by any unique qualities of the girl he has targeted for his attention. This "small adventure" distracts him, furthermore, from "fruitless contemplation of his private grievance" with Anna ($R$ 32). Sophy offers him "an escape from himself"; she is "an object about which his thwarted activities could cluster" ($R$ 53). Her obvious admiration for him soothes his "hurt vanity," while her spontaneity provides a welcome contrast to Anna's cautiousness ($R$ 54). Sophy is "the more engaging, for being so natural," Darrow decides, and "an extraordinary conductor of sensation" ($R$ 32, 40). The girl's receptivity restores his self-esteem. She makes him feel desirable, and consequently she becomes ever more appealing to him: "in the reaction of his wounded vanity he found her prettier and more interesting" ($R$ 46). He delights in her physical responsiveness (the "tremor of pleasure" his glance or touch evokes in her), which contrasts so sharply with Anna's reserve ($R$ 53). In short, Sophy's undisguised liking for Darrow helps to restore his image of himself as an attractive and admirable man, one who deserves (and can get) better treatment from a woman than he has received from Anna.

Sophy is friendly, receptive, and trusting in her behavior towards Darrow, but she makes no overtures to him; it is he, rather, who takes the lead in steering their accidental encounter toward sexual intimacy. He seduces her over a period of several days, employing a favored, often successful, male strategy by lavishing resources on her.[16] He pays for hotel lodgings, restaurant meals, and show tickets, treating her to a luxurious week in Paris that she otherwise could not have afforded. Having discovered her love of theatre, he offers her precisely those benefits she is most eager to obtain. Because she is an outsider in the world of theatre, art, and museums, he impresses her with his education and cosmopolitanism, which are clearly superior to hers. As the provider of almost irresistible benefits, he is able, in addition, to represent himself as a person with the desirable attributes of kindliness and generosity. Darrow speaks to her almost in the voice of a fairy godmother, a benevolent source of wondrous gifts: "'I want you, just for a few days, to have all the things you've never had,'" he tells her (R 66).

There is manifestly deceit in his seductive technique, in that he conceals his ultimate intentions, that is, he does not propose a straightforward exchange of sex for resources. When he urges Sophy to spend a week in Paris at his expense, he declares it to be a "man to man" arrangement, asking her to "trust" him as a "friend" (R 70). All he is suggesting, he explains, is that she "be willing to take a few days' holiday" with him, "just for the pleasure of the thing" (R 70). He tells her, in other words, that he is offering her resources with no strings attached, simply because he likes her — and, by implication, because he himself is an altruistically generous person. "Men looking for casual liaisons compete by mimicking what women desire in a permanent mate," Buss has discovered, and a particularly effective ploy is to "act as if they care about a woman even though they do not really care."[17] When Sophy reacts with enthusiastic gratitude to Darrow's plan ("'you're giving me the only chance I've ever had!'"), clearly overwhelmed by what she interprets as his goodness and magnanimity, he is struck by her naïveté (R 71). Uncomfortable in the role of mendacious seducer, especially with a girl of such apparent disingenuity, he supplements deception with self-deception, reframing his own intentions more idealistically. "She was a child after all," he tells himself, "and all he could do — all he had ever meant to do — was to give her a child's holiday to look back to" (R 71). Reassuring himself, as well as Sophy, that he has no intention of seeking sexual contact with her, he continues to pursue her with an easy conscience. Deluding himself about the disinterestedness of his motives, he is, predictably, all the more successful in deluding her.[18]

There is a high degree of deceptiveness, additionally, in the measures Darrow takes to prevent Sophy from leaving Paris. To obtain the time and propinquity necessary to complete his seduction, he first tempts her to stay in town in order to see a well known actress, "using Cerdine as a pretext" (*R* 44). Dangling new opportunities before her ("'they're giving *Oedipe* tomorrow'"), he reinforces positive inducements for lingering by failing to post her letter to the friends she hopes to join in Joigny (*R* 48). His initial neglect of the errand is presented by Wharton as genuine forgetfulness, showing inconsiderateness for Sophy's situation, perhaps, but no intentional manipulativeness. Realizing that he can exploit the situation to his own advantage, however, he overcomes his initial "twinge of compunction" and undertakes a scheme of deliberate duplicity (*R* 48). Not only does he lie to Sophy about having forgotten her letter, he decides not to mail it at all. Waiting, as she must, for a reply to the unsent missive, she gives him more time to win her confidence and increase her liking. Thus the deception serves his purposes well. In the step-by-step delineation of Darrow's calculated methods of seduction, as Dale M. Bauer notes, Wharton raises "the problem of victimization at the heart of casual affairs like Darrow's with Sophy."[19]

Darrow reconciles himself to his outrageously dishonest plan of action by convincing himself that Sophy must "secretly expect" and wish to remain with him (*R* 55). In particular, he interprets her decision to send a letter, rather than a telegram, as an "artless device to gain more time with him" (*R* 55). He persuades himself that she, too, is maneuvering to prolong their time together. By neglecting to mail her letter, he reasons, he will "be merely falling in with her own hopes," and thus he feels justified in beginning to "plan new ways of detaining her" (*R* 55). In other words, he decides it is acceptable for him to deceive Sophy because she apparently *wants* to be deceived. Rationalizing his duplicity in this manner, Darrow preserves his own self-regard, in particular his image of himself as a morally good person. Darrow is forced to recognize a critical error in his self-serving logic when he discovers that poverty, rather than policy, has caused Sophy to reject the more expensive telegram as a means of communication. Embarrassed and contrite, he admits to himself that his theory that she, too, has schemed to delay her departure is "simply trumped up to justify his own disloyalty: he had never really believed in it" (*R* 64). Despite this moment of honest self-appraisal, he continues to delude himself that Sophy is secretly colluding with his plans. When she accepts his barefaced lies about having mailed her letter, for instance, he considers her very "trustfulness" as "open to suspicion": "Was she not almost too ready to take his word?" (*R* 66). Again he finds himself "ashamed of [his] thought," acknowledging that it is "another pretext to lessen his own delinquency" (*R* 66). By providing such detailed access to Darrow's thoughts, including his moment-by-moment re-evaluation of motives and deeds, Wharton offers shrewd insight into human psychology, illustrating the complex mixture of deceit and self-justification characterizing individual behavior. She demonstrates, too, that the brevity of short-term affairs "dramatically increases the opportunities for deception."[20]

The primary adaptive benefit Darrow, as a male, stands to gain from a short-term affair is obvious, namely, a potential increase in his lifetime total number of offspring. He chooses Sophy as a short-term partner because she is young and attractive, and thus presumably fertile, and because she is available, that is, willing to consent to sex with minimal investment on his part. Her reasons for choosing him, and the benefits she may reap from their brief encounter, are perhaps less readily discernable. They are, in any case, not the same as his; Buss points out that "the adaptive benefits of temporary liaisons differ for each sex."[21] By including information about Sophy's life history and current situation, Wharton enables readers to understand the context in which this young woman makes her choices. She is essentially alone in the world, with no network of kin and friends to support or advise her. She also lacks material resources and must scramble to earn a living on the periphery of an upper-middle-class social community. Necessity has thrown her into dubious company and a "distasteful" environment; she has associated with people whose behavior is ungenteel, if not, indeed, sordid (R 130). Mrs. Murrett's house, in which Darrow first encounters her, clearly is not a place frequented by marriageable girls. Taking into account the disadvantages of her background, Sophy assesses her mating opportunities realistically, concluding that she has little chance of attracting a long-term partner of decent quality. "'I'd like you to see the only men who've ever wanted to marry me!'" she tells Darrow, and proceeds to describe two highly undesirable suitors (R 61). She has little to gain, therefore, by behaving with the sexual reticence that serves the interests of better situated young women: "'girls who've only got to choose!'" as she describes them (R 61). As Sophy realizes, the benefits of sexual withholding accrue principally to women who are otherwise very desirable as wives. The more beautiful, wealthy, well connected, and socially prominent the woman, the more likely she is to profit from a strategy of reticence and restraint. Men of high quality will pursue her because of the advantages she commands, and she can increase her value to them as a long-term mate with behavior that signals future fidelity.

Sophy's chief attractions are her physical appearance and her personality: she is young, pretty, vivacious, and "amusing," but these advantages are insufficient to encourage superior potential mates to make a long-term commitment to her (R 16). Men possessing high status, good genes, abundant resources, and kind personalities are in short supply, inevitably, with respect to the number of women who would like to marry them. Women's choosiness, an evolutionary biologically driven adaptation, "dramatically shrinks the effective pool of eligible men," as Buss explains; "many men are dismissed for failing to pass even the preliminary trials. This leaves just a few survivors — men of high status, high self-confidence, and high resource potential — over whom women then do battle."[22] The higher the social stratum in which this intra-sexual competition for mates occurs, the more striking the shortage of desirable men inevitably becomes. Thus Sophy's options are limited. She can either reduce drastically her standards for a husband (marrying, for instance, the "'deaf widower with three grown-up daughters, who kept a clock-shop'"), or she can accept the short-term attentions of more desirable men (*R* 61).[23] Because men, predictably, *lower* their standards when seeking short-term mates, she, as a woman, can attract *higher* quality suitors if she is willing to settle for encounters involving low investment and low commitment.[24] Although Sophy never articulates, either to herself or to others, a conscious decision to pursue this second option, her participation in a weeklong sexual adventure reveals the choice she does, in fact, make.

The benefits she derives from her brief liaison with Darrow include, most obviously, resources, in the form of otherwise unobtainable luxuries. Wined and dined in Paris, she enjoys cultural opportunities that she very much values but cannot afford. The shared holiday represents a special "treat" for Sophy, her "only chance" to experience a comfortable and sophisticated lifestyle (*R* 69, 71). The advantages Darrow offers are so valuable to her that she would rather have access to them temporarily than not at all. Her willingness to exchange sexual favors for material gain accords with Buss's observation that "the immediate extraction of resources is a key adaptive benefit that women secure through affairs."[25] In addition to on-the-spot material resources, her fling with Darrow offers Sophy potential reproductive gains. That is, she may obtain "superior genes" from her high-status short-term lover.[26] Readers do not observe the couple discussing the possibility of conception, but that possibility clearly exists. If a pregnancy did result from the encounter, Sophy would pay social as well as economic costs: the effort of rearing a child unassisted no doubt would bring added hardship into her life. Bearing a child fathered by Darrow could enhance her reproductive success, nevertheless. If she is correct in assuming that she is unlikely to attract an acceptable husband, then rearing a child out of wedlock is the only means left to her for increasing her direct fitness (which is now zero). She may calculate, further, that her chances of attracting even a short-term partner of better quality than Darrow are slim. If a child results from their affair, at least that child will inherit half its genes from the highest quality male she has yet attracted or seems likely in future to attract.

Thus her decision, conscious or unconscious, to risk pregnancy might well be regarded as adaptive. Darrow hints, furthermore, that he would not leave Sophy entirely unprovided for if conception should occur. His parting request that she "let [him] hear from [her] now and then" suggests that he gives her a way to make future contact with him, while his offer to "help [her] to a start" in a new vocation indicates that he is willing to invest more resources (*R* 148, 170). Euphemistically, he sends the message, 'let me know if you find you are pregnant, and I will help.' Sophy's independent spirit and self-sufficiency in managing her life thus far may make readers doubt whether she would, in fact, apply to Darrow for assistance. Indeed, the uncomplaining resourcefulness she has already demonstrated since assuming self-support at age eighteen offers evidence that she would find a way, if necessary, to cope with pregnancy and a child on her own. Her assessment of Darrow as a wealthy and generous man remains, nonetheless, a factor in her unconscious calculations when she assumes the risk of pregnancy by mating with him. From the standpoint of fitness, she can benefit from bearing a high-quality child whose survival seems probable on two counts: first, she appears capable of supporting it alone and, second, Darrow seems likely to respond favorably to any request for aid.

Her affair with Darrow offers Sophy yet another potential benefit. There is a chance, however small, that the closeness created by sexual intimacy may stimulate enduring affection in her partner, thus transforming him from a short-term to a long-term mate. Since Sophy has little hope of inspiring serious courtship from Darrow, or from any man of similar status, she commands his interest in the only way she can, through sexual accessibility. "Once a woman gains sexual access to a man of her choice," Buss explains, "her proximity offers opportunities for insinuating herself" and eventually, perhaps, winning commitment from him.[27] No matter how slight the likelihood of such an outcome, a woman in Sophy's position nonetheless may be motivated to work toward it. After all, the possible reward is enormous, and the absence of alternative strategies for achieving an equivalent benefit is painfully clear. Sophy's conversations with Darrow later in the novel confirm the impression that he is exactly the kind of man she would choose, if she could, as a husband, thus illustrating Buss's point that "women see casual mates as potential husbands" and therefore "impose high standards for both."[28]

The scene in which Sophy finally yields to Darrow's proposition (that she spend a week in Paris with him at his expense) helps to show that her decision is triggered in part by the hope of attracting his interest on a more permanent basis. Darrow confesses to her his lies about posting her letter, arguing that his duplicity proves how much he wants to prolong his "'good time'" with her (*R* 66). Sophy responds with outrage, retorting that she will have nothing more to do with a man who has so deceived her. She changes her mind immediately, however, when he tells her he is "'depressed'" and acknowledges that her company is helping him to forget his "'bothers'" (*R*

68). The prospect of comforting an "'unhappy'" Darrow causes her to "melt"; she puts her anger behind her, forgives his deceits, and agrees to remain in Paris with him (*R* 68). Why? Once he reveals emotional vulnerability, suggesting he has needs — other than sexual ones — that she may prove able to meet, Sophy sees a chance of becoming important to him. She can provide emotional sustenance that he might, just might, prove reluctant to relinquish. In view of Darrow's expressed neediness, the possible costs to her of the short-term relationship now pale beside its possible benefits. Even if his present unhappiness is indicative of a prior attachment and a lover's quarrel ("'I could see he was thinking of someone else,'" she later tells Anna), there is room for her to hope she may replace that other woman in his life (*R* 309). Sophy does not, of course, secure Darrow as a husband, any more than she conceives a child by him. In the cost-benefit analysis she unconsciously makes before making the decision to accept him as a short-term mate, she nonetheless weighs potential advantages and disadvantages along with those that are certain. As her behavior indicates, sufficiently substantial benefits can exercise a powerful influence on decision-making even when there is no guarantee these will be realized.

Sophy signals availability to Darrow with methods typically employed by women pursuing a short-term strategy. She deliberately draws her physical charms to his attention, as in the scene where she twirls in front of him, "a hand at her hip," asking, "'well, what do you think of me?'" (*R* 34). Her frank admission that she has invented this trick, employing it to fool beholders into thinking she is wearing new clothes, does not detract from the effect of the maneuver, especially since she confesses that this is one of those occasions when she "particularly want[s] to look nice" (*R* 35). Her act of self-display is calculated to inspire Darrow's admiration for her figure more than her clothing. She further allows him to make small gestures of intimacy (to hold her hand or to kiss it, for example), and at the same time she lets him know that he arouses her physically. Darrow notices signs of excitement such as a "tremor" or "tremble," or an increase in "colour" in her face (*R* 53, 58, 65). Buss reports that women signaling "an increased probability of casual sex" exploit eye contact as "a powerful cue" to targeted men, and Sophy employs this method of encouragement as well[29]: when "their eyes met, something passed through hers that was like a light carried rapidly behind a curtained window" (*R* 53). She further indicates availability simply by spending so much time, unchaperoned, with Darrow. She proposes going to the theatre with him alone when she fears he may have trouble getting tickets, for example, despite his conventional offer to take her "'with your friends, of course'" (*R* 31, 32). She also lets him know that he need not invest much time in wooing her; Darrow realizes that "she would waste no time in protestations and objections, or any vain sacrifice to the idols of conformity" (*R* 35).

She communicates receptivity more directly by recounting her history to Darrow, disclosing her unprotected, unsupervised situation and presenting herself without fanfare as a graduate of the school of hard knocks. "She was distinguished from the daughters of wealth," he observes, "by her avowed acquaintance with the real business of living" (*R* 26). She introduces subjects of conversation that disclose her familiarity with romantic intrigue and sexual peccadilloes, gossiping abut the goings-on at Mrs. Murrett's house, teasing Darrow about his pursuit of the infamous Lady Ulrica, and mocking the excessive artifice characterizing the latter's beauty: "'I assure you she took apart like a puzzle'" (*R* 17). She even acknowledges that she has speculated with other members of the Murrett household about the degree of intimacy subsisting between Darrow and Lady Ulrica (did they or did they not consummate their relationship?). Such talk definitively marks Sophy as the reverse of reticent. She shows she is comfortable discussing risqué topics in mixed company, and she demonstrates awareness of sexual activities outside the boundaries of marriage. More important, she reveals strong curiosity about such activities. For obvious reasons, as Buss has observed, men in search of casual sex partners "dislike women who are prudish, conservative, or have a low sex drive."[30] Instead they seek women exhibiting traits dramatically different from those they value in a long-term partner, looking for signs of high sex drive, sexual experience, and promiscuity. Readers see no explicit evidence that Sophy has engaged in any sexual activity prior to meeting Darrow, but she has lived in an erotically charged, promiscuous environment. She conveys, in consequence, both awareness and acceptance of human sexuality. She appears uninhibited, knowledgeable, and responsive — encouraging signs to a man interested in brief dalliance. Finally she is forthright in expressing her own attraction to Darrow: "'I like you,'" she asserts (*R* 69). Verbally and nonverbally, subtly and not so subtly, she provides all the information necessary to make herself desirable to him on a short-term basis.

From the outset, Sophy Viner is presented as Anna Leath's opposite: her openness is juxtaposed against Anna's reserve. Courted by Darrow, Anna is cautious and deliberate, Sophy spontaneous and inviting. The contrast between these two female characters perfectly illustrates the distinction men typically make between sexually faithful women, whom they regard as suitable for long-term commitment, and sexually permissive women, whom they choose for short-term sex requiring minimal investment. The tendency to divide women into good girl-bad girl categories is a clear expression of evolutionary logic; research has confirmed it to be a cross-cultural universal, although individual social communities may define and enforce it with varying degrees of flexibility.[31] The fear of misplaced parental investment strongly discourages men from choosing as wives women who make themselves sexually available to a variety of partners. At the same time, men welcome such readily available women as short-term mates, since low-commitment matings offer them opportunities to increase their reproductive success by siring offspring who may survive even in the absence of paternal care. The optimal reproductive plan for the human male is a mixed strategy: long-term investment in one woman and her children, supplemented by opportunistic short-term affairs with other women.[32] Even men who remain faithful to their wives may exercise a mixed strategy over the course of a lifetime, exhibiting a seduction-and-abandonment pattern of behavior before undertaking marital commitment.

Darrow's casual affair with Sophy, which he pursues in the midst of his serious courtship of Anna, shows how a mixed strategy typically might operate. He seeks out a short-term companion during a period when he is geographically and emotionally distanced from the woman whose long-term regard he is attempting to win. When the temporary misunderstanding between him and Anna has been resolved, and the two are geographically and emotionally reunited, he conceals his interlude of infidelity from her as a matter of course, dismissing it, indeed, from his own mind. Through her handling of plot and setting, however, Wharton arranges for the hidden affair to be revealed. Exploration of its aftermath then becomes the principal stuff of the narrative. Wharton's choice of France as a setting for her American characters is dictated in part, no doubt, by the necessity of discovering Darrow's affair to Anna without sacrifice of plausibility. The smallness of the American community in pre-war France explains how the girl with whom he has dallied in Paris could, realistically, pop up a few months later in Anna Leath's household at Givré, in the dual role of governess to her daughter and fiancée of her stepson. If Wharton had located her cast of characters in New York, the coincidence would seem improbable and contrived. Had Anna been part of an on-the-spot network of New York connections, furthermore, she would not have needed to press Darrow so urgently for information about Sophy's background, which would have been known to her, inevitably, almost from the start. She would quickly have learned enough about Sophy to reject her as a potential caregiver for Effie and, equally important, she would have had so many obviously qualified applicants for the position that the question of employing someone like Sophy never would have arisen. By placing American characters in the relative isolation of expatriate circumstances, Wharton spotlights matters that likely would have remained concealed in the thickly packed, modern social environment of these characters' New York origins.

As the three members of the Anna-Darrow-Sophy triangle confront one another in the wake of awkward revelations, the costs of the mating strategy each has pursued rapidly become evident. The individual who pays the highest costs is, of course, Sophy. Her engagement to Owen Leath shows that she, like Darrow, is attempting to pursue a mixed strategy (i.e., enjoying long-term as well as short-term matings), but her efforts are foiled by disclosure of her prior relationship with Darrow. Having failed to interest Darrow in more than a short-term involvement, Sophy might be expected to establish a pattern of temporary sexual liaisons. When the opportunity to obtain a rich, high-status husband unexpectedly presents itself, however, she seizes upon it. Once again the small size of the American community in France plays a role in Wharton's plot: the paucity of potential mates with whom Owen is likely to share a compatible background helps to explain why he would choose Sophy as wife. Her own pessimistic assessment of her chances of attracting a desirable husband proves inaccurate in the context of an unusual new social environment. Except for the coincidence that brings Darrow to the very household in which she has secured expectations of a more prosperous future for herself, her earlier deviation from the highest standard of feminine sexual reserve presumably would go undetected by her new associates.

Once she is revealed as a woman with prior sexual experience, however, perceptions of Sophy undergo a radical change for the worse. Even in cultures with relatively easy-going sexual mores, Buss observes, "women known as promiscuous suffer reputational damage."[33] Wharton holds up for scrutiny the norms of early twentieth-century America, a culture that reinforces the evolved male preference for premarital chastity with rigid severity. Darrow's discomfort, when he discovers Sophy's position in Anna's domestic circle, is fueled by awareness that Anna would not consider a woman with Sophy's past worthy of educating her daughter or marrying her stepson. Anna presses Darrow for information about the girl's background because she is worried about precisely the kind of impropriety Sophy is concealing. As Owen's suspicion-driven spying gradually discloses the existence of a pre-existing intimacy between Darrow and Sophy, Anna is astonishingly slow to apprehend its sexual nature. Her reluctance to suspect an actual affair stems in part from her own inexperience and in part from her trust in Darrow's loyalty, but it also reflects her strongly negative bias against female sexual license. Casual sex, especially if it involves premarital sacrifice of a woman's chastity, is to her an enormity, and therefore nearly unimaginable.

Anna's intuition nevertheless leads her steadily in the direction her conscious mind rejects. Repeatedly, in the course of several scenes, she asks the two principals in the affair if they know of any *reason* why Sophy should not become Owen's wife (*R* 185). "'There's no reason why he shouldn't marry

her?'" she asks Darrow more than once (*R* 185, 256). Later, in a scene with
Sophy, her persistent probing reaches an anguished crescendo. Over and over
she assures the girl that she will support the marriage, "'if only you'll tell me
there's no reason'" not to do so: "'if there's no reason, no real reason, why
you shouldn't marry Owen'" (*R* 286). Premarital sexual activity on Sophy's
part clearly is the one overwhelmingly "real" reason that weighs with Anna;
in her judgment it constitutes an insurmountable barrier to the girl's union
with Owen. Anna uses sexual conduct to divide women into two camps, and
Sophy's behavior (acknowledged, finally, in "a stream of wordless weeping")
places her unequivocally among those who are disqualified from marriage in
respectable social circles (*R* 286). "An adventuress," Anna at one point dis-
paragingly labels her (*R* 293). Buss discusses at some length how moral judgments based on sexual conduct gain support from women themselves, even
though they perhaps might be expected, on the face of things, to resist such
categorization.[34] Women who choose the long-term strategy of sexual restraint
stand to gain by disparaging more promiscuous women, to preserve their own
advantageous position on the marriage market, for instance, or to protect
their marriages from possible poachers. Anna fears that Darrow's intimacy with
another woman threatens his commitment to *her*, and hence she has a vested
interest in belittling her rival.

In Darrow's mind, his "duty" to protect Sophy's reputation conflicts
with the "equally urgent obligation of safeguarding Anna's responsibility" to
Effie and Owen (*R* 152, 167). To shield his erstwhile lover, he must withhold
facts that he knows would cause Anna to lower her estimate of the girl's character. Although he manifests no unease about hiding his own short-term sexual activity from Anna and thus presenting himself to her in a false light, the
idea of allowing her to regard Sophy in a similar false light is abhorrent to
him. Readers quickly recognize that Darrow shares Anna's bias against the sexually experienced female.[35] He assumes that Sophy's affair with him effectively
removes her from the ranks of the respectable and the eligible. Indeed, she
awakens his "indignation against her" by behaving as if she still properly
belongs to the category of sexually restrained women (*R* 187). By engaging
herself to marry Owen Leath, she has deceived a high-status man about the
kind of woman she is (*R* 187). Darrow wishes "desperately" to prevent the
marriage, which triggers "instinctive recoil" in him (*R* 187). The hypocrisy of
his condemnation of his partner — someone who has behaved, after all, exactly
as he himself has behaved — illumines a psychological mechanism that allows
men to condemn sexually permissive women for the very behavior they themselves encourage and exploit.

Although he initially agrees not to expose Sophy to Anna, Darrow tries
to fulfill his obligations to his fiancée by urging his former lover to disappear

from the scene. If she quits Anna's employ and breaks her engagement to Owen of her own free will, Darrow's problems will evaporate. He will have protected Anna and her kin from the threat represented by an unchaste woman without violating his gentlemanly promise of silence. "It was clear that he owed it to Anna — and incidentally to his own peace of mind — to find some way of securing Sophy Viner's future without leaving her installed at Givré" (*R* 168). The methods he uses to achieve his end are less than straightforward. He does not tell her, outright, that he thinks her unworthy of her present situation and future prospects, but pretends he honestly believes she will be happier elsewhere. Feigning kindly interest in her welfare, he attempts to manipulate her behavior for his own purposes. His deceitful tactics in this portion of the plot mirror those he used in his initial seduction of her. This time, however, his dishonesty is relatively transparent, and she confronts it with unflinching candor. When he suggests that she is not cut out to be a governess and offers to assist her in building "'a different future'" for herself (in the theatre, for instance), she questions his sincerity (*R* 170). Why, she wonders, does he express more concern for her now than before, "'when I was actually, and rather desperately, adrift'" (*R* 171). Later he advances arguments against the match between Sophy and Owen Leath, again ostensibly out of regard for her happiness. "'The essential point to me is, of course, that you should be doing what's really best for you,'" he assures her (*R* 201). She is not impressed with this protestation, nor with his subsequent analysis of Owen as "'too young and experienced'" to give her "'the kind of support'" she needs (*R* 203). Dismissing his self-serving reasoning, she goes to the heart of the matter, putting into words the judgments against her Darrow has made but refuses to acknowledge. "'You think ... I've no right to marry him,'" she charges; "'you'd rather I didn't marry any friend of yours'" (*R* 205). Darrow cannot deny that this is, precisely, his view of the matter.

Sophy recognizes Darrow's manipulative efforts for what they are: a ploy to rid Anna's family of the contagion of her presence. Her humiliation and anger notwithstanding, she goes along, in the end, with his program. Why? Darrow dissuades her from her intended marriage, finally, by suggesting that she is "'not in love'" with Owen but, rather, still in love with Darrow himself (*R* 206). He has guessed ("if certain signs meant what he thought they did") that her feelings for him, stronger from the start than his for her, have been reawakened by his reappearance in her life (*R* 206). Although she first denies that this is so ("you're quite mistaken'"), his words evidently cause her to undertake a comparison of the two men, and of her feelings for both (*R* 206). She concludes that she does prefer Darrow and therefore will not marry Owen — or, indeed, anyone else. She makes a declaration of what appears to be indefinite fidelity to an unobtainable man: "'I want to remember you always.... I've made my choice — that's all: I've had you and I mean to keep you'" (*R* 263). Literally, of course, she cannot "keep" Darrow, who does not want her; the most she can do is demonstrate ongoing commitment to him by refusing to mate with other men. From an evolutionary biological perspective, her decision might seem foolish. Individuals frequently fail to attract their first-choice mates, but in most cases they serve their reproductive interests as best they can by accepting slightly less desirable partners. Owen Leath is by most standards a high-quality husband, and for a girl with Sophy Viner's background he represents a once-in-a-lifetime opportunity to marry well. How, then, can she benefit from rejecting him?

Upon closer examination, however, Sophy's behavior makes Darwinian sense. Her decision to break her engagement might be regarded, first, as a pre-emptive move, a graceful acceptance of the inevitable. Spying and speculating, full of accusations and poorly restrained rage, Owen Leath has shown himself to be a notably jealous man. At the point when Sophy decides to break off with him, he does not yet know that the prior relationship between her and Darrow was a sexual one, but it is clear that the facts of the affair are not going to remain hidden much longer in the face of his persistent investigation. It is unlikely that he would wish to marry Sophy once her unchaste behavior became known to him, nor would it be wise for her to become the object of this temperamental man's wrath.[36] Remembering the case of Nettie Struther in *The House of Mirth* (a girl who finds a decent husband despite a prior sexual involvement with another man), readers may wonder, nonetheless, why Sophy does not try harder to preserve her relationship with her fiancé. Why not insist that Owen, rather than Darrow, is her choice? Such a move on her part would be unlikely to prove successful, however, since her situation differs from Nettie Struther's in important respects. By far the most important reason for a man to reject a woman known for her prior sexual activity is, of course, the danger of future infidelities on her part, with consequent paternal uncertainty. George, who "'knew about'" Nettie's past, is fully aware that she was the naïve victim of a man to whom she thought she would be married; she was seeking a long-term mate and thought she had found one (*HM* 509). Her suitor devoted himself exclusively to her for six months and even gave her "'his mother's wedding ring'" (*HM* 509). In marrying Nettie, therefore, George is not incurring any great risk of cuckoldry: he is obtaining a wife who was foolishly trusting, perhaps, but who responded to undeniably convincing tokens of commitment from a prior suitor. Her experience of betrayal and abandonment in no way suggests that she is given to casual sexual adventures, and George, who has known her for many years, is in a good position to judge this.

In contrast to Nettie, Sophy cannot argue that George Darrow gave her any reason to think he would marry her; he openly proposed a week's holiday, with no strings attached. Since Darrow is there on the spot, a trusted friend of Owen's stepmother, Sophy would not be able to misrepresent her affair with him even if she wanted to try: his version of the week's escapade would be bound to prevail over hers. Unlike Nettie, Sophy willingly employed a short-term mating strategy, and this fact is about to be exposed. Since Owen knows precious little about Sophy's personal history (a point that weighs against the marriage from the start), this revelation is bound to awaken horrid doubts in him concerning her future faithfulness. Her efforts to conceal the affair also tell against her, suggesting a potential for future duplicitousness on her part. Sophy shows good sense, therefore, in concluding that Owen is now highly unlikely to marry her; for her to decide she prefers him over Darrow would serve no purpose. Indeed, it is impossible, at this point, for her to express a preference for Owen without making herself look even worse to him as potential wife material. The more she might try to convince Owen that Darrow meant nothing to her, the more she would be labeling herself as a short-term strategist who had effectively dissociated sex from long-term commitment — hardly the type of woman a man wants to entrust with his genetic legacy.

Sophy is likewise self-protective in concluding that marriage to Owen would keep her in dangerous proximity to Darrow. Familial relations and interactions would push the comparison between the two men to the forefront of her attention on a continual basis, stimulating her desire for another woman's husband. Requiring ongoing "guardedness and deceit," as Gargano points out, the situation would be fraught with potential for costly infidelity, jealousy, even violence, all exacerbated by pseudo-incestuous overtones.[37] This volatile set of circumstances serves as another reason for Sophy to decide, without being regarded as altruistic, "'I could never live here with him'" (*R* 260). Finally, her return at the end of the novel to the employ of Mrs. Murrett suggests that Sophy might in future utilize a short-term mating strategy, despite her current protestations of loyalty to the memory of George Darrow.[38] Readers are given no information, after all, about her future conduct. Certainly she will be re-entering an environment in which opportunities for casual sex abound, an environment in which she might at some point increase her direct fitness with offspring conceived and reared outside of marriage.

Sophy's declaration of an unconquerable preference for Darrow, inextricably linked to her rejection of Owen, might further be construed as a last-ditch effort to attract Darrow's attention on a permanent basis. Her wish to "keep" him conveys the message that he may, if he wishes, *keep* her, that is, assume sole ownership of her reproductive potential. Her stated intention never to take another mate offers Darrow assurance that she belongs solely to him, that his investment, should he choose to make one in her, will be safe. She explains that she had tried to think of their "adventure" as casually as he did, as a pleasant "game" or "joke," only to discover that she has "risked more" than he did in their encounter (*R* 263). From a biological standpoint, it is clear that she did, indeed, risk more (conception and its consequences), although she did not, in the event, become pregnant. Sophy has discovered, however, that her objectives in choosing to mate with him were long-term rather than short-term and thus different from his: she has "risked more" in granting immediate sexual access to a man she would like to attract as a husband, in committing herself before securing a corresponding commitment from him. Believing, as she does, that Darrow was committed to Anna all along — and knowing he has classified Sophy herself as something less than a lady — she can harbor no strong hopes of enticing him away from his fiancée. Nevertheless, she makes her "shining" declaration of permanent devotion just in case the situation changes — just in case there is any chance at all that Darrow may be moved by her dedication of her whole reproductive future to him (*R* 263).

Readers may discern, in addition, a more subtle motivation for Sophy's behavior. If she seals her promise of fidelity to Darrow by breaking off with Owen, her short-term affair is likely to be judged less severely. She will look less promiscuous and more like a one-man woman; with luck, she may be viewed as the hapless victim of Darrow's lust, rather than as the wily exploiter of Owen's love. Clinging tenaciously to her first lover, she will appear much more sexually reserved than if she seemed prepared to move on blithely from a casual affair to long-term involvement with a different partner (especially to a new partner whom she had misled about her premarital sexual activity). In her own mind, and evidently in the estimate of Darrow and Anna as well, Sophy's lapse from chastity is largely redeemed by her self-abnegating decision to remain true to the one man with whom she has enjoyed sexual intimacy. She is "magnificent," Anna, for example, insists (*R* 333). An important benefit Sophy derives from her apparently maladaptive act, therefore, is psycho-social; it enables her to distance herself from the contempt reserved for promiscuous women. Since her abstract fidelity to Darrow, if it indeed continues, obviously will have a deleterious effect on her fitness, her behavior underlines the power of social standards for female chastity, as expressed and enforced in her particular culture, to mold individual psychology. The experience of being regarded as a licentious woman is so painful that Sophy is prepared, at least for the time being, to forego mating opportunities in order to escape it.

The different motivating impulses behind Sophy's seemingly self-injurious behavior work together quite seamlessly, illustrating how a single action may result from a complex interaction of variables. To summarize: she might as well reject Owen, since he is almost certain to reject her. The partner astute enough to desert first usually reaps some social advantage, moreover, forestalling the lowering of status by promulgating a self-interested version of events before the second partner has a chance to do so.[39] She also might as well declare her preference for Darrow, since there is some small chance that he may respond favorably and she loses nothing by the attempt. In fact, she garners some benefit: her announcement of commitment to Darrow, coupled with her simultaneous break-up from Owen, functions as damage control, rescuing her reputation to some degree from the stigma of promiscuity. Finally, she can always change her mind about ongoing fidelity to Darrow, should fitness-enhancing opportunities later present themselves. So examined, her behavior appears to guard her self-interest, present and future, as effectively as possible under trying circumstances. She does not give up anything except what she is nearly certain to lose anyway (marriage to Owen), and she makes no promises that she can be forced to keep (permanent commitment to Darrow). She accrues immediate reputational benefit from her decisions, and she remains free in future to reassess her strategic options. It is true, nonetheless, that of the four principal characters Sophy is in the worst position when the novel ends. More than anything else, her poor prospects reflect her lack of material resources and the absence of a supportive kinship network — the very factors that impelled her to employ a short-term sexual strategy in the first place.[40] With her dramatic act of simultaneous renunciation (of Owen) and devotion (to Darrow), she salvages what she can from circumstances in which she is socially and economically less powerful than those around her.

Like Sophy, Anna pays a price for the mating strategy she employs. The sexual restraint that serves as an important component in her long-term strategy is so extreme that it prevents full development of her erotic nature and, consequently, her adult self. "The reserve which made envious mothers cite her as a model of ladylike repression" is an "impenetrable veil" hanging between Anna and some "vital secret" of life, a barrier between her conscious mind and her animal nature (*R* 86, 84). She is out of touch with some of her deepest impulses. She finds herself envious of young women like Kitty Mayne and Sophy Viner, who express their sexuality more forthrightly, since they seem able to plumb life's pleasures more effectively.[41] They also are able to signal their choices more successfully to men. Comparing herself to such women, Anna "call[s] herself a prude and an idiot" (*R* 87). "'What was she saying to him? How shall I learn to say such things'" she wonders futilely, unable to break free from her inhibitions (*R* 88). Even marriage fails to awaken her erotically, and she is sure that she is missing crucial aspects of human experience. At one point she envies Sophy Viner, who has fulfilled her passion for

Darrow completely, though briefly, while Anna's remains insubstantial and unrealized: "'I shall never know what that girl has known'" (*R* 296). Thus Wharton depicts Anna's anguish in counterpoint to Sophy's. Women in whom sexual inhibition has been strenuously cultivated may attract better quality mates than do their more libertine opposite numbers, but they pay a price, nonetheless, in their "sense of exclusion" from the full range of human emotion and sensuality (*R* 86).[42]

Anna's social environment allows no middle ground between the two opposite ends of the chastity-promiscuity continuum. She has chosen the strategy best calculated to promote her fitness, but she pays interpersonal and psychological costs for her choice, nevertheless. Like any strategy, hers is limiting and, in addition, her community defines female behavior with particular narrowness. Her painful self-doubts illustrate the suffering for which the complexity of the human brain is responsible: she cannot help but second-guess her own choices and envision the possible rewards of alternative tactics. In criticizing the rigidity with which her own society regulates and categorizes female sexual conduct, Wharton helps to demonstrate how social communities have the power to make human adaptations harder — or easier — to live with. A single amorous interlude need not be interpreted as evidence of a woman's incapacity for long-term faithfulness, for instance, just as a woman's desire to communicate future fidelity need not be achieved through crippling suppression of her sexuality. Wharton takes up this topic in a number of her works (most notably in *The Age of Innocence* and *The Old Maid*), expressing her profound dissatisfaction with the social and psychological penalties women pay when license and restraint are interpreted with righteous inflexibility. In *The Reef*, Wharton makes Sophy and Anna equally sympathetic to readers. She provides evidence, in addition, that differences in their chosen mating strategies reflect situational, rather than innate, factors; in many respects the two share, as Anna eventually realizes, "kindred impulses" (*R* 320).[43] Anna's socioeconomic status enables her to select long-term mates from a pool of wealthy, high-status suitors, while Sophy's background effectively excludes her from consideration by this desirable group of men.[44] "'She had the excuse'" for her choices, as Darrow explains, "'of miseries and humiliations that a woman like [Anna] can't even guess'" (*R* 293). Unsurprisingly, the tactic of sexual cautiousness, which serves the interest of a woman in Anna's position, would fail to benefit a woman in Sophy's. Wharton's novel shows that "luck" of circumstance, as Sophy calls it, exercises profound influence upon an individual's choice of behavioral strategies (*R* 24).

It is Darrow's ardency, however, particularly his interest in multiple partners and in short-term, commitment-free liaisons, that proves to be the most potent source of unhappiness for both female characters. Once his affair with

Sophy becomes known to Anna, she is forced to confront important aspects of male sexuality for the first time. She is baffled, first of all, to discover that Darrow's commitment to her does not prevent him from being attracted to other women. Simply knowing in the abstract that men's sexual response differs from women's does not enable her to overcome her feeling of shocked betrayal: how could his lust be trigged by someone else "'at that moment ... when you were on your way here'" (R 115)? Not only has he enjoyed intimacies with another partner while professing commitment to Anna, he has concealed this fact, and his deceit troubles her at least as much as the affair itself. From her point of view, their mutual trust is "disintegrating" in the face of his apparently effortless lies: "he had come to her with an open face and a clear conscience — come to her from this!" (R 294). She senses in his unself-conscious mendacity a "professional expertness" that appalls her (R 294). "No doubt men often had to make such explanations: they had the formulas by heart" (R 294, 293). If men lie about sexual matters, she wonders, can they be trusted in others? "She would never again know," Anna realizes, "if he were speaking the truth or not" (R 325). Surely such mistrust "must corrupt the very source of love" (R 325). These disturbing thoughts lead her to question Darrow's "fitness to become the guide and guardian of her child" and, by implication, of any future offspring the two of them might have (R 325).

Thus discovery of his temporary infidelity causes Anna to re-evaluate Darrow's suitability as a long-term mate. His failure to remain sexually faithful, coupled with his deceptiveness, triggers serious doubts in her mind: is he essentially trustworthy? Is he able to sustain a long-term commitment? Is he good father material? Her anxieties are increased by her suspicions that his behavior may be typically male, rather than uniquely discreditable. If this is so, then simply selecting a different man can in no way guarantee her a husband with a higher degree of integrity and reliability. Thinking back to her life with Fraser Leath, Anna realizes with sudden insight that some of his many trips from home might well have been undertaken for purposes of extra-marital dalliance. Never before has she even considered the possibility that he was secretly unfaithful to her, but her new knowledge about Darrow's behavior prompts painful reconsideration of her deceased husband's: "all men were like that, she supposed" (R 321). She can marry Darrow, it seems to her, only if she can make peace with "a throng of mean suspicions, of unavowed compromises and concessions" (R 334).

What Anna finds most troubling by far about Darrow's involvement with Sophy is his claim that the girl means nothing to him. The more he protests that he feels no lingering emotional attachment to her, that he has not given her a thought since they parted, the more horrified Anna becomes. Her own experiences and emotions provide her with no means of understanding the excuses he offers for his behavior. "What did he mean by 'a moment's folly, a flash of madness,'" she wonders (*R* 294). "How did people enter on such adventures, how pass out of them without more visible traces of their havoc?" (*R* 294). The more he insists that the episode was "'a slight thing,'" the more Anna is inclined to view his behavior as exploitative: undoubtedly, as she realizes, the affair has wrought "havoc" in Sophy's life (*R* 316). His ability to dismiss Sophy so easily from his attention very naturally makes Anna fear what might happen to Darrow's commitment to her, in turn, as she ages and the novelty of his passion for her wears off. What if he should "'grow indifferent to [Anna] as he did to *her*?'" (*R* 347). In short, the male ability to dissociate sexual intimacy from lasting commitment is to Anna frightening, incomprehensible, and repellent. Sophy, too, addresses Darrow on this topic with "wistfulness": "'I wonder what your feeling for me was.... I suppose we ['we' presumably meaning women] don't know much about that kind of feeling. Is it like taking a drink when you're thirsty?'" (*R* 262). With this analogy she identifies masculine sexuality as a primarily physical mechanism: stimulus-response. Darrow invokes a similar metaphor at one point, speaking to Anna about "'the strings that pull us'" (*R* 316). The implicit comparison he makes between humans and marionettes points toward his conviction that sexual desires are not subject to voluntary control. Thus he excuses himself from culpability, judging his behavior to be "'not as black'" as Anna thinks it (*R* 316). He is hurt and frustrated, as well as irritated, by her inability to summon empathy for his perspective on short-term affairs.

These mutual failures in understanding illustrate the "fundamental conflict between [male and female] sexual strategies."[45] Although he is depicted by Wharton as suffering less than either of the two women, Darrow, too, pays a price for the mixed strategy he pursues. He experiences reputational damage, if only within a small circle of people, when his short-term affair with Sophy is discovered; being exposed as a liar and philanderer is humiliating to him. His personal life is painfully complicated, moreover, by the tangle of heated emotions, recriminations, and jealousies at Givré which is the unintended aftermath of his secret affair. That messy situation, in which his loyalty is tugged at from two different directions, proves anxiety-producing and unpleasant for Darrow. A more substantial cost he fears having to pay is, of course, loss of Anna as a long-term mate. He values her as the "crowning felicity" of his life and the "best thing that's ever happened" to him, the highest possible quality wife he could hope to obtain (*R* 128, 120). As a result of his amorous interlude with Sophy, Anna keeps him in protracted, painful suspense, wounding him with her reproaches and repeatedly threatening to break off with him. Her horrified reaction to his affair imposes a further cost in terms of Darrow's own self-esteem. Her reproofs tend to instill guilt (not a comfortable emotion) and undermine the self-justifications he has previously constructed in defense of his behavior. He berates himself for his failure in fidelity, admitting to "self-contempt" for having succumbed to a short-term involvement, and to shame at having "fallen below his own standard of sentimental loyalty" (*R* 152). Sophy's easily exploited preference for him also proves to be a source of some mortification. In the face of her continuing devotion, he is embarrassed to realize that he has "hardly thought of her at all" and never "'cared a straw'" for her (*R* 167, 171). Such psychological and interpersonal costs are not negligible.[46] Indeed, they help demonstrate why men like Darrow typically attempt to conceal their sexual escapades: to avoid precisely such costly outcomes.

The tactic of concealment is in itself a significant focus of intersexual conflict in the novel. Jealousy (Anna's and Owen's) is the principal motivating force behind the investigatory behavior that gradually uncovers the facts of the Darrow-Sophy involvement. Anna is surprised to find herself in the role of "'a ridiculously jealous woman,'" full of "confused apprehensions" and "doubts" (*R* 271, 245). She questions Darrow persistently about Sophy's past and his prior acquaintance with her, ostensibly out of concern for Effie and Owen. The more she detects in him a "'reluctance to speak about her,'" the more strenuously she probes (*R* 271). Her interrogation also includes questions about his failure to answer the letter she sent him in Paris and his subsequent wordless disappearance from her life. She wants to know the reasons behind the hiatus in his courtship, the motives for his hurtful silence. In her urgency to obtain intimate knowledge about her suitor's past behavior, she is compared to "Psyche holding up the lamp" (*R* 111). The Greek myth of Cupid and Psyche provides Wharton with a perfect vehicle to describe Anna's irresistible need to learn the truth about her fiancé.[47] Since her husband comes to her only under cover of darkness and refuses to let her see him, Psyche does not know whether she is married to a god or to a monster. Like Anna, she acts in order to dispel her ignorance about a male who is centrally important in her life. The conclusion of the mythological tale is hortatory, and the knowledge-seeking female is punished: in "holding up the lamp" to behold her husband, Psyche is said to be guilty of a failure of trust and, therefore, of a failure of love.

The hidden truth about Psyche's husband is overwhelmingly positive: he is a god, and he has been worthy, all along, of her trust. Anna's situation, however, proves to be the reverse of Psyche's. The hidden facts she uncovers about her future husband are discreditable, and they indicate that continued trust in him might be misplaced. The more Anna learns about his cavalier treatment of Sophy Viner, the more monstrous Darrow appears to be. "'What are you? It's too horrible!'" (*R* 292). She struggles to come to terms with the gap between his self-presentation ("the man she had thought him") and his behavior ("the man he was") (*R* 302). It is humiliating for her to recognize that "the Darrow she worshipped was inseparable from the Darrow she abhorred" (*R* 302). The meaning of her story, like the meaning of Psyche's, extends beyond the individual circumstance delineated. What is at stake in both instances is women's desire to obtain knowledge about the nature of men. Inevitably, women live on intimate terms with male partners who are biologically and psychologically very different from themselves. In Wharton's novel, as in the Greek myth, a male figure attempts to conceal selected facts from a female partner; he refuses to disclose himself to her fully. Wharton's version of the story suggests that such concealment serves men's interest rather than women's. The Greek original chastises women who act to discover the truth about men. Anna's experience, in contrast, exposes the prohibition against such quests for knowledge as a self-serving device of masculinity. Anna is a Psyche whose pursuit of knowledge about a would-be male partner turns up damaging information.

In some moments Anna almost wishes she had refrained from exploring Darrow's past, telling herself that ignorance would have secured her a simpler and happier future. "Why had she forced the truth out of Darrow?" she asks herself (*R* 322). "But she had probed, insisted, cross-examined, not rested till she had dragged the secret to the light" (*R* 322). Painful though the results may be, Anna's pursuit of information about a potential husband makes excellent sense from the standpoint of fitness. Throughout human evolutionary history, women who refused to subject potential long-term mates to a rigorous process of assessment would have tended to fare badly in terms of reproductive success. It makes equally good adaptive sense, too, for men to conceal their mating objectives and tactics from women if they can do so.[48] Thus Darrow's self-protective efforts to preserve his secrets are countered by Anna's equally self-protective struggles to expose them. Throughout the novel, carefully created patterns of metaphor underline this aspect of intersexual conflict. "Using images of light and shadow," Moira Maynard points out, "Wharton will describe Anna pulling back veils and peering through mists to discover truth, while Darrow, in shadowed hallways and beneath wet umbrellas, will work to conceal truth."[49]

What helps Anna most to muster some sympathetic understanding for the workings of Darrow's sexuality is the awakening of her own erotic nature, an awakening in which Darrow himself is instrumental. During the days he spends with her at Givré, his physical nearness and caresses trigger a "full current of sensation" in her, "a torrent of light in her veins" (*R* 123). "In herself, she discerned for the first time instincts and desires" so powerful that they all but overmaster other considerations (*R* 316–317). As a result, she senses a sharp split between "body and soul," or "complicities between what thought in her and what blindly wanted" (*R* 316, 320). Here Wharton seems to suggest that women's own erotic experiences provide them with the only possible means of achieving empathetic insight into the forces shaping male sexual strategies. This perhaps helps to explain why Sophy Viner expresses more sympathy than Anna does for Darrow, even though it is Sophy who has suffered most directly from exploitation and deceit in his short-term strategy. Her powerful physical attraction to Darrow enables her to judge more gently of male conduct motivated by sexual desire. (Her situation also accounts in part for her forgiving attitude: unlike Anna, Sophy is not being sought by Darrow as a wife. Thus she can afford to idealize him beyond his deserts. If she were in a position to attract him as a potential husband, the issues of long-term reliability and commitment that loom so hugely in Anna's consideration might begin to weigh with her. Since Darrow has made no promises of enduring commitment to Sophy, she has less reason than Anna to feel betrayed by him.) As Anna becomes more aware of the strength of her own passions, even she, who has far more to lose than Sophy, begins to appreciate the "torrent" of desire with which men regularly contend.

When Anna decides, as she eventually does, to accept Darrow as a mate despite his temporary breach of loyalty, she is to some degree subverting her own conscious intentions. The scene in which she allows Darrow to take her to his bed shows her acting with spur-of-the-moment spontaneity, rather than with deliberate calculation. She does not plan her behavior in advance; indeed, the lovemaking occurs directly after she has articulated a definitive, presumably final, rejection of his suit. Anna lets Darrow see that her verbal dismissal is not her real decision by her reluctance to leave his bedroom. Lingering in his presence, reaching out to touch his possessions, she communicates sexual willingness, and he responds to her wordless signals. The scene offers vivid illustration of the exercise of female choice. In choosing Darrow, furthermore, Anna permits physical yearnings to trump the conclusions of her rational, consciously judging mind. In this instance, erotic desires serve as "evolution's executioners" in the mate selection process.[50] For a woman, obviously, sexual intercourse *is* the crucial act of investment, entailing a potentially long-term commitment to pregnancy, lactation, and the ensuing burdens of motherhood. "One she has copulated," Dawkins points out, "she has played her ace — her egg has been committed to the male."[51] Anna cannot admit outright that she is prepared to overlook Darrow's flaws, but by mating with him she indubitably does so. In terms of plot, theme, and character, this is a critical moment.[52]

Even their sexual union does not put a stop to her tortured ambivalence, however. Though she believes she and Darrow now are "as profoundly and inextricably bound together as two trees with interwoven roots," she continues to find it "beyond her power" to prevent moments of mental revulsion and moral abhorrence from recurring (*R* 360). Part of her still wishes to "escape" the prospective marriage and recover her "lost serenity" (*R* 360, 361). The scene in which she and Darrow make love occurs very near the end of the book. It is separated by only two chapters from the novel's final episode, in which Anna seeks out Sophy Viner. Her avowed purpose is to inform Sophy of her renewed determination to leave Darrow, and thus to strengthen her own clearly vacillating will. Anna hopes her pride can assist her in abiding by her plan if Sophy, who has followed through on her own decisions unflinchingly, is witness to it: "'She's kept faith with herself and I haven't'" (*R* 361).[53] Readers are apt to see considerable self-deception in this plan, however. Since Sophy has urged Anna in the strongest terms to forgive Darrow's failings and continue with her marriage plans, it is extremely unlikely that she will now support a decision to leave him. Any expectation that Sophy will "save" Anna from marriage to Darrow is so patently misplaced that it can only bolster readers' supposition that Anna will remain committed to her fiancé (*R* 361). That is, her conscious intentions will continue to be undermined by a mate choice she has already made. She does not, of course, locate Sophy or succeed in speaking with her. Instead, the last pages of the novel portray Anna's interview with Sophy's sister in a tawdry hotel room. There Anna gets a first-hand glimpse of the vulgarity of the environment from which Sophy has emerged, and she also learns of Sophy's return to Mrs. Murrett. Although this episode technically reflects Anna's point of view, it is depicted very impersonally. Dialogue, rather than interior monologue, prevails, so that readers obtain little direct access to Anna's thoughts. The novel ends abruptly, on a rather unpleasant and discordant note, without tying up the ends of the plot. Readers are left wondering whether Anna's opinion of Sophy changes as a result of this face-to-face encounter with her origins.[54]

Readers are left in uncertainty about a good many other matters as well: how will Sophy's future shape itself, for example? Will Anna ever marry Darrow?[55] Wharton has been both praised and blamed for the ambiguity of the novel's conclusion.[56] That ambiguity serves a critically important purpose, however: it mirrors Anna's ambivalence, keeping her see-sawing torment at the forefront of readers' attention. The paucity of action in the novel (particularly in the last eighty pages, after discovery of the affair) contributes to the deliberate inconclusiveness of its ending. Anna becomes enmired in a seemingly endless process of self-search, alternating with interrogative, recriminatory, and self-justifying exchanges with Darrow. Her painful vacillations "create emphatic frustration for the reader," and deliberately so.[57] She is unable to reconcile herself to Darrow's behavior, yet equally unable to disengage herself from him. Once they have consummated the relationship, it seems probable that she will go through with the marriage (in fact, she may already be pregnant with Darrow's child), but the lack of narrative closure serves as a structural equivalent of her psychological unrest. Marriage cannot resolve the problems between men and women that the novel targets for examination. Married or not, Anna will never feel completely comfortable, intellectually or spiritually, with Darrow's sexual conduct; she will always suffer doubts concerning his veracity and trustworthiness. The eternal discontent fostered by biologically based differences between men and women, Wharton's chief topic in the novel, is itself incapable of final resolution.

The Darrow-Sophy affair serves as a magnet, the irresistible center around which other elements of the narrative gather and arrange themselves. It is central in terms of plot, situation, and theme, providing impetus for nearly all the major action. None of the events in the book would play out as they do, had Darrow not enjoyed a fling in Paris with Sophy Viner. Evidently Wharton is making a statement about the disruptive power of short-term sexual liaisons. The narrative supports Anna's contention that such "adventures" are a source of "havoc" in human lives (R 294). The metaphoric resonance of the novel's title likewise points to the destructive potential of casual sexual encounters. Like a "reef," Darrow's affair with Sophy is a fact lurking just below the social surface, a concealed point of danger. "'I've gone aground on it because it *was* on the surface,'" he complains (R 316). The reef metaphor works together with the Psyche allusion to sound a warning about male sexuality: women need to be on the watch. The logic behind men's quest for maximum reproductive success dictates a desire for sexual variety, a desire that tends to be well served by tactics of deception and secrecy; indeed, Buss turns to a metaphor much like Wharton's in discussing the "rocky terrain" of "casual mating."[58] Male ardency, together with its evolved strategies, litters the social landscape with unacknowledged short-term pairings. These byproducts of men's hidden sexual histories pose a perpetual threat to social stability and to human relationships of nearly every kind.

Wharton's narrative puts forward quite a harsh view of male behavior. Darrow's actions appear more exploitative, self-serving, and deceitful, on balance, than those of the two women with whom he becomes involved. Having observed his calculated seduction of Sophy in Paris, as well as his hypocritical manipulation of her later at Givré, readers are unlikely to be as forgiving as she is about her unposted letter and lost marital prospects. When she tells him she's "'always *known*'" she could trust him, readers are apt to judge him all the more negatively because he so patently does not deserve the confidence she places in him (R 174). Of course, Sophy also lies to conceal her part in the affair with Darrow, thereby providing evidence that it is not men alone who resort to deceit as a sexual strategy. In the end, however, she distinguishes herself from him by admitting the affair to Anna. Anna remains ignorant of Darrow's lies about *her* letter, which he never admits that he destroyed unread, and his mendacity in this matter weighs all the more heavily with readers for that reason. There is poignant irony in Anna's later romantic speculation that Darrow uses the note-case she has given him to "carr[y] her letters" everywhere with him (*R* 343).[59]

In addition to observing Darrow's stratagems and comparing them unfavorably with those of the female characters, readers have the opportunity to assess his motives and attitudes from the inside; half of the novel's third-person limited narration is devoted, after all, to his point of view. It is difficult to follow his moment-by-moment reflections as he seduces Sophy, for instance, or lies to Anna, and maintain great sympathy for him. Blaming the weather for his final assault on Sophy's chastity ("but for the rain it might never have happened"), and acknowledging that outside of the bedroom she bores him ("not having to listen to her any longer added immensely to her charm"), Darrow appears narcissistic and self-deluding (*R* 267, 265). At one point he actually congratulates himself on possessing the "more complex masculine nature," which requires two different kinds of women to "minister" to its needs (*R* 25). "He is disposed to assume," moreover, that the two female types "have been evolved, if not designed," for his purposes (*R* 25). His immoderate self-centeredness is, of course, ironically mistaken.[60] Even his self-reproaches, once his deceptions have been exposed, tend to be tinged with complacency. Reviewing his life history, he finds it, on the whole, "creditable" (*R* 128). He argues to himself and to Anna, in what Wolff characterizes as a "smug, self-congratulatory manner," that her condemnation of his secret affair stems chiefly from the "fear" and "hypocrisy" that, in his view, govern her approach to life (*R* 292).[61] His private life, he reassures himself, meets "current standards" of expectation, even "if it had dropped, now and then, below a more ideal measure" (*R* 128). After all, "these declines had been brief, parenthetic, and incidental" (*R* 128). In comparing Sophy Viner to an unimportant parenthesis in an otherwise "creditable" life, Darrow inevitably undermines the sympathy generated by his self-doubts: they are all too easily assuaged. He is quick to conclude that his lapses from "ideal" behavior are insignificant, and he is insufficiently alive to the hurt he has done others.[62]

Nevertheless, Darrow is far from a villain. Two very different women, both of them intelligent and appealing, select him as a mate, indicating his desirability from the female perspective. Evidently his shortcomings are typically masculine and thus, in the long run, inescapable. If she rejects him, Anna realizes, he will be snatched up by "the first woman who cross[es] his path" (*R* 334). As her reflections on Fraser Leath's probable infidelities indicate, no man is likely to be entirely free of behavioral tendencies to manipulate and exploit women. Indeed, Anna's disappointment with Darrow would not be so sharp if her appreciation of him were less profound. She nonetheless experiences many of his attitudes, expectations, and goals as fundamentally alien from her own: he is "a stranger with whom she had not a thought in common" (*R* 301). When she concludes that he and she are not "enemies" but, rather, "beings of different language who had forgotten the few words they had learned of each other's speech," she comes close to articulating an important insight from evolutionary biology (*R* 295): namely, that men and women should be regarded almost as "different species" because their genetic interests are served by such divergent strategies.[63]

Inevitably, individuals are compelled to work intimately with others to succeed in the quest for fitness. A joint reproductive enterprise requires collaboration between members of the opposite sex, that is, between individuals whose goals are incompletely compatible; inevitably such collaboration entails "suspicions," "compromises," and "concessions" (*R* 334). Generally, of course, men and women overcome their mutual distrust long enough to collaborate in securing their genetic legacies, but their individual contentment during that process is by no means assured. Wharton succeeds in showing just how difficult it is for men and women to tolerate biologically based behavioral differences. In the context of her passionate, albeit disillusioning, romance with Morton Fullerton, the real-life Edith Wharton observed that the emotion of "love" signals a competition between opponents with divergent objectives rather than a union of soul-mates with congruent interests. "The basest thing about the state of 'caring' is the tendency to bargain and calculate, as if it were a game of skill played between antagonistics," she laments, adding immediately, "We know it is — soit!" [64] This hard-earned realization demonstrates her essential grasp of Darwinian realities. In *The Reef* she directs readers' sympathies in large measure toward women's predicament, examining in scrupulous detail female responses to male ardency and its ramifications — exploitation, infidelity, deceit — via Anna Leath's "wondering insight into the inconsistent and irrational impulses of her own nature."[65] At the same time, Wharton offers perceptive, often empathetic, insight into men's plight. Her chief object is to highlight the nearly insurmountable obstacles humans face in forging intimate bonds with members of the opposite sex.

The problems she documents emphatically are not susceptible of resolution: they are built into the human condition. Her novel portrays male and female reproductive strategies in illuminating detail, exploring the inevitable conflicts, both within and between individuals, that are the consequence of competing goals and tactics. At the same time, *The Reef* demonstrates how cultural regulation of mating behavior — particularly the expression of female sexuality — can add painfully to the costs of an individual's strategic choices A number of Wharton's readers identify social expectations for female chastity as the major target of her criticism in the novel. Such readers tend to assume that the male concern with female sexual fidelity represents a culturally imposed construct rather than evolved adaptation, and that it is therefore susceptible to social remedy.[66] In fact, the problems Wharton identifies in her novel clearly are rooted in human biology; hence her despair of any resolution. A social community may, as in the environment of *The Reef,* exacerbate the unhappy consequences of intersexual conflict; it does not cause them.

The most remarkable achievement of the narrative, however, is its sensitive depiction of the human mind consciously confronting evolved mating psychology. A furiously active interiority counterbalances the slow pace of external action in the book.[67] Wharton's fictional people are engaged, like one of Pirandello's most famous characters, in "crying aloud the reason of [their] sufferings."[68] As George Darrow's and, especially, Anna Leath's tortured introspections demonstrate, humans are capable of imagining a more dignified, more altruistic kind of love than that which flourishes in the competitive arena of intersexual relationships. "There *was* such love as she had dreamed," Anna insists to herself, even as her disillusionment with her real-life suitor reaches unbearable proportions, "and she meant to go on believing in it ... and never, never would she make of herself the mock that fate had made of her" (*R* 304–05). Cherishing idealized visions of their own making, humans lament the "fate" that is the result of naturally selected adaptations.[69] Wharton's novel fulfills one of the uniquely valuable functions of literary art by creating a special space in which humans can decry, however futilely, the constraints of their own evolved design.

# 3

# The Age of Innocence
*Nepotistic Influences on Mating Behavior*

In her Pulitzer Prize-winning novel, *The Age of Innocence* (1920), Wharton presents readers with a classic love triangle: one man, two women. This situation enables her to focus on female rivalry — the intrasexual competition between May Welland and Ellen Olenska — and on male mate selection, as Newland Archer struggles to choose between two candidates for his investment. The plot sheds light on conditions promoting long-term commitment, as well as those encouraging short-term sexual involvement. It provides at the same time a close view of both male and female courtship behaviors. Wharton scrutinizes the female strategy of sexual reserve with especial thoroughness, noting the emphatic cultural reinforcement of this evolved adaptation under the rubric of "innocence." She highlights the importance of cultural traditions and mores by setting her novel in a recognizable social environment: the upper-class New York community of the 1870's. Placing her fictional characters in a cultural milieu that once existed, she achieves more than mere historical verisimilitude; she makes the point that the social group she depicts is illustrative, unique in some of its features, obviously, but universal in its capacity to influence its members' behavioral choices.[1] The insights her novel offers into the social context of individual behavior hold good beyond the boundaries of time and place. In describing a community that regulates much reproductively oriented activity with extreme strictness, she underlines the magnitude of societal influence on biologically rooted striving. Her plot demonstrates, in addition, that community mores often serve to interpret and enforce adaptive mechanisms. The societal forces thwarting individual happiness with such seeming arbitrariness may be operating, ironically, to promote fitness.

Wharton identifies family as the foundation of society. In the tiny, tightly interconnected community of old New York, not only has everybody "'always known everybody'" (as Granny Mingott observes), everyone is related to nearly everyone else, by marriage if not by blood (*AI* 35). The predilection for using family names as given names serves to indicate the complicated intertwining of kinship: the names van der Luyden, Newland, Thorley, Dallas, and Sillerton, for example, all appear as first names as well as surnames. Thus van der Luyden Newland is Newland Archer's cousin, and both are related to Henry van der Luyden; Sillerton Jackson's name signals kinship with Emerson Sillerton. Undoubtedly confusing, the recycling of family names pushes to the forefront of readers' attention the long history of interbreeding characterizing this social group. The shifting conjunctions of names serve to underline biological connectedness.[2] As informal social historian, Sillerton Jackson derives status from his knowledge of these intricate interrelationships, "all the ramifications of New York's cousinships" (*AI* 19). In fact, Wharton has depicted a community very similar to those that prevailed in the ancestral environment: a small band of families in which cousins have mated cousins haphazardly, but repeatedly, over a long period of time, with the result that nearly everyone in the band shares genes with every other member. Relationships are tangled, the strands of interconnection often multiple. Thus Morris Dagonet is married to a van der Luyden, Henry van der Luyden to a Dagonet. The Reggie Chiverses are part of "the Mingott clan" to which Archer allies himself through his marriage to Mrs. Manson Mingott's granddaughter, and later Archer's daughter marries one of Reggie Chivers's sons, creating yet another link between the two families. And when the Archers appeal to their van der Luyden relatives for social support for Ellen Olenska, on the grounds that she will become Newland's cousin after his marriage to May Welland, Henry van der Luyden observes that Ellen is "'already a sort of relation'" through a different branch of the family (*AI* 57).

Criss-crossed by innumerable ties of kinship, a community such as this one derives cohesive strength from the nepotistic loyalties linking its members with one another. The evolved tendency toward preferential treatment of kin ensures that each individual stands in a relationship of mutual obligation to most of the others in the group. In such circumstances, force of custom is enhanced by biological adaptation. Pressure to conform to collective standards is stronger when "community" is not an abstract concept, but a group of relatives to whom one owes allegiance. Indeed, inhabitants of Newland Archer's little world scarcely distinguish between public good and private interest. When Mrs. Archer remarks, "'if we don't all stand together, there'll be no such thing as Society left,'" the "we" to whom she refers is, above all else, family: family and "Society" are congruent (*AI* 52). In another scene,

Janey Archer attempts to bring her brother into conformity with accepted values by invoking nepotism rather than morality. "'Don't you care about Family?'" she demands, the capital "F" in "Family" conveying the reverence with which she refers to it (*AI* 82). Old New York society is as in-grown and parochial as any band of ancestral hunter-gatherers, a fact that lends extra satiric thrust to Archer's repeated characterization of this elite social group as a "little tribe" or "clan." A collection of closely interconnected extended families, this community defends its interests against outsiders, resisting encroachment on its material resources and its social prestige. Members of the group can raise their status within it through hypergamy, i.e., alliance through marriage to more prominent individuals from "one of the ruling clans" (*AI* 50). Marriage also provides one of the few means of effecting entrée into this elite circle, as the example of Julius Beaufort demonstrates. An outsider of suspect background, he would never have been accepted into old New York society, despite his wealth, had he not managed to marry a member of "one of America's most honoured families" (*AI* 27). His alliance with Regina Dallas, who is "related to the Mansons and the Rushworths," draws him securely into the web of kinship that defines the group (*AI* 27).

Nepotism is a two-edged sword, as events in the novel consistently demonstrate. The benefits accruing from familial loyalty are on some occasions accompanied by costs.[3] The Emerson Sillertons profit from their widespread network of kin, for example, when people who otherwise would shun their "dreary annual garden-parties" feel compelled to attend: "every family on the Cliffs" of Newport is related to the Sillertons through "the Sillerton-Pennilow-Dagonet connection" (*AI* 187). All these "unwilling" guests pay the costs of kinship in social aggravation and wasted time (*AI* 187). When Julius Beaufort's bank fails due to "dastardly" business practices, the disgrace he suffers is visited to some degree upon the relatives he acquired through marriage, since "'poor Mrs. Beaufort is related to every one of you'" (*AI* 221). The seriousness of his crime is exacerbated, moreover, because he is robbing kin rather than anonymous depositors. As Beaufort's case powerfully illustrates, the behavior of any one individual can injure the social standing and economic welfare of those to whom that individual is linked by recognized kinship. Although relatives represent a welcome source of potential assistance, therefore, they also pose a potential threat to individual well-being. Hence the strenuous efforts to ensure that the benefits of nepotism outweigh the costs: individual action is supervised and regulated by "family solidarity," which proves more effective than legal, moral, or religious institutions in influencing conduct in Newland Archer's old New York (*AI* 21).

Wharton's protagonists act out their love triangle, in consequence, in a social universe that imposes limits on individual freedom through the

powerful force of kin selection.[4] The twenty-eight-year-old Newland Archer
inspires romantic feelings in both female protagonists; his desirableness as a
mate provides the necessary stimulus for the rivalry central to the action of
the plot. Interestingly, Wharton offers no physical description of Archer: readers learn no particulars about his height, his build, his complexion, or his facial
structure. It is reasonable to infer that he meets at least average standards for
such measures of attractiveness, but evidently he does not owe the female
attention he enjoys to any exceptional degree of facial handsomeness or of
bodily height and muscularity. The few references to Archer's outward appearance concern his clothing and accessories (the flower in his buttonhole or the
brushes with which he parts his hair), details that mark him as a self-assured
member of an elite social community and that illustrate his conformance to
its sartorial customs. These are small reinforcements of an obvious fact: as a
potential long-term mate, he represents an attractive combination of status
and wealth. He appears to be slightly more highly placed in his community,
tellingly, than either of the women who focus their interest upon him. The
Archers' kinship to the van der Luydens, "who stood above all" others, positions him nearer to the aristocratic apex of the social "pyramid" than May or
Ellen (*AI* 52, 51). Granddaughters of Catherine Manson Mingott, both are
descendants of a "mysteriously discredited" Spicer, the Spicers having been
"raised above their level by marriage" (*AI* 21, 50).

The Archers' family status is supported by wealth; they appear to enjoy
a degree of prosperity fully commensurate with their position in a generally
wealthy circle. As important as the sufficiency of the family fortune, moreover, is Newland's secure control of it. His father being deceased, he has
achieved financial independence at a young age. A reference to "his own
house" suggests, for example, that the family brownstone has passed into his
ownership rather than into his mother's (*AI* 40). An only son, he shares his
inheritance with one sibling, a sister who presumably receives a smaller share
of the whole. From the point of view of attracting a desirable wife, his situation is advantageous: he enjoys the financial autonomy usually associated
with an older man while he still retains the personal appeal of youth. The
uses to which Archer puts his money further enhance his attractiveness. His
family is classified with those who expend their incomes on cultural and intellectual opportunities rather than "the grosser forms of pleasure"; in contrast
to May's and Ellen's Mingott relatives, who focus on "eating and clothes and
money," the Archers are noted for their devotion to "travel, horticulture and
the best fiction" (*AI* 37). Newland carries on the family tradition with dedication, traveling frequently to European destinations and making regular
additions to his personal library. He buys books in subjects ranging from literature to philosophy and science, manifesting the habits of a serious reader.

He rejects invitations to "noisy friendly parties," for instance, because he prefers to spend his leisure time with "new books from his London book-seller" (*AI* 115).

Archer's devotion to arts and letters is sufficiently pronounced to distinguish him from his peers and provide him with a well defined personal identity. "In matters intellectual and artistic" he considers himself superior to other "specimens of old New York gentility," the narrator remarks, for "he had probably read more, thought more, and even seen a good deal more of the world" (*AI* 18). He maintains an acquaintance with New York writers, musicians, and painters; when visiting London or Paris, he seeks out exhibitions and galleries. Such pursuits represent a slight deviation from his community's norms, but of a kind generally respected in his circle, even admired. Culture and education typically are associated with wealth and leisure; they are indicative of resources and often associated with old money. Archer's mother-in-law may regard his love of reading as an "oddity," but in the eyes of the two principal women in his life, his tastes and interests set him apart in a decidedly positive fashion (*AI* 188). For different reasons, both May Welland and Ellen Olenska are drawn to Archer's cultural and intellectual sophistication.

May Welland indicates her admiration for Archer's refined attainments by submitting to his tutelage. "Under his guidance" she begins to develop a "shy interest in books and ideas" (*AI* 47). She is not, fundamentally, either intellectually or artistically inclined, although for a time she manages to convince both Archer and herself that she will come to share his interests. With gentle mockery, Wharton points out the deceptiveness, in self-image and self-presentation, that inevitably plays a part in courtship. May memorizes a poem, for instance, purely for the sake of its romantic associations rather than for the sake of its form or statement: "it was one of the first things he had ever read to her" (*AI* 126). By allying herself with Archer's love of the arts, furthermore, she achieves a heightened sense of social superiority. When he visits her in Florida, he discovers that she has occupied her time wholly with social and athletic activities, neglecting to read the book he has sent her ("Sonnets from the Portuguese"), but she nonetheless expresses delighted condescension toward social peers whose literary education is deficient to hers: "it amused her to be able to tell him that Kate Merry had never even heard of a poet called Robert Browning" (*AI* 126). Rejoicing in the engagement sapphire Archer has selected for her, with its unusual and "beautiful setting," she exclaims: "'I do love you, Newland, for being so artistic!'" (*AI* 80). His "artistic" bent, she clearly indicates, lends extra luster to his appeal. He can give his fiancée presents superior to those received by other women, not because he spends more money but because his aesthetic judgment is better developed than that of other men. May benefits in terms of social prestige by choosing a long-term mate whose leisure activities render him subtly, and attractively, different from his competitors. There appear to be no social penalties attached to Archer's unusualness because it does not result in behavior that threatens group values: he will "accept their doctrine on all the issues called moral" (*AI* 18).

Ellen Olenska likewise appreciates Archer's unusualness; indeed, the tastes and interests that distinguish him from his cohorts constitute a crucial point of compatibility between the two. Archer's cosmopolitan perspective, his intellectual curiosity, and his enthusiasm for the arts make him, as May Welland quickly discerns, "'almost the only person in New York who can talk to [Ellen] about what she really cares for'" (*AI* 109). Accustomed to a culturally sophisticated environment in which she socialized regularly with "painters and poets and novelists and men of science," Ellen responds favorably to Archer's declaration that he "cares immensely" for all "such things" (*AI* 69, 100). Like May Welland, tellingly, Ellen focuses her attention on Archer because he offers an appealing combination of normative and non-normative qualities. He occupies an eminently respectable position in an elite social group, and his allegiance to that group is firm: he values "the old New York note" in matters of conduct and ethics, and "he thanked heaven that he was a New Yorker" (*AI* 88, 37). Since she has fled from Europe avowedly seeking refuge ("'I want to feel cared for and safe'"), Ellen values Archer as much for his conservative, community-oriented attributes as for those suggestive of singularity (*AI* 73). Having enlarged his mental and aesthetic horizons through books and travel, he sets himself apart from community patterns of thought and behavior in just the right measure to create a significant commonality of interests between Ellen and himself.

In sum, both women are interested in Archer as a potential mate because he infuses the safe qualities of status, wealth, and reliability with a slightly exotic flair. Despite his cosmopolitan disposition and intellectual curiosity, he remains securely embedded in a prosperous, prestigious community whose norms he shows no inclination to violate significantly.[5] May is already a member of this community, and she would be highly unlikely to select a husband whose behavior might be expected to threaten her position in it. She regards Archer's bookishness and travel abroad as by-products of his high-status background rather than as predictors of future rebelliousness against collective values; his tastes lend a touch of elegance to his impeccable credentials as a future husband. In choosing Archer, however, it must be acknowledged that May shows a bolder, more imaginative streak to her character than is later manifested by her own daughter, who marries "the dullest and most reliable" of the Chivers sons (*AI* 271). May, too, might have married a more conservative man, one less unusual in his tastes than Newland Archer. She assumes instead a small degree of risk, selecting a mate whose distinctiveness promises to add subtle brilliance to her own social position.

Archer himself occupies the pivotal position in the love triangle that drives the novel's main action. Drawn to two women with nearly equal intensity, he finds himself in the grip of far more inner conflict than does either of his female counterparts. Both May and Ellen fix unhesitatingly on Archer as their preferred partner, and neither waivers in her choice. Archer, in contrast, is a study in protracted vacillation. Repeatedly he chooses, only to second-guess his own desires, embroiling himself in a series of never-final mating decisions. Inevitably, he engages in a process of comparison and contrast, analyzing and evaluating the differences between the two women.

Archer is drawn to May Welland for solid reasons of status and resources, backed up by evidence of her probable fertility and future sexual loyalty. The cherished only daughter of prosperous and socially secure parents, May brings substantial resources to the marriage: her father purchases a large house, as well as a carriage, for the newlyweds ("behaving 'very handsomely'"), signaling from the beginning of the engagement his willingness to transfer wealth to his daughter (*AI* 70). In addition, May's personal appearance and social gifts are sufficiently attractive to secure her a high degree of popularity, leading Archer's mother to conclude "there was no better match in New York than May Welland, look at the question from whatever point you chose" (*AI* 41). Having won the most prized potential mate in his elite community, Archer finds his enjoyment of her sweetened by this victory in intrasexual competition; he savors "the simple joy of possessorship" (*AI* 78).[6] May's already excellent qualifications are further enhanced by her conspicuously advertised chastity. She is described repeatedly as "a Diana," a virgin goddess in modern guise, and Archer is entranced by the prospect of a future with "this whiteness, radiance, goodness" at his side (*AI* 64, 31). He is equally delighted with the promise of future fertility implied by her physical vitality: her "radiant good looks, "her health," and her athleticism (*AI* 47).

Whatever compatibility he looks forward to in a partnership with May is based principally upon community affiliation, which brings with it a shared set of ethical and social values. Thus he is pleased that she is "one of his own kind" (*AI* 37). Education and travel have caused Archer to question the absolute value of practices characterizing his tiny community, however, so that he is repelled by May's strict community loyalty as much as he is drawn to it. The sports-oriented and essentially conformist May does not share Archer's interest in the world of ideas or even his love of travel, while his disposition to mock the limitations of his community's Weltanschauung disturbs and irritates her. He judges their personal compatibility — always an important criterion in mate selection — to be weak.[7] Thus he regards the marked disparity in their views and interests as a problem with which he must cope: "his artistic and intellectual life would go on ... outside the domestic circle" (*AI* 167).

When Archer considers Ellen Olenska's attractions as a mate, he finds himself noticing how radically different she is from May Welland. Novelty itself is a component in the fascination this unusual newcomer exerts upon Archer: she appeals to "the universal male desire for sexual variety."[8] Although she is, like May, a member of the Mingott family, Ellen's status in the community has been compromised by an eccentric upbringing and marriage to a European. Because her Polish husband is legally entitled to retain her money ("their damned heathen marriage settlements take precious good care of that"), moreover, she commands little wealth in comparison with the Wellands (*AI* 91); indeed, her lack of financial resources becomes a source of ongoing problems for her. She is a social hybrid with a suspect background, a person whose behavior fails to conform to community expectations in small but telling instances. Her sense of public decorum is as foreign to Archer's New York as her method of arranging flowers. Although Archer is sometimes distressed by Ellen's rule-breaking, he is captivated by her European sophistication, in particular by her genuine interest in books, music, pictures, history, and architecture. She offers him valuable intellectual and aesthetic companionship. Her outsider's vision of New York also proves to be a significant point of commonality, since Archer himself tends to view the customs of his community with the dispassion of a well read, well traveled, anthropologically-minded observer. Ellen's ability to deflate the self-important vanities of Archer's social circle, revealing its frequent complacencies and parochialisms, constitutes a crucial point of compatibility with a man already partially estranged from a good many of his community's cherished assumptions. Her cosmopolitan perspective and aesthetic interests set her distinctly apart from May Welland.

The physical contrast between Ellen and May is equally striking. Where May is tall, robust, and blond, Ellen is small, slender, and brunette. At twenty-one, May is in the flush of early young womanhood and bursting with vigorous good health, but the twenty-nine-year-old Ellen is generally said to have lost "her early radiance": "she was thin, worn, a little older-looking than her age" (*AI* 61). Archer soon finds himself disagreeing with his community's disparagement of Ellen's looks, however. "There was about her the mysterious authority of beauty," he decides (*AI* 61). She seems to be "full of a conscious power" deriving from an awareness of her own physical charms (*AI* 61). He notes that her posture, her walk, her expression, and her mannerisms all reinforce the impression of self-assurance. Violating New York custom by approaching Archer at the van der Luyden's dinner party, for instance, she demonstrates her willingness to take the initiative "to seek the company" of a man of her own choosing (*AI* 63). Such exercise of "conscious power" indicates her confidence in her own feminine appeal. Her self-presentation could not be more different from May's prominently displayed innocence, often redefined as ignorance ("the young girl who knew nothing") or an oblivious "blankness" (*AI* 46, 79).

Ellen's choice of attire further enhances the exotic quality of her appeal, as well as the "mysterious authority" of her womanliness. Deliberately sophisticated and alluring, her clothing is marked with European flair. She demonstrates no inclination, moreover, to modify her dress to conform to American fashions. While the unmarried May dresses almost entirely in white, with "modest" necklines (*AI* 16), as befits her maidenly identity, Ellen's clothes define her as a sexually mature woman. She selects dramatic colors, sensuous fabrics, and daring designs, defining her bosom and exposing bare flesh. Archer reacts with heightened interest to the stylishly erotic suggestiveness of her clothing. When she receives him in a sleeveless robe of red velvet, trimmed with glossy black fur, he notes that the combination of bare arms and fur collar creates a "perverse and provocative," yet "undeniably pleasing" effect (*AI* 98). There is little actual physical contact between Archer and Ellen, but in critical moments she follows through on the sexual promise implicit in her outward appearance. When Archer embraces her at the end of Book I, she responds with a passion equal to his own, "g[iving] him back all his kiss" (*AI* 146). Later, near the end of Book II, it is she who proposes that they consummate their relationship, and when he agrees to a one-time rendezvous her face is "flooded with a deep inner radiance" that sufficiently indicates a strong erotic component to her feelings for him (*AI* 250).

Although May appears physically more vigorous and voluptuous than Ellen, the image she cultivates is not correspondingly sexually inviting. Even after her marriage, the young Mrs. Archer's style remains demure. She continues to dress chiefly in white and to maintain "the same Diana-like aloofness" (*AI* 179). Her situation in life has changed, but she presents herself as a virginal, sexually unavailable girl rather than as an erotically awakened adult. Indeed, the impression she makes of asexuality is more than superficial. Although Archer is convinced that she has "the capacity" for "feeling," he finds her physically unresponsive (*AI* 179): after two years of marriage he is "weary of living in a perpetual tepid honeymoon, without the temperature of passion" (*AI* 127). In contrast to Ellen, who responds to his embrace against her own better judgment, May "dr[aws] back" from the pressure of his lips when he greets her in St. Augustine (*AI* 125). The warmth of that Florida backdrop sets the coolness characterizing May's temperament into sharp relief. She resembles "a young marble athlete," and kissing her is like "drinking at a cold spring with the sun on it" (*AI* 125). Reiterated use of terms such as coldness, aloofness, and childishness to describe May, both before and after her marriage, all signal low libido. The "vacancy," "emptiness," and "negation" Archer fears to discover in May is an absence of sexual vitality as much as a lack of intellectual, emotional, or imaginative development (*AI* 125, 180).

Yet May's residual reproductive value, as measured by the number of offspring she might potentially bear, clearly is greater than Ellen's, since May is younger by eight years. (When the main action of the novel commences, May is twenty-one and Ellen twenty-nine; by the time events reach their crisis point, Ellen is thirty-one.) May also appears to be the more physically robust of the two. In assessing Ellen's reproductive worth, however, her childlessness is more important than any other factor. After a decade of marriage, and in an era when no reliable contraception is available, her failure to bear children casts strong doubt on her fertility. A further consideration, implicit in information provided about her marriage, is that Ellen's husband is a notorious womanizer ("paying any price" for his "harlots") who conceivably may have infected her with venereal disease (*AI* 2). Available evidence indicates that Ellen is very probably infertile and even, perhaps, a disease-carrier, so that long-term investment in her is likely to result in drastically reduced fitness for her partner. This set of facts can be expected to exert critical influence on Archer's choice — as, indeed, it eventually does: fertility is the bottom line in mate selection. No amount of beauty, status, wealth, or compatibility can compensate for the inability to procreate. No matter what her other attractions may be, Ellen's questionable fertility should be a deal-breaker. Yet it is Ellen, older and "worn," who exudes greater sexual appeal than her younger and more reproductively viable rival. Presenting herself as an erotically mature and inviting woman, Ellen deflects attention away from the reproductively negative results of her sexual activity to date.

It is easy to appreciate how Ellen Olenska's dignified but unmistakable announcement of herself as a sexual being constitutes an important aspect of her attraction for Newland Archer in comparison with May's "boyish" charms, no matter how reassuring the latter prove as indicators of wifely fidelity (*AI* 163). In the context of New York society, nevertheless, there are negative implications to Ellen's dress and behavior, which tend to be construed as indicating an unacceptable degree of sexual availability. A sexually assured self-presentation that is normative for women in European society, to which Ellen has belonged until recently, renders her the subject of harsh gossip in New York. Men universally desire long-term mates who demonstrate good potential for post-marital sexual loyalty, but the specific cues for such loyalty are likely to vary cross-culturally.[9] Wharton's novel effectively illustrates the problems an individual encounters when moving into a new social milieu: all kinds of learned behavioral signals are susceptible to misinterpretation in a different environment. Events and disclosures in the novel make clear that Ellen is not promiscuous. Gossip assigning her a European lover proves to be mistaken, and she refuses advances from married men like Lawrence Lefferts and Julius Beaufort. Everything readers know about her indicates that she is just as likely as May Welland to prove faithful to a future husband.[10] From the moment she appears at the New York opera in a dramatically revealing gown, however, she becomes the target of malicious speculation and the object of pursuit by men desiring short-term mating partners. Once Ellen has moved from Europe to America, the mature sexuality she advertises proves to be disadvantageous: it attracts male attention, to be sure, but it marks her in this new community, with its different norms, as a woman with possibly low potential for fidelity.

With the title she has chosen for her novel, Wharton underlines the thematic centrality of the social concept of "innocence," a cluster of behaviors manifested by marriageable girls in Archer's community to signal premarital chastity. There are good evolutionary biological reasons for men to prefer as long-term mates women who have engaged in little or no prior sexual activity: chastity in a bride inspires paternal confidence.[11] Thus researchers have observed a tendency worldwide for men to value behavioral indicators of virginity in women they court for long-term mating purposes and with the expectation of investment in offspring.[12] When men seek women for short-term involvement, contrastingly, sexual reticence becomes an undesirable trait; it merely wastes time. If long-term investment in a woman and her future offspring is not at stake, men typically prefer women who indicate sexual permissiveness rather than restraint.[13] Women tend to be categorized according to the degree of sexual willingness they project. Those who wish to make themselves available for short-term affairs comport themselves differently from those who seek long-term commitment from a single partner, and generally this disparity in conduct is the source of important social assessments. Archer muses, for example, on the "abysmal distinction between the women one loved and respected and those one enjoyed — and pitied" (AI 89).

In New York, Ellen Olenska finds that she is treated like a woman displaying sexual accessibility, when in fact she does not intend to send that message; her behavior is simply coded to a different set of social signals. Her predicament emphasizes an important point about the intersection of cultural codes and biological adaptations. By demanding exaggerated signals of sexual reserve, this particular community has rendered a set of adaptive impulses much harder to endure. The New York society that reacts so ambivalently to Ellen Olenska's alien manners has effectually denied women the right to present themselves as fully sexual beings. Wharton clearly hopes readers will be angered by the realization that there is no biological necessity for such extreme curtailment of female human nature.[14] The pitifully evanescent power of any one culture to mold human behavior comes to light most prominently in the interchange between Ellen and Archer in the Art Museum. As they contemplate shelves piled with bewildering archaeological relics, "small broken objects" whose use is now "unknown," they are struck by the cruel irony inherent in social change; things once "necessary and important" to "forgotten people" no longer possess signifying power (*AI* 248). Archer and Ellen are confronted in this scene with tangible evidence that cultures come and go, that the rules and rituals shaping human lives in any one time and place are doomed to extinction. The regulatory influence any one society exercises on the choices and activities of its members is to some degree arbitrary and accidental, yet tragically inescapable. Because biological evolution proceeds so much more slowly than does cultural evolution, human adaptations look relatively permanent when viewed in the context of the myriad social systems that have interpreted and reinterpreted them through the ages. A preference for female chastity in a long-term mate, for instance, has influenced human mate selection for millions of years; the actual incidence of virginity, like its social indicators, has varied over time and around the world.[15]

In late nineteenth-century, upper-class New York circles, as Wharton demonstrates, male preference for premarital chastity in women is enforced in notably stringent fashion. Women wishing to signal sexual reserve are required to exhibit an infantile ignorance of a wide range of human experience. Merely refraining from sexual activity will not suffice: a marriageable girl is carefully protected from conversation with sexual content and prohibited, too, from contact with works of art that touch on sexual subjects. Thus Archer looks forward to introducing Goethe's *Faust* to May Welland on their honeymoon, and he smiles with satisfaction at her inability to fathom a seduction scene from Gounod's operatic version of the story: "The darling!" "She doesn't even guess what it's all about" (*AI* 17). Vast portions of Western cultural legacy are forbidden territory to the properly "innocent" girl; her intellectual and aesthetic education is inevitably incomplete. Her emotional development is similarly stunted, since she is "carefully trained not to possess" such important prerequisites for adulthood as "freedom of judgment," "versatility," and "experience" (*AI* 46). Asking why a simple demand for sexual prudence should have such far-reaching consequences for female education, Wharton wonders whether girls raised in the constricting conditions she describes ever can overcome the early deficiencies in their mental, moral, and emotional experience. The famous passage in which Archer likens his fiancée to the Kentucky cave fish, who lose their sight because they have no opportunity to use their eyes, illustrates Wharton's grim predictions for the later lives of girls kept, metaphorically, in the dark. Denied access to information about such vast arenas of human life, history, and culture, women like Augusta Welland, May's mother, lack moral insight and sympathetic compassion. May herself proves to be "incapable of growth," Archer concludes after many years of marriage to her; she is the permanent victim of a "hard bright blindness" (*AI* 274).

The cave fish analogy does not represent Wharton's ideas about biological evolution but, rather, her analysis of society's power to shape individual destiny. Newland Archer's community restricts the lives of women far more sweepingly than the male desire for paternal certainty requires. It may well be advantageous for a young woman to signal virginity, but is it necessary, Wharton demands, for the attendant social codes to suffocate so much of a woman's identity? Nineteenth-century "innocence" encompasses far more than physical chastity: it drains the culturally molded female of enormous developmental potential. The situation of spinsters like Archer's sister Janey illustrates with special pathos the permanent crippling that innocence entails. Because marriage is the only acceptable route to sexual awareness, a woman without a husband is compelled to play an increasingly age-inappropriate role. Naïveté sits awkwardly on a woman in her thirties who is supposed still to be too pure to participate in salacious gossip: "In public Mrs. Archer continued to assume" that any subject with sexual innuendo "was not one for the unmarried" (*AI* 41). Consigned to an "elderly youth," Janey is doomed to inspire a pitying ridicule (*AI* 278). Wharton's depictions of women like Janey Archer and May Welland function as stinging social criticism: culture is the target of her auctorial anger and irony. The constellation of behavioral expectations defined as innocence represents a gratuitously exaggerated societal reinforcement of evolved tendencies.

The result of socially imposed innocence is suffering, both for the women subjected to this social training and for the men they marry. Inevitably, these women make less interesting, less companionable wives than they might have become if their early lives had been less systematically stifled.[16] The critique of innocence is transmitted to readers principally through the consciousness of Newland Archer, since none of the "nice" women in his social world have escaped their fate sufficiently to understand what has happened to them. Thus Archer's plans for liberating May Welland from the limitations of her girlhood education come to nothing: "There was no use in trying to emancipate a wife who had not the dimmest notion that she was not free" (*AI* 167). Once engaged, Archer undergoes a series of increasingly unsettling realizations about his future life with May. He wishes for a "passionate and tender comradeship" that the limitations of her experience preclude (*AI* 46). His recognitions affect readers more powerfully than would criticisms articulated by female characters, since his unhappiness points toward wide-ranging repercussions of female innocence. His dissatisfactions with the ideal mate social custom has prepared for him, "cunningly manufactured by a conspiracy of mothers and aunts and grandmothers and long-dead ancestresses, because it was supposed to be what he wanted," go far to indicate how the entire community suffers from the deliberately depleted human potential of half its members (*AI* 48).

Because it is conveyed through a male character, Wharton's unsparing analysis of innocence, and its implications, no doubt gains in authenticity and persuasive force. Readers notice at once that Archer is not wholly emancipated from the societal norms he has begun to question, however, as his vacillating reactions to May and Ellen repeatedly demonstrate. Ellen attracts him in large measure because she is not a "cunningly manufactured" product of New York society, but her aura of consciously accepted adult sexuality frequently leads him to the same faulty conclusions drawn by the rest of his community. Even as he insists that "women ought to be free — as free as we are," he recognizes his own tacit assumption that women suitable as long-term mates ("'nice' women") will not act upon the freedom "generous-minded men like himself" hypothetically might grant them (*AI* 45, 46). Archer is troubled by Ellen's willingness to spend time with Julius Beaufort, partly because Beaufort's pursuit of her inspires his jealousy, but principally because her tolerance of Beaufort's company makes him wonder if she is, after all, open to transient liaisons. His uncertainty in classifying Ellen (is she wife material, or mistress material?) peaks when he is asked to advise her about the divorce she seeks. Unlike her family, he is initially disposed to be sympathetic to her desire to free herself from her marriage, but his suspicions are triggered by a letter from Count Olenski accusing his wife of adultery. Archer tries to discover whether or not the charge is true, and when his rather obscure questions fail to elicit a definite denial he jumps to the conclusion that she is admitting to the affair: "It flashed across him at that instant that the charge in the letter was true, and that she hoped to marry the partner of her guilt" (*AI* 103). Despite the theoretical freedom he has so "chivalrously conceded" so recently to all women, his reaction is angry, jealous, and judgmental (*AI* 46): "The mere suspicion ... made him feel harshly and impatiently toward her" (*AI* 103).

Suddenly he sees her as an unfaithful wife, and the knowledge that the husband she supposedly betrayed has been guilty of far more flagrant infidelities does nothing to mitigate his judgment against her.[17] Indeed, he acts as the instrument of society enforcing male preferences: a woman of questionable sexual loyalty must not be allowed to enjoy privileges reserved for the "nice." She must not, in this case, be assisted to rehabilitation as a marriageable woman. Concealing his motives, Archer uses all his powers to dissuade

Ellen from divorcing, telling her that "the individual, in such cases, is nearly always sacrificed to what is supposed to be the collective interest" of family (*AI* 103). Wharton lets readers know that family reputation is not his real reason for discouraging her quest for freedom. Obsessing over the embarrassing admission he believes she has just made, he "ramble[s] on" almost unthinkingly, "pouring out ... stock phrases" (*AI* 103). Like George Darrow attempting to persuade Sophy Viner that a marriage to Owen Leath is not in her best interest, Archer is guilty of malicious dissembling in this scene. He has judged Ellen (on insufficient evidence, as he later discovers) and placed her in the category of women whom men do not marry. Unlike Sophy Viner, Ellen fails to see through Archer's deceitful counsel: she has no notion that he would deny her the freedom to remarry because of a supposed sexual indiscretion in her past. She is not entirely his dupe, however, in that she believes she detects a selfish motive in his admonitions. She assumes that his impassioned defense of collective family interest is rooted in his desire to avoid the taint of scandal for himself and May and, ultimately, for their prospective children. She is saddened, though unresentful, that Archer wants her to sacrifice her interests in order to promote his. Had she penetrated his true motives and perceived his dismissive labeling of her as a sexually unreliable female, she might well have proven less amenable to his advice.

Clarification occurs only later, in the scene when he tells Ellen that she is the woman he "would have married if it had been possible" (*AI* 144). She is stunned and angry, since it is he who has effectually prevented their marrying by persuading her not to divorce Olenski. When Archer mentions Olenski's charges of infidelity, she explains that these were completely unfounded; she had "nothing to fear" from them (*AI* 145). There is painful irony in Archer's realization that he is the unwitting author of his own disappointment.[18] His discovery that Ellen is not, in fact, guilty of sexual disloyalty means that his reasons for wishing to prevent her social rehabilitation, and possible re-marriage, do not hold good: he has classified her erroneously. As the person most responsible for persuading Ellen to give up the idea of divorce ("'I've made no secret of having done it for you!'"), he has created a permanent barrier to any socially approved, long-term involvement between the two of them (*AI* 145). Wharton indicates her dissatisfaction with old New York's rigid and punitive regulation of female sexual conduct by making Archer suffer for his unthinking conformity to it.

From the outset, Archer's wavering devotion to May and incipient attraction to Ellen is complicated by kinship alliances and familial interests. Ellen Olenska's family initially supports her re-entry into New York society, risking the danger to the family's collective status that their championship of her entails. Her precarious position as a run-away wife, coupled with the eccentricities of her up-bringing, renders her social position ambiguous, and her nonconformity to New York customs in matters of dress and etiquette add fuel to the general mistrust surrounding her. Quickly spreading rumors concerning her sexual history intensify that mistrust. By bringing Ellen to public performances and private parties, the Mingott family announces that it is standing behind her, vouching for her social respectability. This collective support of Ellen is regarded as a bold testing of the Mingott clan's power (they are "trying it on"): can the family insist upon community acceptance for a member with Ellen's history and situation (*AI* 20)? The Mingotts are known for their "family solidarity," readers learn, their "resolute championship of the few black sheep" in their midst. Their determined nepotism has an evolutionarily sound basis (*AI* 21). It is in the interest of a family to preserve the status of all its members, since one ruined reputation is bound to have a negative effect, however small, on all the rest. Coolly sponsoring Ellen's reinstatement into New York society, the Mingotts are striving to maintain their own collective status by dispelling doubts about their kinswoman's social reputation. The night Ellen first appears in the Mingotts' box at the opera, she is seated beside her white-clad young cousin May Welland, which serves as a public declaration that the family does not consider Ellen a potential threat to May's naïve innocence: what better way for the family to answer questions about the blamelessness of Ellen's sexual past?

May lets Archer know that she understands the role she plays in this scene at the opera. "Her eyes said: 'You see why Mamma brought me?'" (*AI* 25). He demonstrates his agreement with this show of family strength by suggesting that they announce their engagement that very night. By making his alliance-by-marriage with the Welland family public on the same evening that the Wellands launch their public support of Ellen, Archer is letting his community know that he and his family "will all back her up" (*AI* 82). His marriage will unite two extended families, since Archer's relatives now, in effect, become May's. When Lefferts and his confreres decide to boycott the Mingotts' party officially reintroducing Ellen into upper-crust circles, it is Archer, Mrs. Manson Mingott's prospective new grandson-in-law, who calls on his kinship network, using the social power of the extremely high-status van der Luydens to bring the community into line. Henry van der Luyden, the single most socially powerful individual in his community, articulates the theory behind the Mingotts' machinations: "As long as a member of a well-known family is backed up by that family it should be considered—final" (*AI* 57). The Mingotts are convinced that they can muster the social power to enforce acceptance of a relative with a questionable reputation, and they are willing to assume a degree of risk in order to accomplish that goal.

The family's willingness to help Ellen diminishes dramatically when she insists upon seeking a divorce. Her uncles converge upon her to dissuade her from this course, and when she remains stubborn they call upon Archer for assistance. The family's opposition to divorce is based on the late nineteenth-century social context: divorce is considered scandalous, a blot upon the divorcing individual's reputation and, by extension, the individual's family. The threat of a counter-suit by Count Olenski, accusing his wife of adultery, dramatically increases the possible negative impact. There will be media attention, an evil in itself. Mrs. Welland is horrified later at the idea that a photograph of May's wedding might be published in a newspaper; a juicy, gossip-ridden report of Countess Olenska's probable misconduct, however erroneous, would be immeasurably worse. The family willing to incur some costs in order to effect Ellen's reinstatement in the community is decidedly not willing to subject its members to the status-reducing consequences of an ugly contested divorce. All the Mingotts' efforts to support Ellen in her role as blameless victim of a blackguard husband will be undone if Olenski's accusations take tangible form in a court case.[19] Indeed, the Mingotts may suffer more because of their earlier supportive stance: they will appear to be guilty of challenging gender-based behavioral norms that are vitally important in their community.

In the end, the powerful forces of family interest maneuver Ellen into a limbo-like social situation: she forfeits benefits she enjoyed as Olenski's wife, such as "fortune" and "social consideration," yet she is not free to shed her ties with him and remarry (*AI* 109). Her family has ensured that the only mating options available to her will be short-term. Archer is sufficiently honest to see and admit this: "If you'd rather she were Beaufort's mistress than some decent fellow's wife, you've certainly gone the right way about it" (*AI* 128). The Mingotts are anxious that their kinswoman not tarnish the family reputation by carrying on extramarital affairs, but their self-protective refusal to help Ellen free herself from Olenski seem likely to push her toward the very choices they most want her not to make. Her generally nonconformist behavior, from her decision to make her home in an unfashionable part of town to her willingness to attend the "common" Mrs. Struthers's Sunday parties, continues to arouse her relations' suspicions (*AI* 83): "'I'm afraid Ellen's ideas are not at all like ours,'" May's mother laments (*AI* 127). And her apparently easy acceptance of Beaufort as escort and real estate consultant causes particular uneasiness for the ever watchful family look-outs: "A woman engaged in a love affair with Beaufort 'classed' herself irretrievably" (*AI* 122). At any moment, the family collectively realizes, Ellen might embark upon a status-threatening love affair. As one observer slyly remarks, "' Madame Olenska is a great favourite with the gentlemen'" (*AI* 215).

Unsurprisingly, the Mingotts seize the first available opportunity to rid themselves of the potential social liability Ellen increasingly seems to represent to them. When Count Olenski seeks a reconciliation with his wife, asking "only to take her back on her own terms," the Mingotts pressure Ellen to agree to his proposals (*AI* 139). It is easy for them to close their eyes to the unpleasant, even vicious, aspects of the life they expect her to resume, easy for them to believe in Olenski's repentance and probable reformation. Reunited with her husband in Europe, Ellen would no longer require their help, either social or financial, and she would present no awkward reputational threat to her far-off American kin. Reconciliation with Olenski also would silence gossip about her own possible extramarital activity. "After all, a young woman's place was under her husband's roof, especially when she had left it in circumstances that ... well ..." (*AI* 215). So long as Ellen's husband made no move to retrieve her, the Mingotts' best strategy was to offer her their protection; once the husband seeks to recover her, however, supporting the marriage serves their interests better. It is the collective good of kin that motivates the Mingotts, rather than Ellen's personal happiness. When she rejects her relatives' counsel and resists the importunings of a husband who now claims to honor the sanctity of marriage, the Mingotts' attitude toward her changes: she is "no longer in the good graces of her family" (*AI* 215). Scaling back on their efforts to help her establish a social position in their midst, her relatives concentrate on getting her out of New York and back to the social respectability represented by her marriage.

Although their "sense of solidarity" prevents them from sharing their disaffection with outsiders (they have not "proclaimed their disapproval aloud"), the Mingotts take steps to compel Ellen to accede to their wishes (*AI* 215). Because her estranged husband controls nearly all her personal fortune, she is relatively impecunious, dependent upon the generosity of her New York relatives. The family accordingly "reduce[s] Countess Olenska's allowance considerably when she definitely refuse[s] to go back to her husband" (*AI* 217). To their dismay, however, she accepts this decline in her standard of living unprotestingly: they are not able to starve her out. Throughout most of Book II the family continues scheming to effect Ellen's departure. She must be "made to see that it was her duty to go back" (*AI* 241). One of her uncles meets repeatedly with a representative sent by the Count, for example, assuring him that the family supports his interests: "in view of the new proposals ... it is hardly possible for Madame Olenska not to return to her husband" (*AI* 208). Such actions constitute betrayal of a family member for the good of other kin.

The Mingotts pursue their objective with increasing vigor as they begin to sense that Ellen poses a specific threat to her cousin May's marriage. Despite the rarity of their meetings and the precautions Archer takes to keep these private, he does not succeed in concealing his ongoing interest in Ellen from vigilant relatives. He provides a possible clue to his feelings by refusing to join in with family members' attempts to persuade one another, as well as Ellen herself, that she would "be happier with her husband" (*AI* 184). The family is justifiably skeptical that mere altruism can account for Archer's desire to keep this inconveniently embarrassing relative close by, when she easily might be disposed of to the social advantage of her family. Having seen Archer weigh in so successfully to dissuade Ellen from divorce, the Mingotts are suspicious of his unwillingness now to use his proven influence with her for the family's benefit. Even though no actual adultery occurs, the family is correct in assessing the danger that Archer will abandon his marriage in order to take up with Ellen: readers observe him seriously contemplating such a course of action.

Archer's inability to keep his feelings and activities hidden from relatives' observation underlines the similarities between his social community and the small "tribe" to which he frequently compares it. In the EEA, humans lived in small groups, in dwelling conditions that afforded very little privacy. The effectiveness of the surveillance that interferes with Archer's plans demonstrates just how much his prosperous, self-consciously civilized society resembles ancestral bands it likes to describe as "primitive." Eventually Archer realizes that he "has been, for months, the centre of countless silently observing eyes and patiently listening ears" (*AI* 264). Faced with the possible eruption of family scandal, the Mingotts act, offering their collective support to Archer's wife: "the whole tribe had rallied" around May (*AI* 264). "The social body is a highly alert and powerful working system," as Pamela Knights explains.[20] Their decision is inevitable: they are protecting the family's collective genetic interest from a threat emanating from within the family itself.[21]

As first cousins, Ellen and May both are Mrs. Manson Mingott's granddaughters, and their blood relationship to the many Mingott aunts, uncles, and cousins is essentially identical. All things being equal, the family could be expected to offer them similar levels of support. All things are not equal, however, as a quick cost-benefit analysis demonstrates. If Archer abandons his wife to run off with Ellen, the resulting scandal will injure the social reputation of all those connected to them. Since Ellen's family *is* May's family, and May's family has become Archer's via marriage, nepotistic interests converge from several directions to avert this major blow to the extended families' social standing. Still more important is the potential injury to May's reproductive future, should Archer desert her. At a minimum, she would lose precious time out of her expected years of fertility dealing with damage control, extricating herself legally from Archer, and searching for a new partner. As a deserted, perhaps divorced, wife in a society hostile to broken marriages, she would find her options for new mating partners distinctly compromised. It is unlikely that she would be able attract a second husband equal to Archer in status, wealth, and social gifts. In short, the number and quality of children May can produce will be threatened if her current, top-of-the-line husband should leave her. Because May's children will share genes with all the Mingott kin, it is in the family's collective interest to safeguard the valuable resource that May's fertility represents to them.

Ellen's reproductive future, in contrast to May's, already has been foreclosed. "'Her life is finished,'" Granny Mingott remarks at one point, indirectly acknowledging Ellen's childless state and questionable fertility (*AI* 134). In discouraging her from divorce, the Mingotts have prevented Ellen from choosing a new long-term mate with whom there is a chance, however slight, that she might bear children. If they succeed in sending her back to Olenski, to a marriage that has been barren for more than ten years, they consign her to almost certain childlessness. The Mingotts have cut their losses with Ellen, reproductively speaking, channeling their support toward May instead. They are banking on the likelihood that May and Archer will produce children, children who will raise the inclusive fitness of all the people with whom they share genes. From an evolutionary biological perspective, the Mingotts' decision is predictable: they sacrifice a relative with low reproductive potential in order to protect the more valuable reproductive future of another relative. It would be wasteful for them to countenance the transfer of a high-quality mate like Newland Archer to Ellen, especially when coupled with all the disadvantages of a time-consuming, socially stigmatizing re-mating process. Putting the Atlantic Ocean between Ellen and Archer, the Mingotts succeed in removing a significant threat, not just to May herself but to the long-term social and genetic welfare of every one of May's relatives. Hence the elaborate farewell party, at which "the tacit assumption" prevails "that nobody knew anything, or had ever imagined anything" untoward about Newland Archer and Ellen Olenska (*AI* 264). Despite the superficial cordiality, as Archer fully recognizes, Ellen is "a kinswoman about to be eliminated from the tribe" (*AI* 264).

Wharton has incorporated numerous examples of married men's infidelities in her depiction of Archer's social universe, yet none elicit intervention from concerned relatives except the prospective involvement between Archer and Ellen. Julius Beaufort, the most outrageous example, is a persistent womanizer: "his dull and childless marriage had long since palled on him; and in addition to more permanent consolations he was always in quest of amorous adventures in his own set" (*AI* 122). With such a comment, Wharton demonstrates awareness that a barren marriage typically gives extra impetus to the pursuit of extramarital mating opportunities. Lawrence Lefferts engages in frequent affairs with social inferiors (a typist and a postmistress, for instance), calling upon other men to provide him with cover stories. On the night of the farewell party for Ellen Olenska, Lefferts offhandedly requests Archer to connive in such deception: "' do you mind letting it be understood that I'm dining with you at the club tomorrow night?'" (*AI* 269). Since he has just been holding forth like "a young prophet," castigating the enemies of domestic virtue, the timing of his request could scarcely be more ironic (*AI* 269). Engaged in the mixed reproductive strategy often preferred by men whose resources enable them to enjoy the benefits of short- and long-term mating simultaneously, Lefferts and Beaufort do not suffer social penalties for their behavior.[22] Their infidelities subject them to some private censure, "a certain measure of contempt," but they are invited and received everywhere (*AI* 244). Before his marriage, Archer himself indulged in an adulterous liaison which does not injure his opportunities for obtaining a high-status wife. Indeed, it adds to the glamour of his manly appeal. "He knew that his secret love affair with poor silly Mrs. Thorley Rushworth had not been too secret to invest him with a becoming air of adventure" (*AI* 89). Providing extensive evidence of the tacit permission enjoyed by men to engage in extramarital pairings, Wharton articulates a cry of protest on behalf of all women whose communities offer tacit acceptance of male promiscuity.

Given the behavior of men like Beaufort and Lefferts, readers may wonder initially why Archer is held after his marriage to a standard of fidelity that is violated routinely in his community. The answer is not far to seek: Lefferts and Beaufort are not planning to desert their wives for their mistresses, any more than Archer ever hoped Mrs. Rushworth would divorce her husband to marry him. The extramarital liaisons in upper-class New York society are for the most part designed to be short-term, and they are always peripheral, posing no threat to male investment in a long-term mate or in children. Observers sense that Archer is contemplating mate replacement, however, rather than casual dalliance. He is tempted to desert his wife in order to undertake a serious commitment to another woman. Once his doubts about Ellen's prior sexual activity have been painfully corrected at the conclusion to Book I, he is disposed to think of her solely in terms of long-term involvement. When she asks him about his intentions ("'is it your idea that I should live with you as your mistress — since I can't be your wife?'"), he is shocked at the idea that she might play a role in his life similar to that played by Fanny Ring in Beaufort's (*AI* 234). His fantasies center on escape to some far-away place (at one point he mentions Japan!) and exclusive commitment. It is his determination to view Ellen as a potential wife rather than as a possible mistress that makes his case radically different from that of other unfaithful husbands in his social circle. Hence the Mingott family's urgent interference.

The expulsion of Ellen Olenksa is engineered at precisely the moment when she and Archer are on the brink of consummating their relationship. Discussing their options at their meeting in the museum, they first seem disposed "to accept the compromise usual in such cases" and undertake an illicit affair (*AI* 244). Granny Mingott's desire for Ellen's companionship after her stroke will facilitate such an arrangement. Ellen has agreed to move back from Washington D.C. to be with her, and Archer guesses, rightly, that Ellen has acquiesced in her grandmother's wishes partly because of the opportunities for meeting this proximity will provide. The "half-measures" represented by adultery seem "better" to them, on the one hand, than running off together because this more conventional mode of infidelity will "hurt others less" (*AI* 241, 248). On the other hand, neither Ellen nor Archer can overcome the repugnance this scheme inspires: a furtive romance would be, they concur, "detestable" (*AI* 248). They can hardly be said to harbor profound moral scruples about adultery *per se*: Archer does not spend time berating himself for having bedded a married woman (the "silly" Mrs. Rushworth), and Ellen's love for him has not been dampened by her awareness of that incident in his past. They can condone adulterous behavior under certain circumstances, evidently, but not in their own case. Adultery is unacceptable to them not because they have suddenly developed a new set of moral guidelines but because each defines and desires the other as a long-term — not a short-term — mate. They can achieve their goal only if Archer discards his current spouse, yet they shrink from causing such "irreparable harm" (*AI* 249).

As the would-be partners contemplate two unsatisfactory alternatives, Ellen puts forward a startling suggestion. She offers to consummate their relationship "once" — "and then go home" — home, that is, to her philandering husband in Europe (*AI* 249). Her reasons for making such an offer are complicated. She surely knows that the idea of her returning to the arms of Olenski would be utterly unacceptable to Archer. His jealousy is aroused and his mate-guarding impulses stimulated. He must protect this worthy and desirable woman from abuse, at the same time ensuring that another man does not gain sexual access to her: "that was not to be imagined" (*AI* 256). He is thrown into a quandary by her unexpected proposal, which grants him sexual favors but imposes unthinkable conditions. In fact, Ellen's offer bears a curious resemblance to strategies employed by males, albeit less forthrightly. Men in search of short-term sex frequently take off once they have achieved their object, although they usually do not explain their love-'em-and-leave-'em plans in advance. Why is Ellen playing a typically male role here and suggesting an extremely short-term fulfillment of their passion? Certainly she disconcerts Archer, who consents to her suggestion reluctantly, telling himself that he will "have to let her go" afterwards (*AI* 250). Since the rendezvous never takes place, readers do not learn how much self-deception colors his resolution.

Ellen must realize that sexual pleasures will only add fuel to their already passionate feelings. If her ultimate goal is to obtain full-time commitment from Archer, in fact, sexual involvement is likely at this stage to help her toward that end. "Signals of sexual accessibility," as Buss notes, "sometimes are part of a larger strategy to lure a man into a long-term relationship."[23] Archer admits to himself that physical intimacy will make it harder, not easier, for the two of them to part. "Once a woman gains sexual access to a man of her choice, her proximity offers opportunities for insinuating herself ... gradually escalating both the benefits he will receive by staying in the relationship and the costs he will incur if he leaves her."[24] Since Archer has just pressed Ellen to run off with him, such strategizing on her part might seem unnecessary. If her goal is to detach him from May, why not simply consent to "come away" with him (*AI* 249)? Archer has named no definite destination, however, and outlined no plan for their future; he has nothing in mind beyond immediate flight. One purpose physical intimacy might serve is that of prodding him to formulate more specific plans for action once he has appreciated more fully "the benefits he will receive" in choosing Ellen. It is conceivable, too, that Ellen is less disinclined than Archer to disparage the advantages of an illicit liaison in New York, but she can hardly say so outright and still maintain the posture of sexual reserve. Thus she offers a time-limited sexual opportunity, possibly hoping that he will pressure her to continue the affair and then blame himself for failing to keep to his agreement. A secret, short-term involvement would give Ellen more time to test the degree and durability of Archer's commitment to her; as Buss notes, such information is sometimes "difficult to obtain without some level of intimate involvement."[25] They might begin an affair now without forfeiting the option of running off together later, and she then would be in a better position to supervise the details of their eventual departure.

Whatever the motives, conscious or unconscious, behind Ellen's offer of one-time sex, it is impossible to believe that she makes it disingenuously. She is giving an explicitly sexual invitation to a married man, and despite her avowed desire to avoid doing "harm," she must know that adulterous betrayal is not less hurtful simply because it is time-limited. She also must realize that Archer will not be satisfied with a single opportunity to satisfy his desires, any more than he will consent to her returning to Olenski. The threat that she will go back to a marriage she has described as "hell" seems calculated chiefly to incite possessive jealousy in Archer, perhaps spurring him to action (*AI* 139). Presumably she has no intention of rejoining her husband, since she arranges without difficulty for financial support from her grandmother to live independently when she decides, just a day or so after her meeting with Archer, to leave New York. If her childlessness is the result of her husband's sterility rather than her own, moreover, even a single intimate encounter with Archer might result in pregnancy. Such an outcome would help to redirect Archer's commitment from his wife to Ellen. The effect of her invitation for time-limited sexual intimacy, should he accept it, can only be that of further cementing the tie between Archer and herself. Her suggestion is a strategic move in her pursuit of him as a mate.

Ellen is engaged from the beginning in an act of matepoaching, historically a "clearly common mating strategy."[26] Reviewing her behavior toward Archer from the moment of her arrival in Manhattan, readers observe that it is Ellen who initiates the romance from its inception. She invites him to call on her, which he finds strange: "she must know that an engaged man doesn't spend his time calling on married women" (*AI* 26). When he fails to follow through on her initial invitation, she resorts to a stratagem, publicly announcing that she will "expect him" at a certain hour (*AI* 65). As a result of her skillful manipulation, he feels "summoned" (*AI* 67). She has maneuvered him into spending time alone with her and deepening their acquaintance, giving him opportunity to recognize their commonalities in taste and interest. During this first private meeting, she repeatedly lets him know that she looks to him as a kindly protector and wise counselor: "'you must tell me just what to do,'" she says, and "'you'll warn me'" (*AI* 74, 75). When Archer begins to send her yellow roses, she lets him know that she considers his anonymous gifts a sign of romantic attraction. She says nothing until she finds herself beside him at the opera, then speaks up during an emotion-laden scene in which two lovers are parting forever: "'Do you think,' she asked, glancing toward the stage, 'that he will send her a bunch of yellow roses tomorrow morning?'" (*AI* 107). The comment is more than harmless flirtation: she interprets his flowers as a sign that they are embarked upon a love affair that is operatic in scale and intensity. When he follows her to Rhinecliff, she again assigns him the part of acknowledged guardian ("'now you're here to protect me'") and shows him unmistakably that she cares for him (*AI* 117). "'I can't feel unhappy when you're here.... I live in the moment when I'm happy'" (*AI* 119). By any standard of female behavior, she is making great efforts to attract and attach him. Archer's fantasy that she will come "stealing up behind him to throw her light arms about his neck" indicates that he is happy to have her assume the more active role — possibly because it allows him to conceal from himself his growing attraction to her (*AI* 120). During this phase of their relationship, she stays several steps ahead of him, leading and enticing. She keeps assuming that there is more between them than is the case, acts on her assumptions, and thereby causes more to happen. It is she who does the initial wooing, which makes her eventual invitation to Archer to come "once" to her bed less surprising.

After Archer declares himself, when he tells her he "would have married" her had they both been free, Ellen changes her tactics. Her response to his avowal of love is that it is "'too late'" (*AI* 146): he is pledged to May, and she is another man's wife. Now it is Archer who presses ahead. "'Nothing's done that can't be undone,'" he tells her; "'I'm still free, and you're going to be'" (*AI* 145). Extricating himself from his engagement at this point would be socially excruciating, a painful business for both parties and for their families, but he is right in saying it could be done. And Ellen still could decide to sue for divorce. If Archer goes ahead and marries May, dissolution of their union will become immeasurably more difficult: this is therefore the last possible moment for Ellen and Archer to come together with any shred of honor or decency. That being so, why does she push him away at the very moment when he finally proposes to break off with May and marry her instead? Why not seize the prize she has been pursuing so actively, now that it is presented to her? Readers may well wonder why she has bothered to try to attach him to her if she is not prepared to endure social embarrassment and family indignation in the face of his broken engagement. At precisely this point, Ellen switches to a strategy of restraint and retreat. Having rejected Archer's proposal, she withdraws from the scene, eventually moving from New York to Washington. She initiates no more meetings; now it is he who runs after her. She discourages his attentions, telling him that they must not meet or betray the "people who trust them" (*AI* 235). They see less of each other than they did earlier, yet Archer grows more obsessed with her. Employing "the attraction tactic of acting ... unavailable," she stimulates his desire to heightened levels.[27] As he finds himself thwarted, pushed away for the sake of high-minded goals, he experiences increased admiration for the woman who now insists that she is off limits.

Closely examined, Ellen's behavior is characterized by perceptible inconsistency throughout. Although it is generally accurate to say that during the period of Archer's engagement (Book I), she pursues him and that after his marriage (Book II) she evades him, there are repeated breaks in that pattern. Even in pursuit mode, she sometimes repels Archer's increasingly warm responses. "Ah, don't make love to me!" she tells him, for instance (*AI* 144). And when he reacts with agreement to her suggestive comment at the opera about his yellow roses ("'I was thinking of that too'"), she promptly changes the subject by mentioning May (*AI* 107). After his marriage, when Ellen is in retreat mode, she nonetheless admits to Archer that she cannot forget him, that she continues to love and desire him. Driving from the train station in May's brougham ("with the wedding varnish still on it"), Ellen tells him that he "'ought not to have come today,'" then promptly throws herself into his arms, "press[ing] her lips to his" (*AI* 230, 233). Such behavior is not calculated to encourage him to channel his affections toward his wife. If her sincere goal at this point is to discourage Archer's pursuit of her, she could make efforts to deny and conceal her feelings for him, but this she does not do. Buss observes that "playing hard to get is most successful when it is used selectively, that is, when a woman is hard to get in general but is selectively accessible to a particular man."[28] Even as she pushes him away, Ellen lets Archer know that she harbors an overwhelming preference for him and him alone, that she is committed to her love for him although she asserts that they must not act upon their desires.

There are several possible reasons for Ellen to send inconsistent messages. One is strategic: her occasional reserve with Archer in the beginning stages of their relationship are intended to reassure him that she is not too easily obtainable. Later her declarations of ongoing love serve notice that she is available, should Archer muster the courage to leave his marriage. By insisting that they must not even consider such a step, she maintains his image of her as a woman committed to high ethical standards in marital matters. Mixed messages are necessary at this stage if she is to avoid appearing like a short-term partner available for opportunistic sex. In Book I she tells him it's "too late" for him to break his engagement to May, perhaps because urging him to do so, or agreeing too quickly to such a scheme, might make her look over-eager. As an appropriately reserved female, she must reject his plan, but he is not compelled to accept her reaction as final. No matter how strongly Ellen discourages him from breaking his engagement, Archer is still free to do so. Readers surmise that if Archer had freed himself from his fiancée at this point, Ellen would not have resisted his advances, especially if he allowed a decent interval to elapse before paying court to her. Similarly, when Ellen tells Archer in Book II that it would be wrong for him to abandon his wife, she cannot prevent him from doing so. After Ellen's final departure for Europe, he still might choose to follow her. May's announced pregnancy causes Ellen to quit the field, but it is Archer who decides to let fatherhood put an end to extramarital romance. Ellen keeps putting herself in the traditionally female posture of reticence, saying "no, no," but hoping, consciously or not, that he will not take her refusal as final.

Ellen also fears the reputational damage she courts if she plays the socially despised part of *the other woman* by luring Archer away from his marital commitments. She shows her awareness of this danger by mentioning to Archer that her life in Europe has opened her eyes to all sorts of behavior never mentioned in staid New York: "'I've had to look at the Gorgon,'" she tells him, when he expresses amazement at her capacity for hardheaded assessment of realities (*AI* 133). Her allusion to a figure from Greek mythology is more apt that either she or Archer acknowledges. Medusa, the most famous of the Gorgons, assumed the shape of a monster only after she placed herself in intrasexual competition with a goddess. Originally a beautiful girl, she "dared to vie in beauty" with Minerva and was transformed as punishment into a monster with writhing snakes for hair, a being so hideous that the mere sight of her turned beholders to stone.[29] Medusa's story provides a subtle parallel to the intrasexual competition between Ellen and May, a competition that must lead to a miserable outcome for at least one of the competitors. In the course of the novel, perhaps not coincidentally, May is compared at least twice to a different Greek deity — Diana — and her build is described as "goddess-like" (*AI* 255). Given her position as Archer's publicly sanctioned mate, she enjoys an advantage in the competition between the two women; like a goddess fending off a mortal rival, she is in the superior, more easily defensible position. Stating that she has *looked at the Gorgon*, Ellen underscores the disillusioning results of having witnessed, as she did in a different environment, examples of sexual rivalry, marital infidelity, and mate poaching. Such conflicts and betrayals breed misery, she has observed, particularly for the losers. Like Medusa, Ellen is already beginning to take on monstrous lineaments in the perception of those seeking to safeguard May's marriage. She is very conscious, evidently, of the horrific light in which she will be cast, should she and Archer act on their mutual passion. To become a Medusa is to inspire loathing and incur ostracism, a fate she naturally wishes to avoid.

The mixed signals Ellen sends also point toward a powerful internal conflict. On the one hand, she is motivated to maximize her individual fitness by competing for an extremely attractive mate. On the other hand, she is motivated to enhance her inclusive fitness by supporting family members in their reproductive efforts. Conflict occurs because the mate she has selected is the fiancé, initially, and the husband, later, of her own first cousin, a person with whom she shares approximately one-eighth of her genes. If she succeeds in diverting Archer's matrimonial investment from her cousin to herself, she will incur costs as well as benefits. Her own fitness stands to increase, should she and Archer produce offspring. At the same time, however, the social damage the mate switching will cause is bound to hurt Ellen as well as May. And if Archer's abandonment of May causes her to bear fewer children, or children of poorer quality, this will have a negative impact on Ellen's own genetic future. Ellen is pulled in diametrically opposite directions by the operations of two powerful sets of evolutionary forces. The impulse to compete for the best available mate (and thus enhance direct fitness) comes into conflict with the nepotistic impulse to assist kin (and thus enhance indirect fitness).

Ellen's questionable fertility plays an important role in her cost-benefit calculations, exacerbating her ambivalence. An individual tends to favor direct over indirect fitness benefits, but Ellen is a woman who has good evidence for doubting her own reproductive capacity. Typically those leaving a barren marriage can be expected to test their fertility with new partners, given the potential rewards in fitness.[30] If May were not a kinswoman, Ellen's genetic self-interest would best be served by strenuous exertions on her part to secure Archer for herself, no matter how small the probability that the union would produce offspring. Because she has selected a relative's mate, however, she will pay a cost in indirect fitness for this second reproductive chance. And if she proves unable to bear children, there will be no gain in direct fitness to offset that loss. The potential benefit is significant, yet highly uncertain because of her dubious fertility. The cost, in contrast, is nearly inevitable, given May's probable fertility (later proven) and kinship to Ellen. The more likely it is that Ellen is infertile, clearly, the more critically important her relatives' contribution to her fitness becomes. Enticing Archer away from her cousin would be a risky move, guaranteeing Ellen no benefits yet incurring unavoidable costs.[31] The inconsistencies in her behavior to Archer reveal the intensity of her struggles in the face of competing adaptive impulses. The evasiveness characterizing much of her conduct in Book II represents genuine indecision as much as strategic reserve.[32]

May's situation is much less complicated than Ellen's. Her tactics in the two-year intrasexual competition she conducts with Ellen are as predictable as they are effective. Initially secure in Archer's affection, she detects "a difference" in him in the months following announcement of their engagement (*AI* 130). Her response to the unstated but observable waning of his devotion is to offer him his freedom. Perhaps their engagement has been a "mistake," she suggests; he may prefer "some one else" (*AI* 130). May's offer to release her fiancé from their engagement is a strategically prudent move. If he is wavering already in his commitment to her, it is in her best interest to cut her losses now rather than to risk taking on an unreliable long-term mate. The protracted courtship females typically demand enables them to size up a future mate's dependability and reject unsuitable candidates before undertaking costly reproductive projects.[33] The long engagement May's parents expect, and which so irritates Archer, is intended to provide her with useful information about her intended mate. May's willingness to withdraw from the engagement is advantageous to her from another point of view as well: the possibility that she may become inaccessible to Archer immediately increases her desirability to him. Fear of losing the girl he thought he had won makes him want to hold on to his prize rather than seize the opportunity of escape she offers.

Once Archer insists that he remains committed to May and presses for

an earlier wedding date, May never revisits the option of ending the relationship. The rupture of her marriage in their conservative social community
would entail, as earlier discussion already has made clear, enormous reputational and reproductive hardships for May. She fights hard, therefore, to protect her marriage and to keep her husband. Her deathbed admission to her
son — that she once "asked" Archer to give up "the thing [he] most wanted" —
shows that she is consciously aware of the competition between Ellen and herself (*AI* 281); despite her belief that he prefers her rival, moreover, she is
resolved to hang on to her husband. She turns to her kin for assistance, joining without her husband's knowledge in the efforts to send Ellen back to her
husband. Eventually Archer realizes that he is not fully in his wife's confidence:
rather, she has "reported to the family" his comments about Ellen, along with
her suspicions concerning his possibly wandering affections (*AI* 209). Her
single most decisive action is her announcement to Ellen that she is pregnant,
which causes the latter to cancel her rendezvous with Archer and make plans
for immediate departure.

May's announcement is simultaneously duplicitous, in that she is not
"sure" about her condition, and honest (*AI* 270): she is, in fact, pregnant.
Archer's observation of her "slightly heavier outline" and a "slight languor"
in her mood all point to hormonal changes that May herself certainly would
notice (*AI* 255).[34] She is not inventing the idea of pregnancy out of thin air
but reacting to physical changes in her own body. She has real reason to think
she is expecting a child and thus even more to lose if Archer should desert
her at this moment. Telling Ellen she is pregnant is a shrewd move. Ellen can
anticipate that Archer, as a member of a species characterized by high paternal investment, will respond to the prospect of paternity by strengthening his
commitment to May. May expects Ellen to withdraw from the competition,
as she does, rather than wait for Archer to choose reproductive benefits that
are certain and immediate over those that are uncertain and distant. May is
aware, too, that Ellen is a relative, who therefore has a genetic stake in May's
unborn child.[35] To encourage Archer to abandon that child would threaten
Ellen's indirect fitness, providing another reason for her to acknowledge final
defeat in their extended competition for the same man.

The consequences of May's and Ellen's cousinship, clearly, are far-reaching. Indeed, the blood tie linking the two women in Wharton's love triangle
influences plot and theme more decisively than any other element in her auctorial design.[36] On the simple level of narrative economy, kinship between
her two leading ladies allows Wharton to utilize a smaller, more manageable
cast of characters and to weave the threads of her plot more tightly together.
Ellen is thrown in Archer's way so often and so much precisely because she
belongs to his fiancée's family; if she were not his intended's cousin, ironically,

he might not have had opportunity to become so closely acquainted with her. From the moment of her return to New York, Archer is encouraged to be kind to her; he encounters her at family gatherings and at the homes of relatives. When May's grandmother has a stroke, she sends for Ellen — because she is Ellen's grandmother too. It is Ellen's position as a Mingott family member in need of social support that prompts Archer to announce his engagement ahead of schedule. It is only because she is a relative that Ellen is able to assist Archer in persuading May's family to move up her wedding date. If Ellen were not a Mingott, Archer never would have been asked to look into the matter of her divorce. Many more examples might be mentioned, but these should suffice to remind readers of the countless ways, large and small, in which the family relationship connecting Ellen and May affects character interaction and influences the unfolding of events.

The most significant effects of the familial tie at the center of the novel can be summarized easily. If May were not her cousin, Ellen would not suffer such ambivalence in her quest to win Archer as a mate, since her indirect fitness would not be threatened by her pursuit of a man committed to a non-relative. Her motives would be more coherent, in consequence, her strategies more clear-cut and consistent. Furthermore, Ellen's family would be unlikely to take steps to separate her from Archer if he were not the husband of a relative. When a reproductively unsuccessful individual locates a prospective new mate with whom she may make a new try at procreation, her relatives ordinarily would be expected to rejoice, even if this new beginning entails some negative social attention: their inclusive fitness stands to benefit, after all, if the new mating should prove fertile. It is only because Ellen's romance with a prospective new mate threatens the reproductive future of her cousin that her family intervenes. If Ellen's family were not also May's family, no intra-familial conflict of interest would occur. In the event that two unrelated women were competing for Newland Archer, each woman's family could be expected to promote her interests; at a minimum, a family would not work actively against a relative's attempts to secure a mate. Since the Mingotts are related to both women in the love triangle, however, they are forced to make cost-benefit decisions that result in a lopsided division of nepotistic loyalties. Predictably, they cast their support in favor of the reproductively more promising relative of the two. Hence their seemingly cruel behavior to Ellen, who appears to be less capable than her cousin of contributing to family members' inclusive fitness. The initial support they offer Ellen when she returns to New York proves that the Mingotts are not prejudiced against her *a priori*; they withdraw their tribal loyalty only when her behavior challenges the genetic welfare of kin.

By making Ellen and May close relatives, Wharton further highlights her insight that nepotistic loyalties and obligations provide much of the foundation for more broadly conceived social values and social controls. The small, inbred community she depicts, whose members frequently can trace multiple ties of kinship to one another, resembles an ancestral hunter-gatherer group in size and in genetic inter-relatedness. Everyone's choices and activities are susceptible to oversight and, potentially, to interference, since individual behavior — particularly mating behavior — is likely to have an impact on the fitness of nearly everyone else. Social norms reinforce impulses inherent in kin selection because society *is* family, writ large. Nepotism plays a crucial role in the action of the novel, obviously, when May's family exerts its influence to separate Archer from Ellen. Preservation of his marriage serves the genetic interests of May and her family — and thus, to a degree, even Ellen's interests. The plot is resolved when Archer chooses to remain with his pregnant wife; conception is the point at which Archer's self-interest intersects with the nepotistic interests of so many other community members.[37] Just a few hours after he tells himself that "no power could now turn him from his purpose" of following Ellen to Europe, he learns of his wife's pregnancy, and all options except that of committed fatherhood disappear from his radar screen (*AI* 268). May's assumption that pregnancy will prove to be a "victory" for her is well-founded (*AI* 270); the main action ends abruptly at the end of the penultimate chapter with her announcement to her husband that he is about to obtain undeniable fitness benefits from their marriage.

Although Archer tends to think of himself as a passive victim of external forces, it is important to realize that he does, finally, choose between the two women vying for him as a mate. At Ellen's farewell party he sees himself as a "prisoner" in "captivity," forcibly prevented by community members (his "captors") from achieving his heart's desire (*AI* 267, 265). As he takes stock of his life twenty-six years later, in the final chapter of the novel, he consoles himself for "all he has missed" by picturing human life as a lottery in which there is only one first prize: "the chances had been too decidedly against him" (*AI* 274). Such metaphors highlight his self-image as a victim of social machinations or of blind chance.[38] He shows no conscious awareness that the forces frustrating his avowed desires are principally internally based adaptive impulses, abetted by the external pressures of nepotism. The mate choice he finally makes is entirely predictable and — on grounds of fitness, at least — the right one. That is, he chooses the woman with the more viable reproductive future, whose fertility has just been established, the woman more likely to maximize his direct fitness. Staying in his marriage, he elects to maintain his commitment to a reproductive project already launched, to continue his investment in a child of whose paternity he can be certain. In her final chapter, moreover, Wharton provides information that confirms the adaptiveness of Archer's choice. Readers learn that he and May have raised three children, all thriving, and that fatherhood has been one of the great satisfactions of his life. Readers discover at the same time that Ellen has remained childless, further evidence of the evolutionary biological validity of Archer's mating decisions. He is particularly close to his elder son: "the two were born comrades" (*AI* 276). The psychological satisfaction he finds in parenting this son, whose conception decisively divided him from what he "most wanted," points toward the never directly acknowledged biological benefit represented by offspring (*AI* 281). In choosing May, Archer has secured fitness benefits whose value he implicitly acknowledges by rejoicing so plainly in his children.

Because Archer does not locate the source of his frustrations in adaptive mechanisms and evolved preferences, he fails to comprehend that the social pressures he so resents actually are well aligned with his genetic welfare. Family and society conspire to make him stay with May, and this is the same choice genetic self-interest dictates. He imagines that remaining in his marriage is an act of personal renunciation and social responsibility, telling himself that he is yielding to external pressures, but his behavior is nonetheless marked with unmistakable "selfishness" (as defined by Dawkins): maintaining his commitment to his pregnant, twenty-three-year-old wife is more likely to promote his reproductive success than the alternative of running off with a thirty-one-year-old barren mistress. What Archer thinks he wants is not what Archer's genes want.[39] And when he seems inclined to make a choice detrimental to his own fitness, people who share genes with him or with his wife step in, exercising their powers of social suasion. In choosing May, Archer contributes with his eventual offspring to the inclusive fitness of everyone in both their families. Selecting Ellen almost certainly would have resulted, for reasons already discussed, in decreased fitness levels for that same group of people. The resolution of the mate-choice dilemma dominating the novel shows nepotistic interests and community mores operating to reinforce the protagonist's genetic self-interest. Despite the stinging criticism Wharton directs toward Archer's old New York, she provides evidence that its norms support adaptive choices, in this instance, for an individual community member. The intersection of biological and social necessity lends extra poignancy to her tragic recognition that humans cannot escape social systems. There is no "country," as Ellen Olenska reminds Archer, in which humans can evade problems resulting from quests for status and resources, obligations to kin, or competition for mates (*AI* 234); conduct in all these arenas is regulated by the groups in which humans, as social animals, inevitably live.[40]

Archer's ambivalent reflections on his own past from the vantage point of late middle age echo his earlier vacillations. He has missed "the flower of life," that is, he has failed to achieve life's sweetest gifts — which he continues to associate with Ellen Olenska, the mate he wanted but did not select (*AI* 274). Yet he is not completely dissatisfied with his life: he values his contributions to his community, the status he has achieved as "good citizen" and, of course, his children (*AI* 273). He has managed to find some satisfaction in his marriage, too, musing on his wife's virtues along with her limitations: she has been "generous" and "faithful," though "incapable of growth" and "lacking in imagination" (*AI* 274). Tellingly, he dwells on her maternal devotion. She died, readers learn, from a disease she contracted from their youngest child, whom her dedicated care has "snatched from the grave" (*AI* 275). Here is evidence that May fulfilled in glaringly good measure the promise she showed for successful motherhood.

Archer declares himself to be relatively content, in sum, with the choices he has made, yet he also protests that "his life had been too starved" (*AI* 274, 282). He pictures himself as a "grey speck of a man," prudent and ordinary, while earlier he had dreamed of becoming a "ruthless magnificent fellow" (*AI* 279). Eloquently he describes the "packed regrets" that are inevitable in creatures capable of weighing strategic alternatives and choosing between them (*AI* 281). When he committed himself to long-term mating and paternal investment, Archer gave up other reproductive options (specifically, abandonment of his pregnant wife in favor of a socially rebellious, reproductively risky involvement with Ellen), options that now appear more gloriously adventurous than the ones he chose. If his satisfaction in the choices he has made seem somewhat tepid, it is partly because he is able, with his human brain, to imagine alternative routes in life. Having employed what Dawkins calls "the domestic bliss strategy" rather than "the he-man strategy," he cannot help but contemplate the "magnificent" thrills he might have enjoyed had he made wilder, more "ruthless" choices.[41]

In this last, retrospective chapter, when his son sets up an appointment for him to visit Ellen Olenska in Paris, it seems as though Archer needs only to reach out and seize the opportunity to revisit the choices he has made earlier in life. Freed by the death of their former spouses to select new mates, he and Ellen now might enjoy "a quiet harvest of friendship, of comradeship," he fantasizes (*AI* 282). Yet he decides, in the end, not to renew the acquaintance; "inexplicably," as Helen Killoran puts it, he refrains from making the visit.[42] Readers often are puzzled, sometimes exasperated, by his refusal to explore the possibility of obtaining now what he has wanted for so long.[43] Archer articulates a few reasons for his behavior. First, he fears that the very different lives he and Ellen have led in the years since their parting may well have eroded their compatibility. "He thought of the theatres she must have been to ... the people she must have talked with, the incessant stir of ideas..." (*AI* 283). Such thoughts represent a realistic assessment of the effects of time ("more than half a lifetime divided them"), tinged with anxiety about the possibly lackluster impression he may make on her (*AI* 283). He judges his American environment as provincial and culturally deprived compared with the "rich atmosphere" in which she has lived (*AI* 283). He also suspects that Ellen may have enjoyed "tangible companionship" with other men over the years, and he hesitates to place himself in competition with them (*AI* 283). Along with these insecurities, a different kind of motive holds him back: he believes that to see Ellen now might eclipse his fantasies of her, which are based on his memory of her from the past. Any new contact might blur the "edge" of precious recollections (*AI* 285). This fear also seems realistic, especially when he pictures his son being greeted by "a dark lady," overlooking the likelihood that Ellen's once dark hair will have grayed (*AI* 285).

Wharton flies in the face of readers' desire for a delayed but still happy ending by parking her protagonist firmly on his bench in Paris, declining to revisit the love of his life. From a crassly Darwinian perspective, however, Archer's refusal to take up the threads of an old romance is understandable. Ellen is Archer's age, fifty-seven, and distinctly post-menopausal. Any reproductive value she might have had at the age of thirty-one, when they parted, has evaporated in the meantime. Since she can contribute nothing to Archer's fitness, his disinterest in renewing their love affair is adaptive, if disappointing. Perhaps he is more "ruthless," and less sentimental, than he imagines! The death of his wife, which occurs conveniently when the forty-seven-year-old May's years of fertility are drawing to an end, frees him to seek a younger woman with whom he might sire another child or two. Wharton provides no specific evidence that Archer will remarry; already a widower for two years, he has shown no inclination as yet to do so. She indicates his potential for ardor, however, in the romantic fantasies he still conjures up in connection with his youthful romance with Ellen. Certainly he possesses the material resources and the physical vigor to beget and support more children. He has rejected Ellen once in favor of a reproductively more viable mating option; it is consistent that he do so again, even if no particular rival is yet in view. Refusing to visit her in Paris does not guarantee that he will seek out a younger mate but it is an important first step in that direction, since a renewed romantic involvement with Ellen would divert his energies from the search for a new partner. The fact that no social barriers now prevent him from being with her strongly suggests the biological thrust of his motives. Whatever he tells himself, from start to finish, about his reasons for failing to pursue Ellen wholeheartedly, readers cannot help noticing that twice over he avoids committing himself to a woman with low, or depleted, reproductive value.

Because Archer never recognizes the forces driving him, he is not able either to resist them or to formulate adequate complaints about them. He is bewildered to a perceptible degree by the choices he has made in life, baffled by the impulses that override his dreams of happiness. Hence the seeming lack of purposefulness which is a major source of readers' frequently ambivalent responses to him.[44] His plight is eminently human: between the internal workings of evolved impulses, on the one hand, and the external pressures of nepotistic influence and social regulatory mechanisms, on the other, he is scarcely free to design his life along lines that he imagines might best please him. The very strength of readers' desire for the happy consummation of Archer's and Ellen's romance indicates that Wharton's sympathies are ranged against the irresistible combination of biological and social mechanisms thwarting the pair: the novel's outcome is colored with the poignancy of forfeited happiness. Thus the protest Archer is unable to articulate on his own behalf is voiced by his creator.

The social criticism that claims such a central place in Wharton's text meshes logically, moreover, with the evolutionary biological insight she offers into her characters' motives and deeds. Delineating the smug complacency and narrow-mindedness with which Archer's community enforces its norms, she decries the arbitrariness of cultural designs even as she identifies their roots in genetic interest. To a very considerable extent, individuals are prisoners of their time and place, Wharton insists, captives of the social systems they inherit. These social systems derive much of their power from the deep-seated tendencies of kin selection, as family members seek to maximize their fitness by influencing the behavior of relatives. Social approval, material resources, and other forms of support are granted or withheld as a means of compelling individuals to subordinate personal inclination to the welfare of shared genes. Stripped to its essence, *The Age of Innocence* is the story of a genetic victory for the Mingott family: its members succeed in manipulating the behavior of two recalcitrant individuals tempted to waste precious reproductive resources in the pursuit of mere happiness.

# 4

# The Glimpses of the Moon

## A Creative Experiment
## in Long-Term Mating

In *The Glimpses of the Moon* (1922), Wharton builds her plot around an unusual marital experiment. It represents an individually crafted response to dilemmas inherent in human mate selection, dilemmas exacerbated by social pressures that constrain individual choice. In assessing the qualities of potential partners, people in quest of long-term relationships are guided by a number of criteria, including, for example, genetic quality, material resources, personality type, and commitment potential.[1] Wharton places her protagonists in a social environment that encourages a strong bias in favor of resources; other significant factors in the mate-selection process are de-valued or set aside altogether. Hero and heroine launch their experiment in an effort to make a more balanced choice of partners. Paradoxically, their scheme affirms materialistic values even as it evades them; it also includes hazardous ventures into reciprocal altruism, which accordingly comes under auctorial scrutiny. The happy outcome — rare in Wharton's fiction — is achieved only when the experiment fails and her protagonists come to recognize the limitations of the selection criteria promoted in their privileged, upper-class circle. Unsurprisingly, from a Darwinian point of view, Wharton links adaptively revised behaviors and preferences to her characters' heightened interest in their future progeny. They reject environmental pressures once they redefine their relationship (however unconsciously) as a "reproductive union" whose purpose is to produce and nurture children, "the shared vehicles by which genes survive the journey to future generations."[2]

103

Wharton presents readers with two individuals, male and female, who face the same problem in their quest for a mate. Nick Lansing and Susy Branch are affiliated by birth with New York's wealthy upper class, but their families no longer command the extensive resources required to maintain the lifestyle of this financially elite social stratum. Both take for granted, therefore, the necessity of securing a long-term partner with substantial wealth. Inconveniently, as it seems, these two impecunious people find themselves in the grip of a powerful mutual attraction, discovering a unique compatibility, "the one complete companionship" either has ever experienced (*GM* 17). What follows is their decision to enter into an unusual "compact" (*GM* 27). They marry, publicly announcing permanent commitment, but privately agreeing that the arrangement will be contingency-based: they will release each other as soon as either has "a chance to do better," meaning location of a suitably wealthy candidate for remarriage (*GM* 21). Variously referred to as a "mad" adventure, "queer compact," and "absurd agreement," their marital experiment is predicated upon an increased tolerance for divorce, social as well as legal, that will facilitate an exchange of mates when opportunity offers (*GM* 14, 109, 133). Meanwhile they plan to live on the largesse of their community: wedding gifts in the form of "cheques," along with the loan of successive villas, apartments, and estates for a year of "honey-mooning" (*GM* 22, 23). As an added advantage, they plan to exploit their already considerable popularity, which will be enhanced by the "novelty" of their marriage, to "help ... each other ... in the way of opportunities" (*GM* 21).

Wharton's plot very quickly confronts both protagonists with potential new mates who appear to offer exactly the kind of better opportunity they ostensibly seek. Nick and Susy respond positively to these new suitors principally because of their unexpected, and premature, estrangement from each other. Although they have assured each other repeatedly that their "experiment" of a marriage is scheduled to last "at least a year," it dissolves after a brief summer of bliss, approximately two and a half months (*GM* 4). The break-up is precipitated by one partner's inability to tolerate the disadvantages of the "bargain" their marriage represents (*GM* 74). Both Lansings discover that the fantasy of marrying at other people's expense is more agreeable than the reality; for Nick, the burden of favors received quickly becomes insupportable. Depicting the process of disillusionment leading up to Nick's abrupt abandonment of Susy, Wharton explores the workings of reciprocity in great detail. Indeed, problems posed by the Lansings' unusual marital plan are inextricably linked with the risks inherent in reciprocal exchange.

Much of the scientific literature on reciprocal altruism emphasizes its benefits, and understandably so: this "very complex system" of behavior would not have evolved unless it enhanced survival and fitness of participating individuals.[3] The advantages of offering assistance or resources to another individual, with the expectation that in due course reasonably equivalent reciprocation will be made, seems self-evident. Since favors need not be returned immediately or in kind, as Trivers explains, "a diversity of talents" may be fostered.[4] The fact that selective forces have favored the evolution of a system of reciprocity does not mean, however, that transactions invariably prove benign for both exchange partners. Some types of reciprocal alliances, as Nick and Susy Lansing discover, prove more burdensome to one party than to the other. The newlyweds are fully aware that they are the recipients of favors, favors that are merely the extension of many that both have accepted in the past. Perpetual social indebtedness has not been a comfortable experience for them, as readers quickly learn.[5]

Susy, in particular, has suffered in her role as "a poor hanger-on" (*GM* 304). While enjoying the first borrowed honeymoon villa, she reflects on her situation, noting that she has always "detested" the wealthy people among whom she has spent "the greater part of her life" (*GM* 5). Her antipathy stems from "nearly twenty years of dependence" on the largesse of non-kin after her father's death (*GM* 5). These generous acquaintances have become "the people one always had to put oneself out for" (*GM* 5). Having accepted a continuous stream of benefits in the form of housing, travel, and wardrobe, Susy acknowledges the tit-for-tat requirements of reciprocity by paying her debts in the only currency she commands: social compliance and personal service. To some extent, at this point in her life, she is able to compensate her hospitable friends with her companionship and social gifts. She is an attractive, bright young girl, and her company has value. Just as Nick can pay "for good dinners by good manners," Susy can exploit the worth of her "freshness and novelty" (*GM* 17, 176).

As she grows older, Susy recognizes, her social value will decline. She observes the "elderly women" living as "pensioners of her own group, who still wore its livery," who gain access to luxury by assuming "slave-ant offices" (*GM* 176). "More and more," she realizes, she will be "used as a convenience, a stop-gap, writer of notes, runner of errands, nursery governess or companion" (*GM* 176). Even now, at the peak of her youthful vitality and attractiveness, she often is pressured to provide her hosts and hostesses more in the way of compensation than good company. Having entertained Susy as her house-guest in Versailles, for instance, Violet Melrose is very aware of her role as "benefactress"; accordingly, she asks Susy to serve as live-in babysitter for the Fulmer children while she takes a jaunt to Spain with their parents (*GM* 175). Later, Ursula Gillow wants Susy to flirt with her husband to distract him from her own extramarital activities: "'you don't much mind Fred's love-making, do you? And you'd be such a help to me'" (*GM* 200). Ursula makes clear that Susy owes her this service, given the "long vista of favors bestowed" and, more particularly, the "weeks of ecstasy" provided by "the Gillows' wedding cheque": "Ursula was not the woman to forget on which side the obligation lay between them" (*GM* 201). Earlier in the novel, Ursula makes an even more outrageous request: hoping to win Nick Lansing as a short-term partner for herself, she asks Susy to short-circuit her own budding romance with him. Susy complies in the spirit of a person making payment for services rendered. Informing Nick that they must meet no more, she explains that she is honoring "'a business claim'": "'Ursula does a lot for me: I live on her for half the year. This dress I've got on now is one she gave me. Her motor is going to take me to a dinner to-night. I'm going to spend next summer with her at Newport.... so good-bye'" (*GM* 12).

Such examples show that Susy is already a "slave-ant" in training: to meet the expectations of reciprocity, she must sacrifice her time, her plans, her convenience, even her most intimate concerns, to others. In important respects, as she tries to explain to Nick, she is not ... "'free'" (*GM* 10). Susy's predicament illustrates the dangers of entering into reciprocal partnerships characterized by inherent asymmetry. If the goods or services exchanged are not equally necessary or valuable to both partners, the individual providing greater benefits will accrue more power in the relationship. In the absence of her friends' generosity, Susy would not be able to maintain her current lifestyle; thus Ursula, Violet, and their ilk are providing things crucial to Susy's survival in this particular social environment. Because their wealth is so vast, however, Susy's rich friends are conferring benefits that cost them very little, relative to their means. The value of the benefits to her, the recipient, is much greater than their cost to the givers. This would be an ideal situation if the reverse were also true, that is, if Susy could reciprocate by providing something at low cost to herself that would be very valuable to her exchange partners. Clearly this is not the case. As the "sport of other people's moods and whims," she repays her obligations at great personal sacrifice (*GM* 15); she is resentful of their often humiliating demands and clearly does not consider the reciprocation required of her low-cost. Her exchange partners, moreover, most assuredly could survive without Susy's services, which are conveniences rather than necessities. Thus the cost to Susy of the benefits she provides is greater than their value to the recipients.

This asymmetry is reinforced by Susy's lack of options in comparison to those with whom she trades favors: she has no alternative method of achieving the standard of living they provide, whereas they can replace her services. If Susy were to withdraw from her reciprocal partnerships, in a spirit of aggravation or outrage, perhaps, or because her financial circumstances changed, her friends would be merely incommoded: they would and could find other ways to meet the needs to which she has been ministering. There are other pretty girls available to enliven parties and flirt on command, other impecunious acquaintances to mind children or write letters. Since Susy very obviously could not continue her upper-class way of living if her friends ceased to provide her with meals, lodging, transportation, and the like, she has far more to lose if her reciprocal alliances were to rupture. The detestation she harbors for the people who have made her lifestyle possible appears to reflect anger at her own powerlessness.

In a number of details Susy's dilemma echoes that of an earlier Wharton heroine, Lily Bart in *The House of Mirth* (1905). Lily, too, must assume secretarial duties or sit at bridge tables in compensation for expensive hospitality; she, too, is expected to amuse dull conversation partners and provide friends with an infinitely sympathetic ear. Living at other people's expense, she must take on "tiresome things" and undertake "social drudgery" (*HM* 61, 62). Like Susy, Lily finds that her youth and beauty have some exchange value, but that value is dwindling. "'People are getting tired of me,'" she confides to Lawrence Seldon at the start of the novel (*HM* 13). Eventually Lily becomes embroiled in transactions that jeopardize her social standing and reputation, most obviously when she accepts a cruise on the Dorset's yacht in exchange for distracting the husband's attention from his wife's infidelities. The outcome of that exchange is disastrous for Lily, obviously, but for reasons that never come into play in *The Glimpses of the Moon*: an unreliable, or cheating, exchange partner. Bertha Dorset cheats Lily in that she does not do her part in their reciprocal agreement. Lily delivers what Bertha wants, occupying George's attention without actually attempting to secure him as a mate for herself (something Carrie Fisher, at least, thinks Lily might easily have done). When Bertha turns on Lily, accusing her of adulterous behavior and setting her up for social disgrace, she is reneging on her part of their tacit bargain. Not only is she ceasing to provide payment for services rendered (by expelling Lily from the yacht), she goes out of her way to do her harm. Given Bertha's belief that Lily has stolen Lawrence Seldon's affections from her, it appears to on-lookers likely that Bertha never intended to deal honorably with Lily. Indeed, people usually hesitate to enter into reciprocal agreements with enemies, and Lily's friends later berate her for having trusted a person whose ill-will was so evident.

Lily's poor judgment in striking up an alliance with a clearly untrustworthy individual illustrates one of the most often discussed risks of reciprocal altruism. Since altruistic acts typically are repaid at an unspecified later date, and often in unspecified form, subtle and gross forms of cheating are an ever present possibility.[6] Reviewing the case of Lily Bart and Bertha Dorset, readers must be struck by the fact that Wharton's depiction of reciprocal exchange in *The Glimpses of the Moon* excludes the issue of cheating from consideration. Beginning with a young woman whose situation, like Lily's, tempts her to enter into reciprocal partnerships with people whose material resources far exceed her own, Wharton moves the problem of asymmetrical exchange — rather than the problem of cheating — into central position in the 1922 novel. Susy and Nick Lansing do not suffer because their exchange partners are guilty of deceptive dealing; they suffer because their partners exercise power over them. Without the ability to control the nature or timing of the repayment that may be asked of them for benefits conferred, they find their personal freedom and dignity repeatedly threatened.

Wharton indicates that women are particularly, though not exclusively, vulnerable to the dangers of asymmetrical exchange. Readers are able to make detailed comparison of the social and economic circumstances constraining each of the protagonists. Nick Lansing commands few resources in comparison with the rich people with whom he has "knocked about so long" (*GM* 11). By ordinary standards, of course, he is hardly impoverished: from "dwindling family properties" (though large enough to require management by an "agent"), he derives a "meager income" (*GM* 180). Although he speaks of needing to make money, either through his writing or from some kind of "job that will pay," he has spent much of his time since graduating from Harvard engaged in activities that require an outlay of resources (*GM* 187): "distant journeys, the enjoyment of art, the contrast with new scenes and strange societies," poetry and art history projects (*GM* 16). He has spent "rather too much" of the inheritance he regards as a "pittance," and he foresees a future of "poorly paid hackwork, mitigated by brief and frugal holidays" (*GM* 16). To Susy, accustomed to magnificent surroundings, his small, bare apartment suggests a "decent indigence" (*GM* 9). Despite what Nick regards as Spartan features of his lifestyle, however, his small income — buttressed by the opportunities he enjoys to augment his income in ways not open to women — gives him some immunity from the skewed reciprocal alliances in which Susy becomes enmired.

As a man of limited means attempting to socialize with a wealthy crowd, Nick does share Susy's problems sufficiently to understand them: "it was part of his difficulty and of hers that to get what they liked they so often had to do what they disliked" (*GM* 15). To indulge his love of foreign travel, art history, and archaeology, for example, he travels for "'five whole months'" as the guest of the Mortimer Hicks family, people with whom he would not otherwise have spent time (*GM* 57). Later he acknowledges indebtedness to them by devoting time and attention to them when they appear in Venice during his honeymoon. When urged to avoid this gauche, *nouveau riche* family, he invokes the tit-for-tat principle: "'if they bored me occasionally, India didn't'" (*GM*

57). He has purchased *what he liked* (a long and luxurious cruise to the far East) by doing *what he disliked* (associating with dull people far removed from his own social background). In smaller ways and on a day-to-day basis, as he recognizes, he repays lavish hospitality with charming and gracious behavior, including, on occasion, attentiveness to some "dissatisfied fool of a woman" (*GM* 17). He has analyzed the problem of reciprocity carefully and decided which benefits are important enough to him to warrant asymmetrical alliances: "there were things a fellow put up with for the sake of certain definite and otherwise unattainable advantages; there were other things he wouldn't traffic with at any price" (*GM* 26). His gender, as he admits, makes him less susceptible to the degrading transactions that have robbed Susy of so much personal autonomy. "For a woman, he began to see, it might be different. The temptations might be greater, the cost considerably higher, the dividing line between the 'may's' and 'mustn't's' more fluctuating and less sharply drawn" (*GM* 26). Constrained by limited professional opportunities, women are likely to have greater need for the favors to be obtained in hazardous reciprocal alliances; at the same time, their behavior is subject to criticism stemming from culturally dictated, gender-specific expectations. In this novel, as in *The House of Mirth*, Wharton shows that in the early twentieth-century social environment she has targeted for comment, women are far more likely than men to enter into disadvantageous, perhaps demeaning, reciprocal arrangements.

Because of his marriage to Susy, Nick finds himself drawn into new exchange relationships, greater in number and involving more high-cost favors than those he has previously contracted. Initially he ignores the probability that generous friends who have subsidized a year of honeymooning will demand some form of repayment. Basking in moonlight beside a lake in Como, listening to a nightingale from the veranda of a borrowed villa, he enjoys listening to Susy describe how they can "'make it last,'" seemingly oblivious to the consequences of having accepted luxuries he and his bride cannot afford (*GM* 4). When he discovers, three months into his marriage, the price Ellie Vanderlyn has exacted for the loan of her Venetian palace, he is angry and dismayed. In addition to leaving her eight-year-old child for the Lansings to mind, Ellie has asked Susy to mail a series of pre-dated letters to her husband, week by week, effectively concealing from him her absence from home and her adulterous affair with Algie Bockheimer. Susy is horrified that Ellie "would dare to use her in this way"; she finds the request for such a service "unbelievable" and "vile" (*GM* 34).

Upon reflection, however, Susy decides that she is in no position to refuse compliance. She has accepted a very large favor from her absentee hostess: free board and room "all summer" in a fully staffed palace, and not "a particle of expense" for food or incidentals (*GM* 35). Listing these sumptuous benefits, Ellie's note reminds Susy of the expectation of fairness in reciprocal dealings: "'one good turn deserves another'" (*GM* 35). She does not scruple to instill guilt by suggesting that Susy is indebted to her for past favors as well as current ones: "'if you've ever owed me anything in the way of kindness...'" (*GM* 36). Here Wharton illustrates the tenacity with which individuals track benefits given and received, as well as the guilt-inducing tactics so frequently invoked by social creditors to induce repayment.[7] In this instance, Susy must acknowledge that the indebtedness is substantial ("she did owe much to Ellie") and that "this is the first payment her friend had ever exacted" (*GM* 38). She can evade the suddenly distasteful demands of this reciprocal partnership only by rejecting the benefits currently on offer. If she vacates the villa immediately, she can refuse to participate in the elaborate deception Ellie has engineered. The Lansings' lack of resources makes immediate departure highly impractical, however, no matter how attractive from an ethical perspective.

Having no mansion of her own to which she can beat a dignified retreat, Susy needs the hospitality Ellie is extending, and thus she finds herself maneuvered into a form of reciprocation she finds morally repugnant. When Nick learns, after the fact, the "price" she has paid for this particular honeymoon house, he is furious with her, and the resulting quarrel precipitates his abrupt departure (*GM* 109). Susy points out that their marriage is predicated upon the principle of "'give-and-take,'" but he appears never to have considered what kind of *give* might be demanded of those who *take* as largely as he and Susy have done (*GM* 108). Their "'being together'" depends upon what they "'can get out of people,'" she reminds him: "'Did you ever in your life get anything for nothing?'" (*GM* 108). Nick has accepted their situation "'theoretically,'" she argues, noting that "in old times" he himself appeared to make "necessary accommodations" quite readily (*GM* 106, 113). Now, however, the reality of their degraded and powerless position strikes him as untenable. He insists that he has never "'done people's dirty work for them — least of all for favors in return'" (*GM* 108). If transactions such as this one with Ellie Vanderlyn are indeed "the price of ... remaining together," he is convinced that he and Susy must part (*GM* 109).

As a single man, Nick has been able to maintain a "stricter standard" in his reciprocal arrangements, for reasons Wharton carefully has pointed out in advance of this scene (*GM* 108). Susy nevertheless perceives inconsistency in his present position: "When they had entered into their queer compact, he had known as well as she on what compromises and concessions the life they were to live together would be based" (*GM* 109–110). Her reproach is justified from her point of view, although she is not fully aware of the differences between her experiences as a dependent girl and Nick's life as a bachelor. His gender, as much as his personal code of ethics, has prevented him from being drawn into the extremes of personally humiliating reciprocity which have played such a significant role in her own life. At the same time, particularly in light of his earlier admission about the "compromises" necessary in "their wretched lives," Nick appears to be engaging in a certain amount of self-deception when he fails to anticipate that their heavily subsidized marital scheme will require reciprocation — and perhaps in forms not to their liking (*GM* 25).[8] As his cogitations on the "things" he will "put up with for the sake of certain ... advantages" clearly reveal, he has not in the past expected to get something for "nothing" (*GM* 26, 108).[9]

In fact, Nick's tempestuous reaction to Susy's involvement in her friend's "'dirty business,'" as he characterizes it, owes much of its force to emotions he never directly acknowledges (*GM* 107). The nature of the service Susy has rendered can be expected to trigger deep-seated male fears: she has abetted another woman's marital infidelity. Given the problem of paternal uncertainty faced by human males, the prospect of cuckoldry is an ever-present evolutionary threat. Prizing and, indeed, demanding, sexual loyalty in a long-term mate, men are sensitive to signs that this loyalty may be waning. From a Darwinian perspective, it is not surprising that Nick judges his wife to be tainted by the role she has played or that he now questions her potential for fidelity.[10] If Susy had given help to Ellie that did not place her standard of marital loyalty in question, readers surmise, Nick would not have reacted with such rage. He offers no objection, for example, to the time and energy Susy spends caring for Ellie's child. Such service, however onerous, places Susy's capacity for maternal devotion in a favorable light, highlighting her worth as a wife instead of undermining it. Nick is very annoyed with Susy when she tries to make off with Strefford's fancy cigars, to be sure, but he recognizes that it was her "desire to please him, to make the smallest details of his life ... luxurious" that tempted her to this small transgression, and he shows no inclination to desert her because of it (*GM* 33). Nick leaves his wife, finally, because he has re-assessed her capacity for sexual fidelity. The requirements of their heavy social debts have put Susy in the unpleasant position of repaying large favors with "an equivalent" that decreases her own mate value (*GM* 54).

Previously Nick has closed his eyes to a similarly dubious transaction between Susy and the Gillows. He has wondered, but "taken care not to ask," how Susy managed to transform Ursula Gillow's initial resentment of his romance with Susy into wholehearted support: a substantial wedding present in the shape of "a thumping big cheque" (*GM* 71). In fact, as Susy admits to Strefford, she "got Ursula thoroughly frightened" by staging the beginnings of an affair between herself and Ursula's husband: "'I flirted with Fred'" (*GM* 51). Fearing that Susy may steal her husband, Ursula is happy to quash that threat by promoting Susy's marriage to Nick. Nick suspects that something along these lines has occurred, sensing an unspoken "complicity" between Susy and Fred when the latter shows up to visit them in Venice (*GM* 72). Traveling without his wife, who has become interested in yet another young man, Fred disturbs the Lansings' honeymoon tranquility by insisting they have agreed to pay a protracted visit to his estate in Scotland later in the summer. He appears to anticipate further opportunities for dalliance with Susy while she and Nick are his guests. Once they have accepted hospitality from him on a lavish scale, Fred no doubt calculates, he will be favorably positioned to pressure Susy to follow through on her implied promises of sexual favors. When she responds evasively to his urgent invitation, Fred shows signs of "rankling grievance": from his point of view, Susy is backing away from an unspoken agreement (*GM* 73). Clearly she has acted deceptively toward Fred, indicating by flirtatious attention to him that she will allow him future intimacies.

Exercising considerable adroitness, Susy has used the lure of short-term sex to obtain desired benefits from both partners in the Gillow marriage. She is left with the ongoing problem of Fred's thwarted expectations, however, expectations she deliberately raised but has no intention of fulfilling. Suspecting the general outline of Susy's maneuvering, Nick has reconciled himself to it by ignoring it, an act of self-deception that becomes harder to sustain once Fred shows up making obscure claims on Nick's wife. "I'm jealous of Gillow," Nick tells himself, even as he acknowledges that "the time for being jealous ... would have been before his marriage, and before the acceptance of the bounties which had helped to make it possible" (*GM* 74). He realizes that he cannot legitimately reproach Susy for making suggestive overtures to Fred, since her behavior was part of a complex reciprocal transaction from which Nick, too, has benefited. Put in crassest terms, Nick would not now be enjoying a sexual relationship with Susy if she had not bartered the promise of one to Fred Gillow. Indeed, readers observe Nick's passionate enjoyment of the benefits Susy has obtained for them. In the middle of his distressing ruminations about her interactions with Fred, tellingly, she approaches him and presses "her slender length against him" in a lingering embrace, assuring him "with lips close to his" that they need not accept Fred's proffered hospitality in Scotland (*GM* 75). Holding her body against his own, Nick finds that "his doubts and distrust began to seem like a silly injustice" (*GM* 75). Here the powerful immediacy of their physical relationship suffices to quiet his uneasiness about the means she has used to obtain it.

Objectively viewed, Susy's dealings with Fred Gillow appear more likely to stimulate a husband's wrath than the assistance she gives to Ellie Vanderlyn. Her provocative behavior with Fred, loaded with the bait of future sexual access, poses a direct threat to Nick's expectations of sexual exclusiveness.[11] Her activities on Ellie's behalf, in contrast, compromise her only indirectly. The distinction Nick makes between the two situations is based partly on timing. Susy's flirtation with Fred occurred "before" her marriage, before she and Nick had ratified their mutual commitment (*GM* 74). After their marriage, he views her frankly as "his property," and he is less likely to tolerate behavior on her part that suggests openness to short-term straying (*GM* 64). It is probable, too, that the distress evoked by her behavior with Fred, never openly communicated, exacerbates his response to her subsequent willingness to help an unfaithful wife. Susy already has given him reason to worry about her long-term sexual devotion, and the incident with Ellie Vanderlyn pushes his doubts past endurance.

In the midst of their heated quarrel at the Vanderlyns, Susy reminds Nick that his original plan for them had been short-term involvement rather than marriage: "'you were right when you wanted me to be your mistress'" (*GM* 110). In the heat of their mutual attraction, he had suggested to Susy that they should "take their chance of being happy in the only way that was open to them," given their poverty (*GM* 20). She vetoes this idea vehemently, rejecting the "fibbing and plotting and dodging" of a "surreptitious bliss" (*GM* 21, 20). She explains that she intends to marry someday and does not want to enter into matrimony with a past she is compelled to conceal; in other words, she does not want to risk lowering her long-term mate value by indulging in short-term affairs. She wants them, instead, to "belong to each other openly and honorably, if for ever so short a time" (*GM* 21). It is she who is the architect of the "experiment" they then launch, including the provision for release "whenever either of them got the chance to do better" and the scheme of "honey-mooning for a year" at other people's expense (*GM* 21, 23). It is by persuading Nick that her "fantastically improbable" plan is workable that Susy redirects Nick's short-term mating plans toward long-term commitment (*GM* 22).

Susy's plan requires that two short-term adventurers acknowledge and regard each other as long-term partners: this is the Darwinian absurdity at the heart of their peculiar union. It is, after all, the absence of enduring commitment that distinguishes short-term from long-term mating.[12] Once a man has determined not to make prolonged investment of time or resources in a woman and her future children, he has less cause for anxiety if she proves unfaithful to him. Cuckoldry means that some other man may fertilize her eggs, which represents a loss in fitness, to be sure, but the short-term partner is in no danger of misplacing paternal investment, since he intends to make none. Short-term mating intentions also tend to elicit a different set of selection criteria. When interested in a casual affair, men typically prefer sexually enthusiastic and experienced women.[13] If Nick were thinking of Susy as a short-term mate, her sophisticated manipulation of Fred Gillow and discrete assistance to the faithless Ellie Vanderlyn should not have perturbed him as they do. His enraged response to signs of sexual experience and worldly-wise attitudes in his partner reveals that Nick is unable to sustain the image of their marriage as a temporary alliance.

The jealous attention he pays to her sexual behavior is especially revealing, but Nick displays long-term commitment to Susy in a number of other ways as well. He wonders what will happen, for instance, if she should "begin to bore him" or her interests diverge from his (*GM* 65). "It never occurred to him to reflect," the omniscient narrator shrewdly observes, "that his apprehensions were superfluous, since their tie was avowedly a temporary one" (*GM* 69). He worries about their financial future, too, concentrating his efforts as a writer toward potentially lucrative projects. Pleased with "the sense of having someone to look after," he begins to think of himself in the role of provider (*GM* 64). In his conception of her, Susy has "taken her place in the long line of Lansing women who had been loved, honoured, and probably deceived, by bygone Lansing men" (*GM* 64). Evolved adaptations encourage Nick to think of his investment in Susy in one of two well-defined categories, and he discovers he is interpreting his creatively conceived marriage in a thoroughly traditional manner. Despite the lip service he gives to their compact, with its expiration clause and free pass for mate-switching, he finds that "of the special understanding on which their marriage had been based not a trace remained *in his thoughts of her*" (emphasis added): the notion that they might "renounce each other for their mutual good" seems merely "an old joke" (*GM* 69). Since he thinks of Susy as a long-term mate, it follows that he expects her to behave like one.

Nick ends their marriage far in advance of the set term, not because he has found a more desirable partner (the anticipated "better chance") but because Susy's behavior fails to exhibit the sexual reserve men have evolved to value in a long-term mate (*GM* 111). He conceives of her as a prototypically ideal, sexually conservative wife-figure (a mother and ancestress-to-be in the "long line of Lansing women"), and that mental picture lends "a mysterious glow of consecration" to all his strivings (*GM* 64). Her dealings with Fred and Ellie, all too suggestive of an experienced and casual approach to sexuality, are incompatible with the role Nick has assigned her. He realizes, on an intellectual level, that her seemingly loose behavior is the direct result of the asymmetrical reciprocal relationships into which they have entered. Initially oblivious to the risks they were accepting along with palatial entertainment and large gifts of cash, Nick now understands that Susy is meeting demands for repayment from their mutual creditors, demands of a nature he never foresaw. She has flirted and connived only to purchase time with him: "'do you suppose I didn't know it was for me?'" (*GM* 111). To continue the marriage would mean acceding to further degradation of his wife. If he allows her to go on paying for their happiness with "more of the same kind of baseness," he will be giving tacit approval to her un-wifely behavior, and this he refuses to do: "'there are things ... I can't let you put up with for me'" (*GM* 111). When Susy suggests that rather than "'give [him] up,'" she prefers to handle unpleasant demands for reciprocation on her own ("'if you'd only leave it to me'"), he balks: "'men are different,'" he informs her harshly (*GM* 112). Indeed. Although he knows that Susy has acted solely out of loyalty to him, he is unable to override evolved adaptations with logic.

Nick's reactions underline the ease with which adaptive mechanisms can undermine the creative powers of the human intellect. He finds it impossible to overcome deep-rooted male mating patterns, even though doing so would permit him to enjoy many more months of happiness with a woman it pains him to leave. Human psychology (in this case, male psychology) simply does not recognize the idea of a *temporary* long-term mate. Once Nick has placed Susy firmly in the long-term category, her design for the Lansing's marriage founders on a key evolutionary biological fact: sexually permissive wives threaten their husbands' fitness.[14] Wharton's plot reveals, step-by-step, the inevitable collapse of Susy's boldly eccentric plans. Desiring a poor man as a mate, Susy arranges for other people to bear the start-up costs of their relationship. Since such generosity will not sustain itself indefinitely, she declares that the union will be accordingly brief. Yet she is unwilling to engage in a short-term sexual liaison: hence she defines the relationship as simultaneously short- and long-term. She does not realize that she is asking her partner to imagine her in two diametrically opposing roles (wife and mistress), something the male mind is ill-equipped to do. Planning to pay for this romantic adventure via reciprocal exchange, she fails to realize that the payment exacted from her will definitively end her partner's already doubtful ability to accept the ambiguity of her role.

Susy herself does not experience difficulties like those plaguing Nick. She has selected, as many women do, a temporary partner who possesses all the qualities she seeks in a long-term mate except for material resources. "Women's desires in a short-term sex partner strongly resemble their desires in a husband" Buss finds.[15] The atypical feature of her choice is her lover's impecuniousness, since one of the principal benefits women seek in both long-term and short-term relationships is access to resources.[16] It is Nick's relative poverty, coupled with her own, that necessitates the unusual arrangement she invents for them. If Nick were sufficiently wealthy, readers presume, he and Susy might marry in the usual way: there would be no need for a temporary union at other people's expense. Fully aware of her motives as a temporary wife who must pay for the pleasures she has purchased, Susy does not suffer nearly as much as Nick does from the ambiguity of her role. She clearly perceives herself, and intends to be perceived by others, as a suitable long-term mate; thus she is "thrilled with pride" when she learns that Nick's original suggestion that they engage in a casual affair meanwhile has become "unthinkable" to him (*GM* 110). She is irritated by the necessity of flirting with Fred and distressed at being dragged into the ugly details of Ellie's adultery, but she knows that the favors she extends to her reciprocal partners do not undermine her essential loyalty to her husband. Since Nick is not drawn into flirtatious behavior with other women, moreover, Susy's own jealousy is never aroused. If Ursula Gillow had appeared on the scene, for example, trying to extract repayment for her generosity by demanding Nick's attentions, Susy might have reacted angrily to the threat of mate-poaching. Would she watch with equanimity while her husband offered sexual attention to another woman in the name of reciprocal altruism? Readers do not learn the answer to this question, and Susy never imagines such an eventuality. In any case, women tend to be most threatened by the loss of resources to their husbands' extramarital partners; sexual defection is resented less for its own sake than as the prelude to such loss.[17] Nick has no resources to redirect elsewhere, which effectively eliminates a major source of female jealousy. During their brief months of togetherness, nothing occurs to make Susy question Nick's loyalty to her. Because it never poses any comparable threat to her fitness, their "queer compact" does not test her as agonizingly as it does Nick.

Neither Nick nor Susy is consciously aware that it is his doubts of her long-term sexual fidelity that precipitate his departure. His failure to follow through on his promise to write a letter to her is to be explained as much by his confusion about his own motives as by his masculine belief in "the uselessness of writing a letter that is hard to write" (*GM* 179). He only knows that he cannot "tolerate the conditions on which he had discovered their life together to be based.... What more was there to say?" (*GM* 180). At every point when he is most tempted to get in touch with her, moreover, something occurs to arouse his jealousy. Because Nick's departure coincides exactly with Charles Strefford's accession to his family title and fortune, Nick sees newspaper articles about Streff's new wealth and society calendars reporting the latter's social engagements with "Mrs. Nicholas Lansing." Remembering their agreement to separate once they have located appropriately wealthy new mates, Nick immediately suspects that the newly rich earl, whose company had "delighted" Susy when he had nothing, now will prove "irresistible" to her (*GM* 133). The resentment inspired by his jealous fear of losing Susy to another man encourages his tendency to preserve geographical and emotional distance from her. Since his silence only increases the likelihood that his wife will consider his departure permanent and regard herself as free to choose a replacement mate, his jealousy here assumes a self-defeating form of expression.

Separated in spirit, as well as in fact, by their quarrel, both Lansings find themselves actively sought after by exceptionally wealthy individuals. Suddenly they are in a position to achieve the materialistically defined goals they set forth at the beginning of their experiment, and much narrative space is devoted to this testing of their consciously articulated objectives. Susy is courted by Charlie Strefford, the long-time friend unexpectedly propelled into an earldom by the death of his uncle and cousin. As the "possessor of one of the largest private fortunes in England," he discovers that his desirability as a mate has soared (*GM* 133): "now of course every woman is trying for him" (*GM* 212). Nick has attracted the ardent interest of an equally rich would-be partner. Coral Hicks is the only child of an immensely wealthy American businessman. Large enough to fund the expenses of a small nation, her personal fortune wins her a proposal from a member of the German royalty in need of "replenishing the Teutoburger treasury" (*GM* 241). Tempted though they are by the prospect of new marriages that would bring them nearly boundless material resources, Nick and Susy eventually decide against these opportunities. In so doing, they reject clearly articulated community values, which give priority in mate searches to "money, luxury, fashion" (*GM* 134). The Lansings' friend Ellie Vanderlyn provides the most shocking illustration of prevailing social influences when she divorces her husband to marry Algie Bockheimer, who is "so rich, appallingly rich," but whose "small glossy furtive countenance" signals distinctly unappealing physical, psychological, and interpersonal qualities (*GM* 214, 215). No one is surprised that Nick and Susy consider parting in order to re-ally themselves with Coral and Strefford; surprise is expressed only that they hesitate to seize these chances to acquire material abundance. When Susy tells Ellie that the "'experiment'" (meaning her marriage to Nick) has proven "'impossible — for two paupers,'" Ellie assures her that "'we all felt that at the time'"; in the absence of plentiful resources, no alliance is considered viable in this luxury-oriented community (*GM* 212).

The bulk of the novel delineates a fitful, often agonized, process of consideration and reconsideration, as Nick and Susy slowly move away from community-approved standards and practices. Textual details show Nick comparing Coral with Susy, and Susy comparing Strefford with Nick. In these comparative assessments, both protagonists can be observed invoking adaptively significant mate selection criteria, including physical make-up, personality traits, social background, and commitment potential. Physically, Coral is battling against significant liabilities. When the action begins, she has transformed herself from "a fat spectacled school-girl" to "a young lady of compact if not graceful outline" (*GM* 58); even after puberty, evidently, her waist-hip ratio is far from ideal. Her movements tend to be awkward: she springs "clumsily" from a chair (*GM* 94). She is "well dressed," cultivating a "strong" and "assured" image, but she is "not pretty," "never lovely" (*GM* 58, 287). And although she has replaced her spectacles with "a long-handled eyeglass," her myopia continues to remain conspicuous (*GM* 58). She has worked to make the most of distinctly unpromising material: "some miracle of willpower, combined with all the artifice wealth can buy," has transformed her into an "almost handsome — at times indisputably handsome" young woman, Nick reflects (*GM* 185). She has molded her "massive lines" and "blunt primitive build" into a "commanding" presence, but she lacks conventionally feminine appeal: "her big authoritative" manner seems "harsh," out-of-scale, and unwomanly (*GM* 241,185).[18] In contrast to Coral's massiveness, Susy combines an appealing "lightness of line" with "curves" (*GM* 96, 319); she is "fine-drawn" (*GM* 96). Nick can admire the "large beauty" of Coral's arm, but her hands are "muscular" and her ankles "thick" (*GM* 241, 292, 52); he is moved far more by Susy's "slim wrist" (*GM* 320). Susy is, Nick muses, "lovely enough to justify the most irrational pangs" (*GM* 96). He perceives her as "slenderer, finer, vivider" than other women (*GM* 316).

Facially, too, Coral suffers in comparison with Susy. Coral's complexion is "sallow," her cheek "dusky," her face "heavy" (*GM* 185, 287, 92); her smiles are "clumsy" (*GM* 290). Although there is an attractive "thickness" to her lashes, Coral's projecting black eyebrows "nearly met over her thick, straight nose," and she has the suggestion of a mustache, "barely visible black down on her upper lip" (*GM* 288, 185). Nick describes Susy in much more feminine terms: her face is "soft," her smile "exquisite," her lashes long and heavy (*GM* 131, 96). Her complexion and features manifest "a shadowy bloom, a sort of star-reflecting depth" (*GM* 96). Indubitably, Susy exhibits facial and bodily traits of the type generally preferred, whereas Coral's deviate considerably from cross-cultural standards of female beauty established by Buss and other researchers.[19] Coral's defective vision, perhaps heritable (her father also wears corrective lenses), constitutes a specifically disadvantageous trait. More troubling is the generally masculine impression she makes in terms of size, build, and hair distribution: such characteristics point toward possible hormonal imbalance and, perhaps, impaired fertility.

In mental and emotional traits, as well as in physical endowments, Susy outshines her rival. Coral's bodily largeness and ungainliness are matched by a certain ponderousness of intellect. Zealously she accumulates a "store of facts ... carefully catalogued and neatly stored in her large cool brain," but "illuminated by little imagination and less poetry" (*GM* 183). Although Susy is less rigorously educated than Coral, less systematic in her habits of mind, she nonetheless exhibits "swift intelligence," "exquisite insight," and "intuitive discrimination" that serve, in Nick's view, to "shed a new light" on many subjects (*GM* 184). She responds to works of art with an emotional readiness that enthralls him, her own loveliness unconsciously reflecting the beauty of a picture that moves her: Nick sees "the glare of that tragic sky in her face, her trembling lip, the tears on her lashes" (*GM* 184). The workings of her mental faculties, like the workings of her body, are far more graceful and agile than Coral's. She is "the most amusing" as well as "the prettiest" girl Nick has ever met (*GM* 15). The "community of tastes" he shares with Coral cannot compete with the "deeper harmony" he feels with Susy (*GM* 311, 6).

Susy's attractive personal qualities translate, furthermore, into widespread social success. Like Nick himself, she is "'rather unusually popular'" (*GM* 21). The community that values her is the "old crowd" to which she and Nick always have belonged (*GM* 68). He shares with her the "substantial background of old-fashioned cousinships in New York and Philadelphia" (*GM* 47–48). Coral Hicks and her family are not authentic members of this elite social group. They are, rather, *nouveau riche* enthusiasts indulging their taste for archaeology and travel, "common people with big purses" (*GM* 60). Their enormous wealth has enabled them to gain acquaintanceship with many of the people Nick knows, but the Hickses remain a bit "ridiculous," essentially "failures" in their quest for social advancement (*GM* 60). "They were always taking up the wrong people, giving the wrong kind of party" (*GM* 60). In marrying Coral, Nick would be stepping outside his own high-status group and exposing himself to possible social embarrassment. The Hicks family would reap much social benefit from the alliance, Nick none. Despite her "weak wastrel of a father," Susy's social standing is securely high (*GM* 26). Her behavior is marked by an ease and sophistication quite different from the gaucherie Nick often meets when in the company of the Hickses. Marriage to Susy threatens him with no loss of status and poses no risk of community ridicule.

Comparing Strefford with Nick along personal and social dimensions, Susy, too, finds her new suitor inferior to the mate he aspires to replace. Like Coral Hicks, Strefford is physically unattractive. Although he is "tall," the advantage of height is undermined in his case by facial asymmetry (*GM* 45): he has "untidy features" and a "crooked ... face" (*GM* 156, 54).[20] Repeatedly he is said to be "ugly" (*GM* 46, 156, 222). Until he inherits a title and fortune, he is not considered husband material: status and wealth are required to render him eligible. He furthermore describes himself as "elderly," shows symptoms of incipient deafness, and repeats himself so often that Susy wonders if he suffers from "mental infirmity" (*GM* 162, 250). Unlike Nick, who tends to compare Coral's and Susy's physical attributes point by point, Susy does not enumerate Nick's physical characteristics, nor do readers discover by other means any details of his appearance. His looks elicit no special comment, leading readers to infer that Nick is fairly ordinary in appearance: even average looks, however, would mean he is more attractive than the distinctly below-average Strefford. Since Nick is only twenty-eight years old and exhibits good health, his youth and vigor also give him an edge over his rival.[21] Susy expresses preference for Nick in terms of the tactile rather than the visual, remembering his "first kiss," for instance, or wishing "she were in Nick's arms" (*GM* 297, 166). She recalls their intimacy as "the sudden flowering of sensuous joy" (*GM* 194). Her reaction to Strefford's touch is, by way of contrast, violently negative. When he bends "his keen ugly melting face to hers" for a kiss, she flinches in "gasping recoil" (*GM* 222, 223). "Something within her ... resisted" (*GM* 222). Her reasoned decision to accept him as a new mate thus is profoundly contradicted by her feelings, illustrating Wright's observation that "emotions are evolution's executioners."[22]

It is Strefford's personality traits, rather than his looks, that attract Susy — predictably so, as women tend to place less importance on physical attractiveness in a mate than do men.[23] Strefford is, everyone agrees, "delightful" and "charming" company, full of "good humour" and sociability (*GM* 46). What Susy likes best in him, tellingly, are those traits that remind her of Nick, but comparison only serves to underline the latter's superiority. Like Nick, Strefford "writes," but he has less talent (*GM* 56). Susy is sure that Nick will write "something remarkable" someday, but Strefford simply enjoys impressing naïve acquaintances with his "artless attempts at literary expression" (*GM* 56). The two men also share an ironic distance from the goings-on of their crowd. Streff's "malicious commentary on life had always amused Susy because of the shrewd flashes of philosophy he shed on the social antics they had so often watched together. He was in fact the one person she knew (excepting Nick) who was in the show and yet outside of it" (*GM* 219). She nevertheless judges Strefford to be irrevocably committed to the world he mocks: he "could not live without these people whom he saw through and satirized" (*GM* 219–20). He displays "an almost childish satisfaction" in his newly elevated status and prosperity so that, in Susy's estimation, "he seemed to have shrunk" (*GM* 249, 250).

Contrasting the two men, she judges Nick's criticisms of social fads and pretensions to be much more sincere. Nick's visits to art galleries and exhibitions, for example, are motivated by true aesthetic appreciation, whereas Streff's "intermittent interest in art" is triggered only when "everybody ... was sure to be there" (*GM* 225). Given financial independence, Susy believes that

Nick would turn his back upon their "squirrel-wheel of a world" and live more authentically, in tune with individually forged values (*GM* 129). "With Nick how different it would have been!" she muses (*GM* 225); "What a world they would have created for themselves!" (*GM* 220). She trusts "the genuineness of Nick's standards," which are congruent with his actions, whereas Strefford is "untroubled by moral problems" (*GM* 263). Streff is known for his "outspoken selfishness," a "ruthless talent for using and discarding the human material in his path" (*GM* 46, 59). Nick, contrastingly, proves himself to be reliable in interpersonal reciprocity: he is loyal to the Hickses because of their past kindnesses to him, for instance, even when egged on by others to ignore them socially. Comparing their qualities of personality and character, Susy ultimately finds Strefford's less appealing than Nick's.

Susy does stand to gain some social status by marriage to Strefford. As Duchess of Altringham, she would enter an established and prestigious circle of English aristocracy. In the estimate of her upper-class New York community of origin, this would be a step up, particularly when coupled with the inherited wealth accompanying Streff's earldom. At the same time, however, Susy fears that she will not feel at ease in her new position, living in "a huge monument built of ancient territorial traditions and obligations" (*GM* 208). The activities that would fill her days, like the people with whom she would be expected to associate, are alien. The prospect of "the life of heavy country responsibilities, dull parties, laborious duties, weekly church-going, or presiding over local committees" appalls her as much as do the "bridge and debts and adultery" with which she foresees the ancestral halls soon will be "invaded" (*GM* 208). Though seemingly advantageous, the social changes that marriage to Strefford would entail are not necessarily benefits for an individual like Susy who already enjoys membership in an exclusive, high ranking group. If the shift to a new group costs her more in social discomfort than it promises in terms of enhanced status, it is insufficient as an inducement.

The strongest source of the appeal that Coral and Strefford represent — apart from wealth — is their devotion. Their behavior to Nick and Susy, respectively, is marked by demonstrations of kindness, generosity, and concern; they seek to show in every possible way that they offer reliable long-term commitment. "Worldwide," Buss emphasizes, "one of the most highly valued characteristics in a committed mate is kindness"; humans of both genders seek partners who will prove "kind, generous, and understanding." Such behavior gives evidence of the cooperative spirit and committed attitude that foster success in long-term mating.[24] Throughout her acquaintance with Nick, Coral manifests concern for his personal welfare and empathy for his professional ambitions. Her eyes fill with tears at the prospect of Nick's giving up his "real work" in archaeology because of financial pressures (*GM* 93). His opinions and interests matter to her. She makes a point of letting him know, for example, that she has "remembered lots of things" he has said, years before, concerning "Oriental archaeology" (*GM* 58, 59). She arranges employment for him compatible with his interests and undemanding enough to leave him time for writing and research. It's true that she hopes to benefit from this action, since his work on her father's yacht places Nick in close proximity to her and at a distance from his wife, but the fact remains that she provides him with a congenial work environment and takes a sympathetic interest in his vocational aspirations. She proves that he is special to her, "the only man" with whom she can imagine being happy, by showing him a vulnerable side to her otherwise "authoritative" personality (*GM* 291, 185). He experiences "a thrill that was sweet to his vanity" when he sees Coral "soften at his approach, turn womanly, pleading and almost humble" (*GM* 185). In the one gesture of physical intimacy that occurs between them, he takes her hands in his: he feels how her palms "melt[]" in his, indicating a spirit of surrender on her part (*GM* 292). She convinces Nick that she is sincerely and uniquely attached to him, uninterested in rival suitors (such as Mr. Buttles or the Prince of Teutoburg), and dedicated to his professional success.

Strefford provides Susy with similar proofs of empathy and commitment. He comes to see her immediately upon coming into his title and inheritance, responding to news from Susy that she is living apart from Nick. His appearance at a moment when she feels abandoned and adrift indicates genuine concern for her, and with his proposal of marriage he offers her both material security and emotional support. "In the first days of his mourning he had come to Paris expressly to see her, and to offer her one of the oldest names and one of the greatest fortunes in England," she reflects gratefully (*GM* 162). He courts her patiently but assiduously, letting her see the depth of his caring with delicately worded expressions of love: she can hide from him only "'in [his] heart,'" he tells her (*GM* 221). "She is touched" by this declaration and wonders "half exultingly if any other woman" has evoked such tenderness from him (*GM* 222). Strefford convinces Susy that she comes first with him, that she occupies a place in his affections no other woman can fill. Other women, more interested than Susy in becoming Strefford's wife, will "bore" him, he tells her, insisting that she alone can hold his interest (*GM* 325). Significantly, his regard is considered by both Susy and others to have withstood the test of time already: "'Of course I always knew he was awfully gone on you,'" Ellie Vanderlyn states; "'Fred Davenant used to say so ... and even Nelson ... noticed it'" (*GM* 212).

When Susy shrinks from Strefford's kiss, he indicates that he will forego demands for a passionate response from her: "instead of being angry or hurt, he had seen, he had understood, he was sorry for her!" (*GM* 224). He wants her as his long-term partner on any terms, evidently, showing a sympathetic devotion that may not be very wise (since sexual incompatibility tends to undermine the stability of long-term relationships)[25] but certainly makes Susy feel cherished. He is persistent in his pursuit of her, moreover, showing unassailable commitment. When she breaks her unofficial engagement to him, he continues to write her in friendly terms, assuring her of his own unchanged affection and asking her to take time to reconsider her decision. "'Marry me, and find your reason afterward,'" he begs her, having traveled to Paris once again just to see her (*GM* 325). When she protests that she still feels married to Nick despite having been apparently discarded by him, Strefford replies: "'My dear that's rather the way I feel about you'" (*GM* 325, 326).

Susy and Nick find all these proofs of stalwart devotion from Strefford and Coral extremely appealing. The two would-be new partners are offering precisely the assurances of commitment that the Lansings have ceased to give and receive within their marriage. Physical separation, abetted by a complete shut-down in communication, has caused each of them to doubt the other's dedication to the marriage. Each feels alone, ill-used, and directionless. Since they are not receiving sympathy, kindness, or companionship from each other, they grow increasingly receptive to the possibility of obtaining these benefits elsewhere. The quality of commitment and companionship Coral and Strefford offer is no better than that which Nick and Susy provided each other in their marriage; the problem is that the Lansings have withdrawn all signs of caring from each other, on a day-to-day basis and, apparently, indefinitely. Each quickly becomes receptive, in consequence, to courtship from an individual who promises to deliver benefits the current partner is withholding.

In each case, the proposed replacement spouse offers exceptionally abundant resources and reliable long-term devotion packaged with other attributes that are, for the most part, less than ideal. The physical make-up of the new would-be mates constitutes a definite drawback (a point presumably of more importance to Nick than to Susy), for Strefford and Coral are definitively less attractive than their competitors. In personality and intelligence they are adequate, if not outstanding; they promise better than average compatibility and companionability. What makes the protagonists' decision-making process so interesting is that neither Coral nor Strefford can be dismissed out of hand. These extremely available candidates are not absolutely unacceptable as mates; indeed, they have much to offer. They are simply less desirable than those with whom they are competing. Some of the most compelling evidence that their mate value is not equal to that of Nick and Susy comes, intriguingly, from Coral and Strefford themselves, who clearly indicate that they do not expect an enthusiasm equal to their own from the objects of their attentions. Streff lets Susy know that he will "wait for her as long as ... necessary" even though plenty of other marriageable girls are pursuing him, and his eagerness remains unquenched even in the face of her physical revulsion from his caresses (*GM* 207). For her part, Coral assures Nick that she does not require his love; it will be enough if he allows her "just to love" him (*GM* 292). Like Strefford, she has other mating options available to her, suitors much more eager than Nick. In settling for less "love," less ardency, from the individuals they so assiduously court, Strefford and Coral acknowledge that they assess Susy and Nick to be higher in mate value than they are themselves. Despite their great wealth, evidently, the marriage each desires would represent an unequal exchange.[26]

The ardor so conspicuously missing in Nick's and Susy's responses to potential new partners is clearly discernible in their feelings for each other. Their tenderly sensuous, erotically satisfying relationship is in itself evidence that their mutual preference is driven by unconscious adaptive mechanisms rather than by their socially coached, conscious intentions. "Currents" of feeling, simultaneously emotional and physical, "flow[] between them warm and full" (*GM* 352). Frequent scenes from the early part of the novel show them touching, kissing, and embracing, clearly rejoicing in this aspect of marriage. "The impulse which had first drawn them together, in spite of reason," is "deep-seated" and "instinctive" (*GM* 363). Unlike the "temperate" reaction inspired by the proposed replacement mates, their passion is "red-hot" (*GM* 311, 207).

It takes some time, nevertheless, for Nick and Susy to determine that the proposed mate-switching does not serve their best interests. The prospect of actually achieving the prosperous marriages to which, theoretically, they have aspired forces them to reassess their long-held ideas concerning money and marriage. The time frame of the novel is approximately six months, extending from June (when the Lansings are honeymooning at Como) to December (when they take a second honeymoon in Fontainebleau). Nick leaves Susy late in July, so that the two live apart for the greater portion of this period. Their decision to renew and redefine their marital commitment is possible only because both undergo change during their separation. Wharton provides readers access to this dual process by concentrating attention alternately on her two main characters. She employs selective omniscience, filtering the characters' thoughts and feelings through a narrator who draws generously upon dialogue and interior monologue while keeping externally located comment to a minimum. Nick leaves Susy at the end of Chapter 10, and until that moment the alternation between Nick's and Susy's perspectives proceeds fairly evenly, slightly favoring hers: chapters 1, 4, 5–6, 8, and 10 concentrate on Susy, Chapters 2–3, 7, and 9 on Nick. The tendency to devote more narrative space to Susy than to Nick (six chapters as compared with four) increases dramatically once the two protagonists separate: Chapters 11, 13–15,

17–19, 21–23, 25, and 27–29 highlight Susy's point of view, while Chapters 16, 20, 24, 26, and 30 highlight Nick's (Chapter 12 is divided between the two). Of the final twenty chapters, therefore, fourteen and a half are devoted chiefly to Susy, and only five and a half to Nick. There are several reasons for this imbalance.

The process of comparing Strefford with Nick is presented in greater detail than the comparison of Coral to Susy. Wharton likely deemed it impossible to offer lengthy description of Coral's pursuit of Nick, which is, of necessity, more indirect than Strefford's courtship of Susy. Strefford makes an outright proposal of marriage to Susy, which she eventually accepts, allowing word of their unofficial engagement to spread among their acquaintances. The understanding between Nick and Coral, in contrast, never becomes explicit: "though he was not pledged to Coral Hicks ... he meant ... to ask her to marry him; and he knew that she knew it" (*GM* 311). Wharton's plan, obviously, is for both protagonists ultimately to reject the proposed replacement spouses. Susy can break off with Strefford without causing him social injury, but Nick cannot propose to a girl and then cast her aside her with similar impunity. Susy's visceral shrinking from Strefford's caresses, in particular, so useful in demonstrating that her apparent willingness to marry him involves considerable self-deception, cannot be replicated in the romance between Nick and Coral. If Nick were to initiate physical intimacies with Coral and then retreat from marrying her, he would put her reputation for chastity at risk.[27] Given social customs prevalent at the time the novel was published, Wharton cannot portray love scenes between Nick and a young, inexperienced girl without making her protagonist look like a cad.

It is through Susy's eyes, furthermore, that Wharton presents her principal critique of the social environment inhabited by her protagonists. Descriptions, often satiric, of this "little world of unruffled Sybarites" serve to swell the portions of the narrative assigned to Susy (*GM* 131). She, even more than Nick, must learn to reject the values inculcated in her by a wealthy sub-culture if she is to re-establish her marriage successfully.[28] Her union with Nick will endure only if they can be content to live "'differently,'" much more simply and inexpensively than they have heretofore thought possible: "'like work-people,'" as Susy imagines, "'in two rooms, without a servant'" (*GM* 159). Supporting themselves on his small income, augmented by modest earnings, they would cut themselves off from mansions, cruises, motor cars, fancy restaurants, and similar indulgences. Only by accepting a life without such things can they free themselves from the asymmetrical reciprocal exchanges that have operated so destructively on their mutual trust and respect. Susy has always "loved luxury" and "splendid things," however (*GM* 33). Her blueprint for life requires her to seek financial security through marriage. Like Lily Bart, she intends to select a husband from a small circle of rich men, making resources her chief criterion in her choice. She knows that she will have to compromise on other qualities in order to attract a sufficiently prosperous husband: "she was going to wait till she found someone who combined the maximum of wealth with at least a minimum of companionableness" (*GM* 7). She assumes that a less than "splendid" lifestyle, even with an extremely "companionable" man, is not to be contemplated, but she finds that assumption challenged and gradually overturned as a result of the satisfying "mutual understanding" she has experienced with Nick (*GM* 280). Without consciously planning to do so, she begins to revise her estimation of the importance of material resources in all aspects of life, including mate selection criteria.

Socializing with her old crowd in Paris and London, Susy finds herself more and more repelled by the values and pastimes of the super-rich (*GM* 17). The "fluid and shifting figures that composed her world" lack substance (*GM* 46). "Denationalized," they are "universally at home" yet belong nowhere (*GM* 46, 48). Beneath their cosmopolitan surface lies an ethical and spiritual void. Indeed, they are "moral parasites" (*GM* 145). A small, homogenous group, they have "inter-married, inter-loved, and inter-divorced each other over the whole face of Europe, and according to every code that attempts to regulate human ties" (*GM* 47). Sunk in the fresh misery of losing Nick, Susy grows increasingly sensitive to the vacuity of the lifestyle she always thought she wanted. Its passions are "trivial," and its "mysteries" prove "shallow" (*GM* 146). Her prosperous friends are "marionettes," merely "ephemeral beings blown about upon the ... winds of pleasure" (*GM* 47, 143). Repeatedly they are said to be "drifting"; material resources fail to lend purpose or direction to their "communal dawdling" (*GM* 143, 146, 156, 67).[29] Surrounded by "rich aimless people," Susy herself begins to feel more like a shade in the underworld than a living being, "a ghost among ghosts" (*GM* 195, 271). The more time she spends in this environment, the more she is overwhelmed by its "artificiality and unreality" (*GM* 271).

Insistently Wharton's chosen imagery invests Susy's social universe with a hellish quality. Like shades in Hades, its inhabitants lead a disembodied existence. And like the tormented spirits in Dante's *Inferno* (one of Wharton's favorite literary works), they are condemned to repeat their pointless behaviors endlessly.[30] Never satisfied and having "nothing to do," these pleasure-seeking zombies pursue "their inexorable task" in perpetuity, moving restlessly "from one end of the earth to another" (*GM* 195). Susy perceives their culpable "self-absorption" and, more important, their discontent (*GM* 148). Lacking interior resources, they feed off others: Violet Melrose, for example, is a "vampire in pearls" (*GM* 145). They are "agglutinative," incapable of being alone despite their indifference to one another's central concerns (*GM* 66). The leisure they enjoy does not even bring peace: "every hour" must "furnish a motive for getting up and going somewhere else" (*GM* 116). It is "a squirrel-wheel of a world," a "queer social whirligig," but its perpetual motion achieves nothing and arrives no place (*GM* 129, 145). Increasingly Susy discovers that she is exhausted and oppressed by the fruitless activity characterizing this supposedly privileged way of life. It appears drained of emotional, intellectual, and moral significance in comparison with the "paradise" she enjoyed with Nick, which she defines in retrospect as "the one reality she had ever known" (*GM* 265). Throughout the novel, Wharton subtly juxtaposes the robust sensuality of Susy's relationship with Nick to the wraithlike "drifting" and bloodless enervation of those surrounding them.

The brief period of Susy's tacit engagement to Strefford provides her with opportunity to experience the gaudy futility of wealth first-hand. Suddenly she is in a position to purchase jewels and furs, to fulfill the most extravagant of her fantasies. Even better, she is freed at a stroke from the burdens of her previous reciprocal alliances: she need accept no more soul-sapping favors. "Oh, the blessed moral freedom that wealth conferred!" she exults (*GM* 177). Strefford encourages her to view money as the only foundation on which an autonomous life reliably can be built. "'Comforts, luxuries, the atmosphere of ease ... above all, the power to get away from dulness and monotony, from constraints and ugliness'": these are the things that "'last,'" he tells her (*GM* 160). Even "'mortal caring,'" he insists, is bound to fade in the absence of material comforts. His philosophy articulates and ratifies values that Susy "'chose,'" as he points out, "'before [she] was even grown up,'" and for a while the chance to interact as an equal with her former benefactors is a source of exhilaration (*GM* 160). She tries to convince herself that Strefford is right, that wealth alone enables "'one to call one's soul one's own'" (*GM* 177). "Independence with ease" has always been her goal, and marriage to Strefford will secure it (*GM* 19).

She discovers, gradually, that the promise of a chinchilla cloak "softer and more voluminous and more extravagantly sumptuous than Violet's or Ursula's ... not to speak of silver foxes and sables ... nor yet of the Altringham jewels" does not thrill her as much as she had always imagined it would (*GM* 193). "That short interval with Nick" haunts her with its special quality, "a life unreal, indeed, in its setting, but so real in its essentials" (*GM* 194). In place of material wealth, her union with Nick secured her "the sudden flowering of sensuous joy," along with "something graver, stronger, full of future power" (*GM* 194). The contrast between such benefits and those she can expect to obtain through marriage to Strefford is crucial to Susy's re-evaluation of her life's goals. Now that her plan of marrying a rich husband is about to be fulfilled, she finds herself contemplating the significance of other criteria in mate selection — such as compatibility in values and interests, or sexual vigor.[31] She experiences a "disgusted recoil from the standards and ideals of everybody about her" (*GM* 216). Susy's disaffection with "standards and ideals" she had no conscious intention of disowning proceeds with convincing slowness, by fits and starts. Wharton grants readers detailed, moment-by-moment interior access to a character who discovers, against her will, the insufficiency of certain culturally imposed values. This process allows auctorial criticisms of a community dedicated to material excess to emerge all the more powerfully.

Susy arrives at the final stage in her changing ideas about life with the help of the Fulmers. Since their situation is remarkably like that of the protagonists, they serve throughout the novel as a significant reference point. Members of the same social network to which Nick and Susy belong, the Fulmers, too, suffer from relative poverty in comparison with those around them. They share a commitment to the arts (Nat is a painter, Grace a musician) that lends an extra dimension of purpose and pleasure to their tie. In marrying each other, they have chosen compatibility in interests and values over material resources. Their current situation, with five children in a "cramped cottage" in "the wilds of New Hampshire," illustrates with clarity the kind of lifestyle Nick and Susy passionately wish to avoid (*GM* 17). As Nick reflects, "the case of the Fulmers was an awful object-lesson in what happened to young people who lost their heads" (*GM* 18). It is while visiting them that he and Susy formulate the terms of their matrimonial experiment, precisely because they cannot imagine living like these friends. Marked by "disorder and dishevelment," the Fulmers' home is cluttered with "trumpets ... and tadpoles"; they must cope with "slatternly servants, uneatable food and ubiquitous children" (*GM* 18, 132). Personally, Nat and Grace have lost their youthful good looks and "gone to seed so terribly" (*GM* 18). In every way, the "general crazy discomfort" of their lives contrasts decisively with the "luxury and leisure" their wealthy acquaintances take for granted (*GM* 18, 132).

Even as they mock the inadequacies of the Fulmers' material situation ("'how do *they* stand it...?'"), their guests are struck by the happiness the couple radiates (*GM* 19). "Nat had never been such good company, or Grace so free from care and so full of music," they admit to each other (*GM* 18). The Fulmers are better company, certainly, than the languid hosts of "the most opulently staged house party through which Nick and Susy had ever yawned their way" (*GM* 18). It is even possible, they acknowledge, that "Nat and Grace may after all be having the best of it" (*GM* 20). This realization does not deter them from launching their doomed plan, incurring social debts that will render them vulnerable to manipulation by their benefactors-cum-creditors. Witnessing their friends' home life makes Nick and Susy all the more determined to sacrifice nothing except permanency[32]: their marriage will be brief, but it will encompass material comforts such as the Fulmers have foregone, as well as the personal companionability Grace and Nat so obviously are enjoying. In the course of the novel, Susy and Nick undergo a one-hundred-and-eighty degree shift in priorities. Once they have glimpsed the barrenness of luxury that is not shared with a fully desirable life partner — chiefly through the possibility of marriages to Strefford and Coral — they come to regard the Fulmers as role models rather than as bad examples.

Susy has opportunities to interact with the Fulmers in the middle portion of the novel, during the months when she is living in Paris and Nick is away cruising on the Hicks' yacht. Having these friends close at hand influences her re-evaluation of choices during the period of her separation from Nick; this sub-plot is another factor that works to tilt point of view toward her perspective. Wharton may be indicating that though both Lansings need to revise their initial assumptions, it is Susy whose position must undergo the more radical change. Perhaps, too, the intimate conversations Susy holds with Grace on the topic of marital commitment cannot plausibly be imagined as taking place between men, or with a man present. As a person who has "never been afraid of poverty," Grace models for Susy the rewards of a mate choice based on more than material considerations, highlighting "the closeness of the tie" that can be forged "between husband and wife" (*GM* 170). Knowing nothing of the Lansings' peculiar agreement, or of the reciprocal transactions on which it was predicated, Grace assumes that Susy has married Nick for reasons like those that drew her to Nat: "'Seeing us so happy made you and Nick decide to follow our example, didn't it?'" (*GM* 171). Visiting Grace in Paris to dispel the "evil fumes" of shopping sprees with her wealthier acquaintances (another comparison likely inspired by Dante), Susy seeks a "lesson" that will liberate her from the seductions of pointless extravagance (*GM* 168, 174).

It is the unexpected "celebrity" of Nat Fulmer that has brought him and his family from New Hampshire to Europe (*GM* 145). Having been discovered and proclaimed a "Genius" by Violet Melrose and other members of her circle (after "long hard unrewarded years" and a "steadfast scorn of popularity [and] material ease"), Nat has experienced a welcome increase in sales, obtaining commissions and travel opportunities abroad (*GM* 144, 169–70). The potentially didactic note sounded by the presence of this contented but impoverished couple is softened by Grace's frank acknowledgement to Susy of the difficulties inherent in their situation, both before and after Nat's sudden success. Now that their income has increased, Grace confides that she used to spend wakeful nights "'calculating how I [could] make things come out at the end of the month'" (*GM* 172). Susy had never realized that her always "smiling" friend ever suffered from the "tyranny" of material cares (*GM* 172). Still, as Susy learns, money problems never caused Grace to regret her choice of a husband. With a sufficiently companionable partner, evidently, economic woes can be borne, although they do not vanish.

A different kind of problem is posed by Nat's new public popularity. Susy speculates that his recently acquired "honours and prosperity" may entice Nat to discard the wife who has stood by him "at the cost of her own freshness," and these forebodings prove correct, at least to a point. Nat's mate value has gone up rapidly, and he now has access to potential new partners in elite economic circles.[33] Grace admits that Nat has traveled to Italy with Violet Melrose on a "love-journey" (*GM* 170, 299). Although she is pained by her husband's extramarital dalliance, Grace does not by any means regard the damage to her marriage as irreparable. There are several reasons for her equanimity. First, she does not believe Violet's "'sterile flattery'" will hold Nat's interest in the long run; thus she runs no real risk of being deserted in favor of the short-term partner (*GM* 299). Second, no resources are being deflected away from the family: it is Violet who is squandering money on Nat, rather than the reverse. Buss points out that wives are more threatened by loss of resources than by the emotional fall-out from a husband's infidelity,[34] and in this instance Grace's husband is the recipient of money and gifts, not the giver. Finally, Grace's own mate value been boosted by the income and fame she has recently derived from her musical career. Ursula Gillow, always in competition with Violet, has claimed Grace as *her* "discovery," promoting Grace's career as Violet has Nat's (*GM* 198). An important result of her success is Nat's renewed appreciation of his wife's worth: her rising fame "surprised and pleased" him, lending her "a new importance in his eyes" (*GM* 299). "'He was beginning to forget that I wasn't only a nursery-maid,'" she tells Susy, "'and it's a good thing for him to be reminded'" (*GM* 299–300). Because the mate value of both partners has increased by about the same amount, and at nearly the same time, balance is preserved and the marriage remains intact. Nat's casual affair with Violet nevertheless indicates how easily the marriage might have foundered; it is not invulnerable to outside threats. At the same time, however, readers perceive the good judgment Nat and Grace exercised in their initial selection of each other as long-term mates: two working artists chose partners whose professional talents and ambitions equaled their own. It is not entirely accidental that their mate value — in terms of professional success — remains fairly balanced in the long run.

The "lesson" Susy had hoped to learn from Grace is that people who embrace poverty grow indifferent to material cares, or that those who reject materialistic mate-selection criteria are immune from ordinary threats to long-term commitment (*GM* 174). What she learns instead is that married happiness can co-exist with never-to-be-resolved monetary worries, and that long-term commitment frequently must include tolerance for less than ideal behavior in a marriage partner. The Fulmers are not idyllically happy in their circumstances — far from it; rather, they enjoy a believable degree of happiness. Any fears on the part of her readers that Wharton is sending Nick and Susy off into an unrealistic sunset at the novel's conclusion must be assuaged by this portrait of the Fulmers' humanly credible example. Clearly Wharton is not claiming that a marriage like Nick's and Susy's is guaranteed to bring fairy-tale-like happiness or that material welfare is irrelevant to a couple's contentment. She is asserting a more modest hypothesis, namely, that a union between all-around well suited partners is likelier to prove happy and stable than one based too exclusively upon material considerations.

The five Fulmer children contribute as much as do their parents to Susy's revised life goals — possibly more. Once she has given Strefford a final refusal, turning her back on the opportunity to marry for money, Susy goes to Grace "for counsel and comfort" (*GM* 298). "At a loose end, and hard up," she agrees to assume the care of the very children Violet Melrose had tried, unsuccessfully, to bribe her to take on (*GM* 300). "'It will end by interesting you,'" Grace assures her, and this prediction proves correct (*GM* 300). The "arduous apprenticeship of motherhood" forces Susy to grow up, training her to take an active, day-to-day interest in those dependent upon her (*GM* 295). Struggling to satisfy large appetites on a "slim budget," she pays less attention to her own wardrobe, wearing old and cheap garments without a second thought (*GM* 297). Because she is busy with "immediate practical demand[s]" on her time and attention, she grows less self-absorbed; she must set "private cares" aside (*GM* 309). She realizes that in "contracted households," meaning those not supported by substantial incomes, children serve the "useful" purpose of "giving their parents no leisure to dwell on irremediable grievances" of many sorts (*GM* 309). "'What a child I was myself six months ago!'" she marvels, appreciating how two months with a houseful of children have done so much "to mature and steady her" (*GM* 309). She understands now what it means to put the concerns of others before her own. The needs of growing children are indubitably immediate and important, moreover, and this recognition solidifies her disenchantment with the "artificiality and unreality" characterizing the "drifting" lifestyle of her rich friends (*GM* 271, 246).

Susy feels, oddly, that she herself is being "mothered" by her charges (*GM* 298). Spending time with the Fulmers' intelligent and well educated brood, she finds herself "taking her first steps in the life of immaterial values," values which now "seem so much more substantial than any she had known" (*GM* 298). She had responded to Clarissa Vanderlyn with pity, grasping that parental wealth often leads to the neglect of children rather than to superior conditions for child-rearing: "the rich child is exposed to evils unknown to less pampered infancy" (*GM* 45). Eight-year-old Clarissa's values are already shallow and materialistic; full of un-childlike knowledge concerning adultery, deception, and divorce, she craves jewels and dislikes books. Contrasting Clarissa with the young Fulmers, Wharton demonstrates that parental investment encompasses far more than money. Nat and Grace have raised their children in the company of "good music, good books and good talk"—"nothing trivial or dull" (*GM* 298). The children's minds "had been fed only on things worth caring for" (*GM* 297). Although they sometimes "stamped and roared and crashed about," they are alive to "poetry" and "wisdom" and "beauty" (*GM* 298). Unlike little Clarissa, they manifest no "mean envies, vulgar admirations," or "shabby discontents" (*GM* 298). Demonstrating a knowledgeable as well as passionate interest in the arts, the young Fulmers demand to be taken to the Louvre, "where they recognized the most unlikely pictures, and the two elders emitted startling technical judgments, and called their companion's attention to details [Susy] had not observed" (*GM* 302). The result of being raised in that small cottage in New Hampshire, in crowded proximity to their mother's violin and their father's paints, is clearly positive. Steeped in music and the visual arts, these children have received a multifaceted education and cultural legacy from their parents. Seeing this example of successful child-rearing close at hand, Susy feels able to cope, as never before, with "shabbiness and discomfort" in her material surroundings (*GM* 304).

Her experiences with the Fulmer children, in sum, teach Susy that good parenting is compatible with extremely modest resources. Her prolonged contact with Clarissa Vanderlyn suggests, in fact, that vast wealth is more likely to interfere with careful and conscientious child-rearing than it is to foster it. Without thinking in explicitly evolutionary terms, Susy has come to a crucial realization, namely, that the principal reason for seeking a mate with adequate material resources is to ensure the survival of future offspring.[35] Since the Fulmers' supposedly meager resources have proven sufficient for rearing and educating five healthy children, as Susy now sees first-hand, she need no longer consider Nick's and her resources insufficient for long-term involvement. Enjoying her role as ersatz-mother despite "the hurry and fatigue of her days," Susy reflects that if she and Nick had remained together and had children, "their life together might have been very much like the life she was now leading, a small obscure business to the outer world, but to themselves how wide and deep and crowded!" (*GM* 303). The final piece in Susy's rejection of the materialistic values that previously directed her life, therefore, is this insight into the primal and primary importance of reproduction.

The "small ... business" of bearing and raising children is the driving force behind mate selection and, indirectly, nearly every other human activity. In the artificial world of extreme wealth inhabited by Susy's perpetually dissatisfied acquaintances, the quest for material resources has been disconnected from its evolutionary psychological roots. Wealth is no longer used for purposes of parental investment, and thus to enhance individual fitness, but is pursued for its own sake. The result is inadequately nurtured children like Clarissa Vanderlyn, along with discontented adults who fail to understand the reason for their existential emptiness. Wharton's critique of the social environment in which she has set her protagonists is discernibly Darwinian: severing material resources from fitness-based purposes, members of this ultra-rich social group are the victims of maladaptive customs and values. The novel's plot traces the protagonists' fortunate escape from a destructive set of cultural norms.

Wharton's emphasis on progeny as the critical stimulus for a healthy shift in attitude and behavior is clearly deliberate. Focusing on the possibility of rearing a child together with Nick (and leading a life distinctly lacking in chinchilla cloaks and sapphire bracelets), Susy senses that she will gain a "mystic relation to the life she had missed" in her former, luxury-driven days — that is, a life in contact with biological realities and genetic purposefulness (*GM* 304). Because Nick has been from the start less in thrall to the seductions of materialism, the more Susy sheds her consumer-oriented point of view the closer she feels to her absent mate: her emerging new set of values seems to be "a secret shared with Nick, a gift she owed to Nick" (*GM* 265). Metaphorically, Wharton links the "gift" of Susy's emancipation from a biologically deviant social system with conception: "it was almost ... as if he had left her with a child" (*GM* 265). Once her experience with the Fulmer children leads her to think of marriage in terms of procreation, she remembers what she "had known since Nick's first kiss — how she would love any child of his and hers" (*GM* 297). Very clearly she connects the physical ardor he arouses in her, and which Strefford so signally fails to stimulate, with future offspring.

Nick, too, is moved to alter his plans by the idea of parenthood, in particular by the vision of Susy as a maternal figure. He visits her, unannounced, in Paris, planning to procure a divorce and return to propose to Coral Hicks. Watching from across the street, he notices at once that Susy is living in "humble" and "shabby" surroundings: "her look, her dress, her tired and drooping attitude, suggested poverty" (*GM* 318, 320). These signs that she has jettisoned her money-hungry ambitions give him hope. What moves him most, however, is the sight of her holding "a red-cheeked child upon her shoulder" (*GM* 319). "Transformed" and "transfigured" in his eyes, she becomes "the eternal image of the woman and the child" (*GM* 319). "In that instant," readers learn, "everything within him was changed and renewed" (*GM* 319). As Tricia M. Farwell observes, "seeing her as the ideal mother awakens him to her potential."[36] He forgets his tacit understanding with Coral and can think only of a future with Susy.

In creating the climax of her novel, Wharton makes the idea of potential progeny central, even to the point of sending the protagonists off on a second honeymoon encumbered by all five Fulmer children. The children's presence serves as a boisterous reminder of the future the Lansings are choosing: long-term commitment and child-rearing on a slender income. Once they associate their mutual attraction with the prospect of offspring, they are able to cease their agonized wavering. Turning their backs on the "squirrel-wheel" of pointless extravagance Wharton has subjected to such harsh criticism throughout the novel, Nick and Susy are rejecting wealthy replacement mates for discernibly adaptive reasons: they would be trading up only in terms of material advantage; in terms of attributes suggestive of genetic quality and mutually sustainable companionship, they would be trading down. Choosing each other, instead of Coral and Strefford, Nick and Susy improve their chances of producing genetically high-quality children and sustaining a successful long-term marital commitment in which those children may thrive. The positive, forward-looking conclusion would not be possible without the Lansings' new focus on their reproductive future.[37]

Once their "queer" marital compact has been renegotiated along more conventional lines, it is possible in retrospect to see an element of make-believe in Susy's and Nick's initial plan. During the brief weeks of their honeymoon, they often talk of parting, but without the anguish to be expected if they seriously foresaw such an outcome. There is a game-like air to their conversations on the topic: *tell me again, how we'll manage....* They never refer, even indirectly, to the possibility that Susy will become pregnant, and they discuss no contingency plans for that eventuality. This, in itself, is strong evidence that the intention to separate is not serious. "They are deluding themselves" about their motives, Farwell points out, as well as about the probable outcome of their supposedly temporary experiment.[38] They have no long-term solutions to the monetary problems their union presents, however, and they are as yet not reconciled to setting up house on modest means. They engage in an elaborate pretense, consequently, one that enables them to ignore the financial repercussions of their marriage. Further evidence of the insubstantiality of their supposed "bargain" is to be found in their self-deceiving conceptions of divorce. For all their carefree talk about time-limited involvement, both are shocked by the legal and practical realities of divorce law. Their experiment was predicated upon the assumption that marriage could be ended without social or emotional penalty, and the ugly necessities of trumped-up adultery charges horrify them. Susy realizes that her ideas about divorce had been naïve, as if it were "something one went out — or sent out — to buy in a shop: something concrete and portable ... and that it required no personal participation to obtain" (*GM* 253).

Despite their declared intentions, evidently, both partners find themselves making an enduring commitment. Even when they have lived apart longer than they were together, neither feels fully free to accept a new mate or begin a new life. Repeated episodes of jealousy highlight their ongoing emotional investment in each other: Nick is intensely alert to signs of Susy's involvement with Strefford, as Susy is to hints of Nick's with Coral: each demonstrates exactly the kind of jealous reaction that is stimulated by outside threats to a long-term relationship.[39] An individual identified as a former rather than a current mate is not likely to evoke such hyper-vigilance or emotionally charged reactions. Susy's final break with Strefford is triggered by his very natural failure to appreciate the special quality of her relationship with Nick. She is dismayed to learn that he rented the honeymoon villa he had loaned them in June to the adulterous Ellie and Algie for the month of July, thus drawing "a trail of slime across her golden hours" (*GM* 263). Feeling so protective of her "golden" bond with Nick, Susy obviously is not ready to enter into a serious relationship with anyone else. No matter what they persuaded themselves they intended, Nick and Susy have experienced a "mysterious interweaving of their lives which had enclosed them one in the other like the flower in its sheath" (*GM* 255). This subtly erotic comparison aptly describes the union Nick and Susy, apparently unwittingly, have forged. Their often dramatic, sometimes sentimental, descriptions of the "larger and deeper" or "inexorable" attributes of "real love" indicate, more than anything else, the unintended robustness of their mutual commitment (*GM* 339, 348, 340).[40] The consciously crafted rationale for their unusual marriage proves to be incompatible with evolved adaptive mechanisms: they deceive themselves in imagining that they could evade distinctions between casual and committed mating. Their story convincingly illustrates how deeply rooted in human psychology such distinctions lie.

*The Glimpses of the Moon* often has been read as an optimistic re-visioning of *The House of Mirth*, one in which Wharton steers a similarly materialistic heroine through a positive process of re-education. Susy proves able to shake off environmental influences that drag Lily into debt, despair, and death; as result, Susy contents herself with a husband of slender means, while Lily cannot reconcile herself to marriage with Lawrence Seldon. Rough parallels in circumstance and aspiration are balanced by a number of differences between the two characters — in family background, in personality traits, and in historical milieu.[41] The most intriguing point of congruence between the novels, from a Darwinian perspective, is Wharton's indictment of the mal-adaptive influence of a toxic social environment. Both novels portray social communities that foster the over-valuing of wealth, particularly as a criterion in mate selection. In both plots, moreover, the allure of material luxuries proves antithetical to individual fitness. When the quest for wealthy mates leads to reproductive failure, as it does with Lily, or to diminished parental investment, as it does with the Vanderlyns, readers observe that behaviors have been divorced from their intended adaptive functions. Lily's fantasy, in her dying hours, that she is holding a baby — the source of "a gentle penetrating thrill of warmth and pleasure" — may be regarded as an embryonic version of the insights Susy gains while caring for the Fulmer children (*HM* 522).[42] Gradually realizing that rearing children will prove more real, more mean-ingful, to her than a life filled with jewels and furs, Susy provides a better developed example of what Lily, in her drug-induced haze, only faintly begins to intuit.

Once they determine to resist community pressures, Susy and Nick are poised to achieve the "natural and necessary" reproductive success that eluded Lily (*GM* 359). Unlike Lily, they inhabit the post-war world of the 1920's, and this historical accident is an important ingredient in the happy resolu-tion of their mating dilemmas. Wharton shows that between 1905 and 1922 the social universe inhabited by the Barts, the Dorsets, the Trenors, and their ilk has undergone change. Wide-scale disruptions — political, economic, and psychosocial — such as those caused by World War I and its aftermath, enable individuals to question collective prescriptions more effectively.[43] The pres-ence in *The Glimpses of the Moon* of characters such as the Fulmers, whose conduct is to a considerable extent liberated from pressures to accumulate wealth, suggests that cultural norms are undergoing modification. Like Lily, Nick and Susy are products of their time and place; their circumstances are sufficiently altered from her turn-of-the-century environment to make a dif-ferent outcome to their difficulties just barely possible.

The satisfaction readers garner from the optimistic conclusion of *The Glimpses of the Moon* is undercut to some extent by sentiments Nick expresses in the final paragraphs. Specifically, he makes an unfavorable comparison between Susy's current feelings for Strefford and his for Coral: "his mind dwelt on Coral with tenderness, with compunction, with remorse; and he was almost sure that Susy had already put Strefford utterly out of her mind" (*GM* 363–64). He concludes that this difference reflects "the old contrast between the two ways of loving, the man's way and the woman's way" (*GM* 364). To readers of either sex this reflection must seem both snide and unjust. Having definitively broken her engagement with Strefford, Susy has a right to put him out of her mind. Although she has hurt him, she has dealt honorably with him: things are clear between the two of them. Nick, in contrast, is still tacitly engaged to Coral Hicks. He decides against divorce, re-commits himself to Susy, and starts off on a second honeymoon while Coral is still sitting on her yacht anticipating his return to her. When Susy expresses dismay that he has not "told Coral" that his intentions have drastically altered, he reacts with outright callousness: "'what earthly difference does it make?'" he asks (*GM* 349). Nick admits that he has been "a coward" in his dealings with Coral, while Susy has been "sincere and courageous" in hers with Strefford: yet he apparently believes his "remorse" proves that his "way[] of loving" is more sensitive than hers (*GM* 363). In readers' estimation, Farwell notes, he "is not as blameless as he would like to believe."[44] He loses sympathy, too, by proposing to carry Susy off to Fontainebleau *post haste*, leaving her young charges without adequate supervision. When she protests that she "'can't leave the children,'" insisting that she is responsible for them, his reaction falls somewhere "between indignation and amusement" (*GM* 350). He does not label his blithe proposal to dump the children as "the man's way," or her conscientious refusal to abandon them as "the woman's," but readers are likely to judge his indifference to the young Fulmers' welfare harshly. Although he enjoys picturing Susy as "the eternal image" of maternal devotion, he evinces little understanding of the practical realities of parental obligation (*GM* 319).

Concluding her narrative with such examples of Nick's thinking, Wharton spells out a harsh reality, namely, that men's strategies and assumptions are not likely to mesh perfectly with women's, even in marriage.[45] Half realizing this fact, Nick warns himself that "forgotten things, memories and scruples" that he has "swept aside in the first rush of their reunion" are bound to re-emerge in due course, creating occasional problems between him and Susy (*GM* 363). Such problems will be manageable, he believes, because of the long-term commitment they have made: "he and she belonged to each other for always" (*GM* 363). Wharton distinctly avoids saccharine prognostications about the Lansings' future bliss. The couple is likely to experience ongoing struggles with such things as insufficient income, intersexual conflict and, if all goes well, the frustrations of child-rearing. Wharton employs a metaphor drawn from the novel's title to set realistic bounds to her protagonists' projected happiness. They will obtain only "glimpses" of the idyllically perfect moon that elicited rhapsodies from them during their first month together in Como. More typically, as the last lines of the novel insist, the moon will be "labouring upward," casting a "troubled glory" upon a couple that can look forward to a reasonable degree of human contentment, blended with a realistic degree of human woe (*GM* 364).[46] The Lansings have distanced themselves, in any event, from environmental pressures to embrace a sterile, materialistically driven existence. As a corollary, they have freed themselves from destructive, asymmetrical reciprocal alliances. Their life together, however imperfect, will be more natural and more *real* than the one they originally planned. Their "mad," though creative, experiment founders on evolutionary biological facts of human nature, to be supplanted by a more adaptively framed mating commitment.

# 5

# The Old Maid and "Roman Fever"

## *Female Mate Choice and Competition Among Women*

In *The Old Maid* (1924) and "Roman Fever" (1934), Wharton focuses on female mating strategies. She examines women's preferences in long-term partners, at the same time exploring when and why individual women may elect to engage in short-term sexual relationships. The intensity — even ferocity — with which women compete with one another to obtain desirable men emerges with relentless clarity. In these tales, women are active participants in the mate-selection process; undeniably, they exercise choice. They do so, furthermore, in a social environment dominated economically and politically by men. Differentiated chiefly by temporal focus, both works are set in the small, upper-class New York community familiar to readers of *The Age of Innocence. The Old Maid* evokes the 1850's in its fashions and conventions, while "Roman Fever" features technology and customs congruent with its twentieth-century, post-war date of publication. Since this later story reflects on the experiences of three generations preceding the current group of marriageable girls, it effectively incorporates earlier lives and times into its themes, reaching back nearly as far into the past as *The Old Maid*. One effect of the historical sweep Wharton creates in these works is to demonstrate the enduring power of the adaptive mechanisms influencing female mating behavior. Even as she depicts identifiable social environments with meticulous accuracy, she draws attention to psychological processes whose effects transcend time and place.

The two central characters in *The Old Maid*, Delia and Charlotte Lovell, are first cousins who exhibit identical preferences in men but employ diametrically different strategies to attain their goals. Both are drawn to Clement Spender, a charming young man in their own social set. He becomes romantically involved with Delia, initially, but does not offer to marry her. Instead of beginning a profession in "the law" and accumulating means to support a family, he goes off to live in Europe and test his artistic talents (*OM* 17). He is, in general, attuned to pleasures at hand rather than to future concerns, a trait that contrasts appealingly with the "cautious world" of "old New York" (*OM* 3). Exercising neither prudence nor foresight, Clem is "tolerant, reckless, indifferent to consequences, always doing the kind thing at the moment, and too often leaving others to pay the score" (*OM* 36–37). The very qualities that attract Delia to him, obviously, are indicators that he is not likely to prove reliable in the long run. He courts her, encouraging emotional investment on her part, yet shies away from commitment. Delia's reaction is self-protective: she gives up on Clem, who has made neither promises nor plans for a joint future. Assessing her situation and her future prospects, she marries Jim Ralston, a man who exemplifies the "prudent" traits Clem lacks (*OM* 3).

For Delia, Jim represents a next-best choice: he is a reliable and generous provider, a kind if not scintillating companion, a responsible father. Member of a family of "rich and respected citizens," he commands high community status (*OM* 9). More important, he is available—willing and able to invest resources and to offer assurances of long-term devotion. In marrying him, Delia seizes the opportunity to obtain an undeniably good husband immediately instead of waiting to see whether the man she prefers may, perhaps, return and propose. There is danger, after all, in waiting. She has no guarantee that Clem will ever decide to settle into a well-paying profession and make a commitment to her. Meanwhile her reproductive value—and hence her mate value—will diminish. If she refuses Jim Ralston now, she may find herself forced to settle for a considerably lower-quality husband, or even no husband at all, several years down the line. The later she marries, moreover, the more of her reproductive years she will have wasted. She decides not to risk such outcomes, all of which have negative implications for her fitness. Her decision illustrates Buss's observation that most people must make some compromises in their choice of mates. Those compromises are influenced by their awareness, conscious or not, of their current and prospective mate value, relative to others.[1]

Delia's materially prosperous, reliably investing suitor meets female mate-selection criteria more than adequately, yet he fails to stir her deepest feelings. In the opening scene of the novella, readers learn that she remains sexually unawakened; she is confused rather than excited by "the incomprehensible exigencies" of her young husband in their "double-bed" (*OM* 14). In compromising, in marrying prudentially, she has forfeited erotic fulfillment: she is a wife and mother, yet lacks "this last enlightenment" (*OM* 65). If she pays a price in personal fulfillment for her chosen mating strategy, she also reaps tangible benefits: after five years of marriage, she has two healthy children; she has access to abundant resources; she enjoys social respect in her role as wife to a conservative and prosperous Ralston. From an evolutionary biological perspective, it seems, she has chosen wisely. Her two children, bolstered by ample resources to safeguard their well-being in a high-status community, promise to secure Delia a fair degree of direct fitness. Readers learn that both children survive to adulthood and marry "suitably," contracting "irreproachable New York alliances" (*OM* 96). It is possible, though not definitively ascertainable, that Delia's dissatisfaction with the intimate side of her relationship with Jim does exert some negative impact on her fitness. The lack of sexual energy in the marriage means that more offspring are unlikely, even though the Ralstons are young and have been married only five years when the novella begins; in fact, no further children are born in the six years remaining before Jim's death. The small family size may represent a penalty for Delia's mating strategy: as a consequence of settling for a second-choice partner, she experiences reduced sexual drive, which may be the cause of lowered lifetime reproductive success. A small family is better than no family, however. She has ensured that copies of her genes are represented in the next generation, achieving a direct fitness of 1.0.

Charlotte Lovell, whose preferences in men resemble her cousin's, makes radically different choices from Delia's. By her own admission, she has "'always cared'" for the same man Delia loves, but she has even less reason than Delia to suppose that she will obtain long-term commitment from Clem Spender (*OM* 41). During Charlotte's first year as a debutante, Clem focuses exclusively on Delia; Charlotte "'knew there was no hope'" of attracting his affections, but she refuses to consider other suitors: "'I wouldn't marry any one else'" (*OM* 41). When she is courted assiduously by Joe Ralston, a look-alike "copy" of his "second cousin Jim" (Delia's husband-to-be), she does not accept him (*OM* 62, 15). As one of the "poor Lovells," Charlotte needs even more than the wealthier Delia to secure a financially stable husband as soon as possible (*OM* 18). Attending parties and balls in handed-down garments, and further handicapped by unfashionable hair- and eye-color, Charlotte might be considered lucky to have attracted the attentions of a man like Joe Ralston so soon after coming out. Instead of capitalizing on her good fortune, however, she elects to wait — to wait for a man who is in love with someone else and whose behavior, in any case, indicates an aversion to commitment. Charlotte is young still, with "a slim waist, a light foot, and a gay laugh" (*OM* 19):

weighing her assets against her liabilities, she decides she is not desperate enough to settle for second best. Instead of opting for an available, eminently "eligible" husband, therefore, and seizing an opportunity that may not present itself again, she centers her hopes on Clem Spender, a probably unattainable, but distinctly preferable, alternative (*OM* 20). Unlike Delia's prudent course of action, Charlotte's mate search is characterized from the outset by risk-taking behavior.

Quite quickly her strategy pays off, when Clem, disappointed by Delia's marriage to Jim Ralston, turns to Charlotte for companionship: "'he began to notice me, to be kind, to talk to me about his life and his painting...'" (*OM* 42). Even knowing she is valuable to Clem principally as a stand-in for Delia, Charlotte takes advantage of this opportunity to fulfill her dreams of a romance with him. When he goes back to Europe and she finds herself pregnant, she accepts her situation stoically and makes no attempt to coerce him into assuming responsibility for the child: "'He doesn't know of it — why should he? It's none of his business'" (*OM* 42). Since Charlotte is a girl from Clem's own social circle and thus would not be regarded as an appropriate partner for opportunistic sex, he or his family presumably could have been embarrassed into providing some support for his offspring. Charlotte forebears to apply such pressure, for reasons readers are left to guess. From a practical standpoint, it might be more difficult to keep the matter private, and thus to safeguard her reputation for chastity, if she attempted to embroil Clem's family in her predicament. The fewer people who know of her lapse from chastity, the more effectively it can be concealed. From a personal standpoint, it is possible that in getting to know Clem better Charlotte has grown disenchanted with him. She may well judge his capacity for sustained investment of any sort to be unacceptably low. Buss's research suggests that one reason women engage in casual affairs is the hope of converting a short-term relationship into a long-term union.[2] If Charlotte had hoped that by yielding to Clem's seduction she might win his enduring devotion, that hope was dashed once he sailed for Europe. Her comments to Delia suggest that the romantic glow she once felt for him cooled with his departure. "'That's over — all over. It's as if I couldn't either hate him or love him'" (*OM* 42).

Charlotte relies on her family, rather than her lover, to help with her pregnancy. She is packed off to "a remote village in Georgia" in the care of "an old family governess," ostensibly to recover from a case of the same "lung-fever" that caused her father's early death (*OM* 20, 18). Her mother and grandmother provide assistance, material and social, to help her bear her child in secrecy and return to her home in the role of recovered consumptive. The infant is placed with a working-class foster family. Free to return to the social life of a debutante, Charlotte immerses herself instead in good works, exhibiting "a sudden zeal for visiting the indigent" (*OM* 21). As readers learn, her emotional focus has shifted to maternity; instead of renewing the search for a mate, she spends as much time as possible with her unacknowledged child in the local "day-nursery" for paupers (*OM* 21). Her situation seems precarious: as a result of her decision to engage in short-term sex, she has a child she can neither support financially nor acknowledge publicly. She has not obtained Clem as a husband, and her efforts to spend as much time as possible with her child are interfering with her chances to find some other man to marry. All she has obtained from Clem is his genetic contribution to their child, yet Wharton's plot suggests, intriguingly, that this alone may be a sufficiently valuable benefit to compensate for the many penalties Charlotte pays for her initial, risk-laden mating decisions.

When the novella begins, Charlotte appears to be on the way to social and personal recovery from her earlier indiscretion. Despite her "unnatural" new interest in pre-school "paupers," no one appears to suspect the real reason for her year's absence, or to connect her with the mysterious appearance of an upper-class infant in a local handy-man's "hovel" (*OM* 21, 22). Her romance with Joe Ralston has been revived and she is on the point of marrying him. Her married life seems likely to resemble Delia's, as the latter reflects. They are cousins marrying cousins in an in-bred community: "nothing could be safer, sounder or more — well, usual" than such an alliance (*OM* 13). Finally Charlotte is emulating the more prudent Delia, giving up on the elusive Clem and settling for a solid provider instead, a man she "could love ... in another way" (*OM* 37). She has first allowed Clem to seduce and abandon her, however, a fate Delia avoided, and the existence of her unacknowledged child becomes an obstacle to the happy ending apparently in sight for her. Joe and his family have insisted that after her marriage Charlotte must give up all contact with her "poor children," for fear that she may bring "contagion" home to the family she and Joe expect to begin (*OM* 29, 31). To marry Joe, then, means giving up all opportunity to nurture her existing child and oversee its welfare. Many young mothers in Charlotte's position decide to let the first child take its chances, gambling on future offspring in whom a more substantial investment can be made.[3] Charlotte's impassioned insistence that she "can't give up" this baby is a powerful indicator of the value she places on Clem Spender's genes (*OM* 42). She fully expects to conceive offspring with Joe Ralston ("'Oh, yes I shall!'" she exclaims, when Delia suggests that she might not give birth "for some time"), indicating that her behavior is not motivated by any fear of future barrenness. She knows Joe will ensure the material well-being of his children, giving them maximum opportunity to thrive and reproduce, but she evidently anticipates that they will be less attractive, less special, than a child sired by the uniquely desirable Clem (*OM* 31).

Charlotte does not entertain such thoughts consciously, but her decision to maintain her investment in her first child at whatever cost points toward such thinking.[4]

In the second portion of the tale, the pointed contrast between Tina (daughter of Charlotte and Clem) and Delia's son and daughter (sired by Jim) serves to reinforce the idea that Charlotte's brief romance with Clem has garnered her a particularly high-quality child.[5] One of the effects of making two sets of same-sex characters cousins is to demonstrate that Charlotte obtains a truly different kind of offspring from her affair with Clem than she might have through marriage with a Ralston. Since Charlotte is closely related to Delia, and Joe closely related to Jim, Charlotte's putative children by Joe might be expected to share traits with Delia's: their degree of genetic relatedness would approach that of half-siblings. Tina is not at all like Delia's children, however; her highly individual personal qualities reflect, to some degree, the very different genetic influence of her father. (She also shows signs of having inherited some of her mother's propensity for high-risk behavior, it must be noted; in this behavioral tendency, Charlotte and Delia are less alike than Jim and Joe.) Tina's physical appearance, even in the toddler stage, provides evidence of both parents' genetic contribution: she has inherited Charlotte's "pale brown eyes" with "little green spangles," along with curly hair that grows "in points on her high forehead, exactly as Clement Spender's did" (*OM* 49, 50–51). These proofs of Tina's parentage are unmistakable to Delia, yet not so conspicuous that they lead other members of the community to guess the truth. As Tina grows into adulthood, she proves to be "a brilliant and engaging creature," a more "interesting ... specimen" than the typical young woman (*OM* 89). Her personality, as much as her appearance, is "radiant" and vital; she walks with a "dancing step" (*OM* 123, 135). "Admired and sought after," she "attracts" (*OM* 97, 116).

Delia's son and daughter are contrastingly ordinary. "Happy and jolly" children, they grow up to lead successful, but predictable, lives (*OM* 47). Neither their looks nor their characters excite comment; they manifest no special brilliance and are disinclined to defy the "deliberateness" characterizing the community (*OM* 158). Their opinions, like their behavior, are conformist. Delia "always knew beforehand exactly what her own girl would say"; but the "flighty" Tina's "views and opinions were a perpetual delicious shock to her" (*OM* 101, 159). Tina is less concerned than the "traditionalists" around her to hide her feelings behind a façade of propriety (*OM* 5); the force of convention inhibits her less than it does Delia's offspring. In selecting a mate, she differentiates herself from her Ralston cousins with particular emphasis. Reciting details of their highly conventional, perhaps calculatingly advantageous, choices, Wharton's narrator assumes a slyly mocking tone: Delia's son marries "a Vandergrave in whose father's bank at Albany he was to have an immediate junior partnership," while her daughter weds "the safest and soundest of the many young Halseys" (*OM* 96). Less "safely and suitably" inclined, Tina is attracted to the most unconventional of the available young men in her circle (*OM* 96). "Handsomer and more conversable than the rest," Lanning Halsey belongs to the same clan as Delia's daughter's husband, but "among all the sturdy and stolid Halsey cousins he was the only one to whom a prudent mother might have hesitated to entrust her daughter" (*OM* 110, 109). Unsurprisingly, given her parentage and her disposition, Tina's mate choice entails risk. Her vitality and strength of will suggest, too, that she will not "submit tamely" to any interference with her happiness (*OM* 123). When her romance with Lanning Halsey is thwarted by his family, she reacts with frightening intensity. Her "closed and darkened face" suggests to Delia that "the Spender blood in Tina might well precipitate" dangerously reckless behavior (*OM* 163).

Charlotte is correct, evidently, in assuming that with Clem she has produced a different kind of individual than any she would have been likely to create together with Joe Ralston. Indeed, Tina's specialness is crucial to Wharton's plot: it is Clem Spender's child, rather than Clem himself, who becomes the focus of competition between Charlotte and Delia. The two women are equally unsuccessful in their efforts to entice this man into long-term commitment. He courts them in turn, seemingly oblivious to possible emotional or biological consequences. What Clem seeks is short-term romance, rather than marriage. He pursues this goal first with Delia, who refuses him, and then with Charlotte, who yields to him. Charlotte therefore obtains from Clem only what he already has offered Delia — an uncommitted sexual liaison. Yet Delia envies her cousin for having enjoyed the short-term intimacy she herself rejected. In retrospect, after spending years as a Ralston wife and widow, Delia replays that moment of opportunity in her memory, half-wishing that she had selected a different option: "The past was too overwhelmingly resuscitated.... Clement Spender stood before her, irresolute, impecunious, persuasive. Ah, if only she had let herself be persuaded!" (*OM* 115–16). Like any other human animal, Delia finds herself second-guessing past decisions, reconsidering discarded strategies.[6] Now that she has lived with the consequences of mating choices made in her youth, the "clandestine joys" she once rejected as too dangerous appear heartbreakingly desirable (*OM* 137). "Life had passed her by, and left her with the Ralstons" (*OM* 129).

However irrationally, Delia is bitterly jealous of Charlotte's affair with Clem, just as Charlotte remains jealous of Delia for being Clem's first choice (as he apparently made plain even in the heat of their passion).[7] Since Charlotte's brief affair with Clem fails to bring her emotional or social satisfaction in the shape of marriage, readers may well wonder what it is that arouses such intense reaction in Delia. Why is she not congratulating herself on her judicious behavior — and consequent escape from clandestine motherhood and possible social disgrace? Charlotte's fate hardly seems one to envy. What Delia regrets having missed, readers gradually learn, is the opportunity Charlotte seized to combine Clem's genes with her own. To have engaged in sexual relations with the ardent but uncommitted Clem would have meant placing genetic quality above other important mate-selection criteria —fidelity and resources, for example. Delia originally was unwilling to give genes such absolute priority, exercising instead the more typical female preference "for males who offer resources."[8] Her cousin has made a very different decision, with consequences that take tangible form in Tina. From Delia's point of view, Tina represents the baby she might have conceived if she had yielded to Clem's importunities. Readers discern auctorial purposefulness in the women's cousinship: because Charlotte's child is genetically related to Delia, that child not improbably strikes Delia as very like one she herself might have borne if she had consummated her love affair with Clem. Thus there is biological foundation for the symbolic role the child plays in the jealous antagonism that brews between Delia and Charlotte for nearly twenty years. Tina is Delia's might-have-been, the genetic prize she might have obtained if she had made riskier mating decisions.

Covetous of the special child Charlotte has obtained, and which she herself has forfeited, Delia first acts to prevent Charlotte from marrying Joe Ralston. This genetically self-destructive deed is evidence that Delia begrudges her cousin the opportunity to reap benefits from two different mating strategies. "Charlotte has won what Delia has lost," Judith E. Funston observes, "and by insisting so adamantly that Charlotte cannot marry, Delia may be punishing her cousin for taking both her man and her fantasy."[9] If Charlotte marries Joe, she will obtain a faithful, wealthy husband with whom she can raise a family. At the same time, she will enjoy the benefits of a diversified genetic legacy through the daughter she bore out of wedlock. With offspring from short-term as well as long-term relationships, she stands to profit from the mixed strategy so successfully employed by many human males.[10] Textual examples show that men in Charlotte's social environment frequently do engage in exactly this kind of lifetime mating pattern. Just before Charlotte's revelation that she has an illegitimate child, Delia reassures her that she mustn't let "'any little thing in Joe's past'" upset her: "'even if ... he's had a child'" (OM 28). Delia adds that Joe is the kind of man who "would have provided for [a child] before," reassuring her cousin that no further resources will be diverted away from the family he expects to begin with his wife (OM 28). Here Wharton underlines with pointed irony the double standard that has prevailed throughout human evolutionary history: a woman must be prepared to accept premarital sexual activity in a potential husband (so long as his resources are not threatened by his prior activities), but a man cannot be expected to countenance the same behavior in a potential wife.[11] In the words of Wharton's narrator, "social tolerance was not dealt in the same measure to men and to women, and neither Delia nor Charlotte had ever wondered why"; instead, "like all the young women of their class they simply bowed to the ineluctable" (*OM* 66). Worldwide, men value virginity in their brides as a signal of probable future fidelity, Buss emphasizes, and it often serves the interests of monogamous women to expose and denounce promiscuous rivals who have chosen alternative routes to fitness.[12] Taking steps to enforce community standards for female chastity, Delia guards the success of her chosen strategy by thwarting that of her chief competitor.

The competition between Delia and Charlotte is complicated by their tie of kinship. It is true that if Charlotte marries Joe, she will have broken with impunity an important rule governing female behavior in her community. It would appear to be in Delia's interest to support her defiance of convention, however, since Charlotte is her relative. Other kinswomen, including Charlotte's mother and grandmother, help to conceal behavior they know to be socially reprehensible, and they do so for compelling evolutionary biological reasons. If Charlotte marries Joe, she is likely to have more children, and those children will increase the indirect fitness of her relatives. As one of the relatives who stand to benefit from Charlotte's future fecundity, Delia would be expected to rally around her cousin and promote her marriage to a good provider. Nepotistic loyalty is grounded, after all, in genetic self-interest: if by helping a relative to escape punishment for social transgressions, an individual can increase his or her own fitness, then such help typically will be forthcoming.[13] In Delia Ralston, Wharton shows readers an individual so consumed with jealousy that her behavior undermines her fitness instead of enhancing it. Married to Joe, Charlotte might produce several children, thereby increasing her cousin's inclusive fitness, and yet Delia deliberately turns her back on that potential benefit. Viewing Charlotte as a rival more than as a relative, Delia seems determined that her cousin not be allowed to have her cake and eat it too. Never explicitly spelled out, her thinking appears to run along these lines: *She, Delia, made choices and abided by them: she chose a long-term rather than a short-term strategy; she chose the stolid Jim Ralston over the heart-stirring Clem Spender. Why should Charlotte not be compelled to abide by her choices? Why should she be permitted to enjoy the benefits of marriage to a solid citizen after she has reaped the benefits of a short-term alliance with a more exciting man?*

When she speaks to Joe Ralston, Delia has told Charlotte that she will help her but "'must manage it in [her] own way'" (*OM* 55). She leaves Charlotte with the promise that she will persuade her husband to let her, Delia, "take the baby" (*OM* 54). This way around Charlotte's difficulties presumably would mean that Charlotte could marry Joe yet still see Tina regularly, who would grow up under her cousin's guardianship. Instead of carrying out this plan, or even attempting to do so, Delia sets a very different scheme in motion, and without consulting the person most concerned. Quite quickly she realizes that Joe is "very much in love" and that "at a word from Delia ... he would yield, and Charlotte gain her point, save the child, and marry him" (*OM* 65). It would be "easy," Delia realizes, for her to help Charlotte succeed in her quest to have things both ways — to keep her illegitimate child near at hand, well provisioned, and also to become Joe's wife (*OM* 65). Stabbed by a sudden "secret envy" of Charlotte's consummated romance with Clem Spender, however, Delia decides that "it must not be," that "all the traditions of honour and probity" require her to stop this marriage between an upright man and impure woman (*OM* 65). Informing Joe that Charlotte's lung disease has recurred, she hits on an explanation that will secure Joe's co-operation with her plan to separate him from his fiancée: "the bridegroom who had feared that his bride might bring home contagion from her visits to the poor would not knowingly implant disease in his race" (*OM* 72).

Delia's manipulation of events ensures that Charlotte will remain single.[14] She will never enjoy the social privileges matrimony confers upon a woman, never take her place in the community with "the assurance and majesty of a married woman" (*OM* 25). More important, she will not have any more children. At a stroke, Delia has reduced Charlotte's direct fitness definitively, from a potentially high figure if her marriage to Joe had proven fertile, to its present total of .5 (half of Delia's). Invoking "honour and probity," Delia deceives herself, certainly, about her motives for ruining Charlotte's opportunity to marry. She uses moral indignation, as humans so often do, to justify her punitive behavior toward her cousin. "The hallmark of self-deception in the service of deceit," Robert Trivers explains, "is the denial of deception, the unconscious running of selfish and deceitful ploys, the creation of a public persona as an altruist and a person beneffective in the lives of others, the creation of self-serving social theories and biased internal narratives of ongoing behavior which hide true intention."[15] This is a very accurate description of Delia's behavior and accompanying rationalization. It lies well within her power to arrange a happy solution to Charlotte's problem, yet she chooses not to do so. She lies about her machinations to Charlotte both before and after the fact, moreover, setting her actions in a moral framework intended to validate them. Her true motivation — to prevent her cousin from enjoying the benefits of marriage once she has reaped the fruits of short-term sex —

remains concealed from Charlotte, from the community and, to a large extent, from Delia herself.

Following Delia's successful *coup* in separating Charlotte from Joe Ralston, the focus of competition between the two women shifts to Tina. The existence of this child, who represents a reproductive opportunity Delia refused, has "somehow decentralized Delia Ralston's whole life, making her indifferent to everything else, except indeed the welfare of her own husband and children" (*OM* 128).[16] Her own offspring provide her with few satisfactions beyond "a future full of duties" (*OM* 128). She concentrates her maternal energies on Tina from the outset, vying with Charlotte for social and emotional possessorship. Even as she assures Charlotte that Jim Ralston will provide financial support for her and the child, Delia says, with ominous emphasis, "you shall take care of her — for me" (*OM* 80). When Jim Ralston dies young in a riding accident, Delia invites her cousin and her cousin's ward into her own household. Having taken that step, Delia manages easily to make herself, rather than Charlotte, the preferred figure in young Tina's life. Charlotte, after all, is in the uncomfortable position of needing to conceal her maternal relationship to Tina, for the sake of both their social reputations. Displays of motherly affection would risk exposure of her secret. To maximize her credibility in the role of spinster, in addition, she cultivates the appearance and mannerisms of "the typical old maid" (*OM* 87).[17] The repressive, fault-finding persona she creates is hardly calculated to win a child's heart. Yet Tina has become all the more precious to her mother, necessarily so, since the latter was prevented from marrying Joe Ralston. If Charlotte had conceived more offspring, with Joe, her parental investment in Tina almost certainly would have been diluted as a result.[18] Now, however, her reproductive success depends exclusively upon this one child. She suffers the ignominy of having to hide her devotion, while watching another woman usurp her maternal role.

Delia takes full advantage of Charlotte's predicament, offering Tina precisely the kind of motherly warmth Charlotte cannot permit herself to express. Investing Delia with the title of "Mamma," the girl confides in her, exchanges caresses with her, and laments with her about Aunt Chatty's "dreadfully old-maidish" ways (*OM* 86, 91): "'she never understands me, and you always do, you darling dear Mamma'" (*OM* 92). Delia glories in her preferred status, and her victory as mother-figure culminates in official adoption. Transferring Lovell family money to Tina as part of the proceedings, she gives Tina the Ralston name as a means of completing her community acceptance. The money, together with support from a respected family, will enable Tina to overcome the liability of her uncertain origins and, therefore, to marry well. Exalted by a sense of "tremendous purpose," Delia obviously regards this adoption as the final step in her acquisition of her cousin's child, although she avoids defining her motives in such ugly competitive terms (*OM* 152). From an emotional point of view, she had already won the position of Tina's mother, a position now triumphantly buttressed by legal right and social recognition.

The adoption precipitates an open confrontation with Charlotte, who finally gives vent to jealous anger. "'I have no rights, either before the law or in the heart of my own child,'" she tells Delia bitterly (*OM* 154). Her long frustrated maternity abruptly finds passionate expression: "'you've left nothing undone to divide me from my daughter! Do you suppose it's been easy, all these years, to hear her call you 'mother'?'" (*OM* 182). She describes Delia's behavior in harsh terms, pointing out that she has exploited Charlotte's socially enforced powerlessness. Her cousin has lost no opportunity to "'come between'" Charlotte and Tina: "'you've ended by robbing me of my child,'" Charlotte tells her; "'and I've put up with it all for her sake — because I knew I had to'" (*OM* 182–83). Showing clear understanding of Delia's motives, she accuses her outright of perpetuating their rivalry over Clem Spender in a competition for Tina's affections: "'you found your revenge and your triumph in keeping me at your mercy, and in taking his child from me!'" (*OM* 179). When Delia defends herself by reminding Charlotte of all she has "'tried to do'" for her, Charlotte strips away the veils of deceit and self-deception: "'everything you've done has been done for Clement Spender!'" (*OM* 180). That is, Delia's behavior has been motivated by jealousy of Charlotte's intimacy with this man.[19] In annexing their child, the fruit of that intimacy, Delia symbolically supplants Charlotte — in her own mind — as Clem's lover and Tina's mother. Only human animals, with their large and complex mental capacities, are able to redesign external reality in this fashion, embroidering empirical fact with imaginative projection.[20]

As the child of a cousin, Tina does have a blood tie to Delia, and she therefore represents, if only to a limited degree, realization of Delia's unsatisfied reproductive goal: to combine her genes with Clem Spender's. Eagerly presenting herself as Tina's mother, personally and publicly, Delia attempts to deceive herself that success in assuming a social role somehow can enhance the comparatively small coefficient of relatedness linking her to her cousin's daughter. Emotional attachment and legal paperwork notwithstanding, Charlotte's genetic stake in Tina is, and will remain, greater than Delia's. Even Delia is unable to conceal this fact from herself on a sustained basis. Despite her apparent victory in wresting maternal privilege from Charlotte, she often finds herself "envying poor Charlotte's scanted motherhood" (*OM* 105).[21] At times, indeed, "she almost hated Charlotte for being Tina's mother" (*OM* 95). Virtually the only comfort remaining to Charlotte, the "mother who was not a mother," is this ineluctable fact of primary kinship (*OM* 181): "'don't pity me,'" she tells Delia in a moment of tense confrontation; "'she's mine'" (*OM* 95). Delia's envious wish to claim first rights in Tina, a remarkable pheno-type in whom Lovell and Spender genes co-mingle, never can be fulfilled: biologically, Charlotte's tie is pre-eminent. Delia's triumph over her remains forever incomplete. The conclusion of the book, in which she exercises her influence over Tina by instructing her to give her "'last kiss'" to her Aunt Char-lotte before driving off on her honeymoon, shows Delia giving one more turn to the knife in a contest she prolongs but cannot finally win (*OM* 190).

Despite the competitive, jealous spirit that motivates it, Delia's adop-tion of Tina must be regarded as an act of nepotistic loyalty, one with posi-tive consequences for all three major characters. Absent the advantages of the Ralston name and the "little fortune" Delia provides, Tina would not have been able to marry Lanning Halsey, or any other man in the conservative community she inhabits (*OM* 152). Adoption enables the girl to obtain a high-status mate and, in consequence, to anticipate a maximally successful reproductive future. For these reasons the adoption is advantageous in its impact on fitness for all Tina's kin, including Delia herself. The transmission of wealth to Tina is possible, it should be noted, only because Delia com-mands plentiful resources; since there is "money enough to go round," she can enrich Tina without injuring her own children (*OM* 160). Increasing her own inclusive fitness is not Delia's principal goal, however, or she would not have put obstacles, earlier, in the way of Charlotte's marriage to Joe Ralston. In fact, her decision to adopt Tina is by her own admission a back-up plan. Her original idea about Tina's future is that the girl should remain single, "forced to share" Delia's otherwise "lonely" and "purposeless" old age (*OM* 117).

When she and Charlotte discuss Lanning Halsey's "excuses" for not mar-rying Tina, they acknowledge that her dubious personal history renders Tina ineligible for serious courtship by men in their elite community (*OM* 116). Delia already has thought this out: "she had always known that it would be difficult, almost impossible, to find a husband for Tina" (*OM* 117). This real-ity does not dismay her as it does Charlotte; rather, "some inmost selfishness" rejoices in it (*OM* 117). Her suggestion that Tina can be happy remaining at home "with us who love her so dearly" triggers an outburst of protest from Charlotte: "'Tina an old maid? Never!'" (*OM* 117). Charlotte is rejecting, on her daughter's behalf, not only the social stigma and personal loneliness of a spinster's lot but — far more important — the concomitant reproductive fail-ure. If Tina obtains no mate and conceives no offspring, the sacrifices Char-lotte has made to raise her will be rendered purposeless. The risk she assumed to obtain a high-quality child, sired out of wedlock by the exceptionally desirable Clem Spender, is worthwhile only if that child perpetuates Charlotte's lineage. Delia's willingness to acquiesce in Tina's childlessness shows her once again frustrating her cousin's, and thus her own, genetic interest. She would gladly forfeit whatever addition Tina might make to her own inclusive fitness in order to achieve "revenge" (to use Charlotte's term) for her rival's romantic affair with Clem Spender. The best revenge, from an evolutionary biological standpoint, is to ensure that the brief union between Clem and Charlotte remains without issue after the first generation. The goal of minimizing her rival's fitness is more important to Delia than maximizing her own. As a secondary gain (social rather than biological), Tina's spinsterhood would enable Delia to go on playing the role of the girl's preferred mother, in front of Charlotte, for the rest of her life.

Charlotte astutely evades her cousin's sinister program by threatening to remove Tina from Delia's range of influence altogether. She argues that Tina will find a husband only "among plain people" outside her current privileged socioeconomic circle (*OM* 122). Whether the girl could reconcile herself to such changed circumstances, and to a marriage that would appear hypogamous in comparison with her current expectations, is open to question. Delia has no means of preventing Charlotte from acting on her resolution to carry Tina off to a different environment, however, and in her terror at the prospect of losing the girl entirely, Delia forms the decision to adopt her. By putting forward her scheme of taking Tina away, as events demonstrate, Charlotte forces Delia's hand. Delia's adoption of Tina is psychologically painful for Charlotte, but it assures her daughter the best possible chance to obtain economic security and a desirable husband. From the beginning, Charlotte has acted in a fashion calculated to promote Tina's welfare and, in the long run, Charlotte's own fitness. She tells Delia that she "'knew she was giving Tina another mother'" when she applied to her for assistance (*OM* 181). She had "'gambled'" on Delia's continuing affection for Clem Spender, counting on Delia's jealousy as a tool to be used to secure benefits for her daughter (*OM* 181).[22]

Both women manifest mixed emotions as they work toward their separate goals. Charlotte benefits from Delia's adoption of Tina, which promises a better outcome (as measured in fitness) for both mother and daughter than does Charlotte's plan of seeking a new social environment; yet she rages against it, protesting that Delia is stealing her child from her. Delia rejoices in the adoption, which seals her success in alienating Tina from her biological mother; yet this action represents a less complete revenge (as measured in fitness) than her original scheme of keeping Tina at home and unmarriageable. The competition between Delia and Charlotte, which spans two decades, concludes without an explicitly identified victor. Wharton leaves readers to tote up gains and losses on both sides, maintaining a narrative reticence.[23] Delia's most significant triumph takes place early in the plot, when she prevents Charlotte from marrying and having more offspring. With that action she becomes responsible for a dramatic reduction in Charlotte's probable direct fitness. Charlotte's most important triumph also occurs early on, when she gives birth to Tina, a special child sired by a preferred mate. Although Charlotte has fewer children than she might have produced if she had avoided the risk of short-term premarital sex, she is the mother of a particularly attractive child. That child's reproductive success may prove equal to, or even greater than, the success Charlotte might have anticipated from a larger number of mediocre offspring. Insofar as Clem Spender — or rather, Clem Spender's DNA — is the object of the competition, Charlotte is the victor first and last. The adoption itself represents a social and psychological victory for Delia, but an evolutionary biological one for Charlotte. Whatever its interpersonal implications, legal transfer of guardianship does not affect degree of consanguinity. Because Tina shares more genes with Charlotte than with Delia, her improved marriage prospects will affect Charlotte's fitness more significantly than Delia's.

An auctorial decision to tell the story from Delia's point of view is crucial to its impact. Readers are not privy to Charlotte's intentions or anxieties, which are given direct expression only through dialogue. Wharton has chosen to report events from the viewpoint of the prudent woman who makes safe, conventional mating choices, rather than from the perspective of the risk-taking woman who flouts convention.[24] It is Delia's regrets and second thoughts that occupy stage center. As a result of this narrative emphasis, readers are forced to contemplate potentially disturbing topics in the context of a protagonist whose outward behavior is conservative. When an advantageously married young woman suffers from erotic dissatisfaction, covets the pleasures of casual sex, or envies the experience of unwed motherhood, readers cannot dismiss her feelings as those of a criminal or lunatic. "Delia's search for emotional and sexual fulfillment is central to the novella," as Funston points out.[25] In this tale, Wharton plumbs the depths of female psychology, taking as her test case a woman whose life choices appear eminently ordinary. The sexual desires and jealousies driving Delia's behavior, Wharton argues, constitute an indisputably significant part of human nature: the most seemingly conventional of individuals is susceptible to fierce passions and antisocial impulses.[26] Delia's sexual dissatisfactions in her marriage with Jim Ralston, coupled with her yearning for erotic fulfillment in the arms of Clem Spender, provide proximal expression of an ultimate goal: to enhance her direct fitness by conceiving offspring of superior quality. The intensity of her focus on Tina reveals the ultimate motivation working smoothly in tandem with the emotions that serve as proximate mechanisms.

Judging events through Delia's eyes, readers discover the perhaps unsuspected weight women give to genetic quality in assessing potential mates: genetic quality as measured by temperament, appearance, intelligence, and related personal qualities. Folk wisdom claims that women place highest value on a potential mate's material resources, closely followed by the willingness to invest those resources in offspring. There is considerable support for this claim in modern anthropological research as well.[27] Women need resources, obviously, if they are to raise their children to maturity and position them, socially and economically, to obtain good mates of their own. It is futile to select a mate based on his genetically desirable qualities if children of the union fail to thrive because the father cannot or will not make adequate investment in them. If there is reasonable chance that a child can survive without paternal care, however, women may risk choosing genes over resources.[28] Clem Spender exemplifies the genetically superior man with poor investment potential. Having made the decision to choose a more able and willing provider to father her children, Delia spends much of the rest of her life grieving for the superior offspring she might have conceived with the ne'er-do-well but attractive Clem.

Readers may wonder what, exactly, makes Clem Spender so attractive. Except for the "five points" of curls that he passes on to Tina, his physical appearance is left to the imagination. He is artistically inclined, socially rebellious, risk-oriented. Instead of preparing for a future of responsible wage-earning, he scampers lightheartedly off to Europe, paintbrush in hand. He is not inclined to hold others to exacting standards of behavior (Delia is certain that he would not worry about a wife bringing home contagion from paupers), just as he is not much concerned to meet high standards himself. In many arenas of life, he leaves others "to pay the score," as Delia recognizes (*OM* 37). If he had children, for example, they might suffer or die from his lackadaisical attitude toward infectious disease. In Delia's mental universe, he is associated with a pastoral scene depicted on the ornamental clock he delivered to her as a wedding present: she "liked ... to see the bold shepherd stealing his kiss" from the little shepherdess (*OM* 17).[29] Like the painted boy enjoying romance in a utopian world of pastoral artifice, Clem operates as if actions have no consequences — at least for him. He is a thoughtless seducer, intent upon his own pleasure, yet Delia is charmed by his "bold" propensity to "steal" women's affections. As her reaction to him demonstrates, his exploitative tendencies form an inextricable part of the appeal he exerts on potential mates.

A more conventional and more didactic story would denounce Clem as a cad, pronouncing him unworthy, in the end, of women's affection, but Wharton's purposes are more radical. The sterling qualities of Jim Ralston are fully acknowledged, to be sure: despite his conventional outlook, for instance, he is willing to support a child he knows to be illegitimate. Delia learns long after his death that Jim made it his business to find out "whose [Tina] was," and he quietly offers assistance to his wife's unacknowledged kin (*OM* 145). In so doing, Jim literally "pays" another man's "score," underlining the difference between his responsible, altruistic bent and Clem's selfish carelessness. No matter how many virtues he embodies, however, Jim Ralston is not the man to whom Delia is most deeply drawn, not the man she would have liked to choose as her mate. This fact may make readers uncomfortable. The more reliable, more altruistic man ought to be the more desired mate, surely. Revealing that many women actually prefer attractive, devil-may-care men who seduce them charmingly and then cavalierly depart, Wharton exposes an aspect of female mate selection that is hard to reconcile with commonly espoused moral values. The more worthy contender is not always rewarded, even at the end of the story; paradoxically, his very worthiness may signal a lower degree of desirability. There is evidence that less attractive men typically select the role of dependable provider precisely because they are less intrinsically desirable to the opposite sex than their rivals. By the same token, genetically superior individuals (in terms of height, strength, symmetry, intelligence, dominance, and so on) often can obtain access to women without long-term investment.[30] Even when a woman chooses the reliable provider over the delightful bounder, as Delia eventually does, she continues to find the latter more inherently attractive. Her preferences illustrate Dawkins's observation that "one of the most desirable qualities a male can have in the eyes of a female is, quite simply, sexual attractiveness itself."[31]

Lanning Halsey is identified as the Clement Spender of the next generation. In slightly diluted proportions, he manifests personal charm, artistic inclinations, and social rebelliousness reminiscent of Clem's. He, too, is willing to defer marriage and, as events prove, willing to try for casual sexual satisfaction with a girl he has decided not to marry. Only Charlotte's vigilance prevents Tina from becoming Lanning's short-term partner. The "liking" that both Delia and Charlotte express for Lanning confirms female preference for men possessing a certain constellation of desirable traits, even when they fail to meet important criteria for dependably investing husbands (*OM* 113). Both women welcome the opportunity to obtain Lanning as a husband for Tina. Delia views this marriage in highly symbolic terms, readers learn, as the long-awaited consummation of her "unrealized" love affair with Clem Spender (*OM* 184). She creates a mental image of Tina as her "own girlish self," about to enjoy everything Delia "had missed yet never renounced": long-term commitment from a man like Clem (*OM* 185). Delia had had to choose (as did Charlotte) between a short-term mating with Clem and none at all, but she helps her alter ego in the next generation to escape this limited set of options. Tina's marriage thus serves the psychological function of wish-fulfillment for Delia.

Keeping readers firmly focused on Delia's continued yearning for the mate she forfeited, Wharton hints that Charlotte has renounced less than her cousin, and hence has had less to regret. "Because it is [Delia's] point of view through which we experience the story," as Lev Raphael makes clear, "it is not inappropriately her losses that seem greater."[32] Clem Spender *was* Charlotte's mate, if only briefly; genetically, as well as emotionally, she has obtained more in the way of fulfillment from him than Delia. Wharton's narrative perspective again underlines the radical nature of her statement. It is the properly married, supposedly sensible woman who most regrets her past, not her less cautious counterpart who sacrificed a socially and economically secure marriage opportunity for a transitory bliss and illegitimate offspring. Comparing herself to "a cloistered nun," Delia offers readers evidence that it is she, more than her cousin, who should be considered the "old maid" of the novella's title (*OM* 128). Despite the many outward satisfactions of her life, Delia has missed more. She endures what she perceives as a sexually unfulfilled, even sterile, existence: the ordinary offspring she created with Jim Ralston fail to compensate her adequately for the superior phenotypes she might have produced with Clem Spender. Conveying these ideas through interior monologue centered on Delia, Wharton delivers her unexpected insights with maximum impact.

It is easier, of course, to embrace dangerous joys in the realm of fantasy, via regret or projection, than it is to seize them in everyday life. There are signs that Delia's judicious approach to life survives all her lamenting over lost opportunities. She is cautious, tellingly, in supervising her biological daughter's selection of a mate. When she thinks that the "handsome" and "conversable" Lanning Halsey might be paying attention to "young Delia," she feels "apprehension" (*OM* 109, 110, 146). She is "reassured," rather than disappointed, to discover that the girl has no interest in Lanning and prefers "more solid qualities" in a potential husband (*OM* 110). As a mother, Delia is not a risk-taker any more than she was in selecting her own long-term mate. Men like Lanning Halsey and Clem Spender are all too apt to become philandering husbands and even, perhaps, to desert their families. If they sire high-quality offspring, their wives may experience a genetic pay-off, but not without paying a price in terms of economic struggle and social humiliation. Delia does not wish to see her daughter attempting such a hazardous course and gladly consigns her, instead, to a life presumably very like the one she herself claims to have found insufficiently satisfying.[33] Readers may speculate that if her daughter had manifested a more adventurous temperament, falling in love with Lanning or someone like him, Delia might have behaved differently. The fact remains, however, that she not only supports the girl's conservative preferences, she is relieved by them. Vicariously enjoying the high-risk "bliss accepted" of Tina's marriage, she need not test her own willingness to pay, through her daughter, mating costs that in her youth had seemed too high (*OM* 165). Delia's attitude toward mate choices in the next generation underline the hypothetical nature of her retrospective regrets, illustrating just how much mental energy humans expend assessing and re-interpreting their choices in light of the full spectrum of human behavioral options.

Although she does not overcome her innate caution in mate selection, Delia is no timorous creature when she finds herself in the throes of sexual jealousy. She shows herself to be remarkably adept at lying and manipulation, and she does not hesitate to exact vengeance on a relative. If her feelings and actions had been viewed from another character's point of view — from Charlotte's, for instance — she might have come across as a monster. Compelling readers to make discoveries together with Delia and to see things from her perspective, however, Wharton normalizes this character's responses. Sexual jealousy, ferocious competition, and cruel revenge are, evidently, an integral part of female experience. Delia's often expressed compunctions complicate her character, furthermore, winning her a more favorable response from readers. At key moments, she is overcome with shame and reproaches herself for the injuries she has inflicted: "she saw that it was a terrible, a sacrilegious thing to interfere with another's destiny" as she has with Charlotte's (*OM* 186). This insight does not prevent her from continuing her interference, however, even to the very last line of the novella when she orchestrates Tina's farewell to her mother. Delia claims that "pity" for her cousin overrides "every other sensation," but readers easily discern that in this belief she deceives herself (*OM* 178).[34] It is vindictiveness, chiefly, not sympathy, that fuels her dealings with Charlotte. In the after-the-fact competition for a mate that forms the heart of this story, a seemingly ordinary woman executes revenge upon a same-sex competitor, undermining her own inclusive fitness in her efforts to ensure her rival's long-range genetic defeat. By the simple expedient of making Delia's point of view central, Wharton secures her an adequately empathetic response and suggests, at the same time, that her story is not an uncommon one. Delia's experiences support the conclusion that female mate preference may have a stronger bias in favor of genetic quality than often is supposed. More important, the frighteningly powerful desires and aggressively competitive spirit driving her behavior effectively belie sentimental interpretation of female mating strategies.

Like *The Old Maid*, "Roman Fever" depicts females competing for desirable men, highlighting the point that there are not enough such men to go around.[35] The story begins by focusing on competition between Jenny Slade and Barbara Ansley, young women of the 1930's who are dating titled "Italian aviators" (RF 218). It is Barbara who is the more "dynamic" and "brilliant" of the two, and Jenny's mother feels jealousy on her behalf (RF 227, 222). Despite being "extremely pretty," Jenny "has no chance" beside her outstandingly "effective" friend (RF 222, 226, 219); Mrs. Slade even wonders if "poor Jenny" is being used "as a foil" to highlight Barbara's more striking personality (RF 226). Poised to make "one of the best matches in Rome," Barbara triggers long dormant emotions of rivalry in Alida Slade (RF 226). Seeing her daughter so definitively outshone by Grace Ansley's, Alida is forcibly reminded of the intense struggle that occurred twenty-five years earlier between Grace and herself. The object of that competition was Delphin Slade, an ambitious, socially prominent, up-and-coming lawyer. Having married Delphin, Alida is the presumed victor of that contest, but the threat Grace posed to her in the quest for a desirable mate remains vivid in her memory. The bulk of the story consists of a retelling of that long-finished competition, each woman contributing information to which the other was not privy at the time. The revelation of secret actions and unsuspected outcomes lends the story its suspense, powerfully illustrating the aggressiveness with which young women pursue evolutionarily critical goals.

Newly engaged, the young Alida was "'afraid,'" she says, that Grace might steal her fiancé: "'I knew you were in love with Delphin — and I was afraid ... of your quiet ways, your sweetness'" (RF 234). To get Grace "out of the way," Alida lures her to the Colosseum after dark, hoping the chilly dampness there will precipitate serious illness in a girl known for her "delicate throat" (RF 234, 229). To accomplish her ends, she sends a letter purportedly from Delphin, begging Grace to meet him "'alone,'" and signed "'only *your* D.S.'" (RF 232). Alida's ruse works only because she is correct in thinking Grace would like to obtain Delphin for herself. If Grace had not been enamored of him, or if her loyalty to her friend had proved stronger than her romantic attraction, she would not have responded to a letter proposing an illicit meeting. In responding eagerly, as she does, Grace demonstrates how the pursuit of a desirable mate tends to override claims of friendship, morality, and social convention. Alida's initial maneuver demonstrates more clearly, even, than Grace's disloyalty just how far young women are prepared to go to secure attractive partners. Underlining the ferocity of the competition, she sends her rival to the Colosseum, formerly a site of gladiatorial combat, as Lawrence L. Berkove points out.[36] To safeguard her engagement to Delphin, which she perceives to be threatened by Grace, Alida risks the health, perhaps the life, of a young woman with whom she has "been intimate since childhood" (RF 219). In most ethical systems the welfare of a fellow human being rates higher than romantic opportunity, but Wharton's plot points to discrepancies between conventional values and observed behavior. Loyalty to a friend is less adaptively important, in certain situations and at key times of life, than obtaining and keeping the best possible mate.

The story of Grace's "dreadfully wicked great-aunt" reinforces this point with hair-raising emphasis (RF 229). "In love with the same man" as her younger sister, Great-aunt Harriet sends the sister out after dark to gather a night-blooming flower, hoping the sister will contract "the fever" (RF 230). The sister dies of her illness, reportedly, so that Harriet succeeds in clearing the field of a dangerous competitor. In this instance, however, her competitor is a close relative, which means she pays a significant cost in fitness for her victory. Her sister's potential offspring would share one-quarter of her genes, and Harriet's inclusive fitness is accordingly reduced. She is so intent upon obtaining a particularly desirable mate that she is determined to eliminate her rival at any price. If the man is sufficiently desirable, and if her chances of attracting another of almost equal value are low, that price may not be too high — but it is real. She pays a cost in psychological turmoil, readers surmise, as well as in inclusive fitness: why, otherwise, does she "confess[] years afterward" (RF 230)? When impulses fostering kin selection come into conflict with those fostering mate selection, psychological discomfort is a probable result, no matter which option is selected. In fact, Harriet's cost-benefit analysis makes better sense than Delia Ralston's when the latter decides to limit her cousin's reproductive success. Preventing Charlotte from marrying Joe Ralston does not win Delia herself a mate, since she already has one. Her interference reduces the total number of copies of genes Charlotte (and through her, Delia) will pass on to the next generation without in any way increasing or enhancing Delia's own reproductive success. Self-destructively, she assuages her feelings of jealousy with an act of vengeance against a kinswoman, thereby imperiling her own genetic continuance. Although Delia's action is less violent than Harriet's and is supported by noble-sounding social ideals, from an evolutionary point of view she is shooting herself in the foot. Harriet, who actually arranges the death of a person sharing half her genes, at least stands to obtain a desirable mate, and thus to enhance her direct fitness, as a result of her deed.

The anecdote about Great-aunt Harriet occupies little narrative space but extends the reach of the story two generations further into the past, thereby forcing readers to acknowledge that Alida Slade's perfidy is not an aberrant instance of intrasexual rivalry. Throughout history, Wharton hints, women have deceived and injured same-sex competitors in the desperate quest for desirable mates. Indeed, there are no limits to the lengths they will go, as Great-aunt Harriet's story grimly illustrates.[37] It is not accidental that the sororicidal great aunt is Grace's relative, rather than Alida's: the normalcy of Alida's actions is underscored by evidence of underhanded dealings and damaging intentions perpetrated in another woman's lineage. Violent, no-holds-barred tactics are expected as part of male-male competition, but women typically are considered to be "less florid and violent" in their dealings with one another.[38] One of the main effects of "Roman Fever" is to expose the falsity of such assumptions, to characterize women as ruthlessly competing beings in their own right. They are by no means simply the passive objects of male competition; rather, they strive actively against one another for good mating opportunities.[39] "The women of 'Roman Fever' are the drivers of the plots," Rachel Bowlby accurately observes.[40]

As far as Alida knows, her stratagem succeeds exactly as planned: Grace takes to her bed for two months, leaving Alida free to strengthen her hold on Delphin. To her own surprise, she has "gone on hating" the woman she defeated, but this reaction makes psychological sense (RF 235). Since she held on to her man by trickery, she can never be certain that Delphin would have chosen her over Grace, absent intervention. Observing her daughter bested by Grace's in the next generation's struggle for mates, Alida finds her never quite extinguished jealousy reviving. It is jealousy, along with the wish to inflict pain, that prompts her to reveal her long-ago duplicity. She wants Grace to know that she is the victim of Alida's successful machinations and to discover, simultaneously, that Delphin never actually approached her for a secret meeting. When Alida learns that Grace cherished the memory of the faked letter and is devastated at the news that he did not write it, she enjoys a renewed feeling of triumph. She attempts to deepen the wound by instilling guilt, pointing out that Grace had been hoping to meet clandestinely with a man publicly pledged to her friend. Grace acknowledges that she betrayed the demands of reciprocal altruism implicit in friendship, but such acknowledgement only serves to remind both women that Alida is guilty of even more injurious betrayal. "'Of course I was upset when I heard you were so ill afterward,'" she claims, feeling the need "to justify herself" (RF 237, 234).

The plot takes a decisive turn when Alida discovers for the first time that the clandestine appointment she invented, intending to lure Grace out alone into the dangerous night air, actually took place. Sending a secret message to assure Delphin of her compliance, Grace unwittingly sets up the rendezvous. (A certain suspension of disbelief is required of readers at this juncture, since the illicit lovers apparently spend an evening together without discovering any confusion about who proposed the meeting.) Alida is naturally appalled to learn, so long after the event, that her duplicitous maneuver precipitated exactly the kind of romantic encounter between Delphin and Grace that she had hoped to prevent. Hearing that Delphin responded unhesitatingly to

Grace's invitation (he "arranged everything" necessary for them to be "let in" to a private area), Alida has more cause for jealousy than ever before (RF 238). Upon reflection, she realizes that since Delphin did not break his engagement to her she appears to have won the competition all the same: he ratified his choice of her, Alida, as his long-term mate, even though he did take advantage of a casual sexual opportunity on the eve of their marriage. A night of secret pleasure with Grace did not cause him to switch his allegiance. When she voices this point, cruelly (and inaccurately) noting that she "'had everything'" while Grace "'had nothing but that one letter that he didn't write,'" her rival is finally goaded into admitting that she has borne Delphin's child: "'I had Barbara'" (RF 239).

The story now comes full circle. The girl with "rainbow wings" who is competing so successfully against her Jenny is Alida's husband's child (RF 227). She is exactly the kind of daughter Alida had hoped and expected to have as part of her own family, a girl whose exceptional qualities have provoked "envy" in her: "'I always wanted a brilliant daughter'" (RF 227). In one of the many ironies dominating the story, Alida discovers that through her own plotting she has created, unintentionally, a powerful rival who is decreasing her own child's chances to obtain a top-quality mate. It is Grace's daughter who will obtain the best mate in the next generation, and Alida has no one but herself to blame. Her envy of Grace's child, unlike Delia's envy of Charlotte's, is not complicated by any tie of kinship. The unexpected revelation of Barbara's parentage in the story's last line compels readers to revise their judgments (as Alida must hers) about the competition between Alida and Grace. Now revealed as the mother of a child with superior attractions, one who will fare extremely well on the marriage market, Grace appears in the end to have bested Alida.

It is important to realize that Grace's victory is significant only from a Darwinian perspective — a perspective the ironic punch of the story's conclusion encourages readers to share. Alida has had the social victory, after all: twenty-five years as the wife of "*the* Slade," the "famous corporation lawyer," have gratified her social and economic ambitions (RF 222, 221). Together, she and Delphin were regarded as an "exceptional couple," and she takes pride in the achievement her marriage represents (RF 221). Grace, in contrast, has been married to the "exemplary" but staid Horace Ansley, who is dismissed by Alida as a "museum specimen[]" and a "nullit[y]" (RF 221, 219). Horace's social and economic status appear to be acceptably high, since he domiciles his family for many years directly across the street from the Slades, but a "big *coup* in Wall Street," evidence of Delphin's extraordinary ambition and drive, eventually enables the Slades to purchase even more splendid housing (RF 220). Delphin gives Alida an "exciting" life, while Grace spends her days with a much more mediocre, if "irreproachable" man (RF 221, 220). Competing against Alida for commitment from Delphin, Grace obtains only his DNA, and she pays a high price thereafter for her short-term involvement with him. Because she had to find a husband in great haste in order to disguise her pregnancy, she was in no position to pick and choose: "'People were rather surprised,'" as Alida notes, "'they wondered at its being done so quickly'" (RF 236). Grace's triumph over her rival consists solely in having produced a child who is a superior phenotype. In "Roman Fever," as in *The Old Maid*, however, that achievement is presented as one outweighing all other considerations, social or emotional.

Like Charlotte Lovell, Grace derives compensation for the costs of her short-term mating choices in the form of a high-quality child. Because this superior child will enjoy especially good mating opportunities, its mother's genetic future will be enhanced correspondingly. Both tales suggest reasons why women, even high-status women, may choose to employ short-term sexual strategies. It is not difficult to understand why a lower-class, economically disadvantaged woman would find short-term involvement her best, or only, mating strategy. A woman commanding more material resources and social support typically is considered foolish or culpable, in contrast, if she risks opportunities for long-term commitment by engaging in a casual affair. Grace's experience, like Charlotte's, demonstrates that the genetic benefits a woman stands to gain from short-term sex may, in some instances, offer evolutionarily sufficient inducement.[41] Engaging in acts of sexual intimacy without promise of commitment, such a young woman is making shrewd cost-benefit calculations, positing three possible outcomes. If as result of intimacy, the man transfers his affection and commitment to her, the first possibility, she will benefit enormously from the risk she has assumed. If he moves on without making a commitment and she does not become pregnant, the second possibility, she pays a cost only in lost time and emotional turmoil, although there may be a further cost in reputational damage if she fails to keep the liaison private. If he moves on leaving her pregnant, the third possibility, she stands to benefit from the high-quality genetic contribution a very attractive man has brought to the reproductive enterprise. As Charlotte's and Grace's experiences illustrate, that benefit ought not to be underestimated.

If a woman cannot obtain long-term mating commitment from a superior man, but she can obtain access to his sperm, it is not unreasonable for her to decide that that she can best serve her direct fitness by taking what she can get. The more resources and status a woman commands, the greater the probability that she will be able to raise the resulting offspring to maturity without paternal assistance.[42] She may rely on familial aid, as Charlotte does or, like Grace, she may trick a long-term mate into acknowledging and supporting the child. Inevitably, reproductive efforts are laden with risk and uncertainty. High-risk, short-term involvements may not always pay off in the form of a particularly attractive child. Even with the safeguards of marital commitment, as Alida Slade's history demonstrates, there are no guarantees. Mating with the outstanding Delphin, she expected to produce exceptionally dominant and charismatic children: the marriage results in one such child, a son "who seemed to have inherited his father's gifts," along with a less dynamic daughter, the "pretty" but "safe" Jenny (RF 222). "One of the best things a mother can do for her genes is to make a son who will turn out in his turn to be an attractive he-man," Dawkins points out, and Alida appears for a time to have achieved this goal.[43] Then the son dies "suddenly in boyhood," leaving her with one attractive but far less special child (RF 222). There is no controlling the accidents of life, any more than the reshufflings of recombinant DNA.[44]

Risk-oriented behavior like Grace's confers benefits often enough, as Wharton amply illustrates, to remain in the repertoire of human mate-selection strategies. A strategy need not prove one hundred percent successful in order to be adaptive, moreover; it only needs to succeed *on average* more often than it fails.[45] Even though Grace's effort to employ a mixed reproductive strategy (following up a casual liaison with marriage) does not increase the total number of her offspring, she still ends up with a direct fitness equal to that of Alida, the exclusively long-term strategist. In terms of offspring quality, moreover, Grace arguably has the advantage. Like the death of Alida's son, the barrenness of the Ansley marriage could not have been predicted. Chance and circumstance permitting, either woman might have achieved a higher degree of fitness with her chosen strategy.

In choosing to marry Alida rather than Grace, Delphin acts to promote his vocational success and community prestige (and thus, indirectly, to maximize his potential genetic legacy).[46] Alida's more outgoing and assertive personality qualifies her better than her more retiring friend to be the wife of a high-powered lawyer moving in elite circles. Alida revels in her duties as hostess; like Delphin, she possesses superior "social gifts" (RF 221). In temperament and ambition, they are a compatible and well-matched couple: it is easy to understand why Delphin prefers the woman who is more likely to assist him in the quest for increased status. Questions about Grace's sexual loyalty, which will affect Delphin's future paternal confidence, very likely provide an additional reason for his decision to marry Alida. Since Delphin does not know that Alida set up his rendezvous with Grace by means of a forged note, he believes that Grace herself has initiated their secret meeting. A man might well question the future fidelity of a young woman who makes herself sexually available in such a seemingly bold fashion. Even if Delphin were the author of the note, Grace would be violating expectations for premarital chastity in responding to it as she does.[47] Intriguingly, it appears that Alida's ruse proves successful by ways and means she never anticipated: as a result of permitting Delphin sexual intimacy, Grace brands herself as a potentially unfaithful wife, setting off alarm bells in her lover's mind. If Alida had never plotted against Grace with the faked note, thus precipitating a sexual encounter, Delphin's dawning attraction to her rival might, perhaps, have led to a serious involvement. Factors of compatibility likely would have induced him to maintain his initial preference for Alida, but Grace's sexually uninhibited behavior probably seals his decision to remain with his fiancée.

Exploring the repercussions of short-term sex, "Roman Fever" touches on a few topics that never emerge in *The Old Maid*. Grace's hasty marriage to Horace Ansley, for instance, introduces the issues of female deception and paternal uncertainty. Whether or not Horace indeed believes that Barbara is his child, he does acknowledge, support, and raise her as his own. Thus he has made a substantial paternal investment in another man's offspring. This is a fate men typically strive to avoid, and there is not enough information provided in the brief span of Wharton's narrative for readers to learn what led Horace to accept such a destiny.[48] One reason a man might acquiesce in an arrangement like the Ansleys,' for example, is the hope of gaining a higher-quality mate: if Grace is a more attractive girl than Horace otherwise might have hoped to marry, then he stands to gain good-quality offspring from her, offspring that might offset the disadvantage of supporting one child who is non-kin. If this was Horace's hope, it has been frustrated, since the couple produces no children. Perhaps he is simply a gullible man and accepts his wife's seven-month pregnancy without question. The Ansleys' childlessness is another topic that inspires speculation, but the text supplies no basis for preferring one guess over another. The barrenness of the marriage might be ascribed, for example, to low sexual interest on Grace's part, since Horace was a last-resort, last-minute mate choice. Or perhaps Horace has reason to believe he cannot sire children, something that might increase his willingness to assume the social role of father to his wife's child.

In any event, the story does not encourage readers to give much attention to Horace's motives. His childlessness is important from a biosocial perspective, however, because it helps to underline the fact of differential reproductive success in human males.[49] At first glance, it appears that each of the four main characters in the story enjoys equal reproductive success: each is the parent of one child who survives to adulthood. Once the secret of Barbara's parentage is revealed, the numbers look different, obviously, but only for the male characters. Each woman is still the parent of one surviving child (each thereby achieving a direct fitness of .5), but Delphin Slade is the father of two (with a direct fitness of 1.0), and Horace Ansley the father of none (with a direct fitness of zero). Wharton's story confirms the harsh reality that men whom women find especially attractive will obtain more mating opportunities, and hence more offspring, than other men. This inequality of opportunity among males further underlines what is at stake in the competition for mates. Women who succeed in mating with the most desirable men are likely to have offspring who will prove capable, in turn, of attracting the best possible mates available. The potential for progeny to mate advantageously is a critical feature in long-term genetic success and, therefore, in mate selection. The concept of sexual selection was coined to help explain the self-perpetuating nature of qualities perceived as attractive: it is important to choose a mate with these qualities (whether or not they contribute to survival) in the hope of passing them on to offspring.[50] Hence the heated competition for a man like Delphin Slade.

Like Clement Spender in *The Old Maid*, Delphin receives no direct narrative attention. Since Clem is distinctly off-stage in Europe when the main action begins, and Delphin is dead, readers see these male characters only through the memories of women who found them desirable. Just as readers may wonder why the Lovell cousins consider Clem so irresistible, they may question the value of a mate like Delphin.[51] Alida's fiancé appears to be a better prospect as a provider than Clem, certainly, more willing to undertake marital commitment, but he is equally callous in his willingness to exploit women for casual sex. When he receives a message from Grace offering to meet him secretly by night, he accepts her offer and then, all too plainly, decamps. During the "two months" Grace spends on her supposed sick-bed after her assignation with Delphin, he evidently suggests no sequel to their intimacy (RF 236). Not only does he maintain his engagement, he apparently never suspects that the child Grace bears nine months later might be his. If he does suspect, he shows no sign of caring. For many years he lives across the street from his own daughter, moving in a social circle that must be supposed to include encounters with her, yet he appears indifferent to the fact of paternity. His behavior illustrates perfectly the success of the mixed strategy so often employed by human males: he leaves his illegitimate offspring to the care of the mother, who succeeds somehow in rearing the child, while he invests personal care and material resources in his children by his wife. The child in whom he does not invest serves simply as backup, or augmentation, to his principal reproductive efforts. Because Barbara is such an unusual individual, and because his promising son dies young, Delphin gains particularly important fitness benefits from his mixed reproductive strategy. However unpalatable his behavior seems from the perspective of conventional moral judgments, it is undeniably effective from an evolutionary biological standpoint.

Success breeds success, at least in competitions for mates. No wonder young women struggle so ruthlessly for access to the most desirable men! No wonder they often fight for top-quality genetic material as intensely as for plentiful resources and reliable commitment! "'Girls are ferocious, sometimes,'" as Alida acknowledges (RF 237). In much more contracted space than the earlier novella, "Roman Fever" indicates that some women are willing to stake everything on the possibility of a big prize, gambling that the genetic advantage of a truly exceptional child will more than offset the benefits to be realized by a larger quantity of more ordinary offspring. Alida Slade comes close to realizing maximum benefits in a high-stakes contest when she and Delphin produce their high-quality son. As a male, he would have enjoyed a reproductive potential greater than Barbara's. Only the boy's early death prevents Alida from being the unequivocal long-term winner in the competition between the two women. Wharton identifies Grace as the winner of this mating contest even as she underlines the role of chance in deciding the outcome.[52] Grace's victory provides moral comfort to readers in the shape of poetic justice[53]: Alida's malicious intervention boomerangs satisfyingly, resulting in injury to the perpetrator rather than to the intended victim. Moral concerns are not the principal objects of Wharton's attention here, however. Grace's triumph over Alida, like Charlotte's vexed victory over Delia, serves to place premarital sex and short-term mating strategies in a favorable light, creating a happy combination of moral justice and biological success. Shrewdly Wharton arranges for readers to applaud Grace's choices and their outcome — choices that violate conventional ethical prescriptions and that typically earn social condemnation.

# 6

# The Children

## *Social Environment and Parental Investment*

*The Children* (1928) is in important respects Edith Wharton's most modern work of fiction. This novel delineates a ruptured social fabric, kaleidoscopic shiftings of human loyalties, and bizarrely fragmented familial ties. A story line focused on the conduct of parents and offspring, highlighting disturbed intergenerational behavior, portrays the dark side of modernity and at the same time decisively invites biosocial scrutiny. Readers observe adults who cavalierly neglect their offspring, thus jeopardizing their own fitness, or ultimate reproductive success. In response to parental indifference, children themselves embark upon an unusual quest, one that promotes allegiance to non-relatives over actual kin.[1] The plot is driven, and readers' sympathies are engaged, precisely by this deviation on the part of the younger generation from ordinary genetic self-interest. As the action unfolds, Wharton examines both causes and outcomes of behavior that from a Darwinian point of view must be considered maladaptive. She demonstrates that such behavior may perhaps represent an altruistic response to highly unusual circumstances. Her novel provokes interest not only because it explores the workings of biological imperatives but, more intriguingly, because it poses a poignant challenge to them.

Wharton identifies a rapidly changing and in many ways aberrant social environment as the source of much of the biologically senseless behavior she depicts.[2] The action takes place in the period of social upheaval between World War I and the Stock Market crash known as the Jazz Age. We observe a wealthy, upper-class social group, a mixture of Americans and Europeans, coping with dramatic changes in social mores and customs. In the throes of

167

a new permissiveness, the people in this privileged world wander through Europe from one party or cruise to the next, living in hotels, seemingly without any meaningful occupation or stable residence. One character describes this environment as a "wilderness": "packing up our tents every few weeks for another move" (*C* 23). The nomadic domestic arrangements reflect "transient partnerships," undertaken with the avowed intent of long-term commitment but lacking follow-through: "'the marriages just like tents — folded up and thrown away when you've done with them'" (*C* 11, 23). As Blake Nevius notes, the book clearly criticizes "lax notions of marriage and the responsibility imposed by a family,"[3] and at the same time it presents a larger indictment of the environment fostering them. Irresponsibility reigns in this social community overpowered by "wasteful luxury ... vanity ... selfishness ... and greed" (*C* 81, 114). Those who suffer most from the "cross-tangle of divorces" and peripatetic way of life are the offspring of numerous and often ill-considered liaisons: hence the novel's title (*C* 98).

The children at the center of Wharton's tale are a group of seven, thrown together as the result of a complicated series of alliances. The union of the central couple, Joyce and Cliffe Wheater, initially results in a daughter and a set of twins. A divorce ensues, and both partners remarry. In these new unions, Cliffe sires a daughter, and Joyce acquires two stepchildren whose bankrupt and profligate father, an Italian nobleman, afterward proves unwilling to undertake personal care of them. Both of the former Wheater partners eventually become disillusioned with their second marriages and find means to end them. At this juncture, urged by their eldest daughter to reconcile, Joyce and Cliffe remarry and produce a fourth child — actually the seventh child of the group, which now includes four full Wheater siblings, one Wheater half-sibling, and two full Buondelmonte siblings unrelated to the other five. When the novel opens, Judith Wheater, the eldest daughter, is fifteen years old and has been assuming chief responsibility for all six of the others, who range in age from eleven to two. With the assistance of two salaried employees, she provides all hands-on care, organizes the perpetual travels from one pension or hotel to the next, worries and schemes about their common future. Only occasionally are the children in geographic proximity to the adult Wheaters, who are the formal, if not legal, guardians of all seven, and even then the six eldest children are lodged in separate quarters to prevent the parents from being overpowered by their presence.

The children's wanderings are dictated by a jumble of considerations, principally the parents' social schedules, squabbles, and whims. Financial self-interest also plays a role in the hands-off policy exhibited by some of the parents and other adult relatives, particularly the desire to retain alimony or an "allowance" (*C* 65, 266). At unpredictable intervals a parent or step-parent or step-parent-to-be appears, seeking to assert rights to one child or another and sometimes offering bribes to seduce a child's affections. The adults' motives invariably appear selfish, unconnected with any child's actual well-being. For instance, the mother of the Zinnie (the Wheater half-sister) needs to produce the child in order to demonstrate her fertility to her new husband, a wealthy English aristocrat with lands and a title to pass on. In another incident, the newest wife of the Italian nobleman arrives to lay claim to his two children, the Buondelmonte step-siblings. Proudly parading her degree in Eugenics and Infant Psychology, she is demanding custody of her husband's children in order to maintain her image as an expert in childrearing. It is the adult Wheaters themselves, however, who pose the most significant threat to the stability of the children's situation. Their reconciliation and remarriage, crowned though it is with the birth of a healthy boy in whom they obviously, if distantly, rejoice, does not prove stable in this environment of constant "jazzing" (*C* 38). The evidently imminent break-up of their marriage, and both partners' obvious interest in selecting new mates, promises to entail a redistribution of custodial arrangements for the seven children.

Social environment plays a viciously culpable role in Wharton's novel in that it has produced a generation of adults whose parental investment in their offspring is unnaturally low. Some of the parents connected to the Wheater ménage provide financial resources, but virtually none give personal care or responsible supervision of such care. The children's educational needs, including social education, are abysmally neglected, particularly in view of the parents' wealth and social class. Such neglect appears to be injuring their chances to marry well (two daughters, for example, show signs of making hypogamous mate choices by getting involved with hotel staff). Even the most basic of the children's needs — physical survival — is not adequately met. Efforts to get the frail eleven-year-old son to appropriate climates are made almost entirely by his elder sister and tend to be thwarted by parental whim or indifference. Most tellingly, the youngest boy, a "large reliable baby," dies of meningitis at the age of three in the course of yet another family peregrination (*C* 341). The parents' failure to raise this promisingly healthy child to adulthood strongly underscores the inadequacy of their investment in their offspring. The death by suicide of Judith's friend Doll Westway, another child raised under conditions similar to those endured by the Wheaters, demonstrates the widespread prevalence of insufficient parental care in this dangerous new "wilderness," the "world of Palace Hotels" (*C* 23, 46).[4]

Even as they enter middle age, these adults devote their energies preponderantly to the search for new mating opportunities rather than to the nurture of existing children. Such activity is not biologically advantageous, particularly for the females, since their fertile years are coming to an end.

Refusing to "settle down" in age-appropriate fashion, they seek instead the illusion of perpetual youth (with the help of "all these new ways the doctors have of making them young again") and adopt behavior patterns better suited to much younger individuals (*C* 44). Realistically, given the ages of the women involved, most of these proposed matings are unlikely to result in the birth of more children. The evolutionary self-interest of Joyce, Cliffe, and their would-be new partners would be better served by investment of resources and energies in existing offspring than in courtships whose outcomes are very likely to prove sterile. Caught up in a maladaptively youthful lifestyle, the adults in this radically changed environment neglect their children to the point of endangering their own fitness.

Reduced parental investment leads in turn to the formulation of goals on the part of the offspring which ordinarily might seem counter-productive from the standpoint of evolutionary biology. Precociously aware of their parents' essential frivolity and inattention to all serious business of life, the children are understandably disillusioned with adults and adulthood. They do not aspire to join the world of senseless merry-making which has left so many of their own needs unmet. Lacking a home base and any consistent personal parental care, the children have grown into a cohesive and self-sustaining group. The strange and constantly shifting custody arrangements all but the youngest have endured during the parents' various pairings, partings, and re-pairings have left them determined never again to be divided, "bundled up ... and sent from pillar to post, first to one Palace Hotel and then another, wherever one parent or another happened to be" (*C* 25). As a group, they feel a sense of continuity, belonging, and security that nothing else in their lives has provided. Hence their solemn oath, sworn "on Scopy's book," never to be separated (*C* 134). Under leadership of the eldest, who functions partly as pseudo-parent, partly as a child who is simply first among peers, they create a kind of Lost Boys camaraderie, placing prime importance on the continuance of the group as a unit. Including half- and step-siblings in their vision of permanent, familial togetherness, all seven are offering to persons with whom they share no ties of actual kinship the kind of commitment usually reserved for close relatives. Principles of inclusive fitness explain the loyalty extended among them to full and half-siblings, while the allegiance of each child to non-relatives in the group is promoted, presumably, by their having been raised together.[5] Wharton portrays the children's insistent refusal to discriminate between close kin and the biological strangers in their midst as bold, touching, and unexpected; the strength of their collective devotion evokes a heightened emotional response from readers (as from Martin Boyne) precisely because it violates predictions of kin selection theory.

The little Wheaters' determined dedication to the cohesiveness and continuity of their group is particularly astonishing, from a biosocial view-point, because it influences them to cling to one another rather than to expect or accept support from adult relatives. Siblings normally compete for parental attention and resources,[6] but conflict within the Wheater group is confined to jealousy and squabbling over relatively trivial "presents," occasional treats and largesse distributed in the course of infrequent parental visits. When confronted with the inestimably more significant resources presumably associated with actual parental custody, however, the children defy Darwinian predictions by their resistance. The young Buondelmontes cannot be won over with descriptions of the "ancestral palace" they are invited to share, complete with "a modern playroom" and state-of-the-art gymnastics training (*C* 289). And when Zinnie Wheater, five-year-old daughter from Cliffe Wheater's second marriage, is offered the opportunity to go live with her "'own real mother,'" she replies, "'I should like to consult my lawyer first'" (*C* 292, 293). In giving absolute priority to their own "close, self-governing body" even when this priority means rejecting proffered parental resources, the children react in a way that normally might be expected to reduce their individual fitness, but the kind of parental attention they have experienced in the past has proven more harmful than beneficial (*C* 29): they have ascertained that it does not represent genuine investment in their welfare. Experience has taught them that parents are not to be relied on: "'If children don't look after each other, who's going to do it for them? You can't expect parents to, when they don't know how to look after themselves'" (*C* 130). Readers may suspect Wharton of irony in her choice of a title, since the parents she depicts are behaving more like juveniles than the actual children.[7] The little Wheaters have formulated unusual goals in an evolutionarily unusual context. An observer "marvel[s] that the bond [uniting them] ... should be stronger than the sum of [their disparate] heredities. But so it was" (*C* 47).

The member of the group who has sacrificed the most for their common welfare is, of course, the eldest, Judith Wheater. The quasi-maternal role she has assumed not only debars her from many of the normal recreations of adolescence but, she asserts, precludes schooling and marriage. "'There'll always be some of the children left to look after.... I never mean to leave the children — *never!*'" she avers (*C* 60). During the bulk of the action of the novel, therefore, she is shown to be jeopardizing her future individual reproductive success for the sake of siblings and step-siblings. Inclusive fitness theory suggests that this alloparental behavior on her part nonetheless may be adaptive. If Judith succeeds in raising three full siblings and one half-sibling to adulthood, the resulting nieces and nephews may compensate, perhaps more than compensate, for lost fitness as measured by children she might herself have raised. The mathematics of her situation are simple. She shares half her genes with a full sibling (exactly the same percentage she would share with a child), and one-quarter of her genes with a half-sibling. Thus she will share one-quarter of her genes with a niece or nephew, one-eighth with the child of a half-sibling. If each of the siblings whose survival she fosters were to raise exactly two children (a relatively modest expectation), Judith would succeed in getting one and three-quarters copies of her genes into the next generation. She would have to raise four children of her own to improve even slightly on this result. Of course, any children her Buondelmonte step-siblings raise will have no positive impact on her fitness, but once she has made an allo-parental investment in the group of children as a whole, the presence of a couple of non-relatives is of little consequence. Material resources to feed, clothe, and house the children are abundant. Judith is not making a significant additional sacrifice by tending six children rather than four.

It is the allocation of her time and energy that constitutes her principal sacrifice: she is providing child-care instead of seeking an education commensurate with her socioeconomic position or engaging in normal adolescent pre-courtship activities. Postponing her search for a mate, and refusing to prepare herself properly for that search, she is proposing to channel most, perhaps all, of her fertile years into the raising of siblings rather than offspring, as well as decreasing her eventual chances of attracting a high-quality, high-investing mate. Her decision to invest so heavily in siblings shows that she is operating according to what loosely may be termed a bird-in-hand principle: her siblings are already in existence, and she is too young (at the time when she initially assumes her caretaker role) to produce offspring of her own. Thus she is safeguarding copies of her genes that might not be replaceable.[8] At the end of novel, Judith appears to have changed her strategy, partly because she lacks the power to ensure its success and partly because her alloparental function has, for a variety of reasons, come to an end. Most of the other children are no longer physically present to require her assistance, and in consequence she has relinquished, or at least decreased, her all-absorbing foster-mother commitment in order to engage in pre-courtship behavior. She will, of course, still pay the price for her earlier alloparental investment, since she lacks the cultural, intellectual, and social education to attract the kind of mate she otherwise might have obtained.

Wharton generates reader sympathy for the children's goals by introducing their story from the point of view of an outsider. The novel's protagonist, Martin Boyne, accidentally encounters the young Wheater ménage and gradually gains insight into the family complexities that produced the group of seven. Having been acquainted with both the adult Wheaters in his youth (like them, he is a man in early middle age), he might be expected to sympathize with the parental generation. Instead he quickly comes to identify with the children and with their passionate desire to remain together. Having spent most of his adult life on engineering jobs in South America, Boyne is distinctly not a part of the modern Jazz culture in which the Wheaters move. He himself is unmarried and childless, and his appalled reaction to the Wheaters' cavalier treatment of their offspring provides the measure by which readers judge it. Repeatedly he contrasts the Wheater children's lifestyle with the secure and stable conditions of his own childhood, confirming the negative impact of the environmental changes Wharton has targeted for criticism. The children enlist him to intercede on their behalf, and he is able, initially, to persuade the Wheaters to engage a tutor for the elder boy. Later Boyne even agrees to serve as temporary guardian to forestall a breaking-up of the group. Allying himself with their cause and attempting to negotiate for them, he is amazed at the difficulty of getting the Wheaters and assorted other parents to focus even briefly on the subject of the children. The adults are too busy with their partying, in-fighting, and mate-swapping to concentrate on their offspring's present or future welfare; discussions of the topic are repeatedly postponed for the most trivial of reasons: "When all was said and done, all they asked was not to be bothered" (*C* 175). Symptomatic of the peculiar parental priorities is Joyce Wheater's annexing of Terry's new tutor as a potential mate for herself; the tutoring is suspended before it has well begun, as Joyce begins to talk of divorcing her husband (again!) in order to marry her newest partner in the ongoing game of matrimonial musical chairs.

An extended allusion to Greek myth serves to support Wharton's condemnation of the adult behavior blighting these children's lives. Boyne's initial efforts to comprehend the intricately shifting relationships behind the group he encounters on board ship are characterized, metaphorically, as a journey through a maze: "the Wheater labyrinth" (*C* 15). Trying to sort out the marriages, divorces, and remarriages, along with the varying parentage of the children before him, he is "consumed by the desire to see farther into this nursery tangle, and follow its various threads back to the young creature [Judith] at his side" (*C* 14). Which children are the result of which pairings? Who is related to whom? In what order did the different marriages occur? The complex inter-relationships prove "enigmatic," presenting a series of "puzzles" for his solution (*C* 19, 22). Scattered bits of information that come his way only increase his confusion, "land[ing] him in the heart of the labyrinth; the difficulty now was to find his way out again" (*C* 16). Trying to elucidate the tortured matrimonial history of the parental generation, Miss Scope tells Boyne, "'I see that I haven't yet given you all the threads; there are so many'" (*C* 25–26). Gradually Boyne begins to make his way through the "matrimonial tangles" that produced this genetically mixed but socially cohesive group of children (*C* 11).

Wharton's deliberate invoking of the image of a *labyrinth* may suggest even more than the mad complexity of the mating customs which it so aptly renders vivid. The labyrinth in Crete was built by Daedalus to contain a monster, the Minotaur, to whom each year a human sacrifice of Athenian youth was made. It seems more than coincidental that the Wheater group consists of precisely seven members, echoing in abbreviated fashion the formula of "seven youths and seven maidens" familiar from retellings of the myth.[9] In the environment of the novel, children are indeed sacrificial victims, condemned to wander about, lost, in the labyrinthine windings of their parents' marital experiments. From this modern "cross-tangle," furthermore, there is no escape (*C* 98). Theseus-like in his wish to help the youngsters evade their fate, Boyne enters wholeheartedly into the "muddled business," but is helpless to effect the children's release (*C* 23). Their sacrifice is not merely metaphorical, as the deaths of Chip Wheater and Doll Westway so glaringly illustrate. It is worthy of note that the monster itself, the Minotaur of Greek myth, was the product of unnatural desire: the coupling of a woman with a bull. Thus the labyrinth allusion also helps to highlight a fundamental aberrancy in the mating choices characterizing this privileged, post-war world. The adults' maladaptive sexual activity has rendered members of the next generation captive, preparing the way for their monstrous destruction.

There is a Peter Pan-ish quality to the children's doomed quest to preserve their little group intact and untainted by flaws exhibited by nearly all the adults they know. They are seeking to stabilize an inherently unstable situation, unstable not only because of their powerlessness as children to assert themselves effectively in the adult world, but because of the changes they themselves are undergoing: childhood is not a steady state. They are unable to foresee the transformations each of them necessarily must undergo and thus to realize how their group is threatened from within as well as from without. "'It's all hideous and touching and crazy,'" Boyne's fiancée declares, observing the neglected children's struggles (*C* 118). Boyne notes that what "excited his interest and sympathy" in the little Wheaters is "not least the frailness of the tie uniting them, and their determination that it should not be broken" (*C* 45). The precarious quality of the children's bond, their touching resolution to create a social unit based on something other than biological connection, lies at the heart of Wharton's novel. They themselves are aware, on some level, of the unusual nature of their group commitment, as the ritual they devise for affirmation of their loyalty indicates: ordinary, biologically based nepotism does not require "an awful oath" to become operational (*C* 60). The poignancy of their dream is thematically and emotionally central; the novel exists principally to validate its worth even while demonstrating that it cannot prevail. As Nancy Bentley observes, "it is precisely the absence of any clear legal or even blood relation" that elevates their group commitment to a kind of "heroism."[10] Boyne plays a crucial role in this validation of something that can sustain itself, as he says, for "a moment only," as "an episode" (*C* 332); it is "a Utopia," "a dream-paradise of a day," a kind of "fairyland" (*C* 300, 135, 305).

Boyne is the only adult, except for the children's salaried nanny, who takes active steps to abet their schemes and who actually imagines that a happy outcome may prove achievable. Others take for granted that the children's situation at any given moment is provisional. Rose Sellars, for example, refers casually to the moment "'when the break-up comes, as of course it will'" (*C* 178). The general belief that the children's dream must fail is rooted in the conviction that kin selection, aided by social custom and force of law, must and will triumph. Each parent is likely at some point to assert legal, biologically based, rights to his or her child, and these rights will be upheld. Other family members who may step in to offer custodial care for one or more of the group are likely to assist only those with whom they share ties of kinship. In fact, such predictions prove accurate. When parents demand custody of their child or children, they disregard entirely the children's wish not to be separated. Grandmother Mervin (Joyce Wheater's mother), applied to by the children for succor, offers a home only to four of the seven, those who are her own descendants, "'my own dear grandchildren ... cannot assume responsibility step-children'" (*C* 300). Boyne is disappointed but "in his heart not much surprised" by this example of resource allocation based upon preferential treatment of relatives (*C* 300).

There is heartbreaking irony inherent in the children's situation: except in the face of maladaptively low parental investment, they would not have concocted their dream of a togetherness transcending kinship. Biological ties have to a very real extent failed them, so they construct an ideal vision of a different, better kind of bonding. This ideal vision is in turn undercut by critical facts of evolutionary biology, which continue to operate just well enough to prevent realization of the children's dream, if not well enough to prevent the need for the dream in the first place. They are beleaguered, as Carol Wershoven puts it, by "both ... traditional and ... modern" forces.[11] In life, as in fiction, Brett Cooke points out, humans "may occasionally try out behavioral innovations," but "over the long run, [most individuals] are likely to stay close to deep-set tendencies"; in short, "not many individuals can buck inbred tendencies [in themselves or in others] for long."[12]

Thus the children do not succeed in preserving their little group intact. Joyce and Cliffe Wheater divorce, entering into new marriages that, unsurprisingly, prove sterile. Cliffe chooses as his next partner Syb Lullmer ("always chock full of drugs"), mother of the deceased Doll Westway and by any standards the most horrifyingly deficient parent depicted in the novel (*C* 153). Trailing Joyce, the children are dragged from one hotel to the next, never achieving a settled place of residence — that "big house in the country, with lots of dogs and horses" that they dream of (*C* 331). Soon after the Wheaters divorce, moreover, the group begins to scatter. Reclaimed by their father, the two Buondelmonte children are carried off to live with a stepmother in Italy and not heard from again. Terry, whose health remains a question mark, is sent to school in Switzerland. Chip dies. Neither systematic education nor social supervision, apparently, is provided for the remaining three girls. Blanca's precocious and inappropriate behavior grows so outrageous that she is sent away to "a convent," yet eight-year-old Zinnie still is left to spend her days unsupervised in hotels (*C* 341). There she plays games on the elevators, alienates other guests, and cadges cigarettes for the lift boys with whom she in turn is becoming overly friendly. Making her social debut on the international hotel scene rather than in a stable social community, Judith is exposed to the dangers of unchaperoned excursions with persons of unknown background, e.g., "'some P'ruvians ... [with] two Rolls-Royces'" (*C* 343).[13]

Wharton's novel offers evidence that certain kinds of human quests, idealistic in spirit, may originate when basic adaptive mechanisms do not function properly. No matter what threats to fitness are caused by an altered social environment, however, evolved adaptive behaviors are likely in the end to prove more enduring than cultural fads or quirks. (The fate of cultural experiments like that undertaken by the Shakers sufficiently demonstrates the ultimate power of evolutionary forces.) Utopian projects such as the one conceived by the Wheater children illustrate humans' creative response to aberrant social conditions, valorizing their capacity to imagine alternatives to biologically-driven choices. Wharton argues, implicitly, that such visionary quests inspire empathy and awe precisely because they are doomed to be evanescent when ranged against the forces of natural selection. By the same token, her narrative excites readers' interest precisely because it highlights motives and actions deviating markedly from the ordinary. *The Children* thus supports Nancy Easterlin's theory that valued artworks do not merely represent ingrained "biological patterns" of human behavior, but display thought-provoking "divergence from them."[14] In Robert Storey's terms, "the raison d'être of narrative is to deal with departures from the canonical."[15] The comparison Boyne makes at one point between Judith Wheater and Joan of Arc sufficiently indicates how Wharton herself regards the children's conception of a loyalty superseding biological ties (*C* 46): theirs is a courageous and morally admirable project that will end with the martyrdom of the very individuals whose convictions have created and sustained it.

Boyne's own matrimonial designs are folded neatly into the central problem of the Wheater children's future. His awakening concern for the youngsters provokes and "sheds light" upon a quickly developing love triangle.[16] As the novel progresses, he finds himself attracted, nearly simultaneously, to two females, one of whom is just a bit too old to be a biologically plausible mate, the other just a bit too young. The "middle-aged" Rose Sellars very likely will bear Boyne no children, perhaps one at most if they do not delay consummating their union (*C* 91). Certainly her long, childless marriage to Charles Sellars raises questions about her fertility. Boyne's initial impatience with her wish to defer their marriage for the traditional year of mourning perhaps reflects his unarticulated recognition that they are wasting the very last of her rapidly waning reproductive potential. That potential was, of course, considerably higher when he first fell in love with her; it has simply taken him a while to realize that she is no longer as desirable a mate as she was then. His encounter with the much younger Judith Wheater very likely has helped to stimulate that realization. The sight of Chip, the splendidly robust Wheater infant, causes both Boyne and Rose to feel a "pang" of yearning, to associate their planned union with the possible conception of offspring (*C* 131).

From an evolutionary perspective, Rose's obviously low residual reproductive value helps to explain the wavering of Boyne's devotion to her. At the same time, intriguingly, she becomes less desirable to him precisely because she demonstrates so little ability to empathize with the Wheater children's plight and goal. Their divergent reactions to the Wheater children — that is, the clash between his impassioned, idealistic empathy and her refusal to tilt at other people's windmills — indicates a psychosocial incompatibility that serves as a yet another negative predictor for their future as a couple.[17] On one level of Wharton's narrative, Boyne rejects Rose because she does not share his views on a matter of importance to him: she refuses to support a utopian, "crazy," and counter-biological project (*C* 118). On another level, he rejects her because she is unlikely to bear him children. On both levels, his decision follows adaptive logic. A marriage between Rose and Boyne might well be in her reproductive interest, offering her one last small chance to conceive a child, but it would serve his interest much less adequately. Significantly, the novel does not generate much sympathy for Rose, nor are readers disposed to be disappointed by the collapse of her engagement to Boyne. Although he does not mention reproductive considerations explicitly, his ultimate rejection of Rose as a marriage partner corresponds perfectly to Darwinian predictions about mate choice.

Judith, in contrast to Rose, has her full reproductive life ahead of her. Boyne's first impressions of her are connected with fertility: she is surrounded by children. Devoted to the harum-scarum crew "scrambling over her," she is the very image of maternal "solicitude," and he takes pleasure in imagining himself as the partner of such an attractive young mother (*C* 36, 3). The only flaw in the picture she presents to Boyne is that she is *too* young. The infant she holds on her shoulder is "much too heavy for her slender frame," and as child after child appears to join her, Boyne's admiration turns to outrage: "Why, it's barbarous; it ought to be against the law! The poor little thing —" (*C* 3,4). An appealing image of maternal fecundity has been transformed into one of ugly exploitation: the fifteen-year-old Judith now strikes Boyne as a girl forced prematurely into childrearing, condemned to sacrifice her health to burdens to which she is not yet equal. Consequently he cannot feel comfortable thinking of her in erotic terms. The transfer of Boyne's affections from Rose to Judith, biologically explainable in terms of their divergent reproductive value, is thwarted by his sensitivity to the latter's extreme youth. Unlike many males portrayed in history, literature, and myth, he is reluctant to secure a monopoly on her fertile years through a mating commitment that for her would be psychologically and socially premature.

Boyne gives shape to his conception of Judith's intermediary state — half girl, half woman — by comparing her to the figure of Daphne in Greek mythology: "she was like a young Daphne, half emerging into reality, half caught in the foliage of fairyland" (*C* 265). In making this allusion, intriguingly, Boyne reverses the original transformation, picturing tree-into-girl, rather than girl-into-tree. The Greek Daphne is a young woman pursued against her will by a high-status male, the god Apollo, who is determined to possess her sexually: her metamorphosis secures her from the threat of violation. In Boyne's image of Judith, she is "emerging into reality," that is, into the reality of adult sexuality, but, like a developing tadpole, still visibly entrenched in the identity she is in the process of outgrowing. She remains "half caught in the foliage" of childhood, which Boyne redefines as "fairyland," underlining the naïve idealism, the penchant for make-believe, characteristic of that state. Childhood represents chastity, security, magic; adulthood offers the opportunities and dangers of "reality." According to Boyne's reversed pattern of transformation, the young girl gives up the safety of her pre-adult role (her identity as "tree") and with the completion of puberty becomes vulnerable to male ardor and pursuit, with their attendant risks. Not yet having completely outgrown the protective "foliage" of childhood, Judith Wheater is still off limits, not yet fully ripe for courtship although tantalizingly close. Her very nearness to adulthood provides readers with a measure of Boyne's selflessness in giving her up.

As Bulfinch's version of the tale indicates, it is Daphne's freshly developed womanly "form" that stimulates male desire. Apollo admires her hair, her eyes, her lips, her hands, her arms "naked to the shoulder," and is even more excited by "whatever was hidden from view." His "impatient" lust causes him to behave "like a hound pursuing a hare, with open jaws ready to seize." Daphne therefore regards physical metamorphosis as her best hope for escape: "'change my form, which has brought me into this danger!'" she begs her father Peneus, the river god. Even in tree form, Daphne continues for a time to excite her pursuer, so that he caresses her, much against her wishes, in her new state: "He touched the stem, and felt the flesh tremble under the new bark. He embraced the branches, and lavished kisses on the wood. The branches shrank from his lips."[18] Reminding readers of this tale, Boyne emphasizes an unattractive side to male ardency. The picture of Apollo attempting to "seize" the fleeing maiden in his "open jaws" is frighteningly reminiscent of predator-prey violence, but his embracing of the resisting bark and branches of the tree, as he seeks to fulfill his lust with Daphne even after she has lost human form, is even more repellant. To woo Judith Wheater at this stage in her development, Boyne implies, would be a "profanation" equivalent to Apollo's desperate and inappropriate fondling of the helpless, bark-bound Daphne (*C* 312): selfish, opportunistic, grotesque.[19]

From the start, Boyne's interactions with Judith are characterized by ambiguity. The two of them establish a Peter Pan — Wendy relationship, playing the parts of Father and Mother to the other six children in an ongoing game. Judith is, as Rose Sellars explains, a "'little-girl-mother'" (*C* 38). Indeed, her ability to formulate visionary plans, to commit herself so passionately to a naïvely conceived and unobtainable goal, endears Judith to Boyne as much as do any of her other qualities.[20] He acts on his interest in her as a potential mate only when it occurs to him that marriage to her is a possible mechanism, conceivably the only workable one, for achieving the children's dream of togetherness. As their efforts to maintain their group intact increasingly are threatened by the activities of their various parents, he comes up with a possible solution to their problem, namely, a marriage between himself and Judith. Once married, the two of them might assume indefinite guardianship of the other six children. Boyne thinks it probable that the assorted parents and step-parents would agree to such an arrangement, and his assumption appears reasonable. Such a happy resolution of the novel's central problem would require, however, that Judith yield all claim to her role as child. More importantly, she would have to regard Boyne as a mate rather than as a playfellow, elder brother, or foster parent. And this she is unwilling, indeed, unable, to do. The climax of the novel is a tearful scene in which Boyne attempts to comfort Judith about the group's future, explaining that he has thought of a way for them to stay together permanently. She short-circuits his proposal by asking, "'do you really mean you're going to adopt us all, and we're all going to stay with you forever?'" (*C* 309).

Faced with a girl who plainly views him as a fatherly protector rather than as a lover, and who identifies herself as a child despite the maternal responsibilities she has prematurely assumed, Boyne quickly retreats. Her reaction forces him to realize that, as Judith's suitor, he would simply become one more exploitative adult, all too like the others surrounding the young Wheaters. His hope of achieving a simultaneously altruistic and selfish out-come — saving the children by gaining Judith as a sexual partner — can be realized only at her expense. Insofar as his actions as temporary guardian of the seven children represent alloparental care, his behavior up to this point resembles that frequently observed in male primates. As Edward O. Wilson explains, "important differences exist between female and male alloparents. Females generally restrict their efforts to the fondling of infants, play, and 'baby sitting'; males not only perform these roles but under various conditions also affiliate with infants as future sexual consorts."[21] Tempted by such a course of action, Boyne ultimately rejects it, standing alongside Mr. Jarndyce of Dickens's *Bleak House* by renouncing marriage to a quasi-ward who might easily have been coerced out of sheer gratitude into becoming his wife.[22]

Boyne seems also to be responding to incest-avoidance mechanisms, albeit second-hand. Once Judith has signaled that she regards him as a poten-tial adoptive parent, it is clear that she will be uninterested in him as a mate. As numerous studies have shown, the absence of biological ties between two individuals does not prevent them from identifying each other as kin; the *recognition* of another individual as a relative is sufficient to prevent sexual interest from developing.[23] In Boyne's interactions with Judith, both parties play a confused mixture of roles. Sometimes they behave like equals, com-panions and confidants, as Boyne acts out "his desire ... to *be* one of the chil-dren."[24] In other moments he very definitely assumes the adult, parental role and Judith that of child and ward. Claire Preston suggests that Boyne's mem-ory of his youthful flirtation with Joyce Wheater increases his tendency to regard Joyce's children from a quasi-parental perspective: he has a "sense that he might indeed have been their father."[25]

Boyne is, of course, by consent of the Wheaters Senior, Judith's tempo-rary guardian, so that he stands literally in the place of a parent to her. And insofar as he tends to fraternize with the children as a co-equal, treating Judith with "elder-brotherly affection," similar avoidance mechanisms (those selected for to inhibit brother-sister incest) come into play (*C* 247). These inhibiting factors are operating rather one-sidedly, evidently, since Boyne is less unre-servedly inclined to regard Judith as a daughter or sister than she is to view him as a parent or older brother. Such difference is predictable: Richard Dawkins points out that since their investment in any individual child is greater than that of their male partners, females typically will prove to be "more rigid in their adherence to [incest] taboos."[26] Because *his* sexual interest in *her* clearly has not been extinguished ("every vein in his body still ached for her"), it might well serve Boyne's biological self-interest to press his suit, urging Judith into a sexual relationship even against her inclinations (*C* 310). Very probably he could have persuaded her to marry him, using rescue of the other children as leverage. Therefore his decision to repress his ardor in deference to her feelings appears to exhibit an element of altruism.

The significance of Boyne's selflessness at this point in the novel's plot is heightened by the knowledge that Wharton originally projected a radically different outcome to her story line: Judith was to marry Boyne, stipulating that he adopt the other six children. All seven were "always to live under his roof," with Judith in the uncomfortable dual role of wife and "little sister."[27] In rethinking her conclusion, Wharton decided to show Boyne acting a far more disinterested part. Deciding that Judith's filial feelings for him constitute an insurmountable obstacle to fulfillment of his desires, he triumphs over "the pathology of the father-daughter sexual politic," as Elizabeth Ammons states, and rejects "patriarchal incest."[28] He steps aside in order to provide Judith with a "chance to grow up" and "to live ... her own life" for good or for ill: his act in no way guarantees her a happy future, but it "empowers her," Susan Goodman argues.[29] Certainly Boyne's renunciation leaves her free to seek a union unencumbered by the negative emotions associated with evolved adaptations inhibiting inbreeding.

At first glance, at least, his own future looks considerably gloomier. Because marriage to *either* Rose or Judith would give Boyne some chance of future reproductive success, his decision to remain single might appear, in terms of his own fitness, to be the most negative outcome possible. His tendency to be attracted to females who are for a variety of reasons unobtainable makes his continuing bachelorhood psychologically consistent, but still not adaptive from a Darwinian point of view. The fact remains, however, that Boyne's reproductive potential is intact; at the age of forty-nine, he may still at some later period in life choose a fertile mate and sire children in whom to invest. Nothing in Wharton's depiction of him or his state of mind at the conclusion of the novel suggests that such a future is particularly likely for him, but it remains a viable, if hypothetical, option. Readers cannot calculate Boyne's reproductive success with certainty in any case, since he is said to have enjoyed "in the course of his life so much easy love" (*C* 84). If children have resulted from these transient encounters, clearly he has not invested resources or paternal energy of any kind in them. It is nonetheless possible that his genes already are represented in the next generation, without his awareness and in the absence of any contribution on his part to his offspring's survival.

Wharton's emphasis on the extent of Boyne's sexual activity (*"so much easy love"*) helps readers identify him as an ardent male who for most of his adult life has employed short-term mating strategies. His chosen profession, which has taken him to distant, underdeveloped parts of the world, has brought him into contact chiefly with women he would be unlikely to regard as suitable for long-term investment. Thus his actual "amorous episodes had been ... brief and simple," even as he indulged in elaborate romantic fantasies featuring the distinctly unavailable Rose Sellars, whose refusal to betray or leave her husband for Boyne ("faithful in spite of his pleadings") is eminently Madonna-like (*C* 226, 40). "Something apart," she is the "one woman in the world whom he was half-afraid to make love to" (*C* 226, 84). She is, he belatedly recognizes, attractive to him largely because she is so "unattainable" (*C* 40) and hence so worthy of long-range commitment.[30] His brief engagement to the newly widowed Rose, like his thwarted courtship of Judith Wheater, represents an effort on Boyne's part to optimize his fitness by changing his reproductive strategy mid-life. He plans to modify his professional activities, which up until now have been incompatible with long-term mating and paternal investment, to alter a way of life that hitherto has been dominated by low-cost sexual opportunities.[31] Depicting his powerful romantic yearnings — first for Rose, then for Judith — along with his easily activated sympathy for the Wheater children, Wharton illustrates in Martin Boyne the uniquely human ability to envision alternative adaptive options. He is intensely attracted to precisely those reproductive options he has as yet not exercised: investment in a long-term mate and in offspring.

Boyne's renunciation of Judith as a potential mate constitutes the most important moral victory in the novel. He validates her continuing role as child, along with her right to adult protection. At the same time he underscores his support of the children's dream, their ideally envisioned common future in which all seven members of the group, including Judith, are to remain children together indefinitely. His altruism adds to the poignancy of the novel's statement for, of course, his self-denial in no way secures the children their wished-for future, any more than it benefits him personally. The final lines of the novel describe him as a "lonely" man (*C* 347). To some readers, this has seemed a sad, even "bleak" conclusion.[32] Yet within the tragic outlines of its story line, Wharton's novel constitutes a celebration: it lauds the power of the human spirit to forge ideals transcending the constraints of evolutionary biology. The book portrays the deleterious effect of Boyne's disinterestedness on his own future and fitness, just as it describes the children's failure to overcome the force of nepotism in their relatives' behavior or, alternatively, to harness that force for their own benefit. At the same time, however, the narrative accomplishes more than the mere unfolding of these negative findings. It stands as an enduring statement that the children's efforts to establish a "bond" stronger than "heredity" are heroic, that the triumph of altruism over genetic selfishness is admirable (*C* 47). Wharton offers strong support for Storey's contention that "if human life [...] serves the selfish gene, it does so in variegated (and often demonstrably unselfish) ways."[33] In sum, she delineates circumstances in which counter-biological impulses are worthy of honor.

# Conclusion

## Evolutionary Biological Preoccupations in Wharton's Fiction

In creating plots, setting, and situations for her many works of fiction, Wharton revisits key concerns in varied guises, investing them with iterative emphasis. Her abiding preoccupations nearly always demonstrate close connection to reproductive efforts, either direct or indirect. Thus they strongly invite evolutionary biological analysis. She chooses as the principal objects of her attention topics demonstrably central to an Adaptationist perspective: social environment and its effects, kin selection and nepotism, status and reciprocal altruism, mating strategies (male and female) and parental investment, deception and self-deception. This pattern of interest is clearly discernible in varied examples of her work, published over a span of nearly twenty years.

### Social Environment

Exploring the impact of environment on individual destiny, Wharton devotes her attention primarily to cultural forces rather than to natural ones. Climate and landscape tend to exert only peripheral influence on her characters. Action takes place predominantly in prosperous twentieth-century American and European settings, either urban or within reach of urban amenities. No non-human predators threaten the characters' well-being; no earthquakes, tornados, or tidal waves disturb their domestic arrangements. Only on the infrequent occasions when she combines a rural setting with a cast of characters from lower socioeconomic groups does Wharton focus on the vicis-

situdes of nature, indicating the powerful, shaping role these ca
human experience. In the 1912 novella *Ethan Frome*, she offers her mos
orable and poignant picture of humans contending with the elements.
effects of climate on individual striving and on community spirit prove fa
reaching. More typically, Wharton's characters occupy a privileged world in
which nature has been tamed. Well-planned gardens and parks, or mani-
cured, semi-rural estates offer respite and recreation: escape from urban heat
in the warmest months, opportunity for winter sports in the coldest season.
Estates poised on the banks of the Hudson River north of New York City
provide a favorite retreat, as do the Rhode Island beaches near Newport. In
Europe, the movements of Wharton's characters from place to place are guided
by seasonal considerations as well as by fashion. Their quests for better air,
more comfortable temperatures, or varied recreation (tennis, yachting, moun-
taineering) reduce nature to a resource, mined by the wealthy for purposes
of enjoyment.

Culture, in contrast, cannot be tamed or reduced to a pleasing background. Carol J. Singley aptly observes that Wharton "adapted Darwinian
principles to upper-class settings and customs. Wealth, prestige, and tradition become the external forces with which her characters — especially her
women — contend."[1] Always aware that humans are social animals, Wharton
insists that individual lives are knitted into a webwork of collective assumptions, practices, and influences. There is no "country," as Ellen Olenska tells
Newland Archer, in which individuals can free themselves from the shackles
of community expectations (*AI* 234). No matter how desperately they may
sometimes yearn to escape the prescriptions and preconceptions of their social
worlds, they are unable — for good reasons — to do so: humans cannot live in
a social vacuum. In this respect, Wharton's concerns overlap significantly with
those of Adaptationist thinkers and researchers. As Joseph Carroll observes,
"the most important biological concept is the relationship between the organism and its environment.... [T]hat relationship is the necessary presupposi-
tion for the principles of personal psychology, sexual and family relations,
social organization, cognition, and linguistic representation."[2] Portraying the
ineluctable effects of community ethos on individual choice and personal
happiness, Wharton highlights a central irony of the human condition: we
are social animals who often find our deepest impulses regulated, repressed,
or reshaped by the communal structures that define us. The malleability of
cultural norms and practices increases the ironic implications of their potency:
chance alone determines whether individuals are born into a cultural environment advantageous to their phenotypic strengths and limitations, ambitions and needs. "What is truly unique about human evolution, as opposed
say to chimpanzee or wolf evolution," Edward O. Wilson explains, "is that a

large part of the environment shaping it has been cultural.... Members of past generations who used their culture to best advantage ... enjoyed the greatest Darwinian advantage." Wilson acknowledges, too, that "historical accident played a role" in gene-culture coevolution, and it is precisely in this arena of historical accident that Wharton finds the stuff of tragedy.[3]

Musing on broken artifacts labeled "*use unknown*," Ellen Olenska articulates with unusual directness the problem with which so many of Wharton's characters contend (*AI* 248): particular cultural practices are transitory and, to some extent, arbitrary, yet they exercise enormous influence on individual behavioral strategies. At the age of fifty-seven, Newland Archer concludes that his culture has undergone observable change in his lifetime, an incredibly short period of time, and that these changes — in gender role prescriptions, in rules of interpersonal communication, and in mate selection criteria, for instance — represent freedoms that would have made his own youth happier. The young women in the generation of Archer's daughter have been subjected to less stifling physical and intellectual supervision (in the name of premarital chastity) than their mothers; topics that formerly were mentioned only obliquely now are openly named and straightforwardly discussed; persons earlier considered unsuitable as mates in Archer's elite circle — outsiders and those with scandalous family histories, like Fanny Beaufort — now are welcomed into that tight community. Archer has done nothing to make these shifts in cultural norms occur; Wharton indicates that individuals are powerless to effect social change. Furthermore, the changes Archer observes come too late to influence his own life's course.

Historical accident plays a similarly ironic role in the life of Wharton's protagonist in the story "Autres Temps..." (1911). Ostracized from her community of origin for half a lifetime because she divorced her husband, the middle-aged Mrs. Lidcote finds that a shift in values has materially reduced the bias against divorce. This change in social norms means that her daughter, as a member of the next generation, can engage in mate-switching behavior without incurring the social penalties that have overshadowed the mother's life. Wharton twists the knife as her protagonist makes a further discovery: social values may be modified over time, but specific instances of social judgment are much less susceptible to alteration. Not only does increased acceptance of divorce come too late to spare Mrs. Lidcote years of loneliness, in her case acceptance does not come at all. Even though individuals in her daughter's generation now divorce and remarry without causing negative comment, she herself continues to suffer from the stigma associated with her earlier behavior.

In this story Wharton casts unsparing light on the harsh consequences of community disapprobation: having broken an important social rule — though not, by any means, a legal one — Mrs. Lidcote is forced to go into what amounts to exile, making her life on a different continent. She lives far removed from family and former friends, most of whom succumb to social pressure and break off all contact with her. Living despised and outcast with the man for whom she left her marriage, she finds that his love cannot survive in such socially deprived conditions. Her unhappy history illustrates the crucial importance of community to human animals. When social support and companionship are withdrawn, individuals are reduced to a kind of living death; hence the graveyard metaphors used to describe her life. Mrs. Lidcote's experience helps readers to understand why so many of the thwarted characters Wharton portrays hesitate to risk ostracism by defying community mores. Even romantic love, however intense, is not strong enough to withstand the powerful force of social sanctions. Newland Archer is made to feel this dismaying reality at Ellen's farewell party, where his guests appear to him like armed guards prepared to compel obedience by force if necessary. Lily Bart is expelled from her social group when she is judged, justly or not, to have violated its standards of sexual propriety with Gus Trenor and George Dorset. Like the protagonist of "Autres Temps...," Lily endures hostility and loneliness. She finds, in addition, that the negative social judgments leveled against her undermine her material well-being, helping to propel her toward poverty and want. However constraining social structures may prove to be in some circumstances, humans require such structures to preserve emotional and mental health and even, ultimately, to ensure physical survival.

Wharton's characters move between Scylla and Charybdis: those who deviate from socially prescribed behavior pay penalties, often severe, while those who conform may suffer from stifled potential and limited choice. After a lifetime of molding his behavior and bending his preferences to fit with community values, Newland Archer reflects that, "after all, his life had been too starved" (*AI* 282). Delia Ralston, with "no definite notion of what it was [she] had missed" in her prudent but emotionally unsatisfying marriage, is intermittently aware of suppressed yearnings: the "tremor of a muted key-board," a "secret questioning which sometimes beat in her like wings" (*OM* 15, 11). Social pressures to maintain marital commitment, in particular, compel Wharton's characters to stay with unsatisfactory mates unless they are willing to endure shame and disgrace. Rose Sellars from *The Children* chooses the course of conformity and wastes her years of fertility in a loveless and childless marriage, even though she has met a more desirable potential mate (Martin Boyne) who is eager to marry her. Ethan Frome, tied to the prematurely aged Zeena, is pressured by prevailing social norms to maintain his commitment to a personally repulsive, morally reprehensible, and reproductively non-viable partner. Economic considerations certainly influence Ethan's decision not to abandon Zeena for the younger, more attractive (and presumably more fertile) Mattie Silver, but it is clear that community values play a strong role in his agonized weighing of pros and cons.

Human cultures tend over time to reinforce fitness-enhancing behaviors, since those that do not, like that of the Shakers, are bound to vanish. It is possible, nevertheless, as the findings of anthropologists illustrate, to promote human reproductive success through a fairly wide variety of customs and institutions.[4] Wharton locates much personal unhappiness in cultural norms whose function is to support evolved adaptations and behavioral strategies but whose operations exact a high psychological or social price. She turns her attention repeatedly to the issue of premarital female chastity, for example, making it a principal topic of consideration in *The Age of Innocence* and *The Old Maid*. She shows readers a culture that has acceded to biologically based male preferences by extending and exaggerating the hallmarks of chastity in marriageable girls, thereby inhibiting the sensual, emotional, intellectual, and moral development of half its population. Much human misery results from this culturally crafted reinforcement of an evolved adaptation: women are grotesquely infantilized in many significant arenas of experience, and the men who marry them do not find the complete companionship they crave in a lifelong partner. Whether Wharton wishes women could or would resist the demand for premarital chastity altogether is not easily ascertainable from her fiction, but her satiric portrait of the forms that demand assumes in late nineteenth-century American society is scathing.

Wharton's bitterest quarrels with cultural norms occur when their operations undermine the fitness of individuals conforming to them. In novels like *The House of Mirth* and *The Glimpses of the Moon* she targets for severe criticism the overemphasis on material resources which is such a prominent feature of the social values prevailing in her chosen settings. Characters imperil their genetic futures when they make resources the most important criterion in mate selection. Lily Bart is the most striking example of an individual taught by those around her to focus her attention on wealth, rather than on genetic quality, social gifts, or personal compatibility. Nick and Susy Lansing are similarly programmed to assume that only those with super-abundant resources are eligible as long-term mates. Such loaded selection criteria are unlikely to prove fitness-enhancing, as Wharton's mocking descriptions of prospective mates like Percy Gryce, or even her more sympathetic portraits of Coral Hicks and Charles Strefford, sufficiently indicate. In *The Glimpses of the Moon* and *The Children* the focus on wealth is accompanied by a failure in parental investment. An inappropriate extension of youthful courtship behavior into middle age and beyond (assisted by advances in dentistry, makeup, hair color, and similar interventions in personal appearance) contributes to the disruption of long-term commitment and the concomitant neglect of offspring. Wharton roundly condemns such manifestations of maladaptive social values, linking her criticisms to the negative repercussions these values exert on mate choice and parenting behavior.

Although she does not attempt to analyze in detail the origins of the social trends she targets for attack, Wharton indicates that the rapid pace of cultural change ("all these new ways") is largely responsible for behavior deleterious to fitness (*C* 44). Thus she presents the problem in terms understandable from an Adaptationist perspective, as a by-product of the steadily increasing gap between genetic and cultural evolution. As Wilson argues, prior to the emergence of agriculture in the Neolithic period, cultural and genetic evolution preceded in lock-step fashion: "there was time enough for genes and epigenetic rules to evolve in concert with culture." Somewhere between 40,000 and 10,000 years before the present, however, "the tempo of cultural evolution quickened."[5] The result is sometimes a mismatch between social norms and reproductive imperatives. Wharton depicts the struggles of individuals who live in a modern, post-industrial world but find themselves equipped with pre-modern, Paleolithic adaptive mechanisms. In the ancestral environment, for example, efforts to attract a mate with abundant resources made good sense. Choosing a mate for personal compatibility and genetic quality is pointless, after all, if the resources to ensure the survival of offspring are not available. Since the agricultural revolution, however, it has become possible to accumulate resources far beyond anything imaginable in a subsistence-based, hunter-gatherer lifestyle — far beyond what is needed, certainly, to raise offspring successfully. An adaptation favoring mates with resources can go haywire in an environment in which the concept of abundance has been so drastically altered: there is room for cultural norms to set the bar for material resources at an unnecessarily high level.

Repeatedly Wharton shows readers that individual lives are to great extent shaped by the immediate social environment. That environment may, by sheer chance, be dominated by values disadvantageous to any one individual's gifts, ambitions, or wishes. Such collision between cultural norms and individual desires is the root of the human tragedy, as Wharton presents it. It is difficult to challenge prevailing customs, and those who do so generally pay a heavy price. Those who yield to cultural pressures may achieve superficial contentment but generally suffer from a sense of psychological emptiness or suffocation. In addition to frustrating personal dreams, social values at times even may threaten individual fitness by promoting maladaptive values and practices. Some of the most poignant moments in Wharton's fiction are those in which individuals envision creative solutions to the problems with which their culture has presented them. Newland Archer's desperate wish to find a place in which distinctions between "wife" and "mistress" are less absolute is one such moment. Susy and Nick Lansing's plan to evade their culture's materialistic pressures in the mate-selection process — their "mad experiment"— represents more dramatically the kind of individual initiative that captures Wharton's interest. The Wheater children's vision of a utopian bond that transcends kinship is another heroic attempt, admirable but doomed, to counter fitness-threatening norms and usages. Except in *The Glimpses of the Moon*, Wharton's characters fail to elude the psychosocial stranglehold of culture. "While she does not rule out the possibility of human happiness," as Judith E. Funston observes, "she redefines it within the narrow constraints of society; ultimately, it is a happiness muted and greatly diminished."[6] Social structures, seemingly arbitrary in design and at times incompatible with her characters' genetic interests, spell out the conditions of their existence.

## Kin Selection and Nepotism

Wharton's writings attest to the ubiquitous importance of kin in human social life. In countless ways, large and small, her characters offer relatives preferential treatment. They provide social invitations and entertainment; they locate suitable mates; they promote and guard reputations; they offer counsel in times of distress; they connive against common enemies; they foster professional advancement; they give financial help. Readers observe Lawrence Seldon's acts of kindness to his impecunious cousin Gerty, Jim Ralston's efforts to support his cousin Joe in a romantic crisis, and Henry van der Luyden's avuncular assistance to the distantly related Ellen Olenska. Examples of more substantial aid include Granny Mingott's allowance to a granddaughter and Mrs. Peniston's provision of a home (complete with dress allowance) to an orphaned niece. Wharton's narratives abound with incidents in which people give and take help — emotional, social, or financial — from relatives, amply illustrating the adaptive value of such allegiance to kin. Her characters are motivated by a conscious assumption, sometimes directly voiced, that an individual's success in life is tied to the success of kin.

Often a family acts collectively to help individual members, as when the Mingott family acts in concert to effect the newly returned Madame Olenska's social rehabilitation. Family relations established through marriage typically are included in kin support networks. Jim Ralston provides financial assistance to Charlotte Lovell's child, who is no relation to him but who shares genes with his wife and, more important, with his two children. The Archer family offers social support to Newland's fiancée's cousin Ellen because any drop in the Mingott family's status will have a negative impact on Newland's future children. Anna Leath is devoted to the interests of her stepson, who is no kin of hers but is her daughter's half-brother. Julius Beaufort is accepted into an elite social group when he marries a woman with kinship ties to its members: any children of that marriage will share genes with them. By extending the obligations and benefits of kinship in this fashion, as Wharton shows, a family expands its social influence and, at the same time, it increases the number and kind of potential helpers available to its members. Individuals who offer assistance to non-kin within a larger family network are demonstrating nepotistic behavior in an only slightly diluted form: they are helping the relatives of their relatives.

In works such as *The Age of Innocence* and *The Old Maid*, Wharton underscores the social power a large, high-status family can command. It is advantageous to be allied with such a family, since its members benefit from assistance and support of many kinds. Individuals like Henry van der Luyden or Mrs. Manson Mingott, who serve as leaders of powerful families, wield wide-ranging social influence: they decide how family resources will be directed and which enterprises will receive family endorsement. In *The Age of Innocence* Wharton documents with particular force and detail how the entangled web of inter-marriages between extended families, generation after generation, infuses social forms and structures with the force of nepotism. To a large extent, in that novel, "society" and "family" are conflated. Nearly all the important people in any individual's social network are kin, or kin of kin. To violate social custom is to betray family interest, and vice versa. Demonstrating how cultural prescriptions and the claims of kin converge, Wharton suggests that human social life is rooted in the adaptations associated with kin selection. The elite communities she depicts are small and inbred, not unlike the ancestral bands of the EEA. Expulsion from such a community is just as devastating for her characters, moreover, as exile into the wilderness would have been for a Paleolithic nomad.

Wharton's characters are willing to incur costs to assist kin. In addition to the obvious drain imposed by long-term provisioning (such as Lily's aunt or Delia's husband take on), individuals risk social injury in order to preserve a relative's reputation. When Lily Bart is dismissed in disgrace from the Dorset yacht, her cousin Jack takes her in for the night. His assistance is minimal and reluctant, but he would not give it at all if Lily were not a relative. When New York society shows reluctance to accept the exotic Ellen Olenska into its circle, the Mingott family closes ranks to support her, giving entertainments in her honor and compelling hold-outs like Lawrence Lefferts to bend to its will. Families also help to conceal a daughter's premarital sexual activity and any resulting offspring: maternal relatives of Charlotte Lovell and Grace Ansley, for instance, rescue their daughters from potential social catastrophe. It is always clear, in such instances, how a helping individual's self-interest is served by nepotistic loyalty. Since people who lose status may compromise the status of family members, it is reasonable to incur some risk to prevent wide-scale reputational injury. More crucially, people who fail to attract a mate, or a desirable mate—perhaps as the result of a reduction in status—cannot contribute with full effectiveness to their relatives' inclusive fitness. In assisting their daughters to hide out-of-wedlock pregnancies, the mothers of Charlotte and Grace act to maximize their own fitness. Their efforts promote the survival of grandchildren and protect the daughters' reproductive futures.

Individuals who fail to exhibit appropriate nepotistic loyalty, like Lily Bart's mother and Lily herself, suffer in consequence. Mrs. Bart derogates relatives, yet she continues to exploit their loyalty by seeking material assistance from them. Lily follows her mother's example, accepting a home from her aunt but publicly ridiculing her benefactor's taste and defying her advice. Lily's disdainful treatment of her socially clumsy cousin Grace exhibits similar disregard for the claims of kin. Otherwise socially astute, Lily never fully realizes how much her behavior to relatives deviates from the norm: all around her people offer time and resources to family members who seem just as burdensome or unappealing as Grace Stepney. Lawrence Seldon no doubt finds the company of his cousin Gerty less than stimulating, but he nevertheless does his cousinly duty by her. The Silverton sisters impoverish themselves to pay their foolish nephew's gambling debts. With such examples, Wharton makes the point that helping kin usually requires sacrifices—sacrifices Lily is unwilling to make. Observing that Lily's problems are exacerbated because of her failure to behave altruistically to relatives, readers gain insight into the adaptive value of nepotistic behavior.

One result of the complicated webs of kinship Wharton describes is conflicting loyalties. Although the reproductive interests of relatives overlap to a considerable extent, they are not perfectly aligned. When the needs of one relative clash with the needs of another, moreover, families must decide which persons to assist. Generally the degree of loyalty exhibited will correspond roughly with the coefficient of relatedness between the two individuals: people assist children and siblings sooner than cousins, for instance, because they share more genes with them. Those without close kin may suffer, therefore, because the loyalty extended to them necessarily is diluted. Lily Bart, Ellen Olenska, Susy Branch, and Mattie Silver, for example, are orphaned at a young age and must begin adult life without parental support or advice. Although Lily and Ellen have numerous relatives, the family assistance offered them is not of the same quality or intensity as that to be expected from a parent.

Conflicts between the divergent interests of kin are not always resolved by degrees of consanguinity, however. Because self-interest overrides loyalty to kin, when an individual is perceived as too great a liability to relatives, support from kin will be withdrawn. Conflict is especially intense when relatives become sexual rivals, for example, and therefore threaten each other's ability to attract or retain a mate. Readers observe that when Ellen competes with her cousin May, or Great-aunt Harriet with her sister, or Charlotte Lovell with her cousin Delia, or Mattie Silver with her cousin Zeena Frome, nepotistic impulses are overwhelmed by genetic self-interest. Each individual acts to maximize her own genetic legacy. The benefits to be anticipated from reproducing with a desirable mate are greater than those to be anticipated from the reproductive efforts of a cousin or sibling: direct fitness trumps indirect fitness.

When acting collectively, families are guided by the principle of the greatest good for the greatest number. Thus a family may refuse assistance to kin whose behavior threatens the status, resources, or mating efforts of a critical number of relatives. In particular, individuals who incur social opprobrium may be expelled and neglected, as the case of Lily Bart illustrates. Up to a point, families are willing to make sacrifices to preserve the social standing of kin. Thus they may offer assistance to rule-breakers, concealing or defending non-normative behavior. When an individual is publicly observed to have violated important community standards, however, relatives put their own social status — and reproductive opportunities — at risk if they stand by their errant kin. Once they are perceived to threaten the inclusive fitness of relatives, individuals can expect far less help from family support networks. Nepotism is a potent and ineluctable force in the social environments Wharton depicts; sometimes beneficent, sometimes punitive, its workings are nicely calibrated to foster the passing on of shared genes.

## Status

Wharton's characters demonstrate acute awareness of relative status, which is defined, necessarily, in the context of community. High status is valuable precisely because people cannot enjoy it in equal measure. In *The Age of Innocence* Wharton represents social hierarchy with the image of a "small and slippery pyramid" (*AI* 93). Jockeying for position and attempting to move upward, individuals find it hard to maintain secure footing, easy to slide downward to less advantageous placement. Those who occupy desirable positions generally have acquired them through family connections, either inheriting status or acquiring it through marital alliance. Status can be won or lost, enhanced or damaged, in a variety of ways, moreover; in the social environments of Wharton's fiction, the *status quo* is always in flux as newcomers attempt to scale social heights, or highly placed insiders fall in community esteem.

The relationship between status and material resources is fairly tight. Families enjoying high status generally enjoy abundant wealth as well. When one branch of a well positioned family suffers financial reverses, its status tends to drop, though not absolutely. Poor relations typically serve as objects of pity, charity, or gentle ridicule. Many examples in Wharton's fiction illustrate the tendency of money and status to go hand-in-hand: when Strefford unexpectedly inherits a title and a fortune, his status rises dramatically; when Lily Bart's aunt disinherits her, the effects of her social disgrace are exacerbated by the financial disaster. Less affluent members of a community who ally themselves with extremely wealthy families through marriage, as Jack Stepney does when he weds Gwen Van Osburgh, see their status rise accordingly. Outsiders with newly acquired fortunes find that the route to status demands more than resources alone, however: hence the efforts of a Rosedale or a Beaufort to gain social standing via marriage to high-status insiders.

Other examples of the *nouveau riche* seeking membership in elite circles include the Struthers, Hicks, and Hatch families (from *The Age of Innocence*, *The Glimpses of the Moon*, and *The House of Mirth*, respectively). They rely on seemingly altruistic outlays of cash and social opportunities to acquire status, using their wealth to give extravagant entertainments and even to purchase social advice (from a Carrie Fisher, for instance). In such situations Wharton illustrates the operations of reciprocal altruism: people who accept generous hospitality from social inferiors gradually find themselves maneuvered into reciprocal relationships with their hosts. The grand balls and dinner parties hosted by Julius Beaufort are felt by his guests "to compensate for whatever was regrettable in the Beaufort past," as the narrator in *The Age of Innocence* satirically observes (*AI* 27). Material resources can be used effectively in the quest for status because they lure highly placed persons into social indebtedness, thus promoting status-enhancing reciprocal alliances.

Wealth is far from the only means employed by Wharton's characters to ascend the social pyramid. The heads of powerful extended families derive high status from the social influence they command. Individuals who exercise altruistic leadership in community affairs, as the mature Newland Archer so successfully does, can earn an extra measure of social respect. Exceptional social gifts, such as those exercised by Susy Branch, Nick Lansing, or Lily Bart, can be utilized to enhance the status of the possessor: to be charming and conversable is an asset. Social clumsiness, in contrast, is penalized. Those who distinguish themselves by expert competence of various sorts can realize social gains, as Wharton illustrates with numerous examples. Sillerton Jackson is a notably successful instance: his social standing and popularity are increased by the store of information he has amassed in his self-appointed role as community historian. Not all efforts to achieve status through expertise succeed as admirably. Lawrence Lefferts is known for his mastery of fine points in fashion and etiquette, for example, but this arena of knowledge does not command the kind of respect accorded to Sillerton Jackson's magazine of family secrets. Ursula Gillow and Violet Melrose court mockery with their efforts to ally themselves with the latest trends in the arts: they compete for social credit deriving from the discovery of new "Genius." Gerty Farish's conspicuous dedication to charitable works does not win her a noticeable increase in social stature; Percy Gryce's striving for recognition as a collector of Americana fails to compensate for the manifold deficiencies in his self-presentation.

Even physical attractiveness is a factor in an individual's social standing: deficiencies in beauty or dress, such as Medora Manson's rag-tag assemblages of clothing, detract from an individual's reputation, while good looks and good taste bolster status. Women, especially, can affect their social position by their choice of clothing. Here again a strong connection between status and resources is evident: those without the resources to purchase clothes from Worth in Paris, and those who must make do with hand-me-down garments, like Charlotte Lovell, are unlikely to move upward in the social hierarchy. Wealth alone will not ensure success in dress, however: those too far in advance of the fashion, too provocative, too exotic, or too European, forfeit respect. The right degree of flair is rewarded; overly eccentric efforts fail. Lily Bart places high value on her taste in clothing, as in interior decoration, because she rightly assumes that she can utilize it to social advantage. She seeks to obtain through marriage the wealth that will enable her to derive maximum status from her skill in choosing the right fabrics, colors, cuts, and effects.

Status is threatened most critically by violations of social norms or rules of conduct. Even mildly idiosyncratic behavior can have a negative impact on reputation. Although they remain "popular," Ellen Mingott's parents are mocked for their "regrettable taste for travel" (*AI* 59). Medora Manson, with her affinity for cults and gurus, loses stature as a result of her peculiarities. Offenses against propriety, whether real or imagined, occasion a more drastic decline in public approval, as the fates of Lily Bart or Ellen Olenska demonstrate. When Mattie Silver's father is discovered to have stolen money entrusted to him for investment by relatives and friends, his wife and daughter suffer a loss of status as well as a loss of family support. When Julius Beaufort is guilty of the same offence on a larger scale, he and his family are subjected to equally devastating punishment, including exile from the community. In these cases, the betrayal of family is compounded by the legal and social implications of theft. Since successful bids for status often are the fruit of collective efforts by a family, individuals who forfeit status through imprudent behavior are likely to lose the good will of kin in consequence.

## Mating Strategies: Male

Wharton's fiction illustrates the mating preferences and strategies of both sexes, at the same time highlighting problems, personal and social, that occur when male and female sexual strategies come into conflict. Male preferences exhibited by her characters accord with those observed cross-culturally by anthropologists and sociologists: her men appreciate youth and health, facial attractiveness and curvaceous figures (particularly a desirable waist-hip ratio). These are signs of potential fertility. Young women like Susy Lansing, Lily Bart, Mattie Silver (and even the no longer youthful Rose Sellars) give further evidence of vitality through the ease and lightness of their movements, their vigor in sustaining long walks through rural landscapes or the streets of European cities. With their shapely builds, delicately feminine features, and blooming complexions, young women like Susy and Lily appeal to men far more than do homelier rivals such as Coral Hicks or Gerty Farish. When men court and choose middle-aged women, as some do in *The Children*, those choices form part of a larger pattern of cultural malaise.

When selecting long-term partners, men in Wharton's fictional worlds pay attention to status, resources, intelligence, and compatibility as well as to physical attributes; they look, too, for evidence of chastity as a predictor of post-marital fidelity. There are men available to marry the extremely wealthy, socially prominent, and obviously chaste Van Osburgh sisters in *The House of Mirth*, even though the sisters' physical, mental, and social gifts are only average. Men who command plenty of resources, like the newly titled Strefford, have the luxury of choosing poor but attractive girls as wives; those with fewer resources may pay court to wealthier but plainer girls. Men with social ambitions, like Rosedale or Beaufort, try to marry insiders who can help them achieve higher status. May Welland is considered the most attractive match in her community precisely because she unites the qualities of facial and bodily beauty, health and vigor, intelligence and kindness, honesty and fidelity, resources and status, that men desire in a long-term mate. Anna Leath offers a similarly complete package of attractive qualities.

When their demand for sexual loyalty is thwarted, men in Wharton's fiction respond, predictably, with jealousy. Owen Leath, Martin Boyne, and Newland Archer, for example, all manifest suspicion, anger, and resentment when other men seem to be seeking sexual access to women in whom they have a proprietary interest. In her 1900 short story, "The Duchess at Prayer," Wharton represents male jealousy at its most brutal: convinced that his wife is having an affair with another man, the Duke poisons his wife and arranges a slow death by entombment for his rival. Due in large part to the high socioeconomic status of the perpetrator, this double murder remains undetected and unpunished. A year later the Duke remarries, siring six children by this second wife. His story is a male fantasy of jealousy satisfyingly appeased. How does a real man behave when confronted with his mate's infidelity? He acts decisively and ruthlessly to eliminate the threat to his lineage, killing the faithless wife (who may already be pregnant with another man's child) and transferring his mating investment to a new woman. As an added proof of dominance, to discourage any future poaching attempts with Wife Number 2, he murders the man who dared to challenge his exclusive sexual rights to his long-term mate. In this story Wharton exposes the workings of male jealousy in its rawest form, showing the untrammeled rage aroused in men whose mates subvert their desire for paternal certainty.

When selecting short-term partners, Wharton's men exhibit a set of preferences somewhat different from those they use in evaluating potential wives. They still seek signs of fertility such as youth, vitality, womanly shape, and facial beauty, but their standards in such matters may be lower, and they are less concerned with status, resources, and social abilities.[7] Lawrence Lefferts, for example, conducts short-term affairs with a series of women who come from the working lower middle class, women whose social standing is distinctly below his. Darrow's liaison with Sophy Viner shows similar disregard for class: she is pretty and vivacious but, unlike his fiancée Anna, Sophy is not his educational or social equal. The Darrow-Sophy affair is depicted in great detail, allowing readers to notice that sexual openness is a quality men value highly in short-term partners. The restraint and reserve men prize in potential wives as a promise of future fidelity would be merely a hindrance in the conducting of a brief affair.[8] Since Darrow is not thinking in terms of marriage, Sophy's uninhibited approach to erotic intimacy is welcome to him.

Readers do observe a number of short-term involvements between social equals in Wharton's fiction. Bertha Dorset enjoys as much status as does Lawrence Seldon, and she commands more resources. She is attractive and intelligent as well, and thus arguably compatible with Seldon to a considerable degree. Their involvement is short-term, evidently, because it is adulterous; Seldon is taking advantage of the opportunity to enjoy intimacies with another man's wife. Should Bertha become pregnant, presumably her husband would assume paternal responsibilities. Newland Archer's affair with Mrs. Rushworth represents the same kind of adulterous opportunity. It is important to realize that Seldon and Archer are characters who win much reader sympathy: Wharton shows that even the most decent, most desirable men to be found are ready to engage in opportunistic sex when it is available. Clem Spender's affair with Charlotte Lovell, and Delphin Slade's with Grace Ansley, similarly depict young men bedding social equals whom they have no intention of marrying. These men engage in short-term romances that result in pregnancy, but they demonstrate no paternal commitment. Given the prosperous environments they inhabit, chances are good that off-spring will survive without their assistance.

Reviewing the many short-term liaisons in Wharton's fiction, readers find abundant evidence of male characters employing a mixed reproductive strategy. Men like Archer, Beaufort, Lefferts, Darrow, Spender, or Slade make a long-term commitment to one woman and to the children of that union. Either before or during their marriage, however, they engage in affairs with other women to whom they make no commitment. Evidently some men make provision for children born out of wedlock, as Delia assures Charlotte Joe Ralston would have done, and as Darrow hints to Sophy he would do if the necessity arose. Julius Beaufort assumes responsibility for the child of his mistress, readers learn, and perhaps the fact that his marriage is childless increases his motivation to do so. In the small communities Wharton portrays, the presence of so many discarded short-term partners and unacknowledged children cannot be completely hidden. Although participants attempt to keep their activities secret, short-term liaisons are noticed and discussed, if only in private. Despite general awareness of specific instances of infidelity, moreover, no punishment is visited upon the men who are violating their long-term commitments: there is tacit social tolerance for male short-term sexual activity. Men known to be unfaithful to their wives retain their social standing, and they generally retain their wives as well. So long as they make attempts at concealment (Lefferts' lies about dining at his club) and give evidence of ongoing marital commitment (Beaufort's gifts of expensive jewelry to his wife), wives and communities conspire to ignore their philandering. Men who conduct affairs with other men's wives, as Seldon and Archer do, similarly court no significant disapproval.

Men's tactics for attracting partners emphasize displays of dominance, status, resources, intelligence, and kindness. When courting potential long-term mates, they offer evidence of commitment as well. Archer woos May Welland with poetry and compliments, flowers and walks in the park; he also presents her with a handsome ring to symbolize his willingness to lavish substantial resources on her. Strefford courts Susy with much needed emotional support and devoted friendship, coupled with the promise of material prosperity and social prominence. He is eager for her to accept a ring with a "thumping" diamond as public demonstration of his commitment (*GM* 26). When pursuing short-term liaisons, men sometimes rely heavily on resources to attract partners. Beaufort provides a high standard of living for his principal mistress, including a carriage and ponies as well as a house. Approaching Sophy Viner for a brief affair in Paris, Darrow splurges on hotels, restaurants, and theatres. He gives her the kindly attention she craves, though he also employs deceit to keep her close at hand. In his short-term (and unsuccessful) pursuit of Ellen Olenska, Beaufort employs marked machismo, attempting to impress her with shows of dominance that verge on bullying: he insists on escorting her to parties; he demands her attention at all hours; he haunts her residence; he shows up uninvited when she eludes him by leaving town. His very posture, when facing her, reeks of masculine aggressiveness. He tries to win her by the simple expedient of asserting possession. He softens the aggressiveness of his approach with some show of kindness, taking on the task of locating new living quarters for her, but even this aspect of his courtship seems intrusive rather than helpful. More attractive men than Beaufort gain short-term access to women without such crude displays of masculinity. Clem Spender and Delphin Slade, for instance, do very little in the way of courtship: their short-term partners respond to simple indicators of attention, just as Bertha Dorset requires nothing beyond the intrinsic pleasures of clandestine romance from Lawrence Seldon. Wharton's narratives suggest that the most sought-after men frequently can attract desirable partners merely by displaying their high quality.

## Mating Strategies: Female

Female preferences in mates, as illustrated by Wharton, resemble male preferences in most respects: her women look for a variety of qualities ranging from status and resources to intelligence, kindness, commitment, and compatibility. Predictably, they are less interested than their male counterparts in physical appearance[9]: little narrative space is devoted to describing the facial or bodily appearance of male characters. When seeking short-term mates, furthermore, Wharton's women are drawn to men who exhibit most of the same attributes they seek in more permanent partners. Often, as is the case with Charlotte Lovell or Grace Ansley, a woman enters into a short-term liaison with the hope — however slim — of converting it into long-term commitment, or she undertakes an affair as the prelude to mate-switching.[10] Although Sophy Viner assumes from the outset that she has no chance to marry Darrow, he represents a male ideal to her: he is exactly the kind of man she would choose as a husband, given the opportunity.

Relatively few women in Wharton's fiction engage in short-term sex for the purpose of obtaining resources, possibly because Wharton depicts such prosperous social settings: in addition to Sophy Viner, who accepts lavish entertainment from Darrow, there is the example of Carrie Fisher's profitable liaison with Gus Trenor, or Fanny Ring's extravagantly supported life as Beaufort's mistress. Ellie Vanderlyn's affair with the immensely rich Algie

Bockheimer is the most blatant example of mate choice based on resources: she selects him first as an extramarital lover and then divorces her current husband in order to acquire him on a long-term basis, acknowledging that wealth is Algie's chief attraction. Like Ellie's friend Susy, Wharton's readers are shocked at the compromises Ellie makes in order to gain access to the Bockheimer coffers. Algie is an otherwise unprepossessing suitor, whose physical, mental, and social attributes are distinctly below average. Ellie's skewed mate-selection criteria, coupled with the negative effects of her mate-swapping strategy on her parental investment, are the object of auctorial reproach; they provide more evidence that her privileged social environment exercises fitness-threatening effects on its inhabitants. In both *The Glimpses of the Moon* and *The House of Mirth*, Wharton indicates that the overemphasis of material resources in mate selection is a maladaptive modern phenomenon. Protagonists like Lily Bart and Susy Branch assume they must limit their search for husbands to a small group of the super-rich, condemning themselves potentially to genetically second-rate mates.

Repeatedly Wharton makes the point that the genetic quality of a mate, short-term or long-term, is extremely important to women, even when they attempt to deny that this is so. Lily Bart keeps undermining her own efforts to attract rich but otherwise unappealing husbands; she finds herself drawn instead to the superior qualities of Lawrence Seldon despite his inability to support her at the economic level she has targeted. Susy Lansing thinks she is willing to put the intelligent, sensitive Nick aside as soon as a richer potential mate appears, but her conscious plans — like Lily's — are thwarted by unacknowledged, unconquerable preferences. Other evidence that women weigh genetic quality more highly than they do resources is provided by the choices of marriageable girls like Charlotte Lovell and Grace Ansley. These protagonists jeopardize safe and conventional futures in order to obtain exceptionally high-quality fathers for their offspring. They enter into short-term involvements with no assurances of commitment, simply because they find certain men irresistibly attractive. They are not in economically desperate plights, like Sophy Viner, nor need they despair, as she does, of finding husbands: they have family backing, social standing, and personal attractions. Charlotte turns away a serious and respectable suitor (Joe Ralston) to seize the opportunity for short-term intimacy with the commitment-shy Clem Spender.

Instead of condemning the choices made by Charlotte and Grace, Wharton investigates the logic behind them. Mating with exceptionally attractive men, these apparently imprudent women give birth to unusually attractive children. The jealousy these high-quality offspring inspire in rivals underscores the evolutionary benefits of the short-term strategy: Charlotte and

Grace manage to transmit their genes into wildly successful phenotypes in the next generation, emphasizing quality over quantity in their reproductive efforts. Anna Leath makes a similar choice when she allows her sexual passion for Darrow to override her doubts about his loyalty and commitment: yielding to his sexual advances before she has decided to accept him as a husband, she has determined that his genes, at least, are worth having. When Ellen Olenska offers one-time intimacy to Newland Archer, she, too, is risking pregnancy in the absence of commitment, with a man she has singled out as uniquely desirable. The married but childless Bertha Dorset's affair with Lawrence Seldon also may be a bid for good genes. Providing such an array of examples, Wharton sheds unexpected light on women's sexual behavior and its motives. Whether married or single, women engage in short-term affairs more frequently than is supposed, certainly more often than is publicly admitted. Furthermore, many of the women undertaking affairs come from the class and kind regarded as Good Wife material, rather than from the class and kind regarded as prostitutes. Wharton is arguing that short-term sexual strategies often may serve women's reproductive interests effectively. An important piece of her argument, clearly, is that women are more interested in genes, and less interested in resources, than folk wisdom generally maintains. In many instances it is precisely this focus on genetic quality that motivates women to accept short-term attentions from a man they are unlikely to obtain as a husband.

In addition to exposing women's hidden sexual activity, Wharton portrays women behaving assertively to attract and retain mates. Some of the methods they employ are unsurprising: they dress to enhance their physical beauty and show their figures to good advantage; they offer evidence of their capacity for domesticity, fidelity, and maternity; they take sympathetic interest in a man's hobby or vocation; they demonstrate commitment to his interests and values; they express admiration for his behavior and abilities. More surprising is the frequency with which they take the initiative in courtship. Newland Archer does not seek out Ellen Olenska initially: it is she who pursues him. Charlotte Lovell, too, is "the seducer not the seduced," as Linda Costanzo Cahir notes; she "instigates an unconventional liaison."[11] Charlotte's temporary partner, Clem Spender, is married eventually "to a plain determined cousin, who had hunted him down in Rome" (*OM* 130). When Nick Lansing suggests that he and Susy should have an affair, she proposes marriage instead, offering a full-blown plan for their future. Later, while Nick is estranged from Susy, Coral Hicks acts as the aggressor in her efforts to obtain him as a mate: she seeks him out and lures him into her proximity on the Hicks family yacht with the offer of employment. When George Darrow fails to respond to the letter she sends to him in Paris, Anna Leath follows up with a more insistent message, acting assertively to re-establish communication and harmony between them.

Unexpectedly determined in their pursuit of men they have targeted as mates, Wharton's women can be ruthless when competing against other women. They may employ tactics of derogation and disparagement, as the behavior of Rose Sellars or May Archer illustrates. They may undermine a rival's social reputation, as Bertha Dorset and Judy Trenor do Lily Bart's. They sometimes invoke the aid of kin to do battle against competitors, as May Archer marshals the united force of her extended family against Ellen. They may even concoct elaborate plots, like May's against Ellen, or Alida's against Grace, in their efforts to eliminate rivals from the scene. Depicting such behavior, Wharton indicates that women are active participants in the mate-selection process. They do not simply wait passively for whatever potential partners destiny may send their way; they seek out desirable men on their own initiative, rather, and do battle with other women to win them.

Wharton provides abundant evidence that men and women follow divergent routes to fitness. Her narratives illustrate the personal and social implications of conflicts that occur when the reproductive tactics of one sex interfere with those of the other. She demonstrates with special emphasis that the mixed reproductive strategy favored by so many men is a frequent source of problems between the sexes. Men's desire to engage simultaneously in short-term and long-term mating efforts clashes with women's desire for exclusive commitment and investment from a long-term partner.[12] When husbands divert resources to short-term partners (and perhaps to offspring conceived by them), wives must make do with less. Even very wealthy women are reluctant to tolerate such threats to their well-being, as Judy Trenor's resentment of her husband's gifts of money to Carrie Fisher illustrates. Male infidelities stimulate rivalry among women, furthermore, occasionally triggering conflicts that widen to involve family and community. Wharton analyzes the psychological workings and interpersonal effects of the mixed strategy with greatest detail in *The Reef*, attempting to understand ensuing conflicts from both the male and female points of view. Women's efforts to thwart men's philandering impulses, to insist on exclusive commitment, necessarily frustrate their partners' inclination to seize additional reproductive opportunities. Zeena Frome's secret observations of her husband's every move, followed by her careful plans to eject her rival and ensure her husband's fidelity, provide an extreme example of female response to a husband's straying affections. In that narrative Wharton generates sympathy for the male point of view, depicting the psychological oppressiveness generated by female mate-retention tactics.

The female wish to test a suitor's commitment with a long waiting period before allowing sexual intimacy functions as another source of conflict between the sexes.[13] Newland Archer's impatience with the long engagement favored by his fiancée and her family exemplifies the disjunction between men's wish for immediate sexual access and women's wish to approach a high-cost reproductive enterprise with great caution. When Rose Sellars and Martin Boyne decide to marry, she assumes they will enjoy a protracted, long deferred courtship in the idyllic European setting where their reunion occurs; he, in contrast, assumes they will rush to the nearest big city to solemnize their union. Their perspectives are almost comically oppositional: she shocked at his unromantic haste and neglect of proprieties, he uninterested in extending the period of courtship once she has accepted his proposal, and perceiving no benefit to be gained from postponing consummation of the relationship. Like a number of men in Wharton's fiction, Boyne responds to a woman's demand for delay by allowing his attention and affection to wander. He becomes further embroiled in the Wheater children's problems and, simultaneously, more charmed by the teenaged Judith. It is his disinclination to tolerate postponed sexual gratification, as much as his sympathy with the children's problems, that motivates him to assume the role of "trial guardian" without consulting his future partner-in-life. Jealousies and complications, eventually leading to a permanent rift, are precipitated by his unwillingness to accommodate himself to the slower pace his female partner deems necessary in their courtship. George Darrow reacts even more impatiently to Anna Leath's letter putting off his prenuptial visit to her: he uses the enforced period of separation as an excuse for short-term dalliance with a girl he picks up on a train. Manifold entanglements and miseries could have been avoided if he had responded less hostilely to Anna's need to defer their romantic get-together.

Men's efforts to protect themselves from cuckoldry and misplaced parental investment, expressed in a strong preference for signs of sexual fidelity in potential long-term partners, constitute another significant source of intersexual tension.[14] In the social environments Wharton depicts, community expectations strongly reinforce the masculine point of view, restricting women's sexual behavior to an uncomfortable degree. Societal regulations interfere with women's efforts to employ short-term sexual strategies, thus inhibiting achievement of their mating goals. In works like *The Age of Innocence*, *The House of Mirth*, *The Old Maid*, and "Roman Fever," Wharton demonstrates that male strategies and preferences have been culturally validated and institutionalized: hence a double standard that permits men to exercise short-term mating options, both before and during marriage, but penalizes women who do so. The implications of Wharton's analysis are arguably feminist, since a social system that promotes the adaptive advantage of one sex over the other clearly is not equitable. Conflict between male and female reproductive strategies is inevitable, and social mechanisms are established to mitigate the negative effects of this and other forms of human strife. There is no logical reason, however, to valorize one set of biologically-rooted strategies any more than to condemn another. Wharton strongly indicates that social structures can and ought to be examined for evidence of gender-based bias in the regulatory function they exercise.

## Deceit and Self-Deception

Since before Darwin's time, biologists have noticed deceptive strategies practiced throughout the plant and animal kingdoms: false alarm calls and mating signals, for example, or misleading patterns of coloration. Such camouflage and mimicry promote the survival and reproductive future of the deceiver, enabling one organism to manipulate another for its own ends — to achieve pollination, for instance, or to elude predators, or to attract prey.[15] As social animals with a highly developed system of communication, humans enjoy more opportunity for false presentation than do any other creatures on the planet. In the intricate social world of her fiction, Wharton explores the human capacity for deception from many angles, investigating motives behind it and identifying circumstances that foster it. She finds intrigue and dishonesty everywhere: neither gender, nor age, nor status, nor ethical prescription inhibits individuals from exercising guile.

Deception occurs with particular frequency as part of the fierce competition to attract and keep desirable partners. Since genetic survival is at stake, dishonest means may be employed to achieve success.[16] During courtship, for instance, individuals attempt to increase their desirability by expressing sympathies or assuming roles that are actually foreign to them. To please the well-read Newland Archer, May Welland demonstrates an uncharacteristic affinity for poetry; to capture the interest of Percy Gryce, Lily Bart expresses seemingly knowledgeable interest in his collection of Americana; as an excuse for monopolizing Ellen Olenska's time and attention, Julius Beaufort exhibits concern for her housing needs. Even special attention paid to grooming and self-adornment may be interpreted as a relatively innocuous kind of false advertisement, as when Mattie Silver ties a bright red ribbon in her hair on the evening she is to spend alone with Ethan. Such misleading self-presentation is ubiquitous.

Folk wisdom, backed up by considerable scientific research, often charges men with a more serious kind of deceit in their sexual approaches to women.[17] Countless tales and songs illustrate a male tendency to promise enduring commitment when none is intended; successful seducers are accused of acquiring short-term partners by trickery. In the world of Wharton's fiction, however, men rarely resort to deception to obtain short-term sexual opportunities. Typically they are so attractive to their would-be partners that deceit is unnecessary. Charlotte Lovell, bedded and deserted, declares that she has been neither misled nor exploited. Her daughter Tina is prepared to offer intimacy to Lanning Halsey even after he explains that he cannot marry her. Married women like Mrs. Rushworth or Bertha Dorset willingly grant sexual access to desirable men like Archer and Seldon. The adulterous activity that occurs between various pairs of secondary characters in *The Glimpses of the Moon* and *The Children* likewise involves willing female partners. There are no complaints that philanders like Lefferts or Beaufort make false assurances to the various women with whom they are serially involved.

To some degree, at least, Gus Trenor and George Darrow serve as exceptions to this pattern. Trenor's pretense that the gifts of money he makes Lily represent profits on her investments is designed to lure her into obligation, and when she persists in frustrating his attempts at intimacy he constructs a fairly complicated plot to get her in his house alone at night. George Darrow lies to Sophy about having mailed her letter, combining deceit with other tactics to maintain proximity and win her trust. Sophy cannot be regarded as a wholly naïve victim, however, since she gives Darrow many signals indicating availability and is far from dismayed by their intimacy when it occurs. Lily is not Trenor's dupe to any great extent either: although she is aghast at his attempt to force compliance (an attempt she repels without difficulty), she certainly is complicit in the pretense that the money Trenor provides is her own. Nettie Struthers, exploited by a man who promises commitment only to desert her, is one of the few women Wharton portrays who fits the stereotype of female victim. Suggesting that men employ deceit to obtain casual sex less frequently than is supposed, Wharton gives women credit for knowing what they are about. They agree to short-term sex when and if it suits their own mating agendas; like their male partners, they choose this strategy deliberately. As the reproductive outcomes described in several narratives indicate, women are seeking to maximize their own fitness (by obtaining either valuable resources or good genes) rather than suffering defeat from the superior cunning of the opposite sex.

In fact, men in Wharton's world typically practice their deceptions upon their wives and fiancées rather than upon their mistresses. Married or engaged men conceal their short-term liaisons principally to safeguard their long-term relationships and to avoid domestic friction. A betrayed wife is likely to retaliate punitively; she may even abandon her spouse. If a man were to lose his long-term mate in consequence of having conducted a short-term affair, the reproductive benefit he stands to gain from a mixed strategy would be lost: any children he may sire outside marriage are expected to supplement, not to replace, those he will sire with his wife. Often, too, casual partners are of lower quality than wives and fiancées, in terms of attributes ranging from status to appearance, so that a man is apt to lose his most valuable mate if his wife or wife-to-be deserts him.[18] In the wealthy, upper-class environments depicted in the bulk of Wharton's fiction, moreover, men have much to lose socially if their infidelities are discovered. Women in elite groups have status and resources of their own, including families who will support them by ranging their collective social powers against unfaithful mates. An outsider like Julius Beaufort has particularly strong reasons to preserve the outward appearance of loyalty to his wife (that is, to deceive her successfully), since it is his marriage to her that won him membership in an elite group. The price men may pay for exposure of their infidelities includes loss of status, loss of community support, reduced access to resources, and — not least — collapse of marital and familial harmony. Marriage prospects of children may be jeopardized, too, if a cheating husband's lies are discovered by his wife and made a source of public scandal.

Almost certainly a cheating spouse will experience disruption of domestic peace, and this is not a trivial price to pay for extramarital adventuring. In *The Reef* Wharton delineates in agonizing detail the psychological torments a man may undergo if his infidelities come to light. Darrow incurs suspicion, hostility, and reproach as his intended wife questions his essential integrity, forcing him to question it as well. This enforced process of self-evaluation is painful. Instead of basking in emotional closeness and admiration from his partner, he is judged and found wanting. In place of stimulating conversation and peaceful companionship, he finds himself inhabiting an atmosphere charged with rebuke. Because Darrow is committed to Anna, the revelation of his secrets puts her in a powerful position. She keeps him in suspense about her intentions for a protracted period of time, punishing him with her doubts and fears. Exposure of his dishonesty threatens to deprive Darrow of his chosen long-term mate's approbation and, consequently, of the high-quality children that might be expected from their union. His sufferings help readers understand why other male characters devote such energy and care to hiding their extramarital escapades.

Wharton provides abundant illustration of the stratagems men employ. Lefferts arranges cover stories to explain his absences from home; Newland Archer does the same whenever he plans to meet secretly with Ellen Olenksa. Beaufort makes presents of expensive jewelry to his wife to distract her attention from his infidelities. To preserve his engagement to Anna Leath, Darrow first conceals, then brazenly denies his affair with Sophy Viner, at the same time trying to engineer his former lover's departure from Anna's household. Martin Boyne lies to conceal from Rose Sellars a confidential evening stroll he has taken with Judith Wheater. Delphin Slade remains permanently silent about his one-time betrayal of his future wife. Such instances of duplicity, large and small, are motivated by men's desire to pursue a mixed reproductive strategy with impunity; deception assists them in maintaining long-term relationships while pursuing casual mating opportunities.

A sometimes important enabling factor in straying husbands' infidelities is what Newland Archer refers to as "masculine solidarity" (*AI* 246). This unwritten male code of conduct demands that men condone one another's clandestine affairs, sometimes supporting these more actively with false testimony. Archer does not refuse such help even to Lefferts, a man whose infidelities he deems "despicable" (*AI* 245). Uniting men in common cause against their long-term partners, such "male solidarity" is a by-product of intersexual competition, one more weapon in the ongoing conflict between men and women. It is in all men's interest to help conceal infidelities because this collective action allows each individual man to enjoy extra mating opportunities without penalty. Both individually and as a group, Wharton maintains, men lie most consistently to the women with whom they plan to stay rather than to those whom they intend to abandon. (The lying behavior of men who seem somewhat inclined to engage in mate-switching, like Newland Archer or Martin Boyne, demonstrates, at a minimum, their wish to preserve the option of remaining with their current partners.) The duplicities of philandering husbands thus reflect their continuing commitment to their marriages, ironically enough, as well as their desire to evade anger and reproach. Even more important, a wife whose suspicion and jealousy have been aroused will be much more difficult to deceive thereafter, thus curtailing her husband's opportunities for future extramarital affairs. From an evolutionary biological point of view, a talent for deception is advantageous: a husband who lies effectively to his wife is likely to sire more offspring in extra-pair matings than a husband whose lies are less successful.

Like their male counterparts, women very frequently engage in deceit in order to obtain or preserve long-term relationships. Bertha Dorset, Ellie Vanderlyn, and Mrs. Rushworth are unfaithful wives who conceal their adulteries to avoid angering or losing their husbands. Some deceptive maneuvers are more intricate than others: Bertha's accusations of impropriety between Lily and her husband serve mainly to deflect attention from her own affair with Ned Silverton, but they also represent an act of vengeance, payback for Lily's earlier interference between Bertha and Seldon. Alida Slade's plot against Grace is another elaborate example of deception in service of mate-retention. May Archer's premature announcement of pregnancy to Ellen, like the family pressure she organizes to force Ellen back into Count Olenski's arms, is designed to forestall her husband's defection. Delia Ralston's duplicitous interference with her cousin's marriage plans is an act of retaliation, intended to punish Charlotte for mating with the man Delia herself preferred. When the Wheater children, Judith among them, threaten to diffuse Martin Boyne's commitment to her, Rose Sellars conspires with Mr. Dobree to get the youngsters out of the way. Faced with her husband's obvious attraction to a younger and more attractive woman, Zeena Frome uses her illness to justify sending her rival away. Unmarried women like Charlotte Lovell and Grace Ansley hide short-term affairs to protect their reputations for chastity and thus to preserve their future marriage prospects. Concealing her daughter's true paternity, Grace deceives her husband to elicit parental investment from him as well as to safeguard her marriage and her daughter's social standing.

In the world as Wharton presents it, no relationship is free from potential dissimulation. Men lie to wives and potential wives; women lie to husbands and potential husbands. Machinations devised to thwart sexual rivals are rampant. Families undertake collective deception to protect their members, but when necessary they manipulate and betray their own kin. Even children can be victims or perpetrators of deceit. Ellie Vanderlyn draws her eight-year-old daughter into her adulterous intrigues, coaching the child to lie to her father about her mother's jaunts from home. Judith Wheater devises an unsuccessful plan for liberating all seven children from parental supervision, helping herself to her father's cash to finance the scheme of running away. The duplicities practiced upon the Wheater children, severally and collectively, are far more conspicuous than any the children devise, clearly. Assorted parents and step-parents use bribes and lies to convince individual members of the ménage that they are offering altruistic parental care in instances when adult interests, rather than the children's, clearly are being served. In a few instances in Wharton's oeuvre, deception involves a breach of law or financial trust and is related only indirectly to mating concerns. Julius Beaufort, like Mattie Silver's father, solicits investments for fraudulent purposes. The immediate motive for such embezzlement is acquisitiveness. Efforts to accumulate resources do support reproductive efforts, of course, since status and wealth are important both to attract mates and raise offspring. Once discovered, Beaufort's and Silver's deviousness draws intense and widespread moral condemnation, particularly because the perpetrators have duped relatives. To undermine the long-term survival and welfare of people sharing one's genes is perceived as especially unforgivable.

Frequently, though not inevitably, deception is accompanied by self-deception.[19] May Welland convinces herself, as well as her fiancé, that she is developing a love for poetry under his influence; Lily Bart, in contrast, is well aware that she is feigning interest in the Gryce Americana. Wharton's characters deceive themselves either to deceive others more effectively (as the example of May's supposed love of poetry illustrates) or else to avoid psychological discomfort. Susy and Nick Lansing trick themselves into thinking that their marital commitment is not long-term, for instance, in order to avoid confronting the reduced standard of living their marriage will necessitate. For a considerable period of time Martin Boyne manages to deny to himself and others the erotic nature of his attraction to Judith Wheater. So long as he can fool himself into thinking his feelings are brotherly or fatherly, he avoids the problematic implications of romantic involvement with a fifteen-year-old. He likewise avoids having to decide whether or not to break off his engagement with Rose Sellars. Joyce Wheater does not admit to herself, any more than to Boyne, that her eagerness to hire Gerald Omerod as her son's tutor is motivated partly by her romantic interest in him. To confess to herself that she is contemplating adultery with this much younger man would rob her of dignity and spoil her self-image as a devoted mother.

Self-deluding behavior features prominently in *The House of Mirth*, enabling Lily Bart to imagine that she is an innocent victim in her dealings with Gus Trenor. Periodically she admits to herself that she instigated the gift-giving by implying sexual availability to Gus, but she retreats over and over from that recognition: to take full responsibility for bringing about her own social downfall would be too painful. The night she ends her life with an overdose of chloral, her capacity to deceive herself proves fatal. Telling herself that there is "but one chance in a hundred" that an extra dose will prove harmful, that a few drops more "would probably do no more than procure for her the rest she so desperately needed," she disguises from herself the risk she is taking (*HM* 521). Wharton provides equally detailed examples of self-deception in her portraits of George Darrow and Delia Ralston. Darrow is not completely blunted to his failings: he arrives more than once at the conclusion that he has behaved badly to Sophy, or to Anna, but he cannot sustain his self-condemnation for long. Very quickly he returns to his self-image as a kindly man of better-than-average integrity whose sufferings surely are undeservedly harsh. Delia similarly gains periodic insight into her own deviousness, admitting that her intervention in her cousin's life is inspired chiefly by jealousy and malice, but inevitably a more complacent image of herself as kindly helper re-emerges. Clearly Wharton is intrigued by the interior processes that enable even sensitive and intelligent people to evade self-knowledge. When acknowledgement of frailties and mistakes would entail a radical drop in self-esteem, calling into question the individual's worth as a human being, self-deceiving mechanisms take over.[20]

The examples of Lily Bart, George Darrow, and Delia Ralston are essentially tragic: self-deception operates to prevent these characters from correcting their faults or redefining their goals.[21] In some of her short stories Wharton

provides more lighthearted manifestations of the human capacity for constructing and believing lies. She directs deliciously satiric wit towards the ladies
in "Xingu," for instance, who have fooled themselves into thinking they are
well read, highly cultured people. Their misplaced pride in their own cultivation causes them to corroborate Fanny Roby's assertion that they have been
studying the subject of "Xingu." They not only confirm her bold-faced lie,
they fail to recognize it as such: they delude themselves that they are well versed
in a topic with which they are completely unfamiliar. Thus they make themselves ludicrous to readers. When they discover their mistake, after the fact,
they are utterly unwilling to admit their folly; instead they reserve all their
animosity for Mrs. Roby, who has so successfully tempted them to indulge in
self-deception. Thus they avoid the discomfort self-knowledge would entail.

The widowed protagonist of "The Pelican" is similarly a victim of faulty
self-evaluation. Mrs. Amyot earns money to support her young son by giving lectures, a vocation for which she has no gifts whatsoever. Thus the fees
she earns represent charitable hand-outs from kindly audiences who have
heard her heart-warming story. As a result of some internal compartmental-
ization process, Mrs. Amyot manages to deny to herself that she is an inferior lecturer and that no one comes to hear her except out of pity for her
difficulties. Even as she makes sure everyone knows about her child and his
needs, she harbors the illusion that she is competent and popular. She continues to lecture even after the boy has grown up and has repaid his mother
the sums she spent on his Harvard education, and she continues to assure new
audiences that she is working only for her little boy. She enjoys having an
income, which she now spends on luxurious gifts for her son's wife and children, but she enjoys the illusion of professional success even more. She is
accepting money under false pretenses, yet manages to hide this seemingly
obvious fact from herself very effectively. Her self-image is so transparently
inaccurate that she inspires mocking contempt in readers.

Wharton does not shy away from the conclusion that human animals
dissemble to one another and to themselves on a regular basis. Despite the
prevalence of moral codes emphasizing sincerity and integrity, they often use
dishonest means to achieve their ends. When fitness is at stake, either directly
or indirectly, and when straightforward means are inadequate to the occasion, her characters prove adept at lying, cheating, and plotting. Wharton is
both appalled and amused by the evidently ubiquitous phenomenon of self-
deception, which enables individuals to pursue self-interest undetected and,
simultaneously, to escape painful self-examination. The picture she offers of
human nature is not flattering. She delineates with unsparing accuracy the
self-serving impulses underlying social forms and interactions, impulses
accompanied by a pervasive tendency to evade accurate self-assessment.[22]

*  *  *

Considered from an evolutionary perspective, key features of setting, incident, and character in Wharton's fiction come into sharper focus and assume clearer significance. She offers us compelling glimpses into small social environments that in their size and parochialism demonstrate tantalizing resemblance to ancestral bands. Within these relatively closed societies, individuals vie for mates, for status, and for resources, at the same time negotiating an intricate network of kinship obligations and community reciprocities. Readers witness the robustness of nepotistic loyalties, which provide the individual with crucial benefits yet exact painful sacrifices. In countless ways, as Wharton demonstrates, social forms and institutions exercise shaping force on the expression of adaptive mechanisms. She is particularly concerned to illustrate twentieth-century cultural values that prove antithetical to individual fitness: she delineates in exquisite detail, for example, the struggles that occur when evolved strategies for mating or parenting are redirected in a reproductively catastrophic fashion. She depicts individuals caught between customs and adaptations, who seek awkwardly — and sometimes with poignant creativity — to forge solutions to plights for which their evolutionary history has poorly prepared them. Thus her social criticism cannot be separated from her recognition of the biological underpinnings of a universal human nature.

No matter what the cultural context, Wharton's characters contend with furious intensity for the human and material resources necessary to preserve their genetic legacy. They resort frequently to stealth and deception, generally managing to conceal their duplicities even from themselves. Inevitably, Wharton shows, male and female reproductive strategies conflict with one another, so that relations between the sexes often give rise to antagonism and unhappiness. In sum, the individuals she portrays are subject to competing pressures, some deriving from their evolved human nature, others attributable to local environmental conditions. Frequently her protagonists are sufficiently aware of the divergent forces influencing them to engage in self-reflection: they weigh choices and ponder strategies; they mourn options foregone and picture alternatives unexplored; they interpret and reinterpret their own behavior. To indulge in such rumination is the most human of activities, but Wharton supplies plenty of evidence to suggest that readers not be hoodwinked by high-minded, self-justifying musings. The patterns of behavior she depicts are driven, at bottom, by reproductive purposefulness, although her characters often may overlook or deny this reality. The topic to which she returns repeatedly is the endlessly complicated, endlessly vexed inter-relationship between biology and culture.

# Glossary

**Adaptation:** a change in the structure or functioning of an organism that makes it better suited to its environment (i.e., a heritable characteristic that increases the fitness of individuals possessing it).

**Adaptive:** tending to increase the individual's fitness (i.e., conferring an advantage in terms of survival and reproduction). Note: any *adaptation* was, necessarily, *adaptive* at some point in an organism's evolutionary history but changes in environment or ecological niche can reduce the *adaptive* benefit of a formerly advantageous *adaptation*.

**Alloparent:** an individual other than the biological parent who helps to care for juveniles.

**Altruism:** helping behavior provided at a cost to the performer. *(See also* **Selfishness.***)*

**Coefficient of relatedness:** the percentage of genes, on average, that two individuals share by common descent. The coefficient of relatedness between parent and child, or between full siblings, is .5 (i.e., they share one-half of their genes). That between aunts or uncles and nieces or nephews, or between grandparent and grandchild is .25 (they share one-fourth of their genes).

**Fitness:** The reproductive success of an individual, commonly expressed in terms of the number of copies of its genes the individual succeeds in getting into the next generation.

**Genotype:** The genetic constitution of an individual organism (i.e., the organism's full hereditary information). *(See also* **Phenotype.***)*

**Hypergamy:** marrying someone superior to oneself, typically measured by social status or material wealth.

**Hypogamy:** marrying someone inferior to oneself, typically measured by social status or material wealth.

**Inclusive fitness:** The sum of an individual's personal reproductive success and his or her influence on the reproductive success of relatives, weighted according to coefficients of relatedness to the focal individual.

**Indirect fitness:** reproductive success transmitted via relatives with whom the focal individual shares genes.

**Intersexual:** between or among members of the opposite sex (i.e., intersexual conflict = conflict between men and women).

**Intrasexual:** between or among members of the same sex.

**Kin selection:** Selection for genes causing individuals to favor close kin (i.e., selection for behaviors that increase the inclusive fitness of the performer).

**Nepotism:** any discriminative behavior tending to favor an individual's relatives and hence to contribute to that individual's inclusive fitness.

**Parental investment:** any investment by a parent in an individual offspring that increases the offspring's chance of surviving (and future reproductive success) at the cost of parental ability to invest elsewhere.

**Phenotype:** The manifest nature of an organism, including morphological, physiological, and behavioral attributes. *(See also* **Genotype.***)*

**Proximate cause of behavior:** the internal reinforcing mechanism (hormonal or psychological, for instance) that triggers a behavior. *(See also* **Ultimate cause.***)*

**Reproductive value:** an individual organism's expected future contribution to its own fitness.

**Residual reproductive value:** an individual's remaining reproductive value, as measured at a given point in time, taking into consideration age, sex, health, environmental conditions, and other pertinent factors.

**Selfishness:** behavior directed toward maximizing the survival and reproductive success of the performer. *(See also* **Altruism.***)*

**Strategy:** a blind unconscious behavior program.

**Ultimate cause of behavior:** the reason why a specific reinforcing mechanism (i.e., the proximate cause) evolved in the first place. *(See also* **Proximate cause.***)*

# Chapter Notes

## Introduction

1. Here and throughout, references to Edith Wharton's writings are to the editions named in the List of Abbreviations.

2. Wharton to Sara Norton, Paris, 16 March 1908. *The Letters of Edith Wharton*, ed. R.W.B. Lewis and Nancy Lewis (New York: Charles Scribner's Sons, 1988), 136.

3. R.W.B. Lewis discusses Wharton's intellectual debt to Egerton Winthrop, who introduced her to "the extraordinary world of Darwin and Spencer, Huxley and Haickel. It was to Winthrop that she owed such understanding as she reached not only of the theory of evolution, but of the naturalist theory of the implacable power of the environment." *Edith Wharton: A Biography* (New York: Harper and Row, 1975), 56. Hermione Lee traces Wharton's readings in pertinent primary and secondary sources in her biographical study, *Edith Wharton* (New York: Vintage Books, 2008); see 23, 70–71, 102. Marilyn Jones Lyde devotes a chapter to Darwin as one of Wharton's "four awakeners" in *Edith Wharton: Convention and Morality in the Work of a Novelist* (Norman: University of Oklahoma Press, 1959), 39–46. Noting that Wharton "took evolution seriously and abhorred its trivialization by dilettantes," Carol J. Singley examines Wharton's engagement with Darwinism in relation to her spiritual development and religious sensibilities. *Edith Wharton: Matters of Mind and Spirit* (Cambridge: Cambridge University Press, 1995), 10. Donald Pizer addresses the impact of Darwinism in broader terms on American writers of Wharton's era in *Realism and Naturalism in Nineteenth-Century American Literature* (Carbondale: Southern Illinois University Press, 1984). Bert Bender places Wharton in the context of other turn-of-the-century writers, offer-

ing wide-ranging discussion of Darwin's influence on the intellectual and creative life of this period. "It will certainly distort our view of Wharton," Bender warns, "to refer to her in a 'one-to-one' way as a 'naturalist' or Darwinist of any particular variety other than her own, to equate her views ... with those of other writers, or to imagine that her own views remained unchanged throughout her career." Wharton was, he argues, "well aware of the complexities in the Darwinian controversy at the turn of the century." *The Descent of Love: Darwin and the Theory of Sexual Selection in American Fiction, 1871–1926* (Philadelphia: University of Pennsylvania Press, 1996), 317; see especially 33–37, 314–318. Paul J. Ohler discusses Wharton's engagement with Darwin, Spencer, and Huxley in the opening chapter of *Edith Wharton's "Evolutionary Conception": Darwinian Allegory in Her Major Novels* (New York and London: Routledge, 2006), 1–37.

4. Sharon Kim offers a careful and intriguing examination of Wharton's affinity for Lamarckian, rather than strictly Darwinian, theories of evolutionary processes. "Larmarckism and the Construction of Transcendence in *The House of Mirth*," *Studies in the Novel* 38.2 (2006): 187–210.

5. John Tooby and Leda Cosmides, "Conceptual Foundations of Evolutionary Psychology," in *The Handbook of Evolutionary Psychology*, ed. David M. Buss (Hoboken, New Jersey: John Wiley & Sons, 2005), 5.

6. Joseph Carroll, "Literature and Evolutionary Psychology," in *The Handbook of Evolutionary Psychology*, 936.

7. Distilling the findings of twentieth-century scientific research in these fields for a general audience, Edward O. Wilson concludes that they offer "persuasive testimony of a genetically

based human nature." *Consilience: The Unity of Knowledge* (New York: Alfred A. Knopf, 1998), 164.

8. In addition to work by Lyde and Bender, already mentioned, Claire Preston's study helps to place Wharton's evolutionary understandings in the context of her era. *Edith Wharton's Social Register* (Houndmills and London: Macmillan, 2000). Donald Pizer offers specific analysis of two of Wharton's most famous novels in the framework of Darwinism and Naturalism. See "The Naturalism of Edith Wharton's *The House of Mirth*," *Twentieth Century Literature* 41(1995), 241–248 and "American Naturalism in its 'Perfected' State: *The Age of Innocence* and *An American Tragedy*," in *The Age of Innocence: Complete Text with Introduction, Historical Contexts, Critical Essays*, ed. Carol J. Singley (Boston and New York: Houghton Mifflin, 2000), 434–441. Alan Price analyzes *The House of Mirth* from the perspective of evolutionary theory, naturalism, and social determinism in "Lily Bart and Carrie Meeber: Cultural Sisters," *American Literary Realism* 13 (1980), 238–248.

9. Bert Bender applies the concept of sexual selection to his analysis of "The Descent of Man" and *The Reef*. *The Descent of Love*, 314–340. Richard A. Kaye similarly focuses on sexual selection theory, addressing *The House of Mirth*, in particular. *The Flirt's Tragedy: Desire Without End in Victorian and Edwardian Fiction* (Charlottesville: University of Virginia Press, 2002). Paul J. Ohler emphasizes "the sublimation of biological imperatives into social forms — which are themselves adaptive," interpreting her two major novels as an extended "Darwinian allegory" in *Edith Wharton's "Evolutionary Conception."* Tricia M. Farwell discusses Wharton's portrayal of romantic love in the context of — and in juxtaposition to — Darwin's theory of sexual selection. *Love and Death in Edith Wharton's Fiction* (New York: Peter Lang, 2006).

10. Ellen Dissanayake, *Art and Intimacy: How the Arts Began* (Seattle: University of Washington Press, 2000), *Homo Aestheticus: Where Art Comes From and Why* (Seattle: University of Washington Press, 1995), *What Is Art For?* (Seattle: University of Washington Press, 1988); Edward O. Wilson, *Consilience: The Unity of Knowledge* (New York: Alfred A. Knopf, 1998); Joseph Carroll, *Evolution and Literary Theory* (Columbia: University of Missouri Press, 1995), *Literary Darwinism: Evolution, Human Nature, and Literature* (New York: Routledge, 2004); Robert Storey, *Mimesis and the Human Animal: On the Biogenetic Foundations of Literary Representation* (Evanston, Illinois: Northwestern University Press, 1996); Jonathan Gottschall and David Sloan Wilson, eds, *The Literary Animal: Evolution and the Nature of Narrative* (Evanston, Illinois: Northwestern University Press, 2005); Brett Cooke and Frederick Turner, eds, *Biopoetics: Evo-*lutionary Explorations in the Arts* (Lexington, Kentucky: ICUS, 1999); Nancy Easterlin, "Do Cognitive Predispositions Predict or Determine Literary Value Judgments? Narrativity, Plot, and Aesthetics," in *Biopoetics*; Brian Boyd, "Evolutionary Theories of Art," in *The Literary Animal*.

11. Carroll, *Evolution and Literary Theory*, 1.

12. Ibid., 3, 4.

13. Tooby and Cosmides, 13.

14. Ibid., 14.

15. Anne Campbell, *A Mind of Her Own: The Evolutionary Psychology of Women* (Oxford: Oxford University Press, 2002).

16. Ibid., 8.

17. Sarah Blaffer Hrdy, *Mother Nature: A History of Mothers, Infants, and Natural Selection* (New York: Pantheon Books, 1999); Griet Vandermassen, *Who's Afraid of Charles Darwin? Debating Feminism and Evolutionary Theory* (Lanham, Maryland: Rowman and Littlefield, 2005); Janet Radcliffe Richards, *Human Nature after Darwin: A Philosophical Introduction* (London and New York: Routledge, 2000); Douglas T. Kenrick, Melanie R. Trost and Virgil L. Sheets, "Power, Harassment, and Trophy Mates: The Feminist Advantages of an Evolutionary Perspective," in *Sex, Power, Conflict: Evolutionary and Feminist Perspectives*, ed. David M. Buss and Neil M. Malamuth (New York and Oxford: Oxford University Press, 1996); Janet Shibley Hyde, "Where Are the Gender Differences? Where Are the Gender Similarities?" in *Sex, Power, Conflict*; Barbara Smuts, "Male Aggression Against Women: An Evolutionary Perspective," in *Sex, Power, Conflict*; David M. Buss, "Sexual Conflict: Evolutionary Insights into Feminism and the 'Battle of the Sexes,'" in *Sex, Power, Conflict*.

18. David M. Buss, *Evolutionary Psychology: The New Science of the Mind* (Boston: Pearson, 2004), 313.

# Chapter 1

1. Linda Wagner-Martin puts forward the theory that point of view in *The House of Mirth* is not omniscient. She contends that Lawrence Seldon functions as an unreliable narrator whose inadequate perceptions of Lily Bart the reader gradually is compelled to confront (see especially her chapter on "Narrative Voice"). This theory is intriguing, if not altogether persuasive. As Wagner-Martin herself concedes, "much of the narrative does not depend on Seldon's point of view ... because he is so often absent" (19). Linda Wagner-Martin, The House of Mirth: *A Novel of Admonition* (Boston: Twayne Publishers, 1990), 15–21, 19.

2. David M. Buss, *The Evolution of Desire: Strategies of Human Mating* (New York: Basic Books, 2003), 22.

3. Ibid., 19–45.

4. Ibid., 26.

5. Robert Wright, *The Moral Animal: Evolutionary Psychology and Everyday Life* (New York: Vintage Books, 1995), 88.

6. Elizabeth Ammons suggests that Lily lets prospective husbands slip away not only "because she does not love them," but because she "fears ... proprietorship" and "does not want to be owned by any man." *Edith Wharton's Argument with America* (Athens: University of Georgia Press, 1980), 35, 36. Wagner-Martin similarly dubs Lily a "maverick young woman who resists the social code that would coerce her into wifehood." *Novel of Admonition*, 31. Dale M. Bauer concurs with this assessment of Lily: "she cannot accept the restrictions that marriage would place upon her." *Feminist Dialogics* (Albany: State University of New York Press, 1988), 93. Thomas Loebel also discusses Lily as a "misfit" who resists unethical "transactions." "Beyond Her Self," in *New Essays on* The House of Mirth, ed. Deborah Esch (Cambridge: Cambridge University Press, 2001), 109–110.

7. Buss, *Evolution of Desire*, 25–27.

8. Ibid., 25.

9. Elaine Showalter addresses this point, emphasizing that children have been "banished to the margins" of the world Wharton depicts in *The House of Mirth*. "The Death of the Lady (Novelist): Wharton's *House of Mirth*," *Representations* 9 (1985): 138.

10. For a sampling of critical discussions of the baby as metaphoric representation of Lily, see the following: Carol Wershoven, *The Female Intruder in the Novels of Edith Wharton* (Rutherford: Fairleigh Dickinson University Press, 1982), 53–54; Cynthia Griffin Wolff, *A Feast of Words: The Triumph of Edith Wharton* (New York: Oxford University Press, 1977), 181; Susan Goodman, *Edith Wharton's Women: Friends and Rivals* (Hanover and London: University Press of New England, 1990), 57–59; Katherine Joslin, *Edith Wharton* (New York: St. Martin's Press, 1991), 63; Linda Wagner-Martin, *Novel of Admonition*, 47–48; Thomas Loebel, "Beyond Her Self," 126–130; Sharon Kim, "Lamarckism and the Construction of Transcendence in *The House of Mirth*," *Studies in the Novel* 38.2 (2006), 186–190.

11. Richard A. Kaye, *The Flirt's Tragedy: Desire Without End in Victorian and Edwardian Fiction* (Charlottesville: University Press of Virginia, 2002), 171–172. Donald Pizer similarly observes that "what she had not achieved in life, in short, is here achieved in the imagination, and is thus affirmed and even celebrated as a human value even in the face of its actual denial in life." "The Naturalism of Edith Wharton's *The House of Mirth*," *Twentieth Century Literature* 41 (1995), 245.

12. Buss, *Evolution of Desire*, 58, 50.

13. Ibid., 53.

14. Ibid., 57.

15. For discussions of Lily's beauty as "commodity," with emphasis on identity as a product of social construction rather than evolved adaptations, see the following: Thomas Loebel, "Beyond Her Self," 107–112; Ruth Bernard Yeazell, "The Conspicuous Wasting of Lily Bart," in *New Essays on* The House of Mirth, ed. Deborah Esch (Cambridge: Cambridge University Press, 2001), 15–18; Sandra M. Gilbert and Susan Gubar, "Angel of Devastation: Edith Wharton on the Arts of the Enslaved," in *No Man's Land: The Place of the Woman Writer in the Twentieth Century*, Vol. 2, *Sexchanges* (New Haven and London: Yale University Press, 1989), 139–154.

16. Buss, *Evolution of Desire*, 2–8.

17. Ibid., 218.

18. Maureen Howard, "*The House of Mirth*: The Bachelor and the Baby," in *The Cambridge Companion to Edith Wharton*, ed. Millicent Bell (Cambridge: Cambridge University Press, 1995), 141. Buss articulates the matter succinctly: "a woman who overestimate[s] her own value ... suffer[s] costs on the mating market. By setting her standards too high, she ensure[s] that fewer men [will] reach her threshold, and those who [do] might not desire her because they could obtain more desirable women." *Evolution of Desire*, 88–89. Kaye argues that Lily's "treacherously unpractical aesthetic sense" constitutes "the chief obstacle to her economic ambitions." *Flirt's Tragedy*, 167.

19. Buss, *Evolution of Desire*, 218.

20. Cathy N. Davidson explains Lily's declining value to prospective mates as the result of "the 'planned obsolescence' that her society prescribes for women." "Kept Women in *The House of Mirth*," *Markham Review* 9 (1979), 10. Such an argument overlooks the biological roots of male preference.

21. Buss, *Evolution of Desire*, 89.

22. Wolff, *A Feast of Words*, 118.

23. Buss, *Evolution of Desire*, 36, 37.

25. Ibid., 38.

25. Ibid., 36.

26. Marilyn Jones Lyde, *Edith Wharton: Convention and Morality in the Work of a Novelist* (Norman: University of Oklahoma Press, 1959), 134.

27. Buss, *Evolution of Desire*, 39.

28. Geoffrey Cowley, "The Biology of Beauty," *Newsweek*, 3 June 1996, 63–64.

29. Wolff, *A Feast of Words*, 121.

30. Seldon is variously condemned as weak, bloodless, fearful, egocentric, or uncommitted. For discussion of his perceived flaws, see the following critical commentaries: Grace Kellogg, *The Two Lives of Edith Wharton: The Woman and Her Work* (New York: Appleton-Century, 1965), 118–119; Linda Wagner-Martin, The House of Mirth:

*Novel of Admonition*, 18–19, 30–40, 64; David Holbrook, *Edith Wharton and the Unsatisfactory Man* (London: Vision Press, 1991; New York: St. Martin's Press, 1991), 21–37; Blake Nevius, *Edith Wharton: A Study of Her Fiction* (Berkeley, Los Angeles, London: University of California Press, 1976), 59; Katherine Joslin, *Edith Wharton*, 52; Susan Goodman, *Edith Wharton's Women: Friends and Rivals*, 72; Carol Wershoven, *Female Intruder*, 44–54; Cynthia Griffin Wolff, *Feast of Words*, 111, 120–133; Shari Benstock, "'The Word Which Made All Clear': The Silent Close of *The House of Mirth*," in *Edith Wharton's* The House of Mirth: *A Casebook*, ed. Carol J. Singley (Oxford and New York: Oxford University Press, 2003), 138–140; Edmund Wilson, "Justice to Edith Wharton," in *Edith Wharton: A Collection of Critical Essays*, ed. Irving Howe (Englewood Cliffs, New Jersey: Prentice-Hall, 1962), 26–27; Lori Merish, "Engendering Naturalism: Narrative Form and Commodity Spectacle in U.S. Naturalist Fiction," in *Edith Wharton's* The House of Mirth: *A Casebook*, 236–249; Margaret B. McDowell, *Edith Wharton* (Boston: Twayne Publishers, 1976), 22, 45–46; Judith H. Montgomery, "The American Galatea," *College English* 32 (1971), 897–898; Helen Killoran, *Edith Wharton: Art and Allusion* (Tuscaloosa: University of Alabama Press, 1996), 21–24. Joseph Colombe offers a useful summary of critical responses to Seldon, arguing for a more positive view of him as "a nontraditional male character who challenges the dominant literary tropes and cultural stereotypes of [Wharton's] time." "Man or Mannequin? Lawrence Seldon in *The House of Mirth*," *Edith Wharton Review* 13.2 (1996), 3–8 (here 4). Lynne Tillman examines the multifaceted compatibility and mutual attraction that draws Seldon and Lily together, but she concludes that "their attraction to each other is unstable," though "compelling": "the contradictory logic that might make them lovers — both are ambivalent, both want freedom — is precisely what makes them unfit for each other." "A Mole in the House of the Modern," in *New Essays on* The House of Mirth, ed. Deborah Esch (Cambridge: Cambridge University Press, 2001), 149–151.

31. See Buss, *The Evolution of Desire*, 102–103, 179.

32. Paul J. Ohler points out that "what is in her blood is inexpressible" in a social environment which "suppresses the biological will that Lily displays in refusing to marry someone unsuitable." *Edith Wharton's "Evolutionary Conception": Darwinian Allegory in Her Major Novels* (New York and London: Routledge, 2006), 67.

33. Joan Lidoff charges, for instance, that Lily's "visit to the working girl Nettie Struther and her infant and the death scene that concludes the novel are both stock sentimental pieces substituted for scenes of emotional climax or resolu-

tion. "Another Sleeping Beauty: Narcissism in *The House of Mirth*," in *Edith Wharton's* The House of Mirth: *A Casebook*, ed. Carol J. Singley, 184. Bauer argues in the same vein that the scene in Nettie's kitchen "does not conform to the logic of the rest of the novel, for it reveals an ambivalent struggle of sentiment over economics." *Feminist Dialogics*, 124.

34. Wai-Chee Dimock examines how plot and dialogue in *The House of Mirth* highlight "the centrality of exchange." The novel is dominated by talk of expense, price, cost, and payment; exchange is exposed as "a controlling logic, a mode of human conduct and association." Dimock's analysis is in most respects congruent with evolutionary biological principles, emphasizing Wharton's evident dissatisfaction with this particular evolved "mode" of behavior. Dimock speaks, for instance, of Wharton's "hope for an organic life beyond the marketplace" and interprets much of Lily's self-destructive behavior as a "protest against the ethics of exchange." "Debasing Exchange: Edith Wharton's *The House of Mirth*," *PMLA* 100 (1985), 783, 791. Laura K. Johnson focuses on marriage in Lily's (and Wharton's) cultural environment as a "contract" in which exchange of value is regulated by force of law. "Edith Wharton and the Fiction of Marital Unity," *Modern Fiction Studies* 47.4 (2001): 947–976.

35. Buss, *Evolution of Desire*, 144.

36. Wagner-Martin, *Novel of Admonition*, 25.

37. Analyzing the "supposedly romantic alliances" that turn out to be "business deals," Carol Wershoven observes that "the women in the novel ... are in perpetual competition with one another for the best marital deal." *Female Intruder*, 56. Some readers have argued that the exchange of values governing marriage in *The House of Mirth* is a culturally engineered phenomenon and thus susceptible to sociopolitical reform. See, for example, Judith Fetterley's analysis in "'The Temptation to be a Beautiful Object': Double Standard and Double Bind in *The House of Mirth*," *Studies in American Fiction* 5 (1977): 199–211.

38. "In human evolutionary history, reproductive penalties would have been imposed upon women and men who failed to assess their own value accurately." Buss, *Evolution of Desire*, 88.

39. Ibid., 86.

40. Ibid., 71.

41. Ibid., 67, 69, 235.

42. Howard, "The Bachelor and the Baby,"141. Ammons argues that Lily "transgresses ... moral and social regulations with which society expects compliance" because her "real ambitions" are "nonconformist." *Argument with America*, 32. It is difficult to find in Lily's character evidence of conscious sociopolitical rebellion such as Ammons posits, however. Does Lily really want to es-

cape from fashionable New York life, or does she aspire, rather, to command so much social power (based on status and resources) that she can afford to criticize lower-ranking members of her community, or flout with impunity standards to which others are held? In any case, as Wharton makes clear, Lily is unable to envision an alternative way of life for herself, so that her nonconformist impulses remain vaguely conceived and find no outlet.

43. Buss, *Evolution of Desire*, 266–267.

44. Robert Trivers, *Natural Selection and Social Theory: Selected Papers of Robert Trivers* (Oxford: Oxford University Press, 2002), 278.

45. Wolff, *Feast of Words*, 119.

46. "In keeping with Darwinian theory," Carol J. Singley accurately points out, "the seeds of Lily's conflict are planted long ago, first by a managerial mother and then by peers." *Edith Wharton: Matters of Mind and Spirit* (Cambridge and New York: Cambridge University Press, 1995), 69.

47. Buss, *Evolution of Desire*, 15.

48. Perceiving Lily Bart as "the innocent victim of heredity and environment," Lyde points out that one effect of Wharton's determinism is to win reader sympathy for Lily's infatuation with wealth. Since she has been "formed by circumstances beyond her control," her greed and narcissism may be judged less harshly. *Convention and Morality*, 135. Claire Preston interprets Lily as "the Lamarkian victim of a Darwinian universe: no amount of wanting to adapt herself, of willed behaviour toward survival and success, can help her in her struggle with a hostile environment." *Edith Wharton's Social Register* (Houndmills and London: Macmillan, 2000), 57. Donald Pizer argues that "Wharton juxtaposes this conscious deterministic theme of victimization by one's familial and social environment ... with ... alternative forms of belief and value." These alternatives "posit either a transcendent strength ... or a transcendent faith." "The Naturalism of Edith Wharton's *The House of Mirth*," 243. Sharon Kim points to "the prophetic dimension of Lily Bart as an ontogenetic recapitulation of the civilization that produced her." "Larmarckism and the Construction of Transcendence in *The House of Mirth*," 206. Amy L. Blair offers an intriguing analysis of Wharton's original audience, identifying a tendency on the part of many middle class readers to "idealize Lily's environs" and thus "to see Lily's career not as a warning against social aspiration but as a road map...." "Misreading *The House of Mirth*," *American Literature* 76.1 (2004), 166, 168.

49. Buss, *Evolution of Desire*, 18.

50. Showalter comments on Wharton's rejection of "sentimental conventions of nineteenth-century women's literature": "women's relationships in *The House of Mirth* are distant, formal, competitive, even hostile.... Lily sees and treats other women as her allies, rivals, or inferiors in the social competition." "The Death of the Lady (Novelist)," 137, 138. The "lack of female community in [Wharton's] work" has been a source of dissatisfaction to some readers, as Goodman notes. *Edith Wharton's Women*, 48. Julie Olin-Ammentorp argues that strong female characters like Judy Trenor and Bertha Dorset illustrate Wharton's perception that women do, in fact, wield power and influence in a public forum. "Edith Wharton's Challenge to Feminist Criticism," *Studies in American Fiction* 16 (1988): 237–244. Buss emphasizes that "competition among women, though typically less florid and violent than competition among men, pervades human mating systems." *Evolution of Desire*, 9.

51. Diana Trilling, "*The House of Mirth* Revisited," in *Edith Wharton: A Collection of Critical Essays*, ed. Irving Howe (Englewood Cliffs: Prentice-Hall, 1962), 116.

52. Ibid., 116.

53. Edith Wharton, "Introduction to the 1936 Edition of *The House of Mirth*," in *Edith Wharton's* The House of Mirth: *A Casebook*, ed. Carol J. Singley, 33.

54. Richard A. Kaye discusses Lily's failures in Adaptationist terms, pointing to the destructive results of her tactic of endless deferment. In refusing to choose a husband, Kaye suggests, she "throw[s] sexual selection into disarray by prolonging the moment of choice that Darwin discerned as an incremental state in the process of courtship." "Edith Wharton and the 'New Gomorrahs' of Paris: Homosexuality, Flirtation, and Incestuous Desire in *The Reef*," *MFS: Modern Fiction Studies* 43.4 (1997), 872. Trilling observes in this context that "the poignancy of her fate lies in her doomed struggle to subdue that part of her nature which is no better than her culture." "*House of Mirth* Revisited," 109.

## *Chapter 2*

1. Elizabeth Ammons characterizes *The Reef* as "a slow-moving psychological novel," distinctly "unadventurous." *Edith Wharton's Argument with America* (Athens: University of Georgia Press, 1980), 78. "As in James's work," Margaret B. McDowell points out, "the turning points in the lives of the characters derive from an individual's sensitive reaction to scenes in which nothing seems to be happening." *Edith Wharton* (Boston: Twayne Publishers, 1991), 42.

2. Cynthia Griffin Wolff, *A Feast of Words* (New York: Oxford University Press, 1977), 219. Carol J. Singley similarly identifies "the social and moral conditions of love between the sexes" as Wharton's principal concern in the novel. *Edith Wharton: Matters of Mind and Spirit* (Cambridge

and New York: Cambridge University Press, 1995), 129. Singley's analysis emphasizes societal influences on human behavior (the "hypocrisy in early twentieth-century class and gender relations") over biological influences, thus implying that intersexual conflict might be reduced or eliminated through sociopolitical reform. 129.

3. McDowell complains that Wharton fails "to characterize fully Sophy Viner and Owen Leath." *Edith Wharton*, 59. It seems clear, however, that Wharton never intended the younger couple to occupy the foreground of the narrative. Of the four, it is Owen Leath whose character is sketched least completely.

4. In the 1912 Appleton edition, pages 1–77, 125–175, 186–229, and 258–276 are narrated from Darrow's point of view, and pages 81–124, 176–186, 233–258, and 277–367 from Anna's.

5. A. J. Bateman, "Intra-sexual Selection in *Drosophila*," *Heredity* 2 (1. 948), 365. Quoted in Robert Wright, *The Moral Animal: Evolutionary Psychology and Everyday Life* (New York: Vintage Books, 1995), 40.

6. David M. Buss, *The Evolution of Desire: Strategies of Human Mating* (New York: Basic Books, 2003), 19–20.

7. Ibid., 66–90.

8. "Sexual withholding fulfills several possible functions," as Buss points out. "One is to preserve [women's] ability to choose men of high quality, who are willing to commit emotionally and to invest materially." In addition, "scarcity bumps up the price that men are willing to pay." *Evolution of Desire*, 147.

9. Buss, *Evolution of Desire*, 70.

10. Ibid., 12–13.

11. "The idea that Anna's needs are as important as Darrow's is inconceivable" to him, as Singley points out. *Mind and Spirit*, 134.

12. John Keats, "Ode on a Grecian Urn," in *English Romantic Writers*, ed. David Perkins (New York: Harcourt, Brace and World, 1967), 1186. Later, at Givré, when he is securely affianced to Anna, Darrow subtly revisits the Keatsian allusion, contemplating Anna's reserve from a more positive point of view. He decides that "the quality of reticence in her beauty" serves to "suggest[] a fine portrait kept down to a few tones, or a Greek vase on which the play of light is the only pattern" (*R* 126). This reminder and elaboration underline the importance of the allusion, which effectively communicates the ambivalence of Darrow's response to Anna's beautiful remoteness.

13. Buss, *Evolution of Desire*, 116.

14. Ibid., 51–58.

15. Ibid., 59.

16. Ibid., 99–101.

17. Ibid., 105.

18. Trivers discusses "self-deception in the service of deceit" in *Natural Selection and Social Theory: Selected Papers of Robert Trivers* (Oxford: Oxford University Press, 2002), 272–277.

19. Dale M. Bauer, *Edith Wharton's Brave New Politics* (Madison: University of Wisconsin Press, 1994), 19.

20. Buss, *Evolution of Desire*, 98.

21. Ibid., 76.

22. Ibid., 122.

23. A brief Darwinian analysis of the suitors Sophy describes to Darrow is instructive: neither seems likely to contribute positively to her future fitness. The "deaf widower with three grown-up daughters, who kept a clock-shop in Bayswater" has a vocation associated with low status and low income (*R* 61). To make matters worse, his offspring from a previous marriage have a claim on whatever resources he does command. His deafness may be the result of a genetic problem or, more likely, an indicator of his age: he is unlikely to have the health or energy to raise his status or his income in future. Sophy's other suitor, the doctor who was "cashiered from the navy for drunkenness," had in the past presumably enjoyed relatively high status and good income potential (*R* 61). Having forfeited, through alcoholism, the benefits his education and profession otherwise might have brought him, he is now an unreliable provider and a social liability — possibly, too, a source of physical danger to a wife or child.

24. Buss, *Evolution of Desire*, 50.

25. Ibid., 87.

26. Ibid., 76.

27. Ibid., 121.

28. Ibid., 88.

29. Ibid., 119.

30. Ibid., 79.

31. Ibid., 69–70.

32. As Trivers states, "sexual selection ... operates on the male to inseminate females whose offspring he will not raise, especially if another male will raise them instead." *Natural Selection and Social Theory*, 85.

33. Buss, *Evolution of Desire*, 92.

34. Buss elucidates the point as follows: "It is often in the best interests of a woman ... to convince others of the ideal of lifelong love. Promiscuous women pose a threat to monogamous women, siphoning off the resources, attention, and commitment of their husbands." *Evolution of Desire*, 215.

35. Richard A. Kaye offers a provocative interpretation of *The Reef* in which Darrow's affair with Sophy functions as an expression of homoerotic desire, "a 'perversion' of a Darwinian natural order" and "a refusal to assume a predesignated capacity in a Darwinian scheme." Such a reading invests Darrow's affair with the mysterious thrill of the forbidden. If the "subtextual thematics" Kaye discusses do lurk beneath the surface of Wharton's narrative, they serve to

complicate — but do not replace — the significance deriving from a more straightforward reading of sexual identity in the novel. The boyish quality in Sophy's appearance, for instance, is an important feature for Kaye's reading, yet it is limited to Darrow's perceptions of her and not supported by those of other characters. In viewing Sophy as boy-like, Darrow may simply be revealing some of his own self-serving logic (as he assesses Sophy's likely receptivity to a brief liaison) rather than conveying any auctorial intention to blur her gender. Men frequently justify disparagement of short-term partners by casting doubt on their femininity, concocting the convenient argument that sexual freedom is a masculine prerogative: 'true women' remain inaccessible. For full discussion of possible homoerotic overtones in the novel, see Kaye's "Edith Wharton and the 'New Gomorrahs' of Paris: Homosexuality, Flirtation, and Incestuous Desire in *The Reef,*" *MFS: Modern Fiction Studies* 43.4 (1997): 860–897.

36. Buss comments extensively on the causes and consequences of male jealousy in *The Evolution of Desire*, 125–131.

37. James W. Gargano, "Edith Wharton's *The Reef:* The Genteel Woman's Quest for Knowledge," *Novel: A Forum on Fiction* 10. (1976), 43.

38. William R. McNaughton comments on the ambiguity surrounding Sophy's future, given the "licentious environment" of Mrs. Murrett's household. Wharton is warning readers, McNaughton suggests, "not to sentimentalize Sophy's future." "Edith Wharton's *The Reef,*" *The Explicator* 51.4 (1993), 228.

39. Buss, *The Evolution of Desire*, 174.

40. McNaughton observes that "age, education, economic status, and class" are factors that, together with "reasons relating centrally to gender," contribute to "Sophy's powerlessness. "Edith Wharton, *The Reef* and Henry James," *American Literary Realism* 26.2 (1994), 56.

41. McDowell discusses Anna's "jealousy of less inhibited [women]" in this context. *Edith Wharton*, 39.

42. Elizabeth Ammons describes the excessive cultivation of sexual reticence as "society's perversion of ... normal biological needs and desires." "Fairy-Tale Love and *The Reef,*" in *Edith Wharton*, ed. Harold Bloom (New York: Chelsea House Publishers, 1986), 44.

43. Ammons suggests that Sophy and Anna represent "a dichotomous embodiment of one basic identity." She lists the many "similarities and connections" between them, e.g., "both love the same man, Darrow ... both are closely attached to another man, Owen.... [T]hey already share the care of the same child (Effie)." These points of congruence imply "figurative sisterhood," at the same time indicating that the two characters enjoy equal shares of auctorial sympathy. "Fairy-Tale Love and *The Reef,*" 46–47. The

more Wharton brings Anna and Sophy into alignment with one another in this fashion, the more evident it becomes that environmental factors, rather than innate characteristics, dictate their divergent tactics in mate selection and courtship. A number of readers fail to be impressed by the parallels Wharton has so carefully created between her two female characters, however. "Most critics blame the bleak ending on Anna's excessively rigid morality and unforgiving nature," McDowell asserts; "they identify Sophy as the more sympathetic character in the book." *Edith Wharton*, 43. Wolff is one of the most eloquent of these critics, contending that Sophy is the most interesting, significant, and admirable of the novel's characters: she is "what matters, always." *Feast of Words*, 210. McNaughton, in contrast, examines textual evidence that Sophy's behavior is often the result of deliberate calculation, constituting a kind of real-life acting. "Edith Wharton's 'Bad Heroine': Sophy Viner in *The Reef,*" *Studies in the Novel* 25.2 (1993), 213–225.

44. Buss comments on "the sensitivity of mating strategies to early experiences." *Evolution of Desire*, 217.

45. Buss elaborates the point as follows: "Men cannot fulfill their short-term wishes without simultaneously interfering with women's long-term goals. An insistence on immediate sex interferes with the requirement for a prolonged courtship. The interference is reciprocal, since prolonged courting also obstructs the goal of ready sex. Whenever the strategy adopted by one sex interferes with the strategy adopted by the other sex, conflict ensues." *Evolution of Desire*, 13.

46. Lev Raphael examines Darrow's "relentless sense of exposure and inferiority — manifestations of his shame" in detail. *Edith Wharton's Prisoners of Shame* (New York: St. Martin's Press, 1991), 69–71 (here 71). Carol Wershoven points out, in addition, that Darrow will continue to pay interpersonal costs for his affair even after his marriage to Anna, since he will endure "the eternal surveillance of a jealous and disillusioned woman." *The Female Intruder in the Novels of Edith Wharton* (Rutherford: Fairleigh Dickinson University Press; London and Toronto: Associated University Presses, 1982), 107.

47. Wendell Jones, Jr. considers implications of the Cupid-Psyche allusion at length in "Holding up the Revealing Lamp: The Myth of Psyche in Edith Wharton's *The Reef,*" *College Literature* 19.1 (1992): 75–90.

48. Ammons locates "Anna's horror of George Darrow's brief affair" precisely here, in the "deception" which casual sex necessitates and, from the male point of view, even "justifies." "Fairy-Tale Love and *The Reef,*" 43.

49. Moira Maynard, "Moral Integrity in *The Reef:* Justice to Anna Leath," *College Literature* 14 (1987): 292.

50. Robert Wright, *The Moral Animal: Evolutionary Psychology and Everday Life* (New York: Vintage Books, 1995), 88.

51. Richard Dawkins, *The Selfish Gene* (Oxford and New York: Oxford University Press, 1989), 149.

52. Rebecca Blevins Faery observes that some readers (including Lewis, McDowell, Gargano, and Wolff) have overlooked the critical point of this scene, namely, "that Anna does in fact make love with Darrow." Faery suggests that this misapprehension may account for "the widespread failure to make sense of the ending of the novel." "Wharton's *Reef*: The Inscription of Female Sexuality," in *Edith Wharton: New Critical Essays*, ed. Alfred Bendixen and Annette Zilversmit (New York: Garland Publishing, 1992), 95 (note). From a Darwinian perspective, obviously, the act of sexual congress represents a decisive moment for Anna, and hence a major turning point in the plot.

53. Some critics have assumed that Anna's purpose is to "relinquish" Darrow to Sophy. See, for example, McDowell, *Edith Wharton*, 41; Raphael, *Prisoners of Shame*, 77; Ammons, *Argument with America*, 87; Helen Killoran, *Art and Allusion* (Tuscaloosa: University of Alabama Press, 1996), 29. To interpret Anna's intentions in this fashion, however, readers must ignore Darrow's repeated assertions that he would under no circumstances marry Sophy: "'men don't give away their lives like that'" (*R* 316).

54. McDowell, for example, interprets Anna's reaction to the episode in a strongly negative fashion. Sophy's sister is "undoubtedly a courtesan, and she now foreshadows for Anna what Sophy may with the years become. The visit thus provides Anna with the rationale to disregard Sophy as an individual and to reject her as one whose destiny will embrace ... promiscuity." *Edith Wharton*, 41. Blake Nevius likewise reads the scene as providing justification for Anna to "condemn" Sophy of licentiousness. *Edith Wharton: A Study of Her Fiction* (Berkeley: University of California Press, 1976), 140. James W. Gargano argues that Wharton deliberately creates in her final scene a "clinching argument against Sophy and against Darrow," against "the world of easy accommodations." "Genteel Woman's Quest for Knowledge," 48. Bert Bender shrewdly observes that Anna's revulsion in this scene may be interpreted biosocially, the "genetic" tie between Sophy and her sister providing sufficient reason for Anna to reassess her opinion of the girl. *The Descent of Love: Darwin and the Theory of Sexual Selection in American Fiction 1871–1926* (Philadelphia: University of Pennsylvania Press, 1996), 332.

55. James W. Tuttleton is convinced, for instance, that Anna decides "in the end" not to marry Darrow: confronted with the truth about

his "sullied past," she "renounces the possibility of happiness as Darrow's wife." "Mocking Fate: Romantic Idealism in Edith Wharton's *The Reef*," *Studies in the Novel* 19 (1987), 465, 467.

56. An anonymous contemporary reviewer targeted the inconclusive outcome of *The Reef* for special complaint: "all possible solutions are equally unsatisfactory and undesirable." This is, of course, precisely what Wharton wished readers to see, for it is impossible, as this reviewer notes, that Anna and Darrow "should ever be happy together — or apart." Anonymous, review of *The Reef* by Edith Wharton, *Nation* 95 (12 December 1912): 564, quoted in Killoran, 28. The exasperation evident in this comment demonstrates that readers may comprehend Wharton's thematic statement without appreciating its significance, and without admiring the narrative structure that supports it. David Holbrook offers a contrasting opinion, praising "the essential ambiguity of the end of the novel, which must surely be the greatest of Edith Wharton's achievements." *Edith Wharton and the Unsatisfactory Man* (London: Vision Press, 1991; New York: St. Martin's Press, 1991), 191 (see also 63–64). Faery similarly contends that the "indeterminacy" of the novel's ending is "appropriate and inevitable" in the context of Wharton's narrative purposes, "a mark of success rather than disaster." "Inscription of Female Sexuality," 82. Anne MacMaster likewise points out that "by rejecting any easy narrative closure," Wharton demonstrates that the human situation in her novel (particularly the situation of women) defies romantically ideal resolution. "Re-Scripting the Romance: Edith Wharton's Paired Heroines," *Furman Studies* N.S. 37 (1995), 38. For an efficient summary of questions the novel's conclusion appears to leave open, see Jones, "Holding up the Revealing Lamp," 75–76.

57. Killoran, *Art and Allusion*, 30.

58. Buss, *Evolution of Desire*, 77; Dawkins, *The Selfish Gene*, 155.

59. Elizabeth Lennox Keyser examines in detail the leitmotif of letters in the novel. Darrow's cavalier treatment of both Anna's and Sophy's correspondence reveals his consistently egocentric attitude toward the women themselves. "'The Ways in Which the Heart Speaks': Letters in *The Reef*," *Studies in American Fiction* 19.1 (1991): 95–106.

60. Only those traits benefiting the individuals who possess them can be selected for over time; no organism evolves (or can evolve) to serve the interests of genetically unrelated others. Men's preferences are part of the environment in which female adaptations have evolved, to be sure, and thus it may be said that what men want has to some extent influenced what women have become. The reverse is, of course, equally true. As Buss states, "men and women cannot simultaneously reach their goals without coming into

conflict. Conflict stemming from pursuit of mating goals has created recurrent adaptive problems over human evolutionary history." *Evolution of Desire*, 143.

61. Wolff, *Feast of Words*, 211. Gargano, too, sees culpable self-deception in Darrow's characterization of Anna as "someone who is 'still afraid of life.'" "Genteel Woman's Quest for Knowledge," 42.

62. Ammons discusses Darrow's obvious failings in detail, finding Wharton's portrayal of him, and of Owen Leath as well, extremely negative. *Argument with America*, 93–94. Holbrook expresses himself even more strongly on the subject, attributing the wholesale emotional destruction at the end of the novel to "the failure of the man to understand and respect woman." *Unsatisfactory Man*, 76. Henry James accurately observes that the narrative structure tends to support Anna's perspective at the expense of Darrow's: "in the Prologue, as it were, we are admitted so much into the consciousness of the man ... and after the introduction of Anna ... we see him almost only as she sees him." "On *The Reef*: A Letter," in *Edith Wharton: A Collection of Critical Essays*, ed. Irving Howe (Englewood Cliffs: Prentice-Hall, 1962), 149.

63. Wright, *Moral Animal*, 57.

64. Wharton to W. Morton Fullerton, 8 June [1908], *The Letters of Edith Wharton*, ed. R.W.B. Lewis and Nancy Lewis (New York: Charles Scribner's Sons, 1988), 152.

65. Gargano, "Edith Warton's *The Reef*," 46. Bender likewise discusses "sexual entanglements" as the impetus for Anna's inner turmoil: events force her "to confront not only Darrow's but her own sexual reality." *Descent of Love*, 329.

66. For examples of such discussion, see Wershoven, *Female Intruder*, 107, and Ammons, *Argument with America*, 84–85, 95–96.

67. "The richness of the novel," as McDowell states, derives in large part from "the psychic interplay between Anna and Darrow" and from "Anna's anguished introspection." *Edith Wharton*, 40.

68. Luigi Pirandello, *Six Characters Looking for an Author*, 1922, in *Naked Masks: Five Plays by Luigi Pirandello*, ed. Eric Bentley, trans. Edward Storer (New York: E. P. Dutton, 1952), 267.

69. Tuttleton offers a corroborative view, noting that by clinging to unrealized — and perhaps unrealizable — ideals, "the individual may mock the fate that mocks desire." "Mocking Fate," 472.

## Chapter 3

1. As Buss explains, "our evolved strategies of mating are highly sensitive to ... legal and cultural patterns." *The Evolution of Desire: Strategies of Human Mating* (New York: Basic Books, 2003), 15. Paul J. Ohler points to the psychological implications of cultural influence: "while suspecting that rites, rituals, manners, and language narrow his experience, [Archer] cannot create anew his consciousness, which they have molded." *Edith Wharton's "Evolutionary Conception": Darwinian Allegory in Her Major Novels* (New York and London: Routledge, 2006), 180.

2. Claire Preston discusses the recurrence of family names "in various novels, reinforcing the sense of tribal enclosure and genetic inevitability." In all, "20 or so names are welded into a coherent though complex nomenclature across several novels," as she points out, and this nomenclature serves to "denote important alliances through kinship and marriage." *Edith Wharton's Social Register* (Houndmills and London: Macmillan, 2000), 10, 11. Pamela Knights notes that when "the family names reappear in everlasting permutations," the idea of "exclusiveness" is reinforced: the characters belong to "a class reproducing itself without contamination." "Forms of Disembodiment: The Social Subject in *The Age of Innocence*" in *The Cambridge Companion to Edith Wharton*, ed. Millicent Bell (Cambridge: Cambridge University Press, 1995), 27.

3. Judith Fryer characterizes Wharton's view of family as "destructive and oppressive." "Purity and Power in *The Age of Innocence*," in *Edith Wharton: Modern Critical Views*, ed. Harold Bloom (New York: Chelsea House Publishers, 1986), 103. Cynthia Griffin Wolff notes the centrality of "the norms that sustain the family." "The center of Newland's early pieties, the grave enduring traditions of his life, all have to do with family; when he acts without thinking, his automatic behavior affirms the bonds of kinship and familial affection." The result, Wolff contends, is a "social (and moral) inflexibility." *A Feast of Words: The Triumph of Edith Wharton* (New York: Oxford University Press, 1977), 324.

4. "Archer himself is structured by the discourse of Family," Pamela Knights comments. "At every step his life embodies the family design, and the novel takes its form around it. In the narrative of engagement, marriage, and fatherhood, Archer's identity is always positional: he is a son, brother, part of an affianced couple," and finally "a son-in-law." Ellen points out that he can never escape his identity as "the husband of Ellen Olenska's cousin," any more than she can evade the designation of "the cousin of Newland Archer's wife." "Forms of Disembodiment," 23.

5. Although "he prides himself on being different from others," as Carol J. Singley observes, "Archer's tastes and freedoms fall well within the boundaries of New York society." "Bourdieu, Wharton and Changing Culture in *The Age of Innocence*," *Cultural Studies* 17. 3–4 (2003), 506.

6. "Men seek attractive women as mates most simply for their reproductive value but also as signals of status to same-sex competitors." Buss, *Evolution of Desire*, 59.

7. Ibid., 35–37.

8. Ibid., 77.

9. Ibid., 67.

10. Helen Killoran addresses this point, emphasizing that Ellen is "socially innocent of the social codes of New York." *Edith Wharton: Art and Alllusion* (Tuscaloosa: University of Alabama Press, 1996), 58.

11. Buss, *Evolution of Desire*, 67.

12. Ibid., 68.

13. Ibid., 77, 79.

14. Elizabeth Ammons discusses Old New York's exaggerated demand for chastity in political terms, drawing readers' attention to "Wharton's by-now familiar charges against the American patriarchy": training in innocence is part of "a system deliberately designed to arrest female human nature." *Edith Wharton's Argument with America* (Athens: University of Georgia Press, 1980), 147.

15. Buss, *Evolution of Desire*, 68.

16. Katherine Joslin identifies this issue as central to Wharton's social criticism. "The lopsided education and training of men and women make them, in the end ill-suited companions. Community fails because women and men have not been trained to know each other nor to live together as equals." *Edith Wharton* (New York: St. Martin's, 1991), 101. Brian T. Edwards similarly points out that "the removal of women from circulation" proves "debilitating for both men and women." "The Well-Built Wall of Culture: Old New York and Its Harems," in *The Age of Innocence: Authoritative Text*, ed. Candace Waid (New York and London: W.W. Norton, 2003), 503.

17. Kathy Miller Hadley confirms that "for him it is important to keep women in categories." "Ironic Structure and Untold Stories in *The Age of Innocence*," *Studies in the Novel* 23.2 (1991), 266.

18. As Susan Goodman observes, Archer's mistaken assumption that Ellen has had a lover "determines the advice he gives her and his future." *Edith Wharton's Women: Friends and Rivals* (Hanover and London: University Press of New England, 1990), 99.

19. Lev Raphael demonstrates that Old New York society relies heavily on the psychological mechanism of shame to enforce its norms. *Edith Wharton's Prisoners of Shame: A New Perspective on Her Neglected Fiction* (New York: St. Martin's, 1991), 301–317.

20. Knights, "Forms of Disembodiment," 29.

21. Jason Faulkner and Mark Schaller bring new research to bear on the tendency of "kin members lurking behind the scenes" to "monitor relationships likely to affect their inclusive fitness."

"Nepotistic Nosiness: Inclusive Fitness and Vigilance of Kin Members' Romantic Relationships," *Evolution and Human Behavior* 28.6 (2007), 437.

22. Robert Trivers, *Natural Selection and Social Theory: Selected Papers of Robert Trivers* (Oxford: Oxford University Press, 2002), 74. Short-term affairs, as Ohler observes, are "understood within [Archer's] social context as conventional behavior." *Edith Wharton's "Evolutionary Conception,"* 175.

23. Buss, *Evolution of Desire*, 121.

24. Ibid., 121.

25. Ibid., 237. Examining the fictional circumstances here in light of the tolerance for extramarital affairs Wharton demonstrates in *French Ways and Their Meaning*, Julie Olin-Ammentorp speculates that "at some level Wharton felt that Newland's and Ellen's problems could be solved by a discreet long-term affair." *Edith Wharton's Writings from the Great War* (Gainesville: University Press of Florida, 2004), 175.

26. Buss, *Evolution of Desire*, 265.

27. Ibid., 116.

28. Ibid., 116.

29. Charles Mills Gayley, *The Classic Myths in English Literature* (Boston: Ginn, 1893), 225.

30. Buss, *Evolution of Desire*, 175–176.

31. Joslin suggests, intriguingly, that Ellen deliberately exploits her role as potential homewrecker in order to achieve financial independence and personal autonomy: "Ellen is able to use her threat to the Archer marriage to convince her grandmother Catherine Mingott to give her enough money to live an independent life in Paris." So interpreted, her pursuit of Archer functions as a kind of blackmail intended to extract resources from kin. *Edith Wharton*, 103.

32. Many readers are disappointed by the aborted romance between Archer and Ellen, interpreting it as a failure on either his part or hers. Carol J. Singley, for instance, ascribes Ellen's "renunciation of passion" to a combination of Platonic ideals and Puritan tradition: Ellen does not see "that the fulfillment of desire is compatible with higher ideals." *Edith Wharton: Matters of Mind and Spirit* (Cambridge: Cambridge University Press, 1995), 180. James Tuttleton offers a more positive interpretation of Archer's decision to remain with his wife, arguing that "the novel affirms Archer's decision": "it constitutes a recognition that man has institutional, familial, and social responsibilities which cannot be abandoned simply for the gratification of romantic passion." "Edith Wharton: The Archeological Motive," *The Yale Review* 16 (1972), 70. Cynthia Griffin Wolff goes even further, contending that Archer has achieved "an inner peace that transcends time and place": he has "taken the best" of what "his unique moment in history" offered "and built upon it." *A Feast of Words*, 333.

33. Buss, *Evolution of Desire*, 155.

34. As Goodman observes, "although May lies about its technical verification, she does not necessarily lie about her intuition of it." *Edith Wharton's Women*, 100.

35. The announcement of May's pregnancy serves the dual purpose of "reining in Archer just as he is about to stray" and "clinching Ellen's allegiance to a familial order." Dale M. Bauer, "[Whiteness and the Powers of Darkness in *The Age of Innocence*]," *The Age of Innocence: Authoritative Text*, ed. Candace Waid, 480.

36. Alan Price indicates that the cousinship linking the two female protagonists was not part of Wharton's initial scheme; it was introduced, rather, in the "second plan for the novel." "The Composition of Edith Wharton's *The Age of Innocence*," in *The Age of Innocence: Complete Text with Introduction, Historical Contexts, Critical Essays*, ed. Carol J. Singley (Boston and New York: Houghton Mifflin, 2000), 390.

37. Joslin points out that "a pregnancy means the extension of family, an institution jealously protected by the larger community." *Edith Wharton*, 103. Killoran attributes Archer's decision to remain with his pregnant wife to a "medieval sense of honor," and Wolff similarly suggests that "a man without firm moral commitments might almost as easily leave a wife and child as a wife alone." *Art and Allusion*, 360; *"The Age of Innocence*: Edith Wharton's 'Portrait of a Gentleman,'" *The Southern Review* 12 (1976), 653. In this instance, however, moral codes clearly coincide with genetic self-interest.

38. Donald Pizer considers Wharton's evocation of societal constraints on "individual desire and destiny" in terms of literary Naturalism. The novel demonstrates, he argues, that "we live in a contingent universe, that our lives are largely shaped and conditioned by the distinctive social context in which we find ourselves." "American Naturalism in its 'Perfected' State," in *The Age of Innocence: Complete Text with Introduction*, ed. Carol J. Singley, 439, 441.

39. Richard Dawkins, *The Selfish Gene* (Oxford and New York: Oxford University Press, 1989), 4. James A. Robinson observes that Archer's "society marshals all its forces ... to defeat him for his own good." "Psychological Determinism in *The Age of Innocence*," *The Markham Review* 5 (1975), 4. Readers have not been slow to note that the special companionship Archer enjoys with his eldest son serves as "a great compensation" for the sacrifice he has made in remaining with his wife. Olin-Ammentorp, *Edith Wharton's Writings from the Great War*, 176.

40. Readers have noted and commented on the strict demands for conformity to which Wharton's characters are subject. Ohler identifies "the true antagonist" in the novel as "the iron band of class-based rules, rituals, and linguistic practices which are regulative in their capacity to finally elevate the disenchanted Archer to his socially sanctioned roles of husband, father and politician." *Edith Wharton's "Evolutionary Conception,"* 180. Joslin similarly emphasizes that "characters are inextricably bound to [the customs] of their social group." *Edith Wharton*, 91. Drawing on psychoanalytic theory, Pamela Knights underscores Archer's position as a man facing diametrically opposed but equally unappealing alternatives: "to be locked in the family is to buried alive, but ... *loss* of social being is a form of death." "Forms of Disembodiment," 36.

41. Dawkins, *The Selfish Gene*, 149.

42. Killoran, *Art and Allusion*, 61.

43. Readers sometimes criticize Archer's refusal to seek a reunion with Ellen and rekindle their romance, ascribing his behavior to a variety of failings. David Holbrook finds, for example, that Archer is guilty of "cowardice" and lacking in manly ardor: "authenticity is baffled by the failure of the man to be full-blooded and committed." *Edith Wharton and the Unsatisfactory Man* (London: Vision, 1991; New York: St. Martin's, 1991), 120, 14. Joslin contends that Archer "never really wanted comradeship with a woman at all"; his life has been governed by "inertia." *Edith Wharton*, 106. In a similar vein, Jean Witherow argues that Archer "finally recognizes his desire as a fantasy" and realizes that Ellen "symbolizes the lack and failure that have comprised his life." "A Dialectic of Deception: Edith Wharton's *The Age of Innocence*." *Mosaic: A Journal for the Interdisciplinary Study of Literature* 36.3 (2003; ProQuest, Marist College Library). Ammons also judges Archer harshly: "he would rather continue to miss out on life than dare meet Ellen again." *Edith Wharton's Argument with America*, 152. Carol Wershoven suggests that Archer prefers imagined satisfactions to real ones: "the anticipation of a pleasure, the fantasy, is safer and more enjoyable than the realization (and risk) of the pleasure itself." *The Female Intruder in the Novels of Edith Wharton* (Rutherford: Fairleigh Dickinson University Press; London and Toronto: Associated University Presses, 1982), 90. Terrell Tebbetts condemns Archer as "a weak shadow of a man" who "does not deserve Ellen." "Conformity, Desire, and the Critical Self in Wharton's *The Age of Innocence*," *The Philological Review* 30.1 (2004), 36. Other readers respond more sympathetically to Archer's inaction. Wolff, for one, interprets his behavior as validation of the "commitments that have shaped his life for the intervening years.... If he can *now* find a viable world to share with Ellen, then he might have accepted his freedom thirty years before when May offered it." In refusing to visit Ellen, therefore, "he confirms the value of his own life as he has led it." *A Feast of Words*, 331, 333. James A. Robinson similarly maintains that Archer's refusal to visit Ellen constitutes "his first truly free

and moral act," an admission that renouncing her always was the right thing to do. "Psychological Determinism in *The Age of Innocence*," 4. John Arthos reviews the varied interpretations of Archer's "retreat" in detail, concluding that he indeed "sacrifices the reality to keep the dream, but in doing so he has kept the more real thing." "The Court of the Tuileries: Reflections on Archer's Retreat in *The Age of Innocence*," *Edith Wharton Review* 16.2 (2000), 12.

44. Carol J. Singley, for example, asserts that "we feel pity for his acquiescence to a stultifying and deadening existence ... but ... we also understand why he can do no better." "Bourdieu, Wharton and Changing Culture in *The Age of Innocence*," *Cultural Studies* 17.3–4 (2003), 514. Emily J. Orlando maintains that Archer attempts "desperately to preserve" his own "vision" of Ellen as his "only 'reality.'" He is, therefore, "a victim of his own illusions, his misperceptions." "Rereading Wharton's 'Poor Archer': A Mr. Might-Have-Been in *The Age of Innocence*," *American Literary Realism* 30.2 (1998), 72.

## Chapter 4

1. David M. Buss discusses mate selection criteria in chapters 2 and 3 of *The Evolution of Desire: Strategies of Human Mating* (New York: Basic Books, 2003), 19–48, 49–72.

2. Martin Daly and Margo Wilson, *Sex, Evolution, and Behavior*, 2nd ed. (Belmont, California: Wadsworth, 1983), 290; Buss, *The Evolution of Desire*, 221.

3. Robert Trivers, *Natural Selection and Social Theory: Selected Papers of Robert Trivers* (Oxford: Oxford University Press, 2002), 25.

4. Ibid., 34.

5. Lev Raphael analyzes Susy's and Nick's discomfort with reciprocal obligation in terms of shame. Their marriage, as he points out, "will *increase* their shame because it increases their dependence on the very people they have looked down on." *Edith Wharton's Prisoners of Shame: A New Perspective on Her Neglected Fiction* (New York: St. Martin's, 1991) 129.

6. Trivers analyzes cheating behavior as an inevitable hazard in reciprocal behavior. Because the benefits to be obtained by an undetected cheater can be significant, humans have developed complex adaptive mechanisms for keeping track of reciprocal transactions and identifying unreliable exchange partners. *Natural Selection and Social Theory*, 38–46.

7. Trivers considers the adaptive function of guilt in reciprocal partnerships in *Natural Selection and Social Theory*, 41–42. Dawkins discusses the penalties for defection in *The Selfish Gene* (Oxford and New York: Oxford University Press, 1989), 227–228.

8. Trivers comments on the negative impact of self-deception in *Natural Selection and Social Theory*, 286–290.

9. In Claire Preston's judgment, Nick is a "pompous, self-righteous cad, an opportunist and a hypocrite who affects ethical propriety without ever putting himself to the test, making Susy bear all the blame for the 'compromised' existence he has been content, heretofore, to lead." *Edith Wharton's Social Register* (Houndmills and London: Macmillan, 2000), 163.

10. See Buss, *The Evolution of Desire*, 10, 66–70, and Trivers, *Natural Selection and Social Theory*, 85, 102. Tricia M. Farwell accurately observes that Susy's complicity in Ellie's adulterous behavior "implies that Susy takes the marriage pact lightly and that she was not a pure, innocent woman." *Love and Death in Edith Wharton's Fiction* (New York: Peter Lang, 2006), 111.

11. Buss, *The Evolution of Desire*, 173.

12. Helen Killoran notes that Nick's and Susy's "bargain" presupposes "ignoring human experience of the marital bond." *Edith Wharton: Art and Allusion* (Tuscaloosa: University of Alabama Press, 1996), 72. Laura K. Johnson analyzes the problematic nature of the Lansings' marital experiment in the context of early twentieth-century marriage law. "Edith Wharton and the Fiction of Marital Unity." *Modern Fiction Studies* 47.4 (2001), 147–976.

13. Buss, *The Evolution of Desire*, 79.

14. Ibid., 266.

15. Ibid., 88.

16. Ibid., 86–87.

17. Ibid., 127.

18. Killoran argues that the masculinity of Coral's appearance is an indicator of lesbianism: she "is a homosexual woman" whose looks and dress resemble Picasso's famous *Portrait of Gertrude Stein*. *Art and Allusion*, 80. Certainly such speculation underlines Coral's deviation from typical standards of female beauty.

19. Buss, *The Evolution of Desire*, 53.

20. Buss summarizes female preferences in men's facial and bodily types in *The Evolution of Desire*, 39–40.

21. Ibid., 40–41, 48.

22. Robert Wright, *The Moral Animal: Evolutionary Psychology and Everyday Life* (New York: Vintage Books, 1995), 15.

23. Buss, *The Evolution of Desire*, 16.

24. Ibid., 179, 181.

25. Buss comments on the negative impact one partner's sexual disinterest tends to exert upon a marriage. *The Evolution of Desire*, 177.

26. Buss points out that the mate selection process involves assessment of one's own value, as well as that of potential partners. *The Evolution of Desire*, 88–89.

27. Cross-culturally and worldwide, Buss's re-

search shows, men seek evidence of premarital chastity in the women they choose as long-term mates. *The Evolution of Desire*, 66–69.

28. "Wharton's expatriate novels of the twenties are essentially about the contention between soul and purse," Claire Preston explains. Readers witness "the life-cycle of the nomadic rich," the "Playground Europe of F. Scott Fitzgerald." *Social Register*, 158, 162.

29. Preston accurately observes that characters in this novel never mention the war: they occupy "a moral and historical vacuum, in a Europe of expatriates on whose thoughts and conventions the war appears to have made no perceptible impact." *Social Register*, 159.

30. Wharton's "abiding love of Dante" expressed itself in numerous citations and allusions to his work, in her published writing as well as in her letters and diaries. R. W. B. Lewis, *Edith Wharton: A Biography* (New York: Harper and Row, 1975), 139. Hermione Lee notes that Wharton "did not just read Dante, she read a study of the *Paradiso*, and books on Dante and thirteenth-century Catholic philosophy." *Edith Wharton* (New York: Vintage Books, 2008), 102.

31. Buss demonstrates that female mate choice "involves at least a dozen distinctive preferences." *The Evolution of Desire*, 47.

32. Laura K. Johnson points out that "the Lansings' conscious choice to adopt transience as the condition of their life together makes them unwittingly vulnerable to the ceaseless but purposeless fluctuations of the modern world." "Edith Wharton and the Fiction of Marital Unity," *Modern Fiction Studies* 47.7 (2001), 962.

33. Buss explains how a change in one partner's mate value may have a negative impact upon a marriage, threatening its stability. *The Evolution of Desire*, 170–173.

34. Buss, *The Evolution of Desire*, 86–87.

35. Ibid., 22–25.

36. Farwell, *Love and Death*, 120.

37. Wolff finds the Lansings' shift to parental commitment unconvincing, as does Elizabeth Ammons. See *A Feast of Words*, 347, and *Edith Wharton's Argument with America* (Athens: University of Georgia Press, 1980), 161. Ammons is disappointed with what she takes to be Wharton's "conservative position on the woman issue," that is, with her apparent suggestion that "women are meant to be mothers," 160, 162. The conclusion of the novel does not imply, however, that Susy is "meant" to be a mother any more than that Nick is "meant" to be a father. The characters' realizations are biologically rooted and unconnected to gender roles: Nick and Susy have come to comprehend that reproduction, rather than wealth, is the goal driving mating behavior. Thus the novel need not be read as an "endorsement of motherhood," as Ammons supposes (185). It does not glorify patriarchal regulation of women's life

choices; rather, it validates behavioral choices, male *and* female, that enhance fitness.

38. Farwell, *Love and Death*, 103.

39. Buss, *The Evolution of Desire*, 22–25.

40. Johnson draws attention to the care Wharton takes to invest the Lansings' marriage with "a power of its own." "Edith Wharton and the Fiction of Marital Unity," 964.

41. The numerous parallels in situation and incident between *The Glimpses of the Moon* and *The House of Mirth* have generated considerable comment, both positive and negative. Wolff assumes that Wharton is borrowing from her earlier work "probably without entirely realizing it," and she judges Nick and Susy harshly as "almost caricatures of Seldon and Lily Bart." *A Feast of Words*, 346. Claire Preston labels *The Glimpses of the Moon* a "cruder copy of the earlier masterpiece." *Social Register*, 160. Marilyn Jones Lyde finds the novel "an attempt to retell the story of Lily Bart in terms of the gay and brittle postwar international set." *Edith Wharton: Convention and Morality in the Work of a Novelist* (Norman: University of Oklahoma Press, 1959), 170. Helen Killoran makes the case that Wharton has created an "intentional" structure of autoallusion "as a joke on the novel's theme of borrowing houses." *Art and Allusion*, 71. Lev Raphael argues that Wharton is simply following the line of inquiry begun in the 1905 novel, asking: "What would happen when two people heavily dependent on others for their pleasures get married? What are the costs, the challenges, the pressures of such a marriage?" *Prisoners of Shame*, 126.

42. As Preston aptly notes, "Susy's decision to work as a nurserymaid to a troop of children is the more promising equivalent of Lily Bart's last acts — writing out the cheques to pay her final debts and futilely hallucinating herself nurturing new life." *Social Register*, 164.

43. See Julie Olin-Ammentorp's comments in *Edith Wharton's Writings from the Great War* (Gainesville: University Press of Florida, 2004), especially 11 and 233–234.

44. Farwell, *Love and Death*, 121. Raphael, too, finds Nick's reasoning "in no way commendable": "we know," for instance, that his "perception of his own superiority is false; because Susy was so keenly aware of Strefford's humiliation, it seems unlikely that she would forget him." *Prisoners of Shame*, 137.

45. Intersexual conflict occurs when the mating strategies of one sex interfere with those of the other. Buss analyzes such conflict in Chapter 7 of *The Evolution of Desire*, 142–167.

46. Farwell discusses the effect of the moon imagery on the novel's conclusion, emphasizing its role in qualifying the happy resolution of the protagonists' difficulties. *Love and Death*, 121.

## Chapter 5

1. David M. Buss, *The Evolution of Desire: Strategies of Human Mating* (New York: Basic Books, 2003), 218, 170–171.

2. Ibid., 121.

3. Catherine Salmon, "Parental Investment and Parent-Offspring Conflict," in *The Handbook of Evolutionary Psychology*, ed. David M. Buss (Hoboken, New Jersey: John Wiley & Sons, 2005), 508.

4. Richard Dawkins speaks to this point: "If a female can somehow detect good genes in males ... she can benefit her own genes by allying them with good paternal genes." *The Selfish Gene* (Oxford and New York: Oxford University Press, 1989), 157.

5. Buss notes that "it is theoretically possible for women to gain superior genes which are passed on to their children." *The Evolution of Desire*, 90.

6. Joseph Carroll describes how "humans create elaborate mental models of the world and make decisions on the basis of alternative scenarios that present themselves within those modes.... The materials available to the mind and imagination are vast, and the combination of those materials virtually infinite. The possibility for error, uncertainty, and confusion is an ever-present fact of mental life." "Human Nature and Literary Meaning: A Theoretical Model Illustrated with a Critique of *Pride and Prejudice*," in *Literary Darwinism: Evolution, Human Nature, and Literature* (New York: Routledge, 2004), 198.

7. Lev Raphael addresses this issue: "Though smugly superior to Charlotte, her poor cousin, Delia ... also feels deeply and consistently inferior — and that bifurcation will mark their relationship." *Edith Wharton's Prisoners of Shame: A New Perspective on Her Neglected Fiction* (New York: St. Martin's, 1991), 100.

8. Buss, *The Evolution of Desire*, 22.

9. "Clocks and Mirrors, Dreams and Destinies: Edith Wharton's *The Old Maid*," in *Edith Wharton: New Critical Essays*, ed. Alfred Bendixen and Annette Zilversmit (New York and London: Garland Publishing, 1992), 152.

10. Buss discusses female implementation of such a "dual strategy." *The Evolution of Desire*, 90–91.

11. Ibid., 66–70.

12. Ibid., 67, 215.

13. Dawkins discusses behavioral consequences of kin selection at great length in Chapter 6 of *The Selfish Gene,* "Genesmanship," 88–108.

14. "At this point in the novella, Wharton puts Delia in full control of the situation, vesting in her powers denied to the men concerned," Catherine M. Rae observes. "Rapidly emerg[ing] as an accomplished schemer and manipulator,"

Delia ensures that "Charlotte must pay and pay for her night of passion with Clem Spender — to Delia." "Edith Wharton's Avenging Angel in the House," *Denver Quarterly* 18.4 (1984), 122, 121, 122. "Delia's power stems from her socially superior and secure position," Jessica Levine accurately explains; "she is by birth, marriage, wealth, and reputation advantageously placed to assume control of the situation." "Discretion and Self-Censorship in Wharton's Fiction: 'The Old Maid' and the Politics of Publishing," in *Edith Wharton Review* 13.1 (1996), 7.

15. Robert Trivers, *Natural Selection and Social Theory: Selected Papers of Robert Trivers* (Oxford: Oxford University Press, 2002), 276.

16. Delia interprets Tina as a new and fresh version of "her own girlish self," Funston emphasizes, and the girl is therefore "a means by which Delia can experience without inhibition the buried passion of her youth." "Clocks and Mirrors," 150. Cynthia Griffin Wolff similarly identifies Tina with "hope for the future, hope that a beloved someone will enjoy the opportunities that Delia has relinquished." *A Feast of Words: The Triumph of Edith Wharton* (New York: Oxford University Press, 1976), 355.

17. For a fuller discussion of Charlotte's motives in assuming the social role of "old maid," see Judith P. Saunders, "Becoming the Mask: Edith Wharton's Ingenues," *Massachusetts Studies in English* 8.4 (1982). Susan Goodman speculates that Charlotte derives "a covert and superior pleasure" from hiding her persona behind an assumed social role. Given the bitterly accusatory scenes between Charlotte and Delia, however, it is difficult to believe that "hiding the fact of her actual relationship to Tina adds a poignant and enriching resonance to [Charlotte's] life." *Edith Wharton's Women: Friends and Rivals* (Hanover and London: University Press of New England, 1990), 117, 116.

18. Salmon, 508.

19. "An unspoken premiss of the story is Delia's sexual jealousy of Charlotte, who took for herself what Delia was afraid to have," as Claire Preston succinctly explains. *Edith Wharton's Social Register* (Houndmills and London: Macmillan, 2000), 16.

20. Edward O. Wilson's discussion of "gene-culture coevolution" is helpful in understanding Delia's self-deceiving reinterpretation of reality. *Consilience: The Unity of Knowledge* (New York: Alfred A. Knopf, 1998), 127. See especially Chapter 10, "The Arts and Their Interpretation," 210–237.

21. As Funston comments, "Delia's quest for fulfillment through an adopted daughter is clearly inadequate." "Clocks and Mirrors," 157.

22. Funston maintains with justice that Charlotte "is not blameless." She, too, has utilized manipulative means to secure her own ends and is responsible (as she herself admits) for "having set

up Delia to interfere" in her own and Tina's lives. "Clocks and Mirrors," 149, 156.

23. Funston does not regard either protagonist as victorious: Charlotte has become "pitiable" and stunted in her role as old maid, while Delia remains unable to express erotic passion except vicariously, through her identification with Tina. "Clocks and Mirrors," 149. Linda Costanzo Cahir similarly argues that both women have been vanquished: Delia forfeits "life" and her most "vibrant aspirations," while Charlotte experiences "an unredemptive death in life." "Wharton and the Age of Film," in *A Historical Guide to Edith Wharton*, ed. Carol J. Singley (Oxford: Oxford University Press, 2003), 216.

24. "In her one bold, unnarrated, sexual pursuit of Clem Spender," as Cahir notes, Charlotte "rebelled against the sentimental ethos that condemns such behavior in women." "Wharton and the Age of Film," 216.

25. Rae, for one, observes that Wharton's portrait of Delia must be understood as an "attack on the accepted version of sheltered womanhood." "Edith Wharton's Avenging Angel in the House," 121.

26. R.W.B. Lewis explains that the novella was rejected by a number of publishers precisely because it broached topics perceived as "powerful" and "unpleasant." *Edith Wharton: A Biography* (New York: Harper and Row, 1975), 435–436. Levine discusses in detail "the contemporary publishing scene" and its resistance to tales of sexual misconduct. "Discretion and Self-Censorship in Wharton's Fiction," 11.

27. Buss, *The Evolution of Desire*, 22–25.

28. Buss observes that when women enjoy economic independence from men, the incidence of premarital sex increases. *The Evolution of Desire*, 69.

29. For an extended discussion of the ormulu clock, see Funston's essay, "Clocks and Mirrors," 147–149. Funston comments that the clock "is Delia's sole link to the pastoral world of her youthful daydreams, where desires are frankly expressed and satisfied, a world having little connection to ... the kind of life Delia is expected to live in old New York." 147–148.

30. "High dominance traits are ... associated with male promiscuity," as Daniel J. Kruger, Maryanne Fisher, and Ian Jobling observe. "The cues that make cads attractive as sexual partners are, by design, difficult to fake." Thus "a male who pursues a cad strategy without the requisite indicators of genetic fitness may not find much success." "Proper Hero Dads and Dark Hero Cads: Alternate Mating Strategies Exemplified in British Romantic Literature," in *The Literary Animal: Evolution and the Nature of Narrative*, ed. Jonathan Gottschall and David Sloan Wilson (Evanston, Illinois: Northwestern University Press, 2005), 229, 228.

31. Dawkins, *The Selfish Gene*, 158.

32. Raphael, *Edith Wharton's Prisoners of Shame*, 103.

33. Wolff finds that "each life is bitterly incomplete." *A Feast of Words*, 357. An evolutionary perspective leads to a less bleak summing up. Each woman's destiny necessarily is shaped by the mating and reproductive choices she has made — choices entailing costs as well as benefits. To exercise one strategic option, furthermore, is to forego others. In the social environment of old New York, women are strongly discouraged from exercising a mixed reproductive strategy, and in this sense the range of their behavioral options indeed may be regarded as "incomplete." As Claire Preston states, "each pays the price of her choice with a torment: Charlotte's, the agony of unacknowledged motherhood; Delia's, the disturbing sense of being a stranger to her own life ... constantly ambushed by the clandestine world of feelings she can hardly articulate even to herself." *Edith Wharton's Social Register*, 16.

34. Because the narrator does not overtly "chastise" Delia for her repeated interference in Charlotte's life, Funston assumes that Wharton's assessment of Delia's culpability is relatively sympathetic. "Clocks and Mirrors," 149. There is discernible irony, however, in the presentation of Delia's self-justifying self-analyses. Cahir points out in this context that the "departure kiss" Delia commands Tina to bestow upon Charlotte is "ostensibly touching" but in fact "patronizing and darkly ironic." "Wharton and the Age of Film," 216.

35. Buss, *The Evolution of Desire*, 122.

36. Lawrence L. Berkove, "'Roman Fever': A Mortal Malady," *CEA Critic* 56.2 (1994), 59.

37. Berkove notes the "primitive motives" and "deception" at work, as well as the "serious" nature of the "offences" committed by the women in the story. He interprets their behavior as a moral failure (and "the natural human tendency to savagery") rather than as fitness-directed competition for a superior mate. "'Roman Fever': A Mortal Malady," 59, 56, 60.

38. Buss, *The Evolution of Desire*, 9.

39. Ibid., 8–9.

40. Bowlby goes on to claim that it is the female characters, "not the husbands or boyfriends, who control what happens," in "'I Had Barbara': Women's Ties and Wharton's 'Roman Fever,'" *Differences: A Journal of Feminist Cultural Studies* 17.5 (2006), 44. Dale M. Bauer similarly argues that "it depends upon rivalry between the women ... to determine who gets the community 'prize' — the husband." "Edith Wharton's 'Roman Fever': A Rune of History," *College English* 50.6 (1988), 688. Such assertions seem to overstate the case: Delphin Slade plays a decisive role in choosing which of the two young women to marry.

41. Kruger, Fisher, and Jobling suggest that in

"a resource-rich environment," children sired by philanderers have a particularly good chance of survival. "Proper Hero Dads and Dark Hero Cads," 226.

42. Buss, *The Evolution of Desire*, 94.

43. Dawkins, *The Selfish Gene*, 158.

44. Berkove argues that since Jenny and Barbara have the same father, "the genetic difference" between them must be attributed to their mothers. He concludes, therefore, that Jenny's lack of 'brilliance' "reflects negatively on [Alida's] contribution." "'Roman Fever': A Mortal Malady," 158. From a purely biological standpoint, this analysis cannot be correct. It is true that each daughter derives half of her genes from Delphin, but very likely the two girls did not end up with exactly the same set. A father contributes copies of half of his genes to each daughter, but not necessarily the same half, so that he is making a different paternal contribution in each case. Bowlby also draws attention to the "anomalously quiet daughter" born to the Slades, suggesting that the story quietly raises a number of never settled "kinship questions." "'I Had Barbara': Women's Ties and Wharton's 'Roman Fever,'" 46. From a Darwinian perspective, the striking differences between Jenny and her parents simply underscore the randomness of genetic reshuffling in sexual reproduction.

45. "We can regard animals as gamblers," Dawkins suggests. Any reproductive gamble that "*might* have paid off" in existing circumstances represents an evolutionarily viable option for the individual choosing it. *The Selfish Gene*, 118, 119.

46. Bauer argues that the two women are treated as "socially interchangeable" in the contested role of "prospective wife for Delphin Slade"; "for Delphin, it seems, one woman is as good as another." As a result, "competition is forced upon women as a means of escaping their identical status as signs." "Edith Wharton's 'Roman Fever': A Rune of History," *College English* 50.6 (1988), 688. In the end, Delphin does choose between the two women, of course, employing criteria readers can infer from textual details. To say that intrasexual competition is socially imposed, or influenced, may be accurate up to a point, but there is good evidence for regarding such competition from an evolutionary biological perspective, as an adaptation.

47. Buss discusses the costs of casual sex, pointing out that "women risk impairing their desirability if they develop reputations for promiscuity since men prize fidelity in potential wives." *The Evolution of Desire*, 92.

48. The problem of paternal confidence and possible misallocation of male resources is widely discussed in scientific literature. See Trivers, *Natural Selection and Social Theory*, 76, and Buss, *The Evolution of Desire*, 66–67. Among Wharton critics, Berkove raises the issue of Horace Ansley's

apparently passive acquiescence in a scheme that threatens his own fitness: "one wonders what sort of man he was either not to have been aware ... or not to have minded." "'Roman Fever': A Mortal Malady," 59. Bowlby comments that "Horace is merely the accessory groomed for a mother's swiftly pragmatic arrangement of a daughter's wedding." "'I Had Barbara': Women's Ties and Wharton's 'Roman Fever,'" 44.

49. Trivers, *Natural Selection and Social Theory*, 65–67.

50. Dawkins, *The Selfish Gene*, 158–160.

51. Berkove comments on the ethical implications of Delphin's behavior, suggesting that his willingness to rendezvous with Grace casts doubt on the genuineness of his love for Alida. "'Roman Fever': A Mortal Malady," 59.

52. By the end of the story, as Bowlby observes, a subtle power shift has occurred between the two protagonists. It is Grace Ansley, "previously seen as the more timid and passive of the two," who "'begins to move ahead of Mrs. Slade'" as they walk toward the exit" (RF 239). "'I Had Barbara': Women's Ties in Wharton's 'Roman Fever,'" 38–39. Grace's "newly dominant status is signified by changed body language." Alice Hall Petry, "A Twist of Crimson Silk: Edith Wharton's 'Roman Fever,'" *Studies in Short Fiction* 24.2 (1987), 166.

53. Readers have focused much attention on the story's structure, demonstrating that its form supports its theme satisfyingly. Armine Kotin Mortimer draws an elaborate parallel between the suppressed secret of Barbara's paternity and the "submerged" story line that erupts into the surface narrative: "it is the function of the first story to create before the reader the entire second story, insinuated into the devious structures of the first." "Romantic Fever: The Second Story as Illegitimate Daughter in Wharton's 'Roman Fever,'" 188, 191. Bowlby offers an intriguing analysis of parallels between "Roman Fever" and *Oedipus the King*: both are tales of illicit sexuality and mistaken paternity; both investigate "ancient events, showing their significance to be quite different from what participants had imagined." "'I Had Barbara': Women's Ties and Wharton's 'Roman Fever,'" 41.

## Chapter 6

1. For detailed discussion of W. D. Hamilton's theory of kin selection and nepotistic strategy, see Richard Dawkins, *The Selfish Gene* (Oxford and New York: Oxford University Press, 1989), 89–108. Dawkins's discussion of parental investment as an example of kin selection is especially useful (107–08).

2. The environment is "aberrant" in the sense of being extraordinarily unlike that of the so-

called EEA, the environment in which our human ancestors evolved in and in which they consequently were designed to thrive. In Robert Storey's phrasing, the twentieth-century individual is a composite of "various psychological adaptations to an ancient environment that no longer exists." *Mimesis and the Human Animal: On the Biogenetic Foundations of Literary Representation* (Evanston, Illinois: Northwestern University Press, 1996), xix.

3. Blake Nevius, *Edith Wharton: A Study of Her Fiction* (Berkeley: University of California Press, 1953), 213.

4. Elizabeth Ammons examines the cultural-historical implications of Wharton's "indictment of negligent flapper mothers" in *Edith Wharton's Argument with America* (Athens: University of Georgia Press, 1980), 165. It should be noted, however, that the novel provides an equally powerful portrait of negligent fathers.

5. Martin Daly and Margo Wilson, *Sex, Evolution, and Behavior,* 2nd ed. (Belmont, California: Wadsworth, 1983), 306–307.

6. Robert Trivers, *Natural Selection and Social Theory: Selected Papers of Robert Trivers* (Oxford: Oxford University Press, 2002), 143–144.

7. Margaret B. McDowell, *Edith Wharton* (Boston: Twayne, 1991), 120.

8. Dawkins discusses "big sister altruistic behavior" in *The Selfish Gene,* 93–94.

9. Charles Mills Gayley, *The Classic Myths in English Literature* (Boston: Ginn, 1893), 255.

10. Nancy Bentley, "Wharton, Travel, and Modernity," in *A Historical Guide to Edith Wharton,* ed. Carol J. Singley (Oxford: Oxford University Press, 2003), 173.

11. Carol Wershoven, *The Female Intruder in the Novels of Edith Wharton* (Rutherford: Fairleigh Dickinson University Press, 1982; London and Toronto: Associated University Presses, 1982), 111.

12. Brett Cooke, "Biopoetics: The New Synthesis," in *Biopoetics: Evolutionary Explorations in the Arts,* ed. Brett Cooke and Frederick Turner (Lexington, Kentucky: ICUS, 1999), 17, 18.

13. Helen Killoran attempts to interpret this set of outcomes as benign: "most of the children are safe." *Edith Wharton: Art and Allusion* (Tuscaloosa: University of Alabama Press, 1996), 142. Such a reading seems scarcely tenable in light of the horrifying details Wharton offers.

14. Nancy Easterlin, "Do Cognitive Predispositions Predict or Determine Literary Value Judgments? Narrativity, Plot, and Aesthetics," in *Biopoetics,* 243, 246.

15. Storey, *Mimesis and the Human Animal,* 134.

16. Julie Olin-Ammentorp, "Martin Boyne and the 'Warm Animal Life' of *The Children,*" *Edith Wharton Review* 12.1 (1995), 15.

17. See David M. Buss, *The Evolution of De-*

sire: *Strategies of Human Mating* (New York: Basic Books, 2003), 36–37.

18. Thomas Bullfinch, *Bullfinch's Greek and Roman Mythology* (New York: Dover, 2000), 17.

19. See Ammons's analysis (1980) of "the mythicized image of the American child-woman" for discussion of Boyne's dilemma in a wider context, *Argument with America,* 176.

20. See Olin-Ammentorp, "Martin Boyne and the 'Warm Animal Life' of *The Children,*" 16.

21. Edward O. Wilson, *Sociobiology: The New Synthesis* (Cambridge, Massachusetts: Belknap, 1975), 350.

22. Marriages (whether merely contemplated or actually achieved) between male alloparental figures and their female protégés are commonplace in both popular and high literature — from Webster's *Daddy-Long-Legs* or Gilbert's *Mikado* to Austen's *Mansfield Park* and Wharton's own *Summer.*

23. Daly and Wilson, *Sex, Evolution, and Behavior,* 304–307.

24. Ammons, *Edith Wharton's Argument with America,* 77.

25. Claire Preston, *Edith Wharton's Social Register* (Houndmills and London: Macmillan, 2000), 166.

26. Dawkins, *The Selfish Gene,* 163.

27. Quoted in Cynthia Griffin Wolff, *A Feast of Words: The Triumph of Edith Wharton* (New York: Oxford University Press, 1977), 381.

28. Ammons, *Edith Wharton's Argument with America,* 182.

29. Susan Goodman, *Edith Wharton's Women: Friends and Rivals* (Hanover and London: University Press of New England, 1990), 122, 121.

30. See Lev Raphael, *Edith Wharton's Prisoners of Shame: A New Perspective on Her Neglected Fiction* (New York: St Martin's, 1991), 82–85.

31. Judith L. Sensibar argues that Boyne's behavior displays "erotic immaturity." "Edith Wharton Reads the Bachelor Type: Her Critique of Modernism's Representative Man," *American Literature* 60.4 (1988), 375. Biosocial analysis nevertheless shows him making adaptive choices, in context, with the possible exception of his rejection of Judith as a long-term partner. That decision, arguably, may be viewed as altruistic rather than immature.

32. Wolff, *A Feast of Words,* 381.

33. Storey, *Mimesis and the Human Animal,* 177.

## Conclusion

1. Carol J. Singley, *Edith Wharton: Matters of Mind and Spirit* (Cambridge: Cambridge University Press, 1995), 65.

2. Joseph Carroll, *Literature and Evolutionary Theory* (Columbia: University of Missouri Press, 1995), 2.

3. Edward O, Wilson, *Consilience: The Unity of Knowledge* (New York: Alfred A. Knopf, 1988), 166.

4. Ibid., 172.

5. Ibid., 167–168, 168.

6. Judith E. Funston, "Clocks and Mirrors, Dreams and Destinies: Edith Wharton's *The Old Maid*," in *Edith Wharton: New Critical Essays*, ed. Alfred Bendixen and Annette Zilversmit (New York and London: Garland, 1992), 143–157.

7. Buss, *Evolution and Desire: Strategies of Human Mating* (New York: Basic Books, 2003), 78–79.

8. Ibid., 79.

9. Ibid., 47–48, 57.

10. Ibid., 87–89.

11. Linda Costanzo Cahir, "Wharton and the Age of Film," in *A Historical Guide to Edith Wharton*, ed. Carol J. Singley (Oxford: Oxford University Press, 2003), 216, 217.

12. Buss, *Evolution and Desire*, 151.

13. Ibid., 147–148.

14. Ibid., 66–70.

15. Ibid., 153–156.

16. Ibid., 105, 121–122.

17. Ibid., 105.

18. Ibid., 78–81.

19. Robert Trivers, *Natural Selection and Social Theory: Selected Papers of Robert Trivers* (Oxford: Oxford University Press, 2002), 273.

20. Trivers points out that a "major source of self-deception has to do with self-promotion, self-exaggeration on the positive side, denial on the negative," to create and sustain a positive image of the self. *Natural Selection and Social Theory*, 275.

21. One significant cost of self-deception, Trivers observes, "is an impaired ability to deal with reality." *Natural Selection and Social Theory*, 263.

22. "Evolutionary theory promises to provide a firm foundation for a science of self-deception," Trivers anticipates, "which should eventually be able to predict both the circumstances expected to induce greater self-deception and the particular forms of self-deception being induced." *Natural Selection and Social Theory*, 290.

# Works Cited

Ammons, Elizabeth. *Edith Wharton's Argument with America*. Athens: University of Georgia Press, 1980.

_____. "Fairy-Tale Love and *The Reef*." In *Edith Wharton: Modern Critical Views*. Ed. Harold Bloom. New York: Chelsea House Publishers, 1986. 39–50.

Arthos, John. "The Court of the Tuileries: Reflections on Archer's Retreat in *The Age of Innocence*," *Edith Wharton Review* 16.2 (2000): 8–13.

Bauer, Dale M. *Edith Wharton's Brave New Politics*. Madison: University of Wisconsin Press, 1994.

_____. "Edith Wharton's 'Roman Fever': A Rune of History." *College English* 50.6 (1988): 681–693.

_____. *Feminist Dialogics*. Albany: State University of New York Press, 1988.

Bell, Millicent. *The Cambridge Companion to Edith Wharton*. Cambridge: Cambridge University Press, 1995.

Bender, Bert. *The Descent of Love: Darwin and the Theory of Sexual Selection in American Fiction 1871–1926*. Philadelphia: University of Pennsylvania Press, 1996.

Bendixen, Alfred, and Annette Zilversmit, eds. *Edith Wharton: New Critical Essays*. New York and London: Garland Publishing, 1992.

Benstock, Shari. "'The Word Which Made All Clear': The Silent Close of *The House of Mirth*." In *Edith Wharton's* The House of Mirth: *A Casebook*. Ed. Carol J. Singley. Oxford and New York: Oxford University Press, 203. 131–162. First published in *Famous Last Words: Changes in Gender and Narrative Closure*, ed. Allison Booth. Charlottesville: University of Virginia Press, 1993. 230–258.

Bentley, Nancy. "Wharton, Travel, and Modernity." In *A Historical Guide to Edith Wharton*. Ed. Carol J. Singley. Oxford: Oxford University Press, 2003. 147–179.

Berkove, Lawrence L. "'Roman Fever': A Mortal Malady." *CEA Critic* 56.2 (1994): 55–60.

Blair, Amy L. "Misreading *The House of Mirth*." *American Literature* 76.1 (2004): 149–175.

Bloom, Harold, ed. *Edith Wharton: Modern Critical Views*. New York: Chelsea House Publishers, 1986.

Bowlby, Rachel. "'I Had Barbara': Women's Ties and Wharton's 'Roman Fever.'" *Differences: A Journal of Feminist Cultural Studies* 17.5 (2006): 37–51.

Boyd, Brian. "Evolutionary Theories of Art." In *The Literary Animal*. Ed. Jonathan Gottschall and David Sloan Wilson. Evanston, Illinois: Northwestern University Press, 2005. 147–176.

Bullfinch, Thomas. *Bullfinch's Greek and Roman Mythology: The Age of Fable*. Reprint: New York: Dover, 2000.

Buss, David M. *The Evolution of Desire: Strategies of Human Mating*. 1994. Revised Edition: New York: Basic Books, 2003.

_____. *Evolutionary Psychology: The New Science of the Mind*. Boston: Pearson, 2004.

_____, ed. *The Handbook of Evolutionary Psychology*. Hoboken, New Jersey: John Wiley & Sons, 2005.

_____, and Neil M. Malamuth, eds. *Sex, Power, Conflict: Evolutionary Theory and Feminist Perspectives*. New York and Oxford: Oxford University Press, 1996.

_____. "Sexual Conflict: Evolutionary Insights into Feminism and the 'Battle of the Sexes.'" In *Sex, Power, Conflict*. Ed. David M. Buss and Neil M. Malamuth. New York and Oxford: Oxford University Press, 1996. 296–318.

Cahir, Linda Costanzo. "Wharton and the Age of Film." In *A Historical Guide to Edith Wharton*.

Ed. Carol J. Singley. Oxford: Oxford University Press, 2003. 211–228.

Campbell, Anne. *A Mind of Her Own: The Evolutionary Psychology of Women.* Oxford: Oxford University Press, 2002.

Carroll, Joseph. *Evolution and Literary Theory.* Columbia: University of Missouri Press, 1995.

_____. *Literary Darwinism: Evolution, Human Nature, and Literature.* New York: Routledge, 2004.

_____. "Literature and Evolutionary Psychology." In *The Handbook of Evolutionary Psychology.* Ed. David M. Buss. Hoboken. New Jersey: John Wiley & Sons, 1995, 931–952.

Colombe, Joseph. "Man or Mannequin? Lawrence Seldon in *The House of Mirth.*" *Edith Wharton Review* 13.2 (1996): 3–8.

Cooke, Brett. "Biopoetics: The New Synthesis." In *Biopoetics: Evolutionary Explorations in the Arts.* Ed. Brett Cooke and Frederick Turner. Lexington, Kentucky: ICUS, 1999. 3–25.

_____, and Frederick Turner, eds. *Biopoetics: Evolutionary Explorations in the Arts.* Lexington, Kentucky: ICUS, 1999.

Cowley, Geoffrey. "The Biology of Beauty." *Newsweek,* 3 June 1996, 61–66.

Daly, Martin, and Margo Wilson. *Sex, Evolution, and Behavior.* 2$^{nd}$ ed. Belmont, California: Wadsworth, 1983.

Davidson, Cathy N. "Kept Women in *The House of Mirth.*" *Markham Review* 9 (1979): 10–13.

Dawkins, Richard. *The Selfish Gene.* 1976. Revised Edition: Oxford and New York: Oxford University Press, 1989.

Dimock, Wai-Chee. "Debasing Exchange: Edith Wharton's *The House of Mirth.*" *PMLA* 100 (1985): 783–792.

Dissanayake, Ellen. *Art and Intimacy: How the Arts Began.* Seattle: University of Washington Press, 2000.

_____. *Homo Aestheticus: Where Art Comes From and Why.* Seattle: University of Washington Press, 1995.

_____. *What Is Art For?* Seattle: University of Washington Press, 1988.

Easterlin, Nancy. "Do Cognitive Predispositions Predict or Determine Literary Value Judgements?" In *Biopoetics.* Ed. Brett Cooke and Frederick Turner. Lexington, Kentucky: ICUS, 1999. 241–282.

Edwards, Brian T. "The Well-Built Wall of Culture: Old New York and Its Harems." In *The Age of Innocence: Authoritative Text, Background and Contexts, Sources, Criticism.* Ed. Candace Waid. New York and London: W.W. Norton, 2003. 482–506.

Esch, Deborah, ed. *New Essays on* The House of Mirth. The American Novel. Cambridge: Cambridge University Press, 2001.

Faery, Rebecca Blevins. "Wharton's *Reef*: The Inscription of Female Sexuality." In *Edith Wharton: New Critical Essays.* Ed. Alfred Bendixen and Annette Zilversmit. New York: Garland Publishing, 1992. 79–96.

Farwell, Tricia M. *Love and Death in Edith Wharton's Fiction.* New York: Peter Lang, 2006.

Faulkner, Jason, and Mark Schaller. "Nepotistic Nosiness: Inclusive Fitness and Vigilance of Kin Members' Romantic Relationships." *Evolution and Human Behavior* 28.6 (2007): 430–438.

Fetterley, Judith. "'The Temptation to be a Beautiful Object': Double Standard and Double Bind in *The House of Mirth.*" *Studies in American Fiction* 5 (1977): 199–211.

Fryer, Judith. "Purity and Power in *The Age of Innocence.*" In *Edith Wharton: Modern Critical Views.* Ed. Harold Bloom. New York: Chelsea House Publishers, 1986. 99–115.

Funston, Judith E. "Clocks and Mirrors, Dreams and Destinies: Edith Wharton's *The Old Maid.*" In *Edith Wharton: New Critical Essays.* Ed. Alfred Bendixen and Annette Zilversmit. New York and London: Garland Publishing, 1992. 143–157.

Gargano, James W. "Edith Wharton's *The Reef*: The Genteel Woman's Quest for Knowledge." *Novel: A Forum on Fiction* 10 (1976): 40–48.

Gayley, Charles Mills. *The Classic Myths in English Literature.* Boston: Ginn, 1893.

Gilbert, Sandra M., and Susan Gubar. "Angel of Devastation: Edith Wharton on the Arts of the Enslaved." In *No Man's Land: The Place of the Woman Writer in the Twentieth Century.* Vol. 2, *Sexchanges.* New Haven and London: Yale University Press, 1989. 123–168.

Goodman, Susan. *Edith Wharton's Women: Friends and Rivals.* Hanover and London: University Press of New England, 1990.

Goodwyn, Janet. *Edith Wharton: Traveler in the Land of Letters.* New York: St. Martin's Press, 1990.

Gottschall, Jonathan, and David Sloan Wilson. *The Literary Animal: Evolution and the Nature of Narrative.* Evanston, Illinois: Northwestern University Press, 2005.

Hadley, Kathy Miller. "Ironic Structure and Untold Stories in *The Age of Innocence.*" *Studies in the Novel* 23.2 (1991): 262–272.

Holbrook, David. *Edith Wharton and the Unsatisfactory Man.* London: Vision Press, 1991; New York: St. Martin's Press, 1991.

Howard, Maureen. "*The House of Mirth*: The Bachelor and the Baby." In *The Cambridge Companion to Edith Wharton.* Ed. Millicent Bell. Cambridge: Cambridge University Press, 1995. 137–156.

Howe, Irving, ed. *Edith Wharton: A Collection of Critical Essays.* Englewood Cliffs: Prentice-Hall, 1962.

Hrdy, Sarah Blaffer. *Mother Nature: A History of*

*Mothers, Infants, and Natural Selection.* New York: Pantheon, 1999.

Hyde, Janet Shibley. "Where Are the Gender Differences? Where Are the Gender Similarities?" In *Sex, Power, Conflict.* Ed. David M. Buss and Neil M. Malamuth. New York and Oxford: Oxford University Press, 1996. 107–118.

Johnson, Laura K. "Edith Wharton and the Fiction of Marital Unity." *Modern Fiction Studies* 47.4 (2001): 947–976.

Jones, Wendell, Jr. "Holding up the Revealing Lamp: The Myth of Psyche in Edith Wharton's *The Reef*." *College Literature* 19.1 (1992): 75–90.

Joslin, Katherine. *Edith Wharton.* Women Writers. New York: St. Martin's Press, 1991.

Kaye, Rickard A. "Edith Wharton and the 'New Gomorrahs' of Paris: Homosexuality, Flirtation, and Incestuous Desire in *The Reef*." *MFS: Modern Fiction Studies* 43.4 (1997): 860–897.

_____. *The Flirt's Tragedy: Desire Without End in Victorian and Edwardian Fiction.* Charlottesville: University of Virginia Press, 2002.

Keats, John. "Ode on a Grecian Urn." 1819, 1820. In *English Romantic Writers.* Ed. David Perkins. New York: Harcourt, Brace and World, 1967. 1186–1187.

Kellogg, Grace. *The Two Lives of Edith Wharton: The Woman and Her Work.* New York: Appleton-Century, 1965.

Kenrick, Douglas T., Melanie R. Trost, and Virgil L. Sheets. "Power, Harassment, and Trophy Mates: The Feminist Advantages of an Evolutionary Perspective." In *Sex, Power, Conflict.* Ed. David M. Buss and Neil M. Malamuth. New York and Oxford: Oxford University Press, 1996. 29–53.

Keyser, Elizabeth Lennox. "'The Ways in Which the Heart Speaks': Letters in *The Reef*." *Studies in American Fiction* 19.1 (1991): 95–106.

Killoran, Helen. *Edith Wharton: Art and Allusion.* Tuscaloosa: University of Alabama Press, 1996.

Kim, Sharon. "Larmarckism and the Construction of Transcendence in *The House of Mirth*." *Studies in the Novel* 38.2 (2006): 187–210.

Knights, Pamela. "Forms of Disembodiment: The Social Subject in *The Age of Innocence*." In *The Cambridge Companion to Edith Wharton.* Ed. Millicent Bell. Cambridge: Cambridge University Press, 1995. 20–46.

Kruger, Daniel J., Maryanne Fisher, and Ian Jobling. "Proper Hero Dads and Dark Hero Cads: Alternate Mating Strategies Exemplified in British Romantic Literature." In *The Literary Animal.* Ed. Jonathan Gottschall and David Sloan Wilson. Evanston, Illinois: Northwestern University Press, 2005. 225–243.

Lee, Hermione. *Edith Wharton.* New York: Vintage Books, 2008.

Levine, Jessica. "Discretion and Self-Censorship in Wharton's Fiction: 'The Old Maid' and the Politics of Publishing." *Edith Wharton Review* 13.1 (1996): 4–13.

Lewis, R.W.B. *Edith Wharton: A Biography.* New York: Harper and Row, 1975.

_____, and Nancy Lewis. *The Letters of Edith Wharton.* New York: Charles Scribner's Sons, 1988.

Lidoff, Joan. "Another Sleeping Beauty: Narcissism in *The House of Mirth*." In *Edith Wharton's* The House of Mirth: *A Casebook.* Ed. Carol J. Singley. Oxford and New York: Oxford University Press, 2003. 181–207.

Loebel, Thomas. "Beyond Her Self." In *New Essays on* The House of Mirth. Ed. Deborah Esch. Cambridge: Cambridge University Press, 2001. 107–132.

Lyde, Marilyn Jones. *Edith Wharton: Convention and Morality in the Work of a Novelist.* Norman: University of Oklahoma Press, 1959.

MacMaster, Anne. "Re-Scripting the Romance: Edith Wharton's Paired Heroines." *Furman Studies* N.S. 37 (1995): 29–44.

MacNaughton, William R. "Edith Wharton, *The Reef* and Henry James." *American Literary Realism* 26.2 (1994): 43–59.

_____. "Edith Wharton's 'Bad Heroine': Sophy Viner in *The Reef*." *Studies in The Novel* 25.2 (1993): 213–225.

_____. "Edith Wharton's *The Reef*." *The Explicator* 51.4 (1993): 227–230.

Maynard, Moira. "Moral Integrity in *The Reef*: Justice to Anna Leath." *College Literature* 14 (1987): 285–295.

McDowell, Margaret B. *Edith Wharton.* Boston: Twayne Publishers. Revised ed., 1976, 1991

Merish, Lori. "Engendering Naturalism: Narrative Form and Commodity Spectacle in U.S. Naturalist Fiction." In *Edith Wharton's* The House of Mirth: *A Casebook.* 229–270. First published in *Novel: A Forum on Fiction* 29 (1996): 319–345.

Montgomery, Judith H. "The American Galatea." *College English* 32 (1971): 890–899.

Mortimer, Armine Kotin. "Romantic Fever: The Second Story as Illegitimate Daughter in Wharton's 'Roman Fever.'" *Narrative* 6.2 (1998): 188–198.

Nettels, Elsa. "Gender and First-Person Narration in Edith Wharton's Short Fiction." In *Edith Wharton: New Critical Essays.* 245–260.

Nevius, Blake. *Edith Wharton: A Study of Her Fiction.* 1953. Reprint: Berkeley: University of California Press, 1976.

Ohler, Paul J. *Edith Wharton's "Evolutionary Conception": Darwinian Allegory in Her Major Novels.* New York and London: Routledge, 2006.

Olin-Ammentorp, Julie. "Edith Wharton's Challenge to Feminist Criticism." *Studies in American Fiction* 16 (1988): 237–244.

_____. *Edith Wharton's Writings from the Great*

*War.* Gainesville: University Press of Florida, 2004.

_____. "Martin Boyne and the 'Warm Animal Life' of *The Children.*" *Edith Wharton Review* 12.1 (1995): 15–19.

Orlando, Emily J. "Rereading Wharton's 'Poor Archer': A 'Mr. Might-Have-Been' in *The Age of Innocence.*" *American Literary Realism* 30.2 (1998): 56–76.

Petry, Alice Hall. "A Twist of Silk: Edith Wharton's 'Roman Fever.'" *Studies in Short Fiction* 24.2 (1987): 163–166.

Pirandello, Luigi. *Six Characters Looking for an Author.* 1922. In *Naked Masks: Five Plays by Luigi Pirandello.* Ed. Eric Bentley. Trans. Edward Storer. New York: E. P. Dutton and Co., 1952. 211–276.

Pizer, Donald. "American Naturalism in its 'Perfected' State: *The Age of Innocence* and *An American Tragedy.*" In *The Age of Innocence: Complete Text with Introduction, Historical Contexts, Critical Essays.* Ed. Carol J. Singley. Boston and New York: Houghton Mifflin, 2000. 434–441.

_____. "The Naturalism of Edith Wharton's *The House of Mirth.*" *Twentieth Century Literature* 41 (1995): 241–248.

_____. *Realism and Naturalism in Nineteenth-Century American Literature.* Carbondale: Southern Illinois University Press. Revised ed., 1984.

Preston, Claire. *Edith Wharton's Social Register.* Houndmills and London: Macmillan, 2000.

Price, Alan. "The Composition of Edith Wharton's *The Age of Innocence.*" In *The Age of Innocence: Complete Text with Introduction, Historical Contexts, Critical Essays.* Ed. Carol J. Singley. Boston and New York: Houghton Mifflin, 2000. 387–403.

_____. "Lily Bart and Carrie Meeber: Cultural Sisters." *American Literary Realism* 13 (1980): 238–248.

Rae, Catherine M. "Edith Wharton's Avenging Angel in the House." *Denver Quarterly* 18.4 (1984): 119–125.

Raphael, Lev. *Edith Wharton's Prisoners of Shame: A New Perspective on Her Neglected Fiction.* New York: St. Martin's Press, 1991.

Richards, Janet Radcliffe. *Human Nature after Darwin: A Philosophical Introduction.* London and New York: Routledge, 2000.

Robinson, James A. "Psychological Determinism in *The Age of Innocence.*" *The Markham Review* 5 (1975): 1–5.

Salmon, Catherine. "Parental Investment and Parent-Offspring Conflict." In *The Handbook of Evolutionary Psychology.* Ed. David M. Buss. Hoboken, New Jersey: John Wiley & Sons, 2005. 506–527.

Sensibar, Judith L. "Edith Wharton Reads the Bachelor Type: Her Critique of Modernism's

Representative Man." *American Literature* 60.4 (1988): 575–590.

Saunders, Judith P. "Becoming the Mask: Edith Wharton's Ingenues." *Massachusetts Studies in English* 8.4 (1982): 33–39.

_____. "Portrait of the Artist as Anthropologist: Edith Wharton and *The Age of Innocence.*" *Interdisciplinary Literary Studies: A Journal of Criticism and Theory* 4.1 (2002): 86–101.

Showalter, Elaine. "The Death of the Lady (Novelist): Wharton's *House of Mirth.*" *Representations* 9, Special Issue: American Culture Between the Civil War and World War I (1985): 133–149.

Singley, Carol J., ed. *The Age of Innocence: Complete Text with Introduction, Historical Contexts, Critical Essays.* Boston and New York: Houghton Mifflin, 2000.

_____. "Bourdieu, Wharton and Changing Culture in *The Age of Innocence.*" *Cultural Studies* 17.3–4 (2003): 495–519.

_____. *Edith Wharton: Matters of Mind and Spirit.* Cambridge: Cambridge University Press, 1995.

_____, ed. *Edith Wharton's The House of Mirth: A Casebook.* Oxford and New York: Oxford University Press, 2003.

_____, ed. *A Historical Guide to Edith Wharton.* Oxford: Oxford University Press, 2003.

Smuts, Barbara. "Male Aggression Against Women: An Evolutionary Perspective." In *Sex, Power, Conflict.* Ed. David M. Buss and Neil M. Malamuth. New York and Oxford: Oxford University Press, 1996. 231–268.

Storey, Robert. *Mimesis and the Human Animal: On the Biogenetic Foundations Of Literary Representation.* Evanston, Illinois: Northwestern University Press, 1996.

Tebbetts, Terrell. "Conformity, Desire, and the Critical Self in Wharton's *The Age of Innocence.*" *The Philological Review* 30.1 (2004): 25–38.

Tichi, Cecelia. "Emerson, Darwin, and *The Custom of the Country.* In *A Historical Guide to Edith Wharton.* Ed. Carol J. Singley. Oxford: Oxford University Press, 2003. 89–114.

Tillman, Lynne. "A Mole in the House of the Modern." In *New Essays on The House of Mirth.* Ed. Deborah Esch. Cambridge: Cambridge University Press, 2001. 133–158.

Tooby, John, and Leda Cosmides. "Conceptual Foundations of Evolutionary Psychology." In *The Handbook of Evolutionary Psychology.* Ed. David M. Buss. Hoboken, New Jersey: John Wiley & Sons, 2005. 5–67.

Trilling, Diana. "*The House of Mirth* Revisited." In *Edith Wharton: A Collection of Critical Essays.* Ed. Irving Howe. Englewood Cliffs: Prentice-Hall, 1962. 103–118.

Trivers, Robert. *Natural Selection and Social Theory: Selected Papers of Robert Trivers.* Oxford: Oxford University Press, 2002.

Tuttleton, James W. "Edith Wharton: The Archeological Motive." *The Yale Review* 16 (1972): 562–74.

_____. "Mocking Fate: Romantic Idealism in Edith Wharton's *The Reef.*" *Studies in the Novel* 19 (1987): 459–474.

Vandermassen, Griet. *Who's Afraid of Charles Darwin? Debating Feminism and Evolutionary Theory.* Lanham, Maryland: Rowman and Littlefield, 2005.

Wagner-Martin, Linda. The House of Mirth: *A Novel of Admonition.* Boston: Twayne Publishers, 1990.

Waid, Candace, ed. *The Age of Innocence: Authoritative Text, Background and Contexts, Sources, Criticism.* New York and London: W.W. Norton, 2003.

Wershoven, Carol. *The Female Intruder in the Novels of Edith Wharton.* Rutherford: Fairleigh Dickinson University Press, 1982; London and Toronto: Associated University Presses, 1982.

Wharton, Edith. 1920. *The Age of Innocence: Complete Text with Introduction, Historical Contexts, Critical Essays.* Ed. Carol J. Singley. Boston and New York: Houghton Mifflin, 2000.

_____. *A Backward Glance.* New York and London: D. Appleton Century, 1934.

_____. *The Children.* New York and London. D. Appleton, 1928.

_____. *The Glimpses of the Moon.* New York and London: D. Appleton, 1922.

_____. *The House of Mirth.* New York: Charles Scribner's Sons, 1905.

_____. "Introduction to the 1936 Edition of *The House of Mirth.*" In *Edith Wharton's* The House of Mirth: *A Casebook.* Ed. Carol J. Singley.

Oxford and New York: Oxford University Press, 2003. 31–37.

_____. *The Letters of Edith Wharton.* Ed. R.W.B. Lewis and Nancy Lewis. New York: Charles Scribner's Sons, 1988.

_____. *The Old Maid (The 'fifties). Old New York.* New York and London: D. Appleton, 1924.

_____. *The Reef.* New York: Charles Scribner's Sons, 1914.

_____. "Roman Fever." In *The World Over.* New York and London: D. Appleton-Century, 1936. 215–239.

Wilson, Edmund. "Justice to Edith Wharton." In *Edith Wharton: A Collection of Critical Essays.* Ed. Irving Howe. Englewood Cliffs, New Jersey: Prentice-Hall, 1962. 19–31.

Wilson, Edward O. *Consilience: The Unity of Knowledge.* New York: Alfred A. Knopf, 1998.

_____. *Sociobiology: The New Synthesis.* Cambridge, Massachusetts: Belknap, 1975.

Witherow, Jean. "A Dialectic of Deception: Edith Wharton's *The Age of Innocence.*" *Mosaic: A Journal for the Interdisciplinary Study of Literature.* 36.3 (2003). 9/18/08. ProQuest, Marist College Library.

Wolff, Cynthia Griffin. "*The Age of Innocence*: Wharton's 'Portrait of a Gentleman.'" *The Southern Review* 12 (1976): 640–658.

_____. *A Feast of Words: The Triumph of Edith Wharton.* New York: Oxford University Press, 1977.

Wright, Robert. *The Moral Animal: Evolutionary Psychology and Everyday Life.* New York: Vintage Books, 1995.

Yeazell, Ruth Bernard. "The Conspicuous Wasting of Lily Bart." In *New Essays on* The House of Mirth. Ed. Deborah Esch. Cambridge: Cambridge University Press, 2001. 15–41.

# Index